children guessed (but only a few
and down they forgot AS UP THEY GREW
autumn winter spring summer) —e. e. cummings

Autobiographical Essays
Edited by Herbert R. Coursen, Jr.

AS UP THEY GREW
Autobiographical Essays

Herbert R. Coursen, Jr.
Bowdoin College

Scott, Foresman and Company

Acknowledgments

"First Light" from *The Edge of Day, A Boyhood in the West of England*, by Laurie Lee. Reprinted by permission of William Morrow and Company, Inc., Publishers. Copyright © 1959 by Laurie Lee.   "A New England Boyhood" from *The Education of Henry Adams* by Henry Adams. Reprinted by permission of Houghton Mifflin Company, publishers.   "Nightmare" from *The Autobiography of Malcolm X*, by Malcolm X. Reprinted by permission of Grove Press, Inc. Copyright © 1964 by Alex Haley and Malcolm X. Copyright © 1965 by Alex Haley and Betty Shabazz. "Death and Life" by Maxim Gorky reprinted by arrangement with Citadel Press, Inc.   "Knoxville: Summer 1915" from *A Death in the Family* by James Agee, Copyright © 1957 by James Agee Trust. First published in *The Partisan Review* (August-September 1938, Vol. 5 No. 3.) Reprinted by permission of the publisher Grosset & Dunlap, Inc.   "Playmates" from *Lanterns on the Levee*, by William Alexander Percy. Copyright 1941 by Alfred A. Knopf, Inc. Reprinted by permission. "The Dump Ground" from *Wolf Willow* by Wallace Stegner. Copyright © 1959 by Wallace Stegner. Reprinted by permission of The Viking Press, Inc.   "The Last Threshing in the Coulee" and "David and His Violin" reprinted with permission of The Macmillan Company from *A Son of the Middle Border* by Hamlin Garland. © The Macmillan Company 1962. Copyright by Hamlin Garland 1917, Copyright renewed 1945 by Mary I. Lord and Constance G. Williams.   "The Farm" by Mark Sullivan reprinted from *The Education of an American* by permission of Mark Sullivan, Jr.   From *The Innocent Eye* by Sir Herbert Read reprinted by permission of the publisher, Horizon Press, from *The Contrary Experience:* Autobiographies by Sir Herbert Read. Copyright 1963.   "Then What Was It?" reprinted from *Coming of Age in Mississippi* by Anne Moody. Copyright © 1968 by Anne Moody and used by permission of the publisher, The Dial Press, Inc.   "Christmas in Maine" reprinted by permission of Robert P. T. Coffin, Jr.   "A Small-Town Street" reprinted from *Sherwood Anderson's Memoirs: A Critical Edition*, ed. by Ray Lewis White, by permission of the University of North Carolina Press.   "The Day We Flew the Kites" by Frances Fowler reprinted from *Parents' Magazine*, New York, with permission of the publisher.   "When I Was a Child" reprinted from *Killers of the Dream* by Lillian Smith. By permission of W. W. Norton & Company, Inc. Copyright 1949, © 1961 by Lillian Smith.   "Reminiscences of Childhood" from Dylan Thomas, *Quite Early One Morning*. Copyright 1942 & 1954 by New Directions Publishing Corporation. Reprinted by permission of New Directions Publishing Corporation.   From "The Dogwood Tree: A Boyhood" by John Updike from "Five Boyhoods," edited by Martin Levin. Copyright © 1962 by Martin Levin. "The Plot Where the Garden Lived" from *A Mass for the Dead* by William Gibson. Copyright © 1968 by Tamarack Productions Ltd., George S. Klein and Leo Garel as trustees under three separate deeds of trust. Reprinted by permission of Atheneum Publishers.   "The White Gate" and "Aunt Mi" reprinted from *The White Gate* by Mary Ellen Chase. By permission of W. W. Norton & Company, Inc. Copyright 1954 by Mary Ellen Chase.   "Coast Children of the Nineties" from *A Goodly Heritage* by Mary Ellen Chase. Copyright 1932 © 1960 by Mary Ellen Chase. Reprinted by permission of Holt, Rinehart and Winston, Inc.   "A Step-Daughter of the Prairie" by Margaret Lynn, Copyright © by The Atlantic Monthly Company, Boston, Mass. Reprinted by permission.   "A Boy in Old Russia" from *Speak. Memory* by Vladimir Nabokov. Reprinted by permission of the author.   "A Christmas Memory" by Truman Capote © Copyright 1956 by Truman Capote. Reprinted from *Breakfast at Tiffany's*, by Truman Capote, by permission of Random House, Inc.   "Brownsville" by Alfred Kazin from *A Walker in the City*, copyright 1951, by Alfred Kazin. Reprinted by permission of Harcourt, Brace & World, Inc.   "Lady" from *My Land Has a Voice* by Jesse Stuart. Copyright © 1966 by Jesse Stuart. Used with permission of McGraw-Hill Book Co.   "The Son of Nick Massimo" used by permission of the author, Herbert R. Coursen, Jr.   "Marcia and the Celebrity" from *Grandfather Stories*, by Samuel Hopkins Adams. Copyright 1951 by Samuel Hopkins Adams. Reprinted by permission of Random House,

Preface

While I hope that many students will use this book to learn how to write about their experiences, it is designed to be read, with no goal other than the reader's enjoyment. The reader will not be encumbered with "Suggestions for Further Study," "Topics for Composition," or artificial categories like "Town and Country" and "Black and White." The essays of this anthology should not be insulted by an "apparatus" devised by a mere English teacher. Nor should they be smothered in the pall of a "textbook atmosphere."

I have made some divisions in the material, but have resisted the impulse to impose a title upon each section. The groupings seem to me to cohere thematically, but the reader will find more within each group than any title might imply, and will recognize that each selection comments on selections in other sections as well as upon those in its own grouping. In other words, I have not narrowed this anthology to what only one mind may see in its components.

I have enjoyed selecting these essays. I can only hope that the reader derives comparable enjoyment from them. The only pain involved in the process has been the necessity of excerpting from works which deserved to be more fully represented. I hope that the reader will go to some of the longer works from which many of these selections have been culled.

Herbert R. Coursen, Jr.

Contents

Part Four

Part Five

Part Six

To the Student

"You want me to write about myself? But nothing interesting has ever happened to me!"

This student is wrong. Maybe he didn't drive an ambulance across a battlefield, or survive the sinking of the *Andrea Doria*, or escape from a POW camp, or land a jet dead-stick on a dirt road. Such dramatic events occur in few lives. But everyone has experience. And everyone has language. This book shows what happens when language and experience come together. It shows also that excitement is not a product of external events, of things that happen *to* someone, but is, instead, a measure of the person living a life, a product of his vision, insight, and sense of humor. The claim that life is dull says nothing about life but does say something about the person making the statement.

Students complain of a "generation gap" and blame their elders for it (with some reason). But students, too, suffer from a generation gap. They are too often detached from their *own* past experience. They rush toward the future, forgetting that the past—where they have been—often determines the future—where they will be. The past often contains within it the vectors of possibility which the student can only pursue if he recognizes them. And those vectors are different for everyone. Therefore, a careful look at the past can have enormously positive results for that ever moving present in which everyone lives.

Too many students are right now shrinking toward the "adult" described by E. E. Cummings:

> children guessed (but only a few
> and down they forgot as up they grew . . .

and by William Dean Howells:

> from his third to his eleventh year [a boy] seldom, if ever, catches a glimpse of life much higher than the middle of a man, and has the most distorted and mistaken views of most things. He may then indeed look up to the sky, and see heaven open, and angels ascending and descending; but he can only grope about on the earth, and he knows nothing aright that goes on there beyond his small boy's world. Some people remain in this condition as long as they live, and keep the ignorance of childhood, after they have lost its innocence; heaven has been shut, but the earth is still a prison to them.

Growing up, then, can involve more loss than gain. We grow, and "shades of the prison-house begin to close" around us, as Wordsworth says, until the vision of childhood dies, to fade "into the light of common day."

One way of maintaining contact with the power of the vision Wordsworth describes—when "every common sight . . . did seem/ Appareled in celestial light"—is by recreating it in language. And if a childhood will not support the transcendent values which Wordsworth found in his, the exploration of the past *will* be valuable for a student, particularly in an America where the process of growing is too often begun *before* we have had a chance to be children.

The children of the affluent often mimic "adult" patterns, becoming teen-agers in thought and habit even before their ages achieve two digits. They play with Barbie and her boyfriend Ken and all the accouterments accompanying these plastic personalities. The playhouse world evolves effortlessly toward the commuting, golf-playing husband and the beautiful wife with her Villager clothes, paneled estate wagon, and roll-around dishwasher.

The children of poverty have often been denied a childhood and may seek escape from the past through the panacea called "education." But they never really escape. If they achieve affluence, yet ignore their pasts, these pasts continue to operate, negatively, rendering them emotional cripples who pretend that their lives began upon graduation from college and attainment of "that first good job." Their former lives remain a part of their experience, whether they like it or not, an unperceived but powerful force.

Happily, many students have come to recognize these tendencies in their lives. The affluent have become aware of the hollowness at the heart of suburbia. Black students have rejected a future as "Uncle Tom" for the pride of their heritage, for the positive value to be discovered in the experience to which they and their people have been subjected. The "disadvantaged" student who faces his past squarely often translates it into a positive system of intentions. One disadvantaged white student said to me recently, "I want an education so I can go into social work and help kids like me." The "advantaged" student must face his past honestly, must penetrate the protective façades he has inevitably placed between himself and the realities of hunger, cold, and pain which his less affluent contemporaries have known, must determine his direction by looking back to see what it has been and what it can be.

This anthology speaks, I believe, to those who want to do more than drift into the future, who want to live the "examined life," the only life worth living. Even if the student is not moved to emulate these essays in his own writing he will learn something about himself by finding his own experience stimulated into recognition by the vibrantly recorded experiences of the writers represented here.

But the answer to the question Who am I? is better found by an individual's shaping of his past into form and language. How? Each of the selections suggests the answer more adequately than can my generalizations. The selections record "not facts but experiences," as Roy Pascal says in his book about autobiography. They are the products of senses—which all students have—and of the translation of sensory and emotional data into language—which all students have. To write well about his past, the student must transmit experience to his reader, who also has senses and language. The process, then, involves a student's meeting a reader on the shared ground of their human attributes. It is a *creative* process, which André Malraux describes in his introduction to *Anti-Memoirs*:

> memory . . . does not recreate a life in its original sequence. Lit by an invisible sun, nebulae appear which seem to presage an unknown constellation. Some of them belong to the realm of imagination, others to the memory of a past which appears in sudden flashes or must be patiently probed; for the most significant moments in my life do not live in me, they haunt me and flee from me alternately. No matter. Face to face with the unknown, some of our dreams are no less significant than our memories.

Finally, even though a student may say (correctly) that "English has always been my worst subject," that student *can* write. It may be that he has never been asked to write about anything *he* was interested in. Students do have language—no matter how "ungrammatical"—and they do have experience—no matter how "undramatic." If a student doubts that the two can combine for him into good writing he might notice that among the great names (Twain, Thomas, Baldwin, Nabokov, Capote, *et al.*) of this anthology are unknown names, the names of students like himself who write well and honestly about their own lives.

Many writing courses ask their students to perfect the techniques required for "Success" with a capital dollar sign in the Great Economy just outside the classroom. This anthology suggests something more exciting —that the student learn to move to the rhythms of his own drummer.

To the Teacher

Surely we are tired of the essays our students write. Depending upon the format of our course in freshman English or expository writing, we receive either bored and superficial "analyses" of poems, some with footnotes sprinkled here and there like raisins, or glib and superficial essays on free speech or how the ad-men are killing us, paraphrases of the four or five glib essays collected under the headings "Problems of a Democracy" or "Media and Culture in the Post-McLuhan Age." When we work on these essays, asking marginal questions and registering interlinear objections, writing final comments about structure, evidence, and syntax, we *are* helping our students. They should be able to grind out well-organized and reasonably coherent term papers for their economics major work and to present succinct and specific reports for their future superiors in the Great Economy. But is not ours a narrow and degraded service? Aren't we really helping our students become more effective parts in the modern machine? Aren't we involved in a profoundly anti-humanistic enterprise? As Robert Hutchins says, "to the extent to which an educational system pretends to get the student ready for something, to that extent is it likely . . . to cause him to think he has been deceived. . . . An educational system directed to economic growth will regard the people as instruments of production and teach them to regard themselves as such."

But we teachers of English should be able to help our students develop their writing abilities. What do I purpose? Nothing radical. Most of us have tried it once we dispatched the "service" aspects of our courses. I suggest a "free topic," with the proviso that the subject matter be the life of the student, preferably his earlier life (and certainly not "My Life So Far," or "What I Did on My Summer Vacation"). The student would recreate a moment in his past, giving language to what eight or twelve years before had been merely impression. The essay could treat a home town, an important event—a birth, a death, a trip to the beach, a summer's day, moving, the return to school. Above all, it would appeal to a reader's senses and through his senses to his emotions. It would recreate the feeling of being there.

What are the advantages to this approach? First, grammatical and usage problems often arise in our students' writing because we place them in false situations. We expect them to write like little social or literary critics, and they resent this, automatically if unconsciously. One result is stilted, artificial language, modeled on something the student is not and probably does not want to be (and probably *won't* be after we get through with him). When we demand analyses of poems we demand bad writing. Instead of giving the student a poem or a problem to examine, we might send him seeking into his own past, there to discover the dynamics of his being. The subject should interest him, and we know that the interested student writes better prose.

Second, the student can write in something closer to *his* language. Teachers grow older, while students retain perpetual youth. Thus we teachers find it increasingly difficult to speak to students in their language. Yet we insist that they speak to us in ours. Most students can express themselves. *We* reduce them to silence. Some students, of course, quickly learn the game and send back reassuring reflections of ourselves. The others are "insensitive clods, with no appreciation for the finer things." But have the clods nothing to say? And what of the students from other backgrounds, particularly the children of poverty who may soon break the middle-class monopoly on our classrooms? Does it make sense to ask a bright young man from the ghetto to write about a poem? He may well have a rich and beautiful language, but it will be the *patois* of the streets, uninformed by the jargon of the "critical essay." Does it not make sense to have him tell us, in his language, about his own experience? Once he puts something down on paper we can move him toward more formal subjects and usages—if that is a relevant direction for him.

Third, the reminiscent essay can develop in several ways, depending on the talents and inclinations of the student and teacher. This type of essay is a valid *genre* in itself, as the selections in this anthology suggest. There is much to be said for the student's reworking of a promising first version until it fulfills its potential. The reminiscent essay *can* move toward the sociological or cultural essay. But here the student uses himself as the starting point, basing his generalizations on his lived experience, whether amid the opulence of the upper middle class or the squalor of a wind-invaded rural shack. Few students, after reading *Essays for Our Times*, relate themselves to the problem. Instead, they grind out another assignment, writing vaguely about other people in other places. And the reminiscent essay can develop toward fiction, showing the student that he has the stuff of fiction within his own experience, that fiction does not necessarily emerge from overtly dramatic events, but often from careful observation and description of "daily life," from emotions boiling behind the impassive faces of people.

Each of these potential directions—the reminiscent essay *per se,* the social essay, the short story—emerges from the premise that the past is prologue. Our students, plunging toward the mirages beckoning on the future's horizon, tend to ignore the fact of the past. If they neglect the power of their pasts over their presents and futures, they do so at their peril. They cannot go home again, perhaps, but they can explore what that home meant and means. If this drive toward self-knowledge implies a goal beyond that of most English courses, so be it. Kant says that "man's highest task is to learn what one must be to be a human being." Today, a man must learn who *he* is before he can embrace the Kantian imperative.

Obviously, there are disadvantages to this program. Some students, thoroughly indoctrinated by "practical" courses, may demand to know "what good will this do *me?*" Rather than stultify the course at the outset by rationalizing it into practicality, it should be allowed to justify itself in its own terms as it goes along. And for some students it may not. The program will also be hard to sell to administrations which deal in tangibles—like rows of letters on transcripts. Certainly the course will look suspicious to the presidents, deans, and chairmen who believe "creative" courses are like pets that the children pestered and pestered to get, pets to be kept in little dog houses in the curriculum's backyard and fed mostly bread crumbs.

Ideally the course should not be graded. The work is important *per se*, not the number it receives. Surely there is a philosophical inconsistency in placing a number on a creative or imaginative effort. To give a short story, however inadequate, a B— is to debase it, to reduce it to that lower world where decimal points lurk. But some must comply with such systems. As long as our students know that the grade we must give is not the end toward which the course has driven, that the grade does not translate their efforts into so much IBMable data, perhaps the student will feel the vectors of the course continuing to push him toward further creativity—whether defining himself and his relationships to the world or in developing his writing beyond the June or January in which the course has formally ended.

The essays in this anthology have been grouped according to similar patterns and themes, but I have not imposed upon these groupings a simplistic title which would exclude as much truth as it enclosed. To me, the groupings represent an "evolutionary" sequence, from the first probings of the senses into the world's imagery (I); to the increasing complexity of the problems and questions which the developing consciousness encounters (II); to the doubts and insecurities which the child knows so much more intensely than the adult (III); to the relationships which the child creates and rejects with other people, and with his own fears and feelings (IV); to more formal structures of education and initiation (V); and, finally, to the assumption of adulthood (often involuntary) and to the awareness of the past by the new adult (VI). The last three essays, each in a different way, cast a retrospective look back on youth, hence on all the essays that have preceded them in this anthology. But that, as I said, is only what I see there, and only part of what I see.

Nor have I constructed an "apparatus" for each selection. If the essays do not speak for themselves (with the amplification of alert student and skillful teacher), then any effort to speak for them would be useless. If they do, such an effort would be superfluous. And I would guess that the kind of teacher attracted by the autobiographical approach would usually ignore someone else's apparatus anyway. Then, of course, a "textbook atmosphere" is death to creativity—a teacher's *and* a student's.

Thus the teacher who uses this anthology as the basis for a writing course cannot push a button and watch his course function automatically. He must identify each student, must work individually with each student, must encourage what is unique in each student to emerge and grow. But while this undertaking is difficult and exhausting, it should finally prove more rewarding than the conventional program. Here we are not producing walking footnotes. Here we may be helping potential human beings become human.

It might be helpful were I to discuss a final question—"How do you get the student started?" My answer (and I'm sure that other teachers have better ones) is contained in an introduction I wrote for *Growing Up in Maine*, an anthology of writings by Upward Bound students at Bowdoin College:

One of my colleagues on the Upward Bound staff at Bowdoin College says that our program "reaffirms the radical notion that young people are worth listening to." Too often our educational system delivers "the word" to its students, translating them gradually into complacent plodders. Those who don't plod are pushed to the side of the highway. Why do students write book reports or critical essays sprinkled with those terrifying things called footnotes? Not merely because we English teachers are attempting to receive reassuring reflections back from our better students, but because the Great Economy demands persons who can write clear and concise analytical prose. And our schools and colleges, obviously, are subservient to the demands of the society surrounding them.

The Upward Bound student has already been rejected by his school and his society. His school has branded him a failure, or has decided that, because of his poverty, he is "not college material," and therefore deserves no further attention. Society also pushes him aside. One girl, writing in our Bowdoin Upward Bound newspaper, *Rebound*, said, "In my town people laugh and snicker at you if you don't have much money and do have a large family." And when our Director once asked at a gas station for directions to one of our Upward Bound families, the attendant said, "You don't want to go there," and refused to tell her. This in one of the poorest towns in one of the nation's poorest states!

I worked with about twenty of these students during the summer of 1968 in a course called "Rhetoric and Composition." Since most of the students will go on to college, I was tempted to give them something resembling a freshman English course. But then I thought of where these students come from—from a town long ago abandoned by the railroad, now a mere junction of rusting iron, from a shack in a group of shacks called "the Happy Valley" by more affluent townsfolk whose euphemism coats their social consciences, from hovels at the edges of dirt roads, hovels invaded by the winter winds and filled with coughing children, from rooms where the first thing a child sees against the darkness of the morning is his own breath probing the air. They come from the French valleys of the north where English is seldom heard and from the abject reservations which the state has bestowed upon its Indians. They come from back country Maine, never seen in the splendid spreads of the *National Geographic*, where cold is their constant companion, where they begin working in the potato fields full-time at age six, where hunting out of season or cutting timber on another man's land sometimes means survival, where illness must usually go untreated, where fathers too often drink themselves to divorce or early death. I knew nothing of this world. I decided to listen.

The most difficult part of the course was the beginning—getting them to write. I did not spend much time on justifying their work in the *genre* of the reminiscent essay. I felt that the course would provide its own justification as it developed, and I feel that the essays included in this anthology are their own justification. I did two things at the outset, neither very original. First, we read good autobiography—Henry Adams, James Baldwin, Gorky, Joyce, Thomas, Nabokov, *et al.* Second, the students completed seemingly simplistic assignments in class—"Describe a house." Then we moved towards their experience; "Take a significant moment in your past—when you were ten or so—and describe it in the language available to you now," or "Describe a typical day in your life at age ten or twelve." In a few cases, the original "house" assignment became the essay topic.

Once the students began to develop their subjects, they read their essays to the class. Here the class took over, teaching each other. We weren't dealing with a novel by Hardy or a poem by Housman. We were working with a student's experience described in his language. Thus the other students were able and usually eager to participate in the process of evaluation. And often they sounded like English teachers ("I think she should expand here," "He needs to go into more detail there").

The range of ability represented by the students was wide—from 257 to 595 points in verbal aptitude, with most falling towards the bottom of the spectrum. Few had written in their schools, an occasional book report being the limit of their effort. Only two had ever attempted to write about their own experiences before. One boy said, "No English teacher has ever felt that anything *I* did was important." I had hoped for one "finished" essay from each student, feeling that he would learn more from the process of revising and rewriting one essay, expanding this and eliminating that, than from making several unfulfilled beginnings. Some of the essays reflect this process. Others appear as they came from the pen, written by students who at the last minute decided they had something to say. Their essays, of course, remain "unfinished" but represent a victory for the writers—these essays are the first gropings of their experience into language. If they are also the last, then at least it has been done once. If they are the first of more, then they are a beginning, a movement towards the joy of working well with what all students and all people have—language and experience.

Since several of these essays are included in this volume, the English teacher can judge for himself the validity of the autobiographical approach.

ONE

LAURIE LEE

Laurie Lee was born in the Cotswolds, England, in 1914. As a teen-ager he led a dance band and, later, he went to Spain and supported himself by playing the violin in the streets and cafés. Like George Orwell (also represented in this volume), he fought with the International Brigade in the Spanish Civil War. During the Second World War he worked for the British Ministry of Information. He is best known as a poet, but besides his volumes of poetry he has written *A Rose for Winter* (1955), a book about Spain, and an autobiography, *The Edge of Day* (1960), from which the following selection comes.

First Light

I was set down from the carrier's cart at the age of three; and there with a sense of bewilderment and terror my life in the village began.

The June grass, amongst which I stood, was taller than I was, and I wept. I had never been so close to grass before. It towered above me and all around me, each blade tattooed with tiger skins of sunlight. It was knife-edged, dark and a wicked green, thick as a forest and alive with grasshoppers that chirped and chattered and leapt through the air like monkeys.

I was lost and didn't know where to move. A tropic heat oozed up from the ground, rank with sharp odours of roots and nettles. Snow clouds of elderblossom banked in the sky, showering upon me the fumes and flakes of their sweet and giddy suffocation. High overhead ran frenzied larks, screaming, as though the sky were tearing apart.

For the first time in my life I was out of the sight of humans. For the first time in my life I was alone in a world whose behaviour I could neither predict nor fathom: a world of birds that squealed, of plants that stank, of insects that sprang about without warning. I was lost and I did not expect to be found again. I put back my head and howled, and the sun hit me smartly on the face, like a bully.

From this daylight nightmare I was wakened, as from many another, by the appearance of my sisters. They came scrambling and calling up the steep rough bank and, parting the long grass, found me. Faces of rose, familiar, living; huge shining faces hung up like shields between me and the sky; faces with grins and white teeth (some broken) to be conjured up like genii with a howl, brushing off terror with their broad scoldings and affection. They leaned over me—one, two, three—their mouths smeared with red currants and their hands dripping with juice.

"There, there, it's all right, don't you wail anymore. Come down 'ome and we'll stuff you with currants."

And Marjorie, the eldest, lifted me into her long brown hair, and ran me jogging down the path and through the steep rose-filled garden, and set me down on the cottage doorstep, which was our home, though I couldn't believe it.

That was the day we came to the village, in the summer of the last year of the First World War. To a cottage that stood in a half-acre of garden on a steep bank above a lake; a cottage with three floors and a cellar and a treasure in the walls, with a pump and apple trees, syringa and strawberries, rooks in the chimneys, frogs in the cellar, mushrooms on the ceiling, and all for three and sixpence a week.

I don't know where I lived before then. My life began on the carrier's cart which brought me up the long slow hills to the village, and dumped me in the high grass, and lost me. I had ridden wrapped up in a Union Jack to protect me from the sun, and when I rolled out of it, and stood piping loud among the buzzing jungle of that summer bank, then, I feel, was I born. And to all the rest of us, the whole family of eight, it was the beginning of a life.

But on that first day we were all lost. Chaos was come in cartloads of furniture, and I crawled the kitchen floor through forests of upturned chairlegs and crystal fields of glass. We were washed up in a new land, and began to spread out, searching its springs and treasures. The sisters spent the light of that first day stripping the fruit bushes in the garden. The currants were at their prime, clusters of red, black and yellow berries all tangled up with wild roses. Here was bounty the girls had never known before, and they darted squawking from bush to bush, clawing the fruit like sparrows.

Our Mother too was distracted from duty, seduced by the rich wilderness of the garden so long abandoned. All day she trotted to and fro, flushed and garrulous, pouring flowers into every pot and jug she could find on the kitchen floor. Flowers from the garden, daisies from the bank, cow parsley, grasses, ferns and leaves—they flowed in armfuls through the cottage door until its dim interior seemed entirely possessed by the world outside—a still green pool flooding with honeyed tides of summer.

I sat on the floor on a raft of muddles and gazed through the green window which was full of the rising garden. I saw the long black stockings of the girls, gaping with white flesh, kicking among the currant bushes. Every so often one of them would dart into the kitchen, cram my great mouth with handfuls of squashed berries, and run out again. And the more I got the more I called for more. It was like feeding a fat young cuckoo.

The long day crowed and chirped and rang. Nobody did any work, and there was nothing to eat save berries and bread. I crawled about among the ornaments on the unfamiliar floor—the glass fishes, china dogs, shepherds and shepherdesses, bronze horsemen, stopped clocks, barometers, and photographs of bearded men. I called on them each in turn, for they were the shrines and faces of a half-remembered landscape. But as I watched the sun move around the walls, drawing rainbows from the cut-glass jars in the corner, I longed for a return of order.

Then, suddenly, the day was at an end, and the house was furnished. Each stick and cup and picture was nailed immovably in place; the beds were sheeted, the windows curtained, the straw mats laid, and the house was home. I don't remember seeing it happen, but suddenly the inexorable tradition of the house, with its smell, chaos and complete logic, occurred as though it had never been otherwise. The furnishing and founding of the house came like the nightfall of that first day. From that uneasy loneliness of objects strewn on the kitchen floor, everything flew to its place and was never again questioned.

And from that day we grew up. The domestic arrangement of the house was shaken many times, like a snowstorm toy, so that beds and chairs and ornaments swirled from room to room, pursued by the gusty energies of Mother and the girls. But always these things resettled within the pattern of the walls, nothing escaped or changed, and so it remained for twenty years.

Now I measured that first growing year by the widening fields that became visible to me, the new tricks of dressing and getting about with which I became gradually endowed. I could open the kitchen door by screwing myself into a ball and leaping and banging the latch with my fist. I could climb into the high bed by using the ironwork as a ladder. I could whistle, but I couldn't lace my shoes. Life became a series of experiments which brought grief or the rewards of accomplishment: a pondering of patterns and mysteries in the house, while time hung golden and suspended, and one's body, from leaping and climbing, took on the rigid insanity of an insect, petrified, as it were, for hours together, breathing and watching. Watching the grains of dust fall in the sunny room, following an ant from its cradle to the grave, going over the knots in the bedroom ceiling—knots that seemed to dilate and run in the half-light of dawn and form the fluid shapes of monsters, or moved stealthily from board to board; but which settled again in the wax light of day no more monstrous than fossils in coal.

These knots on the bedroom ceiling were the whole range of a world, and over them my eyes went endlessly voyaging in that long primeval light of waking to which a child is condemned. They were archipelagoes in a sea of blood-coloured varnish, they were armies grouped and united against me, they were the alphabet of a macabre tongue, the first book I ever learned to read.

Radiating from that house, with its crumbling walls, its thumps and shadows, its fancied foxes under the floor, I moved along paths that lengthened inch by inch with my mounting strength of days. From stone to stone in the trackless yard I sent forth my acorn shell of senses, moving through unfathomable oceans like a South Sea savage island-hopping across the Pacific. Antennae of eyes and nose and grubbing fingers captured a new tuft of grass, a fern, a slug, the skull of a bird, a grotto of bright snails. Through the long summer ages of those first few days I enlarged my world and mapped it in my mind: its secure havens, its dust-deserts and puddles, its peaks of dirt and flag-flying bushes. Returning too, dry-throated, over and over again, to its several well-prodded horrors: the bird's gaping bones in its cage of old sticks; the black flies in the corner, slimy dead; dry rags of snakes; and the crowded, rotting, silent-roaring city of a cat's grub-captured carcass.

Once seen, these relics passed within the frontiers of the known lands, to be remembered with a buzzing in the ears, to be revisited when the stomach was strong. They were the first tangible victims of that destroying force whose job I knew went on both night and day, though I could never catch him at it. Nevertheless I was grateful for them. Though they haunted my eyes and stuck in my dreams, they reduced for me the first infinite possibilities of horror. They chastened the imagination with the proof of a limited frightfulness.

From the harbour mouth of the scullery door I learned the rocks and reefs and the channels where safety lay. I discovered the physical pyramid of the cottage, its stores and labyrinths, its centres of magic, and of the green, spouting island-garden upon which it stood. My Mother and sisters sailed past me like galleons in their busy dresses, and I learned the smells and sounds which followed in their wakes, the surge of breath, air of carbolic, song and grumble, and smashing of crockery.

How magnificent they appeared, full-rigged, those towering girls, with their flying hair and billowing blouses, their white-mast arms stripped for work or washing. At any moment one was boarded by them, bussed and buttoned, or swung up like a wriggling fish to be hooked and held in their lacy linen.

The scullery was a mine of all the minerals of living. Here I discovered water—a very different element from the green crawling scum that stank in the garden tub. You could pump it in pure blue gulps out of the ground; you could swing on the pump handle and it came out sparkling like liquid sky. And it broke and ran and shone on the tiled floor, or quivered in a jug, or weighted your clothes with cold. You could drink it, draw with it, froth it with soap, swim beetles across it, or fly it in bubbles in the air. You could put your head in it, and open your eyes, and see the sides of the bucket buckle, and hear your caught breath roar, and work your mouth like a fish, and smell the lime from the ground. Substance of magic—which you could tear or wear, confine or scatter, or send down holes, but never burn or break or destroy.

The scullery was water, where the old pump stood. And it had everything else that was related to water: thick steam of Mondays, edgy with starch; soapsuds boiling, bellying and popping, creaking and whispering, rainbowed with light and winking with a million windows. Bubble, bubble, toil and grumble, rinsing and slapping of sheets and shirts, and panting Mother rowing her red arms like oars in the steaming waves. Then the linen came up on a stick out of the pot, like pastry, or woven suds, or sheets of moulded snow.

Here, too, was the scrubbing of floors and boots, of arms and necks, of red and white vegetables. Walk into the morning disorder of this room and all the garden was laid out dripping on the table. Chopped carrots like copper pennies, radishes and chives, potatoes dipped and stripped clean from their coats of mud, the snapping of tight pea-pods, long shells of green pearls, and the tearing of glutinous beans from their nests of wool.

Grown stealthy, marauding among these preparations, one nibbled one's way like a rat through roots and leaves. Peas rolled under the tongue, fresh cold, like solid water; teeth chewed green peel of apples, acid sharp, and the sweet white starch of swedes. Beaten away by wet hands gloved with flour, one returned in a morose and speechless lust. Slivers of raw pastry, moulded, warm, went down in the shapes of men and women—heads and arms of unsalted flesh seasoned with nothing but a dream of cannibalism.

Large meals were prepared in this room, cauldrons of stew for the insatiate hunger of eight. Stews of all that grew on these rich banks, flavoured with sage, coloured with Oxo and laced with a few bones of lamb. There was, it is true, little meat at those times; sometimes a pound of bare ribs for boiling, or an occasional rabbit dumped at the door by a neighbour. But there was green food of great weight in season, and lentils and bread for ballast. Eight to ten loaves came to the house every day, and they never grew dry. We tore them to pieces with their crusts still warm, and their monotony was brightened by the objects we found in them—string, nails, paper, and once a mouse; for those were days of happy-go-lucky baking. The lentils were cooked in a great pot which also heated the water for the Saturday-night baths.

Our small wood fire could heat sufficient water to fill one bath only, and this we shared in turn. Being the youngest but one, my water was always the dirtiest but one, and the implications of this privilege remain with me to this day.

Waking one morning in the white-washed bedroom, I opened my eyes and found them blind. Though I stretched them and stared where the room should be, nothing was visible but a glare of gold, flat on my throbbing eyelids. I groped for my body and found it there. I heard the singing of birds. Yet there was nothing at all to be seen of the world save this quivering yellow light. Was I dead? I wondered. Was I in heaven? Whatever it was, I hated it. I had wakened too soon from a dream of crocodiles and I was not ready for this further outrage. Then I heard the girls' steps on the stairs.

"Our Marge!" I shouted, "I can't see nothing!" And I began to give out my howl.

A slap of bare feet slithered across the floor, and I heard sister Marjorie's giggle.

"Just look at him," she said. "Pop and fetch a flannel, Doth—'is eyes've got stuck down again."

The cold edge of the flannel passed over my face, showered me with water, and I was back in the world. Bed and beams, and the sun-square window, and the girls bending over me grinning.

"'Oo did it?" I yelled

"Nobody, silly. Your eyes got bunged up, that's all."

The sweet glue of sleep; it had happened before but somehow I always forgot. So I threatened the girls I'd bung theirs up too; I was awake, I could see, I was happy. I lay looking out of the small green window. The world outside was crimson and on fire. I had never seen it looking like that before.

"Doth?" I said, "what's happening to them trees?"

Dorothy was dressing. She leaned out of the window, slow and sleepy, and the light came through her nightdress like sand through a sieve.

"Nothing's happening," she said.

"Yes it is then," I said. "They're falling to bits."

Dorothy scratched her dark head, yawning wide, and white feathers floated out of her hair.

"It's only the leaves droppin'. We're in autumn now. The leaves always drop in autumn."

Autumn? In autumn. Was that where we were? Where the leaves always dropped and there was always this smell. I imagined it continuing, with no change, for ever, these wet flames of woods burning on and on like the bush of Moses, as natural a part of this newfound land as the eternal snows of the poles. Why had we come to such a place?

Marjorie, who had gone down to help with the breakfast, suddenly came tumbling back up the stairs.

"Doth," she whispered; she seemed excited and frightened; "Doth . . . 'e's turned up again. 'Elp on Loll with 'is clothes and come on down, quick."

We went down and found him sitting by the fireside, smiling, wet and cold. I climbed up to the breakfast table and stared at him, the stranger. To me he did not so much appear to be a man as a conglomeration of woody things. His face was red and crinkled, brilliant like fungus. There were leaves in his mud-matted hair, and leaves and twigs on his crumbling clothes, and all over him. His boots were like the black pulp you find when you dig under a tree. Mother gave him porridge and bread and he smiled palely at us all.

"It must have been cruel in the wood," said our Mother.

"I've got some sacks, ma'am," he said, spooning his porridge. "They keep out the wet."

They wouldn't; they'd suck it up like a wick and wrap him in it.

"You oughtn't to live like that," said Mother. "You ought to get back to your home."

"No," smiled the man. "That wouldn't do. They'd jump on me before you could say 'knife.'"

Mother shook her head sadly, and sighed, and gave him more porridge. We boys adored the look of the man; the girls, fastidious, were more uncertain of him. But he was no tramp or he wouldn't be in the kitchen. He had four bright medals in his pocket, which he would produce and polish and lay on the table like money. He spoke like nobody else we knew, in fact we couldn't understand many of his words. But Mother seemed to understand him, and would ask him questions, and look at the photographs he carried in his shirt and sigh and shake her head. He talked something of battles and of flying in the air, and it was all wonderful to us.

He was no man from these parts. He had appeared on the doorstep one early morning, asking for a cup of tea. Our Mother had brought him in and given him a whole breakfast. There had been blood on his face and he had seemed very weak. Now he was in a kitchen with a woman and a lot of children, and his eyes shone brightly, and his whiskers smiled. He told us he was sleeping in the wood, which seemed to me a good idea. And he was a soldier, because Mother had said so.

I knew about war; all my uncles were in it; my ears from birth had been full of the talk of it. Sometimes I used to climb into the basket chair by the fire and close my eyes and see brown men moving over a field in battle. I was three, but I saw them grope and die and felt myself older than they.

This man did not look like a soldier. He had a beard and his khaki was torn. But the girls insisted he was a soldier, and said it in whispers, like a secret. And when he came down to our house for breakfast, and sat hunched by the fire, steaming with damp and coated with leaves and dirt, I thought of him sleeping up there in the wood. I imagined him sleeping, then having a go at the battle, then coming down to us for a cup of tea. He was the war, and the war was up there; I wanted to ask, "How's the war in that wood?"

But he never told us. He sat drinking his tea, gulping and gasping, the fire drawing the damp out of his clothes as if ghosts were rising from him. When he caught our eyes he smiled from his beard. And when brother Jack shot at him with a spoon, saying, "I'm a sodger," he replied softly, "Aye, and you'd make a better one than me, son, any day."

When he said that, I wondered what had happened to the war. Was he in those rags because he was such a bad soldier? Had he lost the war in the wood?

When he didn't come any more, I knew he had. The girls said some policemen had taken him away in a cart. And Mother sighed and was sad over the poor man.

In weather that was new to me, and cold, and loud with bullying winds, my Mother disappeared to visit my father. This was a long way off, out of sight, and I don't remember her going. But suddenly there were only the girls in the house, tumbling about with brooms and dishcloths, arguing, quarrelling, and putting us to bed at random. House and food had a new smell, and meals appeared like dismal conjuring tricks: cold, raw, or black with too much fire. Marjorie was breathless and everywhere; she was fourteen, with all the family in her care. My socks slipped down, and stayed down. I went unwashed for long periods of time. Black leaves swept into the house and piled up in the corners; it rained, and the floors sweated, and washing filled all the lines in the kitchen and dripped sadly on one and all.

But we ate; and the girls moved about in a giggling flurry, exhausted at their losing game. As the days went by, such a tide of muddles mounted in the house that I didn't know which room was which. I lived free, grubbing outside in the mud till I was black as a badger. And my nose ran free, as unchecked as my feet. I sailed my boots down the drain, I cut up sheets for puttees and marched like a soldier through the swamps of leaves. Sensing my chance I wandered far, eating all manner of raw objects: coloured berries, twigs and grubs; sick every day, but with a sickness of which I was proud.

All this time the sisters went through the house, darting upstairs and down, beset on all sides by the rain coming in, boys growing filthier, sheets scorching, saucepans burning, and kettles boiling over. The doll's house became a madhouse, and the girls frail birds flying in a wind of chaos. Doth giggled helplessly, Phyl wept among the vegetables, and Marjorie would say, when the day was over: "I'd lie down and die, if there was a place to lie down in."

I was not at all surprised when I heard of the end of the world. Everything pointed to it. The sky was low and whirling with black clouds; the woods roared night and day, stirring great seas of sound. One night we sat round the kitchen table, cracking walnuts with the best brass candlestick, when Marjorie came in from the town. She was shining with rain and loaded with bread and buns. She was also very white.

"The war's over," she said. "It's ended."

"Never," said Dorothy.

"They told me at the Stores," said Marjorie. "And they were giving away prunes." She gave us a bagful, and we ate them raw.

The girls got tea and talked about it. And I was sure it was the end of the world. All my life was the war, and the war was the world. Now the war was over. So the end of the world was come. It made no other sense to me.

"Let's go out and see what's happening," said Doth.

"You know we can't leave the kids," Marge said.

So we went too. It was dark, and the gleaming roofs of the village echoed with the buzz of singing. We went hand in hand through the rain, up the bank and down the street. A bonfire crackled in one of the gardens, and a woman jumped up and down in the light of it, red as a devil, a jug in her hand, uttering cries that were not singing. All down the other gardens there were other bonfires too. And a man came up and kissed the girls and hopped in the road and twisted on one toe.Then he fell down in the mud and lay there, working his legs like a frog and croaking a loud song.

I wanted to stop. I had never seen a man like this, in such a wild good humour. But we hurried on. We got to the pub and stared through the windows. The bar seemed on fire with its many lamps. Rose-coloured men, through the rain-wet windows, seemed to bulge and break into flame. They breathed out smoke, drank fire from golden jars, and I heard their great din with awe. Now anything might happen. And it did. A man rose up and crushed a glass like a nut between his hands, then held them out laughing for all to see his wounds. But the blood was lost in the general light of blood. Two other men came waltzing out of the door, locked in each other's arms. Fighting and cursing, they fell over the wall and rolled down the bank in the dark.

There was a screaming woman we could not see. "Jimmy! Jimmy!" she wailed. "Oh, Jimmy! Thee s'll kill 'im! I'll fetch the vicar, I will! Oh, Jimmy!"

"Just 'ark at 'em," said Dorothy, shocked and delighted.

"The kids ought to be in bed," said Marjorie.

"Stop a minute longer. Only a minute. It wouldn't do no 'arm."

Then the schoolhouse chimney caught fire. A fountain of sparks shot high into the night, writhing and sweeping on the wind, falling and dancing along the road. The chimney hissed like a firework, great rockets of flame came gushing forth, emptying the tiny house, so that I expected to see chairs and tables, knives and forks, radiant and burning, follow. The moss-tiles smouldered with sulphurous soot, yellow jets of smoke belched from cracks in the chimney. We stood in the rain and watched it, entranced, as if the sight had been saved for this day. As if the house had been saved, together with the year's bad litter, to be sent up in flames and rejoicing.

How everyone bellowed and scuffled and sang, drunk with their beer and the sight of the fire. But what would happen now that the war was over? What would happen to my uncles who lived in it?—those huge remote men who appeared suddenly at our house, reeking of leather and horses. What would happen to our father, who was khakied like every other man, yet special, not like other men? His picture hung over the piano, trim, haughty, with a badged cap and a spiked moustache. I confused him with the Kaiser. Would he die now the war was over?

As we gazed at the flaming schoolhouse chimney, and smelt the burning throughout the valley, I knew something momentous was occurring. At any moment I looked for a spectacular end to my already long life. Oh, the end of the war and the world! There was rain in my shoes, and Mother had disappeared. I never expected to see another day.

HENRY ADAMS

Henry Adams, a great nineteenth-century historian and influential observer of the America of his era, was born in Boston in 1838, the great-grandson of John Adams and the grandson of John Quincy Adams. An Adams of *the* Adams family (as opposed to the more humble stock from which Samuel Hopkins Adams, also represented in this anthology, sprang), Henry had every right to expect that someday he would be summoned to greatness. But times changed. Jacksonian democracy and the expansion of America westward from Boston left Henry Adams an observer, a role he brilliantly describes in his monumental *Education of Henry Adams* (1906), from which this brief selection is taken. He taught history at Harvard and published volumes of articulate and carefully researched history, the most interesting of which is, perhaps, his *Mont-Saint-Michel and Chartres* (1904), a profound analysis of the dynamics of medieval life. While he thought that history had passed him by, his works refuse to grant him obscurity. He died in 1918.

A New England Boyhood

The chief charm of New England was harshness of contrasts and extremes of sensibility—a cold that froze the blood, and a heat that boiled it—so that the pleasure of hating—one's self if no better victim offered—was not its rarest amusement; but the charm was a true and natural child of the soil, not a cultivated weed of the ancients. The violence of the contrast was real and made the strongest motive of education. The double exterior nature gave life its relative values. Winter and summer, cold and heat, town and country, force and freedom, marked two modes of life and thought, balanced like lobes of the brain. Town was winter confinement, school, rule, discipline; straight, gloomy streets, piled with six feet of snow in the middle; frosts that made the snow sing under wheels or runners; thaws when the streets became dangerous to cross; society of uncles, aunts, and cousins who expected children to behave themselves, and who were not always gratified; above all else, winter represented the desire to escape and go free. Town was restraint, law, unity. Country, only seven miles away, was liberty, diversity, outlawry, the endless delight of mere sense impressions given by nature for nothing, and breathed by boys without knowing it.

Boys are wild animals, rich in the treasures of sense, but the New England boy had a wider range of emotions than boys of more equable climates. He felt his nature crudely, as it was meant. To the boy Henry Adams, summer was drunken. Among senses, smell was the strongest—smell of hot pine-woods and sweet-fern in the scorching summer noon; of new-mown hay; of ploughed earth; of box hedges; of peaches, lilacs, syringas; of stables, barns, cow-yards; of salt water and low tide on the marshes; nothing came amiss. Next to smell came taste, and the children knew the taste of everything they saw or touched, from pennyroyal and flagroot to the shell of a pignut and the letters of a spelling book—the taste of A-B, AB, suddenly revived on the boy's tongue sixty years afterwards. Light, line, and color as sensual pleasures, came later and were as crude as the rest. The New England light is glare, and the atmosphere harshens color. The boy was a full man before he ever knew what was meant by atmosphere; his idea of pleasure in light was the blaze of a New England sun. His idea of color was a peony, with the dew of early morning on its petals. The intense blue of the sea, as he saw it a mile or two away, from the Quincy hills; the cumuli in a June afternoon sky; the strong reds and greens and purples of colored prints and children's picture-books, as the American colors then ran; these were ideals. The opposites or antipathies, were the cold grays of November evenings, and the thick, muddy thaws of Boston winter. With such standards, the Bostonian could not but develop a double nature. Life was a double thing. After a January blizzard, the boy who could look with pleasure into the violent snow-glare of the cold white sunshine, with its intense light and shade, scarcely knew what was meant by tone. He could reach it only by education.

Winter and summer, then, were two hostile lives, and bred two separate natures. Winter was always the effort to live; summer was tropical license. Whether the children rolled in the grass, or waded in the brook, or swam in the salt ocean, or sailed in the bay, or fished for smelts in the creeks, or netted minnows in the salt-marshes, or took to the pine-woods and the granite quarries, or chased muskrats and hunted snapping-turtles in the swamps, or mushrooms or nuts on the autumn hills, summer and country were always sensual living, while winter was always compulsory learning. Summer was the multiplicity of nature; winter was school.

The bearing of the two seasons on the education of Henry Adams was no fancy; it was the most decisive force he ever knew; it ran through life, and made the division between its perplexing, warring, irreconcilable problems, irreducible opposites, with growing emphasis to the last year of study. From earliest childhood the boy was accustomed to feel that, for him, life was double. Winter and summer, town and country, law and liberty, were hostile, and the man who pretended they were not, was in his eyes a schoolmaster—that is, a man employed to tell lies to little boys.

MALCOLM X

Malcolm X was born Malcolm Little in Omaha, Nebraska, in 1925. One of the most powerful and perceptive black leaders in America, he became a Black Muslim ("X" being the symbol of his Muslim name) and one of the most outspoken critics of racist America. He became disenchanted with the Muslim leader, Elijah Muhammad, however, and, after his return from Mecca, he began to develop a position which called for some accommodation with white society rather than the absolute separatism preached by the Black Muslims. He was assassinated in New York City in 1965, apparently in retaliation by more extremist elements in the black movement. The following selection is the first chapter of *The Autobiography of Malcolm X* (1964).

Nightmare

When my mother was pregnant with me, she told me later, a party of hooded Ku Klux Klan riders galloped up to our home in Omaha, Nebraska, one night. Surrounding the house, brandishing their shotguns and rifles, they shouted for my father to come out. My mother went to the front door and opened it. Standing where they could see her pregnant condition, she told them that she was alone with her three small children, and that my father was away, preaching, in Milwaukee. The Klansmen shouted threats and warnings at her that we had better get out of town because "the good Christian white people" were not going to stand for my father's "spreading trouble" among the "good" Negroes of Omaha with the "back to Africa" preachings of Marcus Garvey.

My father, the Reverend Earl Little, was a Baptist minister, a dedicated organizer for Marcus Aurelius Garvey's U.N.I.A. (Universal Negro Improvement Association). With the help of such disciples as my father, Garvey, from his headquarters in New York City's Harlem, was raising the banner of black-race purity and exhorting the Negro masses to return to their ancestral African homeland—a cause which had made Garvey the most controversial black man on earth.

Still shouting threats, the Klansmen finally spurred their horses and galloped around the house, shattering every window pane with their gun butts. Then they rode off into the night, their torches flaring, as suddenly as they had come.

My father was enraged when he returned. He decided to wait until

I was born—which would be soon—and then the family would move. I am not sure why he made this decision, for he was not a frightened Negro, as most then were, and many still are today. My father was a big, six-foot-four, very black man. He had only one eye. How he had lost the other one I have never known. He was from Reynolds, Georgia, where he had left school after the third or maybe fourth grade. He believed, as did Marcus Garvey, that freedom, independence and self-respect could never be achieved by the Negro in America, and that therefore the Negro should leave America to the white man and return to his African land of origin. Among the reasons my father had decided to risk and dedicate his life to help disseminate this philosophy among his people was that he had seen four of his six brothers die by violence, three of them killed by white men, including one by lynching. What my father could not know then was that of the remaining three, including himself, only one, my Uncle Jim, would die in bed, of natural causes. Northern white police were later to shoot my Uncle Oscar. And my father was finally himself to die by the white man's hands.

It has always been my belief that I, too, will die by violence. I have done all that I can to be prepared.

I was my father's seventh child. He had three children by a previous marriage—Ella, Earl, and Mary, who lived in Boston. He had met and married my mother in Philadelphia, where their first child, my oldest full brother, Wilfred, was born. They moved from Philadelphia to Omaha, where Hilda and then Philbert were born.

I was next in line. My mother was twenty-eight when I was born on May 19, 1925, in an Omaha hospital. Then we moved to Milwaukee, where Reginald was born. From infancy, he had some kind of hernia condition which was to handicap him physically for the rest of his life.

Louise Little, my mother, who was born in Grenada, in the British West Indies, looked like a white woman. Her father *was* white. She had straight black hair, and her accent did not sound like a Negro's. Of this white father of hers, I know nothing except her shame about it. I remember hearing her say she was glad that she had never seen him. It was, of course, because of him that I got my reddish-brown "mariny" color of skin, and my hair of the same color. I was the lightest child in our family. (Out in the world later on, in Boston and New York, I was among the millions of Negroes who were insane enough to feel that it was some kind of status symbol to be light-complexioned—that one was actually fortunate to be born thus. But, still later, I learned to hate every drop of that white rapist's blood that is in me.)

Our family stayed only briefly in Milwaukee, for my father wanted to find a place where he could raise our own food and perhaps build a business. The teaching of Marcus Garvey stressed becoming independent of the white man. We went next, for some reason, to Lansing,

Michigan. My father bought a house and soon, as had been his pattern, he was doing free-lance Christian preaching in local Negro Baptist churches, and during the week he was roaming about spreading word of Marcus Garvey.

He had begun to lay away savings for the store he had always wanted to own when, as always, some stupid local Uncle Tom Negroes began to funnel stories about his revolutionary beliefs to the local white people. This time, the get-out-of-town threats came from a local hate society called The Black Legion. They wore black robes instead of white. Soon, nearly everywhere my father went, Black Legionnaires were reviling him as an "uppity nigger" for wanting to own a store, for living outside the Lansing Negro district, for spreading unrest and dissension among "the good niggers."

As in Omaha, my mother was pregnant again, this time with my youngest sister. Shortly after Yvonne was born came the nightmare night in 1929, my earliest vivid memory. I remember being suddenly snatched awake into a frightening confusion of pistol shots and shouting and smoke and flames. My father had shouted and shot at the two white men who had set the fire and were running away. Our home was burning down around us. We were lunging and bumping and tumbling all over each other trying to escape. My mother, with the baby in her arms, just made it into the yard before the house crashed in, showering sparks. I remember we were outside in the night in our underwear, crying and yelling our heads off. The white police and firemen came and stood around watching as the house burned down to the ground.

My father prevailed on some friends to clothe and house us temporarily; then he moved us into another house on the outskirts of East Lansing. In those days Negroes weren't allowed after dark in East Lansing proper. There's where Michigan State University is located; I related all of this to an audience of students when I spoke there in January, 1963 (and had the first reunion in a long while with my younger brother, Robert, who was there doing postgraduate studies in psychology). I told them how East Lansing harassed us so much that we had to move again, this time two miles out of town, into the country. This was where my father built for us with his own hands a four-room house. This is where I really begin to remember things—this home where I started to grow up.

After the fire, I remember that my father was called in and questioned about a permit for the pistol with which he had shot at the white men who set the fire. I remember that the police were always dropping by our house, shoving things around, "just checking" or "looking for a gun." The pistol they were looking for—which they never found, and for which they wouldn't issue a permit—was sewed up inside a pillow. My father's .22 rifle and his shotgun, though, were right out in the open; everyone had them for hunting birds and rabbits and other game.

After that, my memories are of the friction between my father and mother. They seemed to be nearly always at odds. Sometimes my father would beat her. It might have had something to do with the fact that my mother had a pretty good education. Where she got it I don't know. But an educated woman, I suppose, can't resist the temptation to correct an uneducated man. Every now and then, when she put those smooth words on him, he would grab her.

My father was also belligerent toward all of the children, except me. The older ones he would beat almost savagely if they broke any of his rules—and he had so many rules it was hard to know them all. Nearly all my whippings came from my mother. I've thought a lot about why. I actually believe that as anti-white as my father was, he was subconsciously so afflicted with the white man's brainwashing of Negroes that he inclined to favor the light ones, and I was his lightest child. Most Negro parents in those days would almost instinctively treat any lighter children better than they did the darker ones. It came directly from the slavery tradition that the "mulatto," because he was visibly nearer to white, was therefore "better."

My two other images of my father are both outside the home. One was his role as a Baptist preacher. He never pastored in any regular church of his own; he was always a "visiting preacher." I remember especially his favorite sermon: "That little *black* train is a-comin' . . . an' you better get all your business right!" I guess this also fit his association with the back-to-Africa movement, with Marcus Garvey's "Black Train Homeward." My brother Philbert, the one just older than me, loved church, but it confused and amazed me. I would sit goggle-eyed at my father jumping and shouting as he preached, with the congregation jumping and shouting behind him, their souls and bodies devoted to singing and praying. Even at that young age, I just couldn't believe in the Christian concept of Jesus as someone divine. And no religious person, until I was a man in my twenties—and then in prison—could tell me anything. I had very little respect for most people who represented religion.

It was in his role as a preacher that my father had most contact with the Negroes of Lansing. Believe me when I tell you that those Negroes were in bad shape then. They are still in bad shape—though in a different way. By that I mean that I don't know a town with a higher percentage of complacent and misguided so-called "middle-class" Negroes—the typical status-symbol-oriented, integration-seeking type of Negroes. Just recently, I was standing in a lobby at the United

Nations talking with an African ambassador and his wife, when a Negro came up to me and said, "You know me?" I was a little embarrassed because I thought he was someone I should remember. It turned out that he was one of those bragging, self-satisfied, "middle-class" Lansing Negroes. I wasn't ingratiated. He was the type who would never have been associated with Africa, until the fad of having African friends became a status-symbol for "middle-class" Negroes.

Back when I was growing up, the "successful" Lansing Negroes were such as waiters and bootblacks. To be a janitor at some downtown store was to be highly respected. The real "elite," the "big shots," the "voices of the race," were the waiters at the Lansing Country Club and the shoeshine boys at the state capitol. The only Negroes who really had any money were the ones in the numbers racket, or who ran the gambling houses, or who in some other way lived parasitically off the poorest ones, who were the masses. No Negroes were hired then by Lansing's big Oldsmobile plant, or the Reo plant. (Do you remember the Reo? It was manufactured in Lansing, and R. E. Olds, the man after whom it was named, also lived in Lansing. When the war came along, they hired some Negro janitors.) The bulk of the Negroes were either on Welfare, or W.P.A., or they starved.

The day was to come when our family was so poor that we would eat the hole out of a doughnut; but at that time we were much better off than most town Negroes. The reason was we raised much of our own food out there in the country where we were. We were much better off than the town Negroes who would shout, as my father preached, for the pie-in-the-sky and their heaven in the hereafter while the white man had his here on earth.

I knew that the collections my father got for his preaching were mainly what fed and clothed us, and he also did other odd jobs, but still the image of him that made me proudest was his crusading and militant campaigning with the words of Marcus Garvey. As young as I was then, I knew from what I overheard that my father was saying something that made him a "tough" man. I remember an old lady, grinning and saying to my father, "You're scaring these white folks to death!"

One of the reasons I've always felt that my father favored me was that to the best of my remembrance, it was only me that he sometimes took with him to the Garvey U.N.I.A. meetings which he held quietly in different people's homes. There were never more than a few people at any one time—twenty at most. But that was a lot, packed into someone's living room. I noticed how differently they all acted, although sometimes they were the same people who jumped and shouted in church. But in these meetings both they and my father were more intense, more intelligent and down to earth. It made me feel the same way.

I can remember hearing of "Adam driven out of the garden into the caves of Europe," "Africa for the Africans," "Ethiopians, Awake!" And my father would talk about how it would not be much longer before Africa would be completely run by Negroes—"by black men," was the phrase he always used. "No one knows when the hour of Africa's redemption cometh. It is in the wind. It is coming. One day, like a storm, it will be here."

I remember seeing the big, shiny photographs of Marcus Garvey that were passed from hand to hand. My father had a big envelope of them that he always took to these meetings. The pictures showed what seemed to me millions of Negroes thronged in parade behind Garvey riding in a fine car, a big black man dressed in a dazzling uniform with gold braid on it, and he was wearing a thrilling hat with tall plumes. I remember hearing that he had black followers not only in the United States but all around the world, and I remember how the meetings always closed with my father saying, several times, and the people chanting after him, "Up, you mighty race, you can accomplish what you will!"

I have never understood why, after hearing as much as I did of these kinds of things, I somehow never thought, then, of the black people in Africa. My image of Africa, at that time, was of naked savages, cannibals, monkeys and tigers and steaming jungles.

My father would drive in his old black touring car, sometimes taking me, to meeting places all around the Lansing area. I remember one daytime meeting (most were at night) in the town of Owosso, forty miles from Lansing, which the Negroes called "White City." (Owosso's greatest claim to fame is that it is the home of Thomas E. Dewey.) As in East Lansing, no Negroes were allowed on the streets there after dark—hence the daytime meeting. In point of fact, in those days lots of Michigan towns were like that. Every town had a few "home" Negroes who lived there. Sometimes it would be just one family, as in the nearby county seat, Mason, which had a single Negro family named Lyons. Mr. Lyons had been a famous football star at Mason High School, was highly thought of in Mason, and consequently he now worked around that town in menial jobs.

My mother at this time seemed to be always working—cooking, washing, ironing, cleaning, and fussing over us eight children. And she was usually either arguing with or not speaking to my father. One cause of friction was that she had strong ideas about what she wouldn't eat—and didn't want *us* to eat—including pork and rabbit, both of which my father loved dearly. He was a real Georgia Negro, and he believed in eating plenty of what we in Harlem today call "soul food."

I've said that my mother was the one who whipped me—at least she did whenever she wasn't ashamed to let the neighbors think she was killing me. For if she even acted as though she was about to raise her hand to me, I would open my mouth and let the world know about it. If anybody was passing by out on the road, she would either change her mind or just give me a few licks.

Thinking about it now, I feel definitely that just as my father favored me for being lighter than the other children, my mother gave me more hell for the same reason. She was very light herself but she favored the ones who were darker. Wilfred, I know, was particularly her angel. I remember that she would tell me to get out of the house and "Let the sun shine on you so you can get some color." She went out of her way never to let me become afflicted with a sense of color-superiority. I am sure that she treated me this way partly because of how she came to be light herself.

I learned early that crying out in protest could accomplish things. My older brothers and sister had started to school when, sometimes, they would come in and ask for a buttered biscuit or something and my mother, impatiently, would tell them no. But I would cry out and make a fuss until I got what I wanted. I remember well how my mother asked me why I couldn't be a nice boy like Wilfred; but I would think to myself that Wilfred, for being so nice and quiet, often stayed hungry. So early in life, I had learned that if you want something, you had better make some noise.

Not only did we have our big garden, but we raised chickens. My father would buy some baby chicks and my mother would raise them. We all loved chicken. That was one dish there was no argument with my father about. One thing in particular that I remember made me feel grateful toward my mother was that one day I went and asked her for my own garden, and she did let me have my own little plot. I loved it and took care of it well. I loved especially to grow peas. I was proud when we had them on our table. I would pull out the grass in my garden by hand when the first little blades came up. I would patrol the rows on my hands and knees for any worms and bugs, and I would kill and bury them. And sometimes when I had everything straight and clean for my things to grow, I would lie down on my back between two rows, and I would gaze up in the blue sky at the clouds moving and think all kinds of things.

At five, I, too, began to go to school, leaving home in the morning along with Wilfred, Hilda, and Philbert. It was the Pleasant Grove School that went from kindergarten through the eighth grade. It was two miles outside the city limits, and I guess there was no problem about our attending because we were the only Negroes in the area. In those days white people in the North usually would "adopt" just a few

Negroes; they didn't see them as any threat. The white kids didn't make any great thing about us, either. They called us "nigger" and "darkie" and "Rastus" so much that we thought those were our natural names. But they didn't think of it as an insult; it was just the way they thought about us.

One afternoon in 1931 when Wilfred, Hilda, Philbert, and I came home, my mother and father were having one of their arguments. There had lately been a lot of tension around the house because of Black Legion threats. Anyway, my father had taken one of the rabbits which we were raising, and ordered my mother to cook it. We raised rabbits, but sold them to whites. My father had taken a rabbit from the rabbit pen. He had pulled off the rabbit's head. He was so strong, he needed no knife to behead chickens or rabbits. With one twist of his big black hands he simply twisted off the head and threw the bleeding-necked thing back at my mother's feet.

My mother was crying. She started to skin the rabbit, preparatory to cooking it. But my father was so angry he slammed on out of the front door and started walking up the road toward town.

It was then that my mother had this vision. She had always been a strange woman in this sense, and had always had a strong intuition of things about to happen. And most of her children are the same way, I think. When something is about to happen, I can feel something, sense something. I never have known something to happen that has caught me completely off guard—except once. And that was when, years later, I discovered facts I couldn't believe about a man who, up until that discovery, I would gladly have given my life for.

My father was well up the road when my mother ran screaming out onto the porch. *"Early! Early!"* She screamed his name. She clutched up her apron in one hand, and ran down across the yard and into the road. My father turned around. He saw her. For some reason, considering how angry he had been when he left, he waved at her. But he kept on going.

She told me later, my mother did, that she had a vision of my father's end. All the rest of the afternoon, she was not herself, crying and nervous and upset. She finished cooking the rabbit and put the whole thing in the warmer part of the black stove. When my father was not back home by our bedtime, my mother hugged and clutched us, and we felt strange, not knowing what to do, because she had never acted like that.

I remember waking up to the sound of my mother's screaming again. When I scrambled out, I saw the police in the living room; they were trying to calm her down. She had snatched on her clothes to go with them. And all of us children who were staring knew without anyone having to say it that something terrible had happened to our father.

My mother was taken by the police to the hospital, and to a room where a sheet was over my father in a bed, and she wouldn't look, she was afraid to look. Probably it was wise that she didn't. My father's skull, on one side, was crushed in, I was told later. Negroes in Lansing have always whispered that he was attacked, and then laid across some tracks for a streetcar to run over him. His body was cut almost in half.

He lived two and a half hours in that condition. Negroes then were stronger than they are now, especially Georgia Negroes. Negroes born in Georgia had to be strong simply to survive.

It was morning when we children at home got the word that he was dead. I was six. I can remember a vague commotion, the house filled up with people crying, saying bitterly that the white Black Legion had finally gotten him. My mother was hysterical. In the bedroom, women were holding smelling salts under her nose. She was still hysterical at the funeral.

I don't have a very clear memory of the funeral, either. Oddly, the main thing I remember is that it wasn't in a church, and that surprised me, since my father was a preacher, and I had been where he preached people's funerals in churches. But his was in a funeral home.

And I remember that during the service a big black fly came down and landed on my father's face, and Wilfred sprang up from his chair and he shooed the fly away, and he came groping back to his chair—there were folding chairs for us to sit on—and the tears were streaming down his face. When we went by the casket, I remember that I thought that it looked as if my father's strong black face had been dusted with flour, and I wished they hadn't put on such a lot of it.

Back in the big four-room house, there were many visitors for another week or so. They were good friends of the family, such as the Lyons from Mason, twelve miles away, and the Walkers, McGuires, Liscoes, the Greens, Randolphs, and the Turners, and others from Lansing, and a lot of people from other towns, whom I had seen at the Garvey meetings.

We children adjusted more easily than our mother did. We couldn't see, as clearly as she did, the trials that lay ahead. As the visitors tapered off, she became very concerned about collecting the two insurance policies that my father had always been proud he carried. He had always said that families should be protected in case of death. One policy apparently paid off without any problem—the smaller one. I don't know the amount of it. I would imagine it was not more than a thousand dollars, and maybe half of that.

But after that money came, and my mother had paid out a lot of it for the funeral and expenses, she began going into town and returning very upset. The company that had issued the bigger policy was balking at paying off. They were claiming that my father had committed suicide. Visitors came again, and there was bitter talk about white people: how could my father bash himself in the head, then get down across the streetcar tracks to be run over?

So there we were. My mother was thirty-four years old now, with no husband, no provider or protector to take care of her eight children. But some kind of a family routine got going again. And for as long as the first insurance money lasted, we did all right.

Wilfred, who was a pretty stable fellow, began to act older than his age. I think he had the sense to see, when the rest of us didn't, what was in the wind for us. He quietly quit school and went to town in search of work. He took any kind of job he could find and he would come home, dog-tired, in the evenings, and give whatever he had made to my mother.

Hilda, who always had been quiet, too, attended to the babies. Philbert and I didn't contribute anything. We just fought all the time—each other at home, and then at school we would team up and fight white kids. Sometimes the fights would be racial in nature, but they might be about anything.

Reginald came under my wing. Since he had grown out of the toddling stage, he and I had become very close. I suppose I enjoyed the fact that he was the little one, under me, who looked up to me.

My mother began to buy on credit. My father had always been very strongly against credit. "Credit is the first step into debt and back into slavery," he had always said. And then she went to work herself. She would go into Lansing and find different jobs—in housework, or sewing—for white people. They didn't realize, usually, that she was a Negro. A lot of white people around there didn't want Negroes in their houses.

She would do fine until in some way or other it got to people who she was, whose widow she was. And then she would be let go. I remember how she used to come home crying, but trying to hide it, because she had lost a job that she needed so much.

Once when one of us—I cannot remember which—had to go for something to where she was working, and the people saw us, and realized she was actually a Negro, she was fired on the spot, and she came home crying, this time not hiding it.

When the state Welfare people began coming to our house, we would come from school sometimes and find them talking with our mother, asking a thousand questions. They acted and looked at her, and at us, and around in our house, in a way that had about it the feeling—at least for me—that we were not people. In their eyesight we were just *things*, that was all.

My mother began to receive two checks—a Welfare check and, I believe, a widow's pension. The checks helped. But they weren't enough, as many of us as there were. When they came, about the first of the month, one always was already owed in full, if not more, to the man at the grocery store. And, after that, the other one didn't last long.

We began to go swiftly downhill. The physical downhill wasn't as quick as the psychological. My mother was, above everything else, a proud woman, and it took its toll on her that she was accepting charity. And her feelings were communicated to us.

She would speak sharply to the man at the grocery store for padding the bill, telling him that she wasn't ignorant, and he didn't like that. She would talk back sharply to the state Welfare people, telling them that she was a grown woman, able to raise her children, that it wasn't necessary for them to keep coming around so much, meddling in our lives. And they didn't like that.

But the monthly Welfare check was their pass. They acted as if they owned us, as if we were their private property. As much as my mother would have liked to, she couldn't keep them out. She would get particularly incensed when they began insisting upon drawing us older children aside, one at a time, out on the porch or somewhere, and asking us questions, or telling us things—against our mother and against each other.

We couldn't understand why, if the state was willing to give us packages of meat, sacks of potatoes and fruit, and cans of all kinds of things, our mother obviously hated to accept. We really couldn't understand. What I later understood was that my mother was making a desperate effort to preserve her pride—and ours.

Pride was just about all we had to preserve, for by 1934, we really began to suffer. This was about the worst depression year, and no one we knew had enough to eat or live on. Some old family friends visited us now and then. At first they brought food. Though it was charity, my mother took it.

Wilfred was working to help. My mother was working, when she could find any kind of job. In Lansing, there was a bakery where, for a nickel, a couple of us children would buy a tall flour sack of day-old bread and cookies, and then walk the two miles back out into the country to our house. Our mother knew, I guess, dozens of ways to cook things with bread and out of bread. Stewed tomatoes with bread, maybe that would be a meal. Something like French toast, if we had any eggs. Bread pudding, sometimes with raisins in it. If we got hold of some hamburger, it came to the table more bread than meat. The cookies that were always in the sack with the bread, we just gobbled down straight.

But there were times when there wasn't even a nickel and we

would be so hungry we were dizzy. My mother would boil a big pot of dandelion greens, and we would eat that. I remember that some small-minded neighbor put it out, and children would tease us, that we ate "fried grass." Sometimes, if we were lucky, we would have oatmeal or cornmeal mush three times a day. Or mush in the morning and cornbread at night.

Philbert and I were grown up enough to quit fighting long enough to take the .22 caliber rifle that had been our father's, and shoot rabbits that some white neighbors up or down the road would buy. I know now that they just did it to help us, because they, like everyone, shot their own rabbits. Sometimes, I remember, Philbert and I would take little Reginald along with us. He wasn't very strong, but he was always so proud to be along. We would trap muskrats out in the little creek in back of our house. And we would lie quiet until unsuspecting bullfrogs appeared, and we would spear them, cut off their legs, and sell them for a nickel a pair to people who lived up and down the road. The whites seemed less restricted in their dietary tastes.

Then, about in late 1934, I would guess, something began to happen. Some kind of psychological deterioration hit our family circle and began to eat away our pride. Perhaps it was the constant tangible evidence that we were destitute. We had known other families who had gone on relief. We had known without anyone in our home ever expressing it that we had felt prouder not to be at the depot where the free food was passed out. And, now, we were among them. At school, the "on relief" finger suddenly was pointed at us, too, and sometimes it was said aloud.

It seemed that everything to eat in our house was stamped Not To Be Sold. All Welfare food bore this stamp to keep the recipients from selling it. It's a wonder we didn't come to think of Not To Be Sold as a brand name.

Sometimes, instead of going home from school, I walked the two miles up the road into Lansing. I began drifting from store to store, hanging around outside where things like apples were displayed in boxes and barrels and baskets, and I would watch my chance and steal me a treat. You know what a treat was to me? Anything!

Or I began to drop in about dinnertime at the home of some family that we knew. I knew that they knew exactly why I was there, but they never embarrassed me by letting on. They would invite me to stay for supper, and I would stuff myself.

Especially, I liked to drop in and visit at the Gohannas' home. They were nice, older people, and great churchgoers. I had watched them lead the jumping and shouting when my father preached. They had, living with them—they were raising him—a nephew whom everyone called "Big Boy," and he and I got along fine. Also living with the Gohannas was old Mrs. Adcock, who went with them to church. She was always trying to help anybody she could, visiting anyone she heard was sick, carrying them something. She was the one who, years later, would tell me something that I remembered a long time: "Malcolm, there's one thing I like about you. You're no good, but you don't try to hide it. You are not a hypocrite."

The more I began to stay away from home and visit people and steal from the stores, the more aggressive I became in my inclinations. I never wanted to wait for anything.

I was growing up fast, physically more so than mentally. As I began to be recognized more around the town, I started to become aware of the peculiar attitude of white people toward me. I sensed that it had to do with my father. It was an adult version of what several white children had said at school, in hints, or sometimes in the open, which really expressed what their parents had said—that the Black Legion or the Klan had killed my father, and the insurance company had pulled a fast one in refusing to pay my mother the policy money.

When I began to get caught stealing now and then, the state Welfare people began to focus on me when they came to our house. I can't remember how I first became aware that they were talking of taking me away. What I first remember along that line was my mother raising a storm about being able to bring up her own children. She would whip me for stealing, and I would try to alarm the neighborhood with my yelling. One thing I have always been proud of is that I never raised my hand against my mother.

In the summertime, at night, in addition to all the other things we did, some of us boys would slip out down the road, or across the pastures, and go "cooning" watermelons. White people always associated watermelons with Negroes, and they sometimes called Negroes "coons" among all the other names, and so stealing watermelons became "cooning" them. If white boys were doing it, it implied that they were only acting like Negroes. Whites have always hidden or justified all of the guilts they could by ridiculing or blaming Negroes.

One Halloween night, I remember that a bunch of us were out tipping over those old country outhouses, and one old farmer—I guess he had tipped over enough in his day—had set a trap for us. Always, you sneak up from behind the outhouse, then you gang together and push it, to tip it over. This farmer had taken his outhouse off the hole, and set it just in *front* of the hole. Well, we came sneaking up in single file, in the darkness, and the two white boys in the lead fell down into the outhouse hole neck deep. They smelled so bad it was all we could stand to get them out, and that finished us all for that Halloween. I had just missed falling in myself. The whites were so used to taking the lead, this time it had really gotten them in the hole.

Thus, in various ways, I learned various things. I picked strawberries, and though I can't recall what I got per crate for picking, I remember that after working hard all one day, I wound up with about a dollar, which was a whole lot of money in those times. I was so hungry, I didn't know what to do. I was walking away toward town with visions of buying something good to eat, and this older white boy I knew, Richard Dixon, came up and asked me if I wanted to match nickels. He had plenty of change for my dollar. In about a half hour, he had all the change back, including my dollar, and instead of going to town to buy something, I went home with nothing, and I was bitter. But that was nothing compared to what I felt when I found out later that he had cheated. There is a way that you can catch and hold the nickel and make it come up the way you want. This was my first lesson about gambling: if you see somebody winning all the time, he isn't gambling, he's cheating. Later on in life, if I were continuously losing in any gambling situation, I would watch very closely. It's like the Negro in America seeing the white man win all the time. He's a professional gambler; he has all the cards and the odds stacked on his side, and he has always dealt to our people from the bottom of the deck.

About this time, my mother began to be visited by some Seventh Day Adventists who had moved into a house not too far down the road from us. They would talk to her for hours at a time, and leave booklets and leaflets and magazines for her to read. She read them, and Wilfred, who had started back to school after we had begun to get the relief food supplies, also read a lot. His head was forever in some book.

Before long, my mother spent much time with the Adventists. It's my belief that what mostly influenced her was that they had even more diet restrictions than she always had taught and practiced with us. Like us, they were against eating rabbit and pork; they followed the Mosaic dietary laws. They ate nothing of the flesh without a split hoof, or that didn't chew a cud. We began to go with my mother to the Adventist meetings that were held further out in the country. For us children, I know that the major attraction was the good food they served. But we listened, too. There were a handful of Negroes, from small towns in the area, but I would say that it was ninety-nine percent white people. The Adventists felt that we were living at the end of time, that the world soon was coming to an end. But they were the friendliest white people I had ever seen. In some ways, though, we children noticed, and, when we were back at home, discussed, that they were different from us—such as the lack of enough seasoning in their food, and the different way that white people smelled.

Meanwhile, the state Welfare people kept after my mother. By now, she didn't make it any secret that she hated them, and didn't want them in her house. But they exerted their right to come, and I have many, many times reflected upon how, talking to us children, they began to plant the seeds of division in our minds. They would ask such things as who was smarter than the other. And they would ask me why I was "so different."

I think they felt that getting children into foster homes was a legitimate part of their function, and the result would be less troublesome, however they went about it.

And when my mother fought them, they went after her—first, through me. I was the first target. I stole; that implied that I wasn't being taken care of by my mother.

All of us were mischievous at some time or another, I more so than any of the rest. Philbert and I kept a battle going. And this was just one of a dozen things that kept building up the pressure on my mother.

I'm not sure just how or when the idea was first dropped by the Welfare workers that our mother was losing her mind.

But I can distinctly remember hearing "crazy" applied to her by them when they learned that the Negro farmer who was in the next house down the road from us had offered to give us some butchered pork—a whole pig, maybe even two of them—and she had refused. We all heard them call my mother "crazy" to her face for refusing good meat. It meant nothing to them even when she explained that we had never eaten pork, that it was against her religion as a Seventh Day Adventist.

They were as vicious as vultures. They had no feelings, understanding, compassion, or respect for my mother. They told us, "She's crazy for refusing food." Right then was when our home, our unity, began to disintegrate. We were having a hard time, and I wasn't helping. But we could have made it, we could have stayed together. As bad as I was, as much trouble and worry as I caused my mother, I loved her.

The state people, we found out, had interviewed the Gohannas family, and the Gohannas' had said that they would take me into their home. My mother threw a fit, though, when she heard that—and the home wreckers took cover for a while.

It was about this time that the large, dark man from Lansing began visiting. I don't remember how or where he and my mother met. It may have been through some mutual friends. I don't remember what the man's profession was. In 1935, in Lansing, Negroes didn't have anything you could call a profession. But the man, big and black, looked something like my father. I can remember his name, but there's no need to mention it. He was a single man, and my mother was a widow only thirty-six years old. The man was independent; naturally she admired that. She was having a hard time disciplining us, and a big man's presence alone would help. And if she had a man to provide, it would send the state people away forever.

We all understood without ever saying much about it. Or at least we had no objection. We took it in stride, even with some amusement among us, that when the man came, our mother would be all dressed up in the best that she had—she still was a good-looking woman—and she would act differently, lighthearted and laughing, as we hadn't seen her act in years.

It went on for about a year, I guess. And then, about 1936, or 1937, the man from Lansing jilted my mother suddenly. He just stopped coming to see her. From what I later understood, he finally backed away from taking on the responsibility of those eight mouths to feed. He was afraid of so many of us. To this day, I can see the trap that Mother was in, saddled with all of us. And I can also understand why he would shun taking on such a tremendous responsibility.

But it was a terrible shock to her. It was the beginning of the end of reality for my mother. When she began to sit around and walk around talking to herself—almost as though she was unaware that we were there—it became increasingly terrifying.

The state people saw her weakening. That was when they began the definite steps to take me away from home. They began to tell me how nice it was going to be at the Gohannas' home, where the Gohannas' and Big Boy and Mrs. Adcock had all said how much they liked me, and would like to have me live with them.

I liked all of them, too. But I didn't want to leave Wilfred. I looked up to and admired my big brother. I didn't want to leave Hilda, who was like my second mother. Or Philbert; even in our fighting, there was a feeling of brotherly union. Or Reginald, especially, who was weak with his hernia condition, and who looked up to me as his big brother who looked out for him, as I looked up to Wilfred. And I had nothing, either, against the babies, Yvonne, Wesley, and Robert.

As my mother talked to herself more and more, she gradually became less responsive to us. And less responsible. The house became less tidy. We began to be more unkempt. And usually, now, Hilda cooked.

We children watched our anchor giving way. It was something terrible that you couldn't get your hands on, yet you couldn't get away from. It was a sensing that something bad was going to happen. We younger ones leaned more and more heavily on the relative strength of Wilfred and Hilda, who were the oldest.

When finally I was sent to the Gohannas' home, at least in a surface way I was glad. I remember that when I left home with the state man, my mother said one thing: "Don't let them feed him any pig."

It was better, in a lot of ways, at the Gohannas'. Big Boy and I shared his room together, and we hit it off nicely. He just wasn't the same as my blood brothers. The Gohannas' were very religious people. Big Boy and I attended church with them. They were sanctified Holy Rollers now. The preachers and congregations jumped even higher and shouted even louder than the Baptists I had known. They sang at the top of their lungs, and swayed back and forth and cried and moaned and beat on tambourines and chanted. It was spooky, with ghosts and spirituals and "ha'nts" seeming to be in the very atmosphere when finally we all came out of the church, going back home.

The Gohannas' and Mrs. Adcock loved to go fishing, and some Saturdays Big Boy and I would go along. I had changed schools now, to Lansing's West Junior High School. It was right in the heart of the Negro community, and a few white kids were there, but Big Boy didn't mix much with any of our schoolmates, and I didn't either. And when we went fishing, neither he nor I liked the idea of just sitting and waiting for the fish to jerk the cork under the water—or make the tight line quiver, when we fished that way. I figured there should be some smarter way to get the fish—though we never discovered what it might be.

Mr. Gohannas was close cronies with some other men who, some Saturdays, would take me and Big Boy with them hunting rabbits. I had my father's .22 caliber rifle; my mother had said it was all right for me to take it with me. The old men had a set rabbit-hunting strategy that they had always used. Usually when a dog jumps a rabbit, and the rabbit gets away, that rabbit will always somehow instinctively run in a circle and return sooner or later past the very spot where he originally was jumped. Well, the old men would just sit and wait in hiding somewhere for the rabbit to come back, then get their shots at him. I got to thinking about it, and finally I thought of a plan. I would separate from them and Big Boy and I would go to a point where I figured that the rabbit, returning, would have to pass me first.

It worked like magic. I began to get three and four rabbits before they got one. The astonishing thing was that none of the old men ever figured out why. They outdid themselves exclaiming what a sure shot I was. I was about twelve, then. All I had done was to improve on their strategy, and it was the beginning of a very important lesson in life—that anytime you find someone more successful than you are, especially when you're both engaged in the same business—you know they're doing something that you aren't.

I would return home to visit fairly often. Sometimes Big Boy and one or another, or both, of the Gohannas would go with me —sometimes not. I would be glad when some of them did go, because it made the ordeal easier.

Soon the state people were making plans to take over all of my mother's children. She talked to herself nearly all of the time now, and there was a crowd of new white people entering the picture—always asking questions. They would even visit me at the Gohannas'. They would ask me questions out on the porch, or sitting out in their cars.

Eventually my mother suffered a complete breakdown, and the court orders were finally signed. They took her to the State Mental Hospital at Kalamazoo.

It was seventy-some miles from Lansing, about an hour and a half on the bus. A Judge McClellan in Lansing had authority over me and all of my brothers and sisters. We were "state children," court wards; he had the full say-so over us. A white man in charge of a black man's children! Nothing but legal, modern slavery—however kindly intentioned.

My mother remained in the same hospital at Kalamazoo for about twenty-six years. Later, when I was still growing up in Michigan, I would go to visit her every so often. Nothing that I can imagine could have moved me as deeply as seeing her pitiful state. In 1963, we got my mother out of the hospital, and she now lives there in Lansing with Philbert and his family.

It was so much worse than if it had been a physical sickness, for which a cause might be known, medicine given, a cure effected. Every time I visited her, when finally they led her—a case, a number—back inside from where we had been sitting together, I felt worse.

My last visit, when I knew I would never come to see her again—there—was in 1952. I was twenty-seven. My brother Philbert had told me that on his last visit, she had recognized him somewhat. "In spots," he said.

But she didn't recognize me at all.

She stared at me. She didn't know who I was.

Her mind, when I tried to talk, to reach her, was somewhere else. I asked, "Mama, do you know what day it is?"

She said, staring, "All the people have gone."

I can't describe how I felt. The woman who had brought me into the world, and nursed me, and advised me, and chastised me, and loved me, didn't know me. It was as if I was trying to walk up the side of a hill of feathers. I looked at her. I listened to her "talk." But there was nothing I could do.

I truly believe that if ever a state social agency destroyed a family, it destroyed ours. We wanted and tried to stay together. Our home didn't have to be destroyed. But the Welfare, the courts, and their doctor, gave us the one-two-three punch. And ours was not the only case of this kind.

I knew I wouldn't be back to see my mother again because it could make me a very vicious and dangerous person—knowing how they had looked at us as numbers and as a case in their book, not as human beings. And knowing that my mother in there was a statistic that didn't have to be, that existed because of a society's failure, hypocrisy, greed, and lack of mercy and compassion. Hence I have no mercy or compassion in me for a society that will crush people, and then penalize them for not being able to stand up under the weight.

I have rarely talked to anyone about my mother, for I believe that I am capable of killing a person, without hesitation, who happened to make the wrong kind of remark about my mother. So I purposely don't make any opening for some fool to step into.

Back then when our family was destroyed, in 1937, Wilfred and Hilda were old enough so that the state let them stay on their own in the big four-room house that my father had built. Philbert was placed with another family in Lansing, a Mrs. Hackett, while Reginald and Wesley went to live with a family called Williams, who were friends of my mother's. And Yvonne and Robert went to live with a West Indian family named McGuire.

Separated though we were, all of us maintained fairly close touch around Lansing—in school and out—whenever we could get together. Despite the artificially created separation and distance between us, we still remained very close in our feelings toward each other.

MAXIM GORKI

Maxim Gorki is the pen name of Alexei Maximovitch Pyeshkov, born in 1868 in Nizhni Novgorod, Russia. The following selection is from the first volume of his autobiographical trilogy (*Childhood*, 1913; *In the World*, 1915; and *My University Days*, 1923). Gorki (which means "bitter one") was the first Russian writer of any stature to support the Bolsheviks, and headed their propaganda bureau. Later, like many of his fellow revolutionaries, he was exiled from Russia, but he returned to take part in the 1917 Revolution. He remained faithful to the Communist Party until his death in 1936, although at Stalin's "purge trials" of 1938 it was alleged that he had been poisoned as an enemy of the state. Regardless of his fate as an old Bolshevik, he is perhaps the greatest Russian writer of the twentieth century.

Death and Life

On the floor, under the window, in a small, shuttered room, lay my father, dressed in a long white garment I had never seen him in before. His feet were bare and the toes were strangely distended, while the fingers of his hands, resting on his breast, were curled in. The blackened disks of two copper coins covered his eyes, shutting out their accustomed, cheerful gleam. All the light had gone out of his still face. But what scared me most was the snarl his open mouth showed with the teeth bared.

Beside him, on her knees, was my mother, in an undergarment. She was combing his long, fine hair back from his forehead to the nape of his neck. The comb she was using was the one with which I scraped edible shreds from watermelon rinds. As she combed away, she talked to him without stopping, through tears that fell without stopping, until it seemed that they must finally flood her eyes out of their sockets.

I saw all this holding on to the hand of my grandmother, whose dark head and eyes and nose looked enormous—the nose shapeless and pitted like a sponge—but a gentle, yet vividly interesting, woman. She, too, wept with sobs that were like cadences to my mother's. Shuddering herself, she pushed me toward my father, but I was too terrified to let go and clung to her.

This was the first time I had ever seen grown-ups cry, and I could not understand her repeated bidding, "Say good-by to your father. You'll never see him again. He's dead before his time."

I, myself, was just out of sickbed after a long, hard illness. It was still fresh in my mind how my father had done all he could to amuse me; and then how his place at my bedside had suddenly been taken by that old woman, then a stranger to me, my grandmother.

I asked her where she came from, using the verb form which implies coming by foot.

"From up north, from Nizhny," she replied, "but I didn't walk it; I came down by boat. You don't walk on water, you little scamp."

This made no sense to me at all. Upstairs there lived a gaily-dressed Persian who wore a beard; and downstairs, in the cellar, there lived a withered, yellow Kalmuck who dealt in sheepskins. And I got up to one and down to the other by way of the banisters; and if I had a fall, I just rolled down. But there was no place for water. So her "down" from "up north" on water could not be true; but it was a delightful muddle.

"Why do you call me a little scamp?" I asked.

"Because you make so much noise, that's why," she said, with a laugh.

Her voice was sweet and her words were merry and I made friends with her at once.

Now, clinging to her, all I wanted was for her to hurry and get me out of the room.

My mother caught me to her with a burst of weeping and moaning that frightened me. I had never seen her so before, this strong, composed, reserved woman, always so glowing and neat, strongly-framed like a horse and with tremendous power in her arms. Now, quivering and puffy, she looked utterly stricken. Her hair had shaken out of its gaily-trimmed cap and out of the usual tidy coil around her head and was streaming over her shoulder, and the part of it that remained in braid tracked across my father's still face. All this time she had not given me even a look, unable to tear herself away from her grief-stricken combing of my father's hair.

Then a policeman and some grave-diggers appeared at the door. "Get a move on!" bellowed the policeman.

A draft had filled the shawl that curtained the window, filled it like a sail. That picture came to me because my father had taken me sailing, once, and the sail had filled out the same way, in a sudden gust. With it had come a clap of thunder and my father had pulled me to his knee to reassure me and, laughing, had said, "It's nothing; don't let it frighten you."

All at once my mother dropped to the floor and immediately turned over, her hair in the dirt. Her mouth came open on her now-livid face so that her teeth were bared like my father's. In a terrifying voice she ordered me out, and the door to be shut.

Pushing me aside, grandma rushed to the door crying out, "Friends, there's nothing to be alarmed about; it's not the cholera; she's giving birth. For the love of God, leave us! Good people, go away."

Hidden behind a big box in a corner I saw my mother moving convulsively over the floor, panting through clenched teeth. Grandma hovered over her with soothing, cheering words, "Patience, Barbara . . . Holy Mother of God, be her protection!"

I shook with fright. In their frantic movements they bumped against my father, they groaned and shrieked into his unmoved, even smiling, face. For a long time this thrashing about on the floor went on. And all through it, rolling in and out like a big, black woolly ball went grandma on her errands.

Suddenly there was a whimper of a child. "Thank God!" grandma called out, "it's a boy!" and got up to light a candle.

And at that point, I must have fallen asleep in the darkness behind the box, because that was all I remembered.

My next memory is a solitary spot in a cemetery, in the rain. Standing beside a muddy pile of earth, I looked down into the hole in which they had sunk my father in his coffin. Frogs splashed in the water that had seeped in, and two were perched on the yellow coffin lid. Beside me were grandma, the drenched sexton and a pair of grave-diggers with shovels.

The sexton ordered the grave to be filled and moved off. Grandma wailed into an end of her head-shawl. Bent nearly double, the grave-diggers shoveled lumps of earth over the coffin, kicking the frogs who were trying to hop out, back into the grave.

"Come, Alex," said grandma, her hand on my shoulder, but I was too absorbed and slipped away.

"What next, O Lord!" grandma complained, half to me, half to God, and stood there in silence, with a dejected droop of her head.

Not till after the grave had been filled and the diggers' shovels had clanged to the ground and a sudden scurry of breeze had spattered us with raindrops, did she stir. Then, leading me by the hand, she took me to a church some distance away, over a path bordered by occasional dim crosses.

As we left the graveyard, she asked me, "How is it you're not crying? You ought to."

"I don't want to," I replied.

"You don't? Well, you don't have to," she said, gently.

It was a surprise to me that I was expected to cry. My crying had been always more out of temper than sadness. Father had laughed my tears away and mother had forbidden them. "Don't you dare to cry!" And so I seldom cried.

Afterwards we rode down a broad, but filthy street in a drozhky between rows of houses all painted dark red. On the way I asked grandma, "Can those frogs ever get out?"

"Never, God bless them."

God came more frequently and familiarly into her conversation, it occurred to me then, than He ever did in my father's or mother's.

Several days later I found myself, together with mama and grandma, in a tiny steamboat cabin. On a table, in the corner, lay the corpse of my little brother, Maxim, in white trappings held together with red tape. The porthole had the appearance of a horse's eye; I climbed up our piled luggage to look through. All there was to see was muddy froth. It charged against the glass, at one moment, with such force that it splashed in, and I scrambled down to the floor.

"There's nothing can harm you," said grandma lightly, lifting me back upon the baggage in her caressing arms.

Gray and brooding over the water, the fog thinned, now and then, to let a distant bulk of the shore loom through like a shadow, only to be lost again in mist and spume. Everything seemed to be aquiver except mother. With her hands clasped behind her head she stood rigid against the wall, with a grim, iron-hard face. Mute and expressionless, she seemed far away from us, an utter stranger. Even her clothes looked unfamiliar.

Gently, now and then, grandma would say, "Barbara, have a bite to eat." Mama did not so much as stir.

To me grandma spoke in whispers; to mama she spoke aloud, but infrequently, and in a timorous manner. Her fear of my mother was something I understood and made me feel closer to grandma.

A sudden, harsh exclamation from mama startled both of us. "Saratov. Where's that sailor?"

Saratov. Sailor. New words to me.

The sailor turned out to be a broad-shouldered, gray-haired man in blue. He carried in a box in which grandma laid my brother's body. She could not get through the door with it, being too broad, and came to a perplexed and ludicrous halt.

"Oh, mama!" exclaimed mama angrily, and took the little coffin from her. Both disappeared and I was left with the man in blue.

"Well, matey," he said, "your little brother has left you."

"Who are you?"

"I'm a sailor."

"Who's Saratov?"

"Saratov's a city. You can see it through the porthole."

From the porthole, the land seemed to shimmer. Dim and crusty, as it steamed in the fog, it made me think of a slice of bread fresh off a hot loaf.

"Where's grandma?"

"She's gone out to bury the little fellow."

"In the ground?"

"That's right."

Then I told the sailor about the frogs that had been buried alive with my father.

Lifting me up he fondled me, "Poor kid, you don't understand. Pity your mother, not the frogs. You don't know what unhappiness is crushing her."

From above came a howl that I recognized as the voice of the ship, so I wasn't frightened. But the sailor put me down at once and left me, shouting, "I must be off!"

I had an impulse to get away. I looked out—the passageway was dark and empty. Nearby glittered the brass plates of steps. Looking up the stair, I saw passengers with valises and bundles, evidently leaving the boat. I thought this meant I must leave, too.

But, at the gangway, in the crowd of debarking peasants, I was met with yells, "Whose boy is he? Who do you belong to, boy?"

Nobody knew me, and I didn't know what to answer. I was hauled from hand to hand until the sailor came up, took hold of me and explained, "It's that Astrakhan boy, the one in the cabin."

He brought me back there, sat me on the baggage and went off threatening me with his forefinger and the words, "I'll give it to you."

The ship's voice, overhead, quieted down; the vibrations of the boat and its movements in the water stopped. Dripping walls opposite the porthole shut off the air and the light, and the cabin grew stifling and dark. The bundles among which I had been placed seemed to grow larger and harder, and I began to feel crushed by them. A fear that I had been left all alone and for good in that empty ship possessed me.

I tried the door, but the metal handle was unbudging. I picked up a bottle of milk and put all my strength in the blow I gave it to make it turn; but all I accomplished was to break the bottle and spill the milk, which splashed over me and trickled down my legs. Sobbing with exasperation, I cried myself to sleep on the bundles.

I woke to find the boat in motion and the porthole round and glowing like a sun. Beside me sat grandma, combing her hair back from her knitted brows and muttering to herself. Her blue-black hair was remarkable for its abundance. It came below her knees and even reached the ground. She had to hold it up with one hand while, with the other, she drew an almost toothless comb through the heavy mass. The strain made her lips purse and brought an exasperated sharpness to her eyes. There was something almost bitter in her expression; yet, when I asked why her hair was so long, it was in her usual melodious words and with her customary tender intonations that she answered, "God must have given it to me to punish me. It's combed out but look at it! When I was a girl I was proud of that mane but now I curse it. But sleep, child. It's early yet. The sun's barely up."

"I want to get up."

"Well then, get up," she said. As she braided her hair she glanced toward my mother who lay rigid on her bunk. "How did you happen to break that bottle? Tell me, but be quiet about it."

That was her way. Her words were like music and like flowers. They bloom in my memory like everlasting blossoms. I remember her smile as a dilation of her large eyes and a cheerful flash of her white teeth that gave her face an inexpressible charm. Despite her wrinkles and her weathered complexion she looked young and even glowing. All that spoiled her appearance was her bulbous red nose with its splayed-out nostrils, the result of a weakness for drink and her snuff-taking; her black snuff box was almost always in her hand.

Outwardly she looked dark, but within burned a vigorous, inextinguishable flame of which the radiance in her eyes was a reflection. She was so stooped as to be almost hunchbacked, yet her motions were gliding and light like those of a great cat; and she was soft and caressing like a cat.

I felt that I had been asleep and in darkness until she came, and that then I woke and was led into the light. It was she who provided the threads with which my mind wove its multi-colored patterns. And by this she became my lifelong friend, the dearest and most understanding and the closest to my heart. Nourished by her wise love for every living thing, I gained the strength to face a hard life.

JAMES AGEE

James Agee was born in Knoxville, Tennessee, in 1909. He worked as a harvest "stiff" in the wheat fields of Kansas and Nebraska during vacations from Exeter and Harvard. At Harvard he edited the *Advocate* and received its poetry prize. An assignment for *Fortune* magazine led to his moving documentary book about the life of a sharecropper's family, *Let Us Now Praise Famous Men* (with photographer Walker Evans). For several years, Agee wrote cogent movie reviews for *Time* Magazine and *The Nation.* The following selection first appeared in *Partisan Review* (1938) and became the first chapter of Agee's posthumously published Pulitzer Prize-winning novel, *A Death in the Family* (1956). Agee died in 1955.

Knoxville: Summer of 1915

We are talking now of summer evenings in Knoxville, Tennessee in the time that I lived there so successfully disguised to myself as a child. It was a little bit mixed sort of block, fairly solidly lower middle class, with one or two juts apiece on either side of that. The houses corresponded: middle-sized gracefully fretted wood houses built in the late nineties and early nineteen hundreds, with small front and side and more spacious back yards, and trees in the yards, and porches. These were soft-wooded trees, poplars, tulip trees, cottonwoods. There were fences around one or two of the houses, but mainly the yards ran into each other with only now and then a low hedge that wasn't doing very well. There were few good friends among the grown people, and they were not poor enough for the other sort of intimate acquaintance, but everyone nodded and spoke, and even might talk short times, trivially, and at the two extremes of the general or the particular, and ordinarily nextdoor neighbors talked quite a bit when they happened to run into each other, and never paid calls. The men were mostly small business-men, one or two very modestly executives, one or two worked with their hands, most of them clerical, and most of them between thirty and forty-five.

But it is of these evenings, I speak.

Supper was at six and was over by half past. There was still daylight, shining softly and with a tarnish, like the lining of a shell; and the carbon lamps lifted at the corners were on in the light, and the locusts were started, and the fire flies were out, and a few frogs were flopping in the dewy grass, by the time the fathers and the children came out. The children ran out first hell bent and yelling those names by which they were known; then the fathers sank out leisurely in crossed suspenders, their collars removed and their necks looking tall and shy. The mothers stayed back in the kitchen washing and drying, putting things away, recrossing their traceless footsteps like the lifetime journeys of bees, measuring out the dry cocoa for breakfast. When they came out they had taken off their aprons and their skirts were dampened and they sat in rockers on their porches quietly.

It is not of the games children play in the evening that I want to speak now, it is of a contemporaneous atmosphere that has little to do with them: that of the fathers of families, each in his space of lawn, his shirt fishlike pale in the unnatural light and his face nearly anonymous, hosing their lawns. The hoses were attached at spiggots that stood out of the brick foundations of the houses. The nozzles were variously set but usually so there was a long sweet stream of spray, the nozzle wet in the hand, the water trickling the right forearm and the peeled-back cuff, and the water whishing out a long loose and low-curved cone, and so gentle a sound. First an insane noise of violence in the nozzle, then the still irregular sound of adjustment, then the smoothing into steadiness and a pitch as accurately tuned to the size and style of stream as any violin. So many qualities of sound out of one hose: so many choral differences out of those several hoses that were in earshot. Out of any one hose, the almost dead silence of the release, and the short still arch of the separate big drops, silent as a held breath, and the only noise the flattering noise on leaves and the slapped grass at the fall of each big drop. That, and the intense hiss with the intense stream; that, and that same intensity not growing less but growing more quiet and delicate with the turn of the nozzle, up to that extreme tender whisper when the water was just a wide bell of film. Chiefly, though, the hoses were set much alike, in a compromise between distance and tenderness of spray, (and quite surely a sense of art behind this compromise, and a quiet deep joy, too real to recognize itself), and the sounds therefore were pitched much alike; pointed by the snorting start of a new hose; decorated by some man playful with the nozzle; left empty, like God by the sparrow's fall, when any single one of them desists: and all, though near alike, of various pitch; and in this unison. These sweet pale streamings in the light lift out their pallors and their voices all together, mothers hushing their children, the hushing unnaturally prolonged, the men gentle and silent and each snail-like withdrawn into the quietude of what he singly is doing, the urination of huge children stood loosely military against an invisible wall, and gently happy and peaceful, tasting the mean goodness of their living like the last of their suppers in their mouths; while the locusts carry on this noise of hoses on their much higher and sharper key. The noise of the locust is dry, and it seems not to be rasped or vibrated but urged from him as if through a small orifice by a breath that can never give out. Also there is never one locust but an illusion of at least a thousand. The noise of each locust is pitched in some classic locust range out of which none of them varies more than two full tones: and yet you seem to hear each locust discrete from all the rest, and there is a long, slow, pulse in their noise, like the scarcely defined arch of a long and high set bridge. They are all around in every tree, so that the noise seems to come from nowhere and everywhere at once, from the whole shell heaven, shivering in your flesh and teasing your eardrums, the boldest of all the sounds of night. And yet it is habitual to summer nights, and is of the great order of noises, like the noises of the sea and of the blood her precocious grandchild, which you realize you are hearing only when you catch yourself listening. Meantime from low in the dark, just outside the swaying horizons of the hoses, conveying always grass in the damp of dew and its strong green-back smear of smell, the regular yet spaced noises of the crickets, each a sweet cold silver noise three-noted, like the slipping each time of three matched links of a small chain.

But the men by now, one by one, have silenced their hoses and drained and coiled them. Now only two, and now only one, is left, and you see only ghostlike shirt with the sleeve garters, and sober mystery of his mild face like the lifted face of large cattle enquiring of your presence in a pitchdark pool of meadow; and now he too is gone; and it has become that time of evening when people sit on their porches, rocking gently and talking gently and watching the street and the standing up into their sphere of possession of the trees, of birds hung havens, hangars. People go by; things go by. A horse, drawing a buggy, breaking his hollow iron music on the asphalt; a loud auto; a quiet auto; people in pairs, not in a hurry, scuffling, switching their weight of aestival body, talking casually, the taste hovering over them of vanilla, strawberry, pasteboard and starched milk, the image upon them of lovers and horsemen, squared with clowns in hueless amber. A street car raising its iron moan; stopping; belling and starting, stertorous; rousing and raising again its iron increasing moan and swimming its gold windows and straw seats on past and past and past, the bleak spark crackling and cursing above it like a small malignant spirit set to dog its tracks; the iron whine rises on rising speed; still risen, faints; halts; the faint stinging bell; rises again, still fainter; fainting, lifting, lifts, faints forgone: forgotten. Now is the night one blue dew.

Now is the night one blue dew, my father has drained, he has coiled the hose.
Low on the length of lawns, a frailing of fire who breathes.
Content, silver, like peeps of light, each cricket makes his comment over and over in the drowned grass.
A cold toad thumpily flounders.
Within the edges of damp shadows of side yards are hovering children nearly sick with joy of fear, who watch the unguarding of a telephone pole.
Around white carbon corner lamps bugs of all sizes are lifted elliptic, solar systems. Big hardshells bruise themselves, assailant: he is fallen on his back, legs squiggling.
Parents on porches: rock and rock: From damp strings morning glories: hang their ancient faces.
The dry and exalted noise of the locusts from all the air at once enchants my eardrums.

On the rough wet grass of the back yard my father and mother have spread quilts. We all lie there, my mother, my father, my uncle, my aunt, and I too am lying there. First we were sitting up, then one of us lay down, and then we all lay down, on our stomachs, or on our sides, or on our backs, and they have kept on talking. They are not talking much, and the talk is quiet, of nothing in particular, of nothing at all in particular, of nothing at all. The stars are wide and alive, they seem each like a smile of great sweetness, and they seem very near. All my people are larger bodies than mine, quiet, with voices gentle and meaningless like the voices of sleeping birds. One is an artist, he is living at home. One is a musician, she is living at home. One is my mother who is good to me. One is my father who is good to me. By some chance, here they are, all on this earth; and who shall ever tell the sorrow of being on this earth, lying, on quilts, on the grass, in a summer evening, among the sounds of the night. May God bless my people, my uncle, my aunt, my mother, my good father, oh, remember them kindly in their time of trouble; and in the hour of their taking away.

After a little I am taken in and put to bed. Sleep, soft smiling, draws me unto her: and those receive me, who quietly treat me, as one familiar and well-beloved in that home: but will not, oh, will not, not now, not ever; but will not ever tell me who I am.

WILLIAM ALEXANDER PERCY

William Alexander Percy was born in Greenville, Mississippi, in 1885. He was the son of Senator LeRoy Percy and was educated at the University of the South (Sewanee) and Harvard Law School. He was one of the leaders of the successful fight against the Ku Klux Klan when it tried to take over Greenville in 1922. His autobiography, *Lanterns on the Levee,* from which the following selection comes, was published in 1941. He died in 1942.

Playmates

Any little boy who was not raised with little Negro children might just as well not have been raised at all. My first boon-companion was Skillet, the small dark son of Mère's cook. He was the best crawfisher in the world and I was next. Instead of closed sewers our town had open ditches, which after an overflow swarmed with crawfish, small clear ones, quite shrimp-like, whose unexpected backward agility saved them from any except the most skilful hands, and large red ones, surly and whiskered, with a startling resemblance to the red-nosed old reprobates you saw around the saloons when you were looking for tobacco tags in the sawdust. When these rared back and held their claws wide apart, Skillet said they were saying: "Swear to God, white folks, I ain't got no tail." Theoretically it was for their tails that we hunted them, because when boiled and seasoned and prayed over they made that thick miraculous pink soup you never experience unless you have French blood in the family or unless you dine at Prunier's. Of course anyone could catch crawfish with a string and a lump of bacon, and anyone knows their family life is passed in holes, like snake-holes, from which they must be lured; but who except Skillet had ever observed that a hollow bone lying on the bottom of a ditch is bound to be occupied by one? Maybe he sat there as in a summerhouse thinking or catching a nap or saying to himself: "These boys will never think of this." If you waded up noiselessly and clapped both hands suddenly and simultaneously over both ends of the bone, he was yours and went into the bucket outraged and blowing bubbles, nothing appeased that his high destiny was to contribute his bit to a bisque d'écrevisses.

Skillet's sister Martha was a virago. Like Goneril she never reformed and so kept the plot boiling. She constantly threatened to do away with our crawfish in some low diabolical manner. This led to a painful incident. After an especially successful day we decided to hide from Martha our water-bucket brim-full of the simmering live catch and chose for that purpose an obscure corner behind the bookcase in Mère's parlor. Black fate decreed that on that very night Mère should give what was called a soirée. Now, the parlor was the hallowed place to receive guests, gay and beribboned and with splendid bustles. Fruit punch seemed to make them as lively as cocktails do now (I think Père spiked it). Mrs. Holland sang the Jewel Song from *Faust* and as an encore "Three Little Pigs Went to Market." Everyone said she should have joined the New Orleans Opera instead of marrying Mr. Holland, as obviously she would have had a succès fou in *Mignon* or *L'Africaine,* but Mother insisted she was a natural comèdienne and would have been irresistible in *Orphee aux Enfers* or *Les Cloches de Corneville.* Then someone began playing dance music, which, if I recollect accurately, was as enticing and stimulating as the radio, but in a nice way, and without interpolations concerning liver pills and tooth paste. After the dancing, Mother and Mr. Harry Ball were to have sung a duet—they had "parlor voices, but sweet"—and it may have been sung, but I was not destined to hear it. At that moment a ladylike scream stopped the music and threw the gathering into consternation. Mrs. Holland had stepped on a large red crawfish in the attitude of "Swear to God, white folks." It made a crunchy sound. Another was discovered and another; they were all over the place. Mère was indignant, but Mother, though she retired me hastily, and in bad odor, really wanted to laugh. Skillet and I were in disgrace; Martha—need I say?—escaped unscratched.

Crawfishing was not Skillet's only excellence. As a conversationalist he outdistanced any white child in inventiveness, absurdity, and geniality. In Mère's back yard we would sit in a row-boat, a relic of the last overflow, and for hours ply imaginary oars toward an imaginary land that we described and embellished as we approached. These voyages afforded endless opportunity for discussions. One in particular drifts back to me across long years. It was one of those still, hot days when earth things lie tranced at the bottom of a deep sea of summer sun. We were resting on our oars at the moment. Far, far up buzzards circled dreamily, their black wings motionless, tilting, banking, coasting in wide arcs, somnambulistic symbols of the drowse and delight of deep summer. Watching them, Skillet observed in a singsong: "If they was to ever light, the world would burn up." As the birds seemed fixed at their vast altitude, this was a safe prophecy. But I was skeptical, as could have been expected of any horrid little white realist. Skillet, though, was so eloquent in citing reasons and authorities that my disbelief weakened and by degrees I was convinced, for the old excellent reason that I wanted to be. As we watched, the buzzards, careening and narrowing their circles, began to descend. It was exciting to see them drop lower and lower and to think what might happen. At last we could discern their horrible necks and heads. Skillet rose in a kind of ecstasy, thrusting out his arms, flexing his knees, and chanting: "Don't let 'em light, God, don't let 'em light." The flames of a consuming world were practically around us. Only the fire music as it came to Mime about the time Siegfried rushed in with the bear could have expressed our abject and delicious terror. They were hovering over our own back yard and, last touch of horror, there lay one of Mère's chickens dead—indeed, more than dead—their target, stark and untidy on the crust of the earth so unconcerned and so doomed. One of the ghastly creatures suddenly rocked, flapped its wings, and settled down awkwardly on the fence between us and the Fergusons'. "Look, I told you so, the world didn't burn up," I almost sobbed, torn between relief and disappointment. "He lit on a fence. He ain't never teched the ground," whispered Skillet. The buzzard gave an ungainly bound and landed on the too, too solid earth. "Look," I wailed. "He lit on a chip," Skillet observed affably. I was outraged.

Calling to mind with gratitude those to whom we are indebted on our journey is not only a sort of piety, but one of the few pleasures that endure without loss of luster to the end. I like to imagine that Skillet is not in jail or dead, but that he lords it in a Pullman car or pulpit, or perhaps has a farm of his own and many little crawfishers—in fine, that the swooping dark wings continue for him to light on a chip. He is all my memory records of what must have been long months of my childhood; all others it seems were lay figures.

Equally treasurable were Amelia's children on Aunt Nana's farm in Virginia, where I was deposited so many summers. I don't remember the house well except that it was square, airy, and very old, with a corridor behind leading to the kitchen, storerooms, and Amelia's sleeping-quarters; the old furniture and woodwork made no impression whatever. All around were cornfields and dabs of woods, and a few hundred yards in front the small cool river. I must have seen it rain there often, but like a sundial I remember only sunlight, acres and acres of it: sometimes merely pale and fresh and still on the pasture; or heavy like a great depth of blue sea-water on the undulating rows of corn, which, tired of the weight, sagged limply; or in splotches and scarves and sudden widths of glitter on the river; or, best, early in the morning, when it slanted in long gray panels through the orchard and barely silvered the small yellow pears with a sweat of cold dew on them and dew on the grass where they lay. Quantities of little wiggly paths, cow-paths likely, meandered everywhere and nowhere, bordered by straggling colonies of tawny lilies and bushes of pokeberry, indispensable for war-paint on our Indian days. They too were sunny, but managed to make every patch of shade a port of call, and two of them met in the little wood where an old fox-grape vine with the kindliness and humor of old age crooked one arm into a perfect swing. The swing itself would be in shadow, of the breezy arrowy kind, all shreds and patches on you as you swung through it, but you looked out from under the branches across all that shining clearness that lay on the fields and the aspen woodland to the old house far off to the left, and you knew you needed nothing else. When your peace is without grayness, it comes seldom and does not stay long; some are still hunting for it and some are trying to find it again, but know they won't.

At Aunt Nana's there were so many fascinating spots you couldn't make the round of them in a week, and all of them smelled good. The dairy, round, with thick walls and no windows, where the crocks of milk and clabber and cream stood in live spring-water, smelled cold and slightly sour. The corn-bin had a warm yellow smell like a loaf of bread at the moment Amelia opened the oven and pawed it out with the edge of her apron. The barn, from the pile of manure in front (which Père said Uncle George was too lazy to scatter over the fields, and it was beautiful manure) to the stalls, soggy with corn-shucks and urine, had an exciting smell, like autumn, but the smell was definitely good. Of course the kitchen was so full of things to whiff and sniff and inhale with eyes closed that you could stay there all day, only you were always being shooed out, on lucky occasions with the batter-bowl to lick. The best smell, however, was undoubtedly at the mill. That mill was none of your modern contraptions, spotless and intricate and unintelligible. You saw how it worked when it worked, which was occasionally. There was the dam, and the mill-pond above and behind it; there was the huge water-wheel which sloshed and turned when the sluice was opened; there were the great millstones, likely the very ones the gods used to use, between which the corn filtered to its golden doom; and there was the miller, a bit sweaty and covered with a lovely creamy dust of meal, especially his eyebrows and mustache. Sometimes I was allowed to ride behind Reuben when he took a sack of corn to be ground. We would wait till the resulting sack of meal was ready to be put over the pommel and jogged home to Amelia, by her to be manipulated into corn-pones of unspeakable crunchiness and savor. The meal would be still damp and warm when turned over to us, and it was hard not to eat it raw, like chickens, so rich and sweet and really fundamental it smelled.

Reuben was too old to be interesting, perhaps eighteen, but Amelia's children—Ligey, Martha, Cora, Friday, and a few more I've forgotten—were exactly the right ages. They seem to have arrived precisely a year apart and all were dark, but some were darker, and no two of them looked alike. I often wondered who and where their father was, and once put the question to Aunt Nana, but she developed one of those little attacks of hurry and said, as well as I could gather, he was a traveling man. However, it must have been a fine father or set of fathers, because they were fine children and as playmates perfection. Small satyrs and fauns could not have been more instructive or resourceful or absurd.

We harried the hillsides for arrow-heads and found many splendid ones—training I found invaluable years later when between showers I hunted sea-shells in Bora-Bora. Sometimes we spent days on end in full flight from a murderous band of gypsies. Cora's cries on one occasion when she was almost captured were so blood-curdling we rushed off down the road and abandoned her to her fate, quite forgetting the plot she furthered with such histrionic fervor. Friday had a genius for discovering hornet-nests. Silvery and rather Burmese in design, one would be hanging on a tree conveniently low, its irascible inmates in a stew and a lather, storming in and out. Led by Friday, we would approach as near as we dared and let fly our barrage against the patiently built castle of the poor earnest insects. But they, unadvised of the other-cheek doctrine we have so long been beseeching one another to follow, would sally forth in the best modern echelon formation, armed to the tip, and we, sounding precipitate and individual retreat, would scatter yowling. If someone was not badly stung, to be borne lamenting loudly to Amelia's soda and scarifying invective, it was a disappointing adventure.

In our milder moods the river was a favorite haunt. It was the right sort of river. With the dam closed, it could be waded and was all pools and trickles and slimy shelving rocks. Although not scorning such lesser quarry as eels, leeches, water-snakes, and frogs, our constant ambition was to discover a giant sturgeon. This ambition was unlikely but not impossible of fulfillment, because one had found its way into our river as a result of the Johnstown flood and we had seen it with our own eyes hanging from the ceiling of the tool-house, its tail sweeping the floor, glittering in the lamplight, magnificent even in death. We noticed when it was split open that with just a little more room Jonah could have sat inside. We discussed this and kindred issues for days afterwards.

During one of these theological sessions I swallowed a persimmon seed. Doctors had recently discovered appendicitis, attributed it to the swallowing of a seed, and considered it fatal. Solemn with this medical erudition, I explained the grisly situation and announced my approaching demise. All accepted the news with delight and prepared for the end. I lay on the ground and my faithful retainers knelt around me, in the manner of sundry versions of the Assumption of the Virgin. I closed my eyes, and fervent prayers rose loudly. Nothing happened. Nothing ever did happen. Reviving was undignified and bitterly disappointing to all concerned. As a corpse I was a fiasco, but as mourners my colored entourage displayed genius. Racially they are the best diers in the world anyway: they put more force and enthusiasm into the scene, being seriously aware it is the climax of the show, their curtain. If Friday had swallowed my persimmon seed, he would beyond question have died outright and to perfection, although it's a role one can't rehearse.

So many things to do and each summer so short. To chase rats in the barn, a dangerous and slightly sickening enterprise; to teach the kitten to play circus (our cats were Manx, with stubs for tails and bouncing rabbit motions); to climb the roof of the corridor and watch the ducks file out to the pond, cracking dry mirthless jokes to one another and sometimes laying an egg, shamelessly and without stopping, on the bare ground with no thought of a nest; to be allowed to help with the cider press where all the apples with a rotten spot, those claimed and contended for by the yellow-jackets, disappeared into the hopper and gushed out the sides in a seethe of bubbly brown liquor, fit for Ceres; to hunt in the mold of the wood-pile for the turquoise bits that were fox-fire and find instead a land-terrapin closed up safe from the mad world in his neat hinged box, and to devise means to make him come out—so many things to do, and summer so short.

Supervised play and summer camps came after my time. I missed learning the principles of team work and many games which must be helpful if you can think of nothing to do. Instead, Friday's accent, Cora's intonation, and Ligey's grammatical uses contaminated beyond hope of purification the wells of what should have been my pure English undefiled. That was their only evil influence. Of nastiness and bad manners they taught me nothing; older boys of my own color and caste were later to be my instructors in those subjects. From Amelia's children I learned not only gaiety and casualness and inventiveness, but the possibility that mere living may be delightful and that natural things which we ignore unless we call them scenery are pleasant to move among and gracious to recall. Without them it would probably never have occurred to me that to climb an aspen sapling in a gale is one of those ultimate experiences, like experiencing God or love, that you need never try to remember because you can never forget. Aspens grow together in little woods of their own, straight, slender, and white. Even in still weather they twinkle and murmur, but in a high wind you must run out and plunge among them, spattered with sunlight, to the very center. Then select your tree and climb it high enough for it to begin to wobble with your weight. Rest your foot-weight lightly on the frail branches and do most of your clinging with your arms. Now let it lunge, and gulp the wind. It will be all over you, slapping your hair in your eyes, stinging your face with bits of bark and stick, tugging to break your hold, roaring in your open mouth like a monster sea-shell. The trees around you will thrash and seethe, their white undersides lashed about like surf, and sea-music racing through them. You will be beaten and bent and buffeted about and the din will be so terrific your throat will invent a song to add to the welter, pretty barbaric, full of yells and long calls. You will feel what it is to be the Lord God and ride a hurricane; you will know what it is to have leaves sprout from your toes and finger-tips, with satyrs and tigers and hounds in pursuit; you will never need again to drown under the crash of a maned wave in spume and splendor and thunder, with the white stallions of the sea around you, neighing and pawing. That must have been the very wood old Housman had in mind when he sang "We'll to the woods no more." But when he found his way to it he was alone, and it was autumn.

DAVID MARQUIS

David Marquis was born in Frenchville, Maine, in 1950. He attended Wisdom High School in St. Agatha and is now pursuing a program in Constructional Drafting at Northern Maine Vocational Technical Institute in Presque Isle. His essay first appeared in *Growing Up in Maine,* a collection of essays published by Bowdoin College Upward Bound Students in 1968.

My Spud Day

My mother, sister, and brother had been picking potatoes for two and one half weeks now, but this day was to be my day. I was only five years old but when mom came to wake me up I felt ten feet tall. After all I was getting up at five o'clock for the first time in my life. My grandmother used to babysit for me when I stayed home, and sure enough, today she wouldn't have to watch over me. I was a big boy now.

It was cold outside my warm comfortable bed, but I had to come out. I shivered as my feet touched the cold boards of my room. I went downstairs and went right next to the wood stove where everybody else was. I brought my clothes with me and my mother offered to help me but I refused any help from anybody. I could do it myself.

After I had dressed up, I went to the table, which was right next to the wood stove, and ate breakfast. For breakfast my mother had prepared me a hot bowl of oatmeal covered with sweet maple sugar.

With the hot stove shedding its heat over my body and the hot oatmeal warming my stomach, I was almost hoping that my cousin would not show up. But then I heard his horn honking outside. "There's Danny," mom said. "Let's go everybody." Then she looked at me and said, "Vien temps, David."

Then everyone went outside in the cold air. I was shivering but I wasn't sure if it was from fear or because it was cold out. Just in case it was from fear, I kept away from mom and I think nobody noticed it.

My cousin came out of the cab and helped me get on the rear of the truck which was covered with barrels. As the truck started to move forward, the cold air pierced my clothes. Now I noticed how small I was because I could easily duck down into a barrel and keep some of that cold air away from me. In that barrel, I realized that my spud day had begun.

Even though I had ridden on that road before, the ride from home to the potato field seemed to be a long one because I couldn't see a thing around me. I could only feel the bumps and hear the tires whistle on the roads the truck moved on.

By the time we got to the potato field my whole body was so frozen that I could hardly move. I got out from my barrel and jumped off the truck. That time I knew I was shivering from the cold and not from fear. And so from that moment on I had one objective for that day; it was to recondition my body to the temperature outside. Potatoes were just not interesting to me.

I soon figured out a way to warm my body up. This was to turn a barrel over my head. It was effective in some ways but there were exceptions to the rule. The air soon became stale in the barrel and my continual movement caused dust particles to fly around. My nose and throat soon became dried up and I could hardly breathe. I also received plenty of dust in my eyes. I only found a few years later that I shouldn't have been under that barrel as a truck could easily run over me.

While I was in the barrel I kept peering through a knot hole in one of the planks. It happened to be turned toward the potato pickers, and I watched them with extreme curiosity. Most of the time I was watching my mother because she seemed to be the fastest moving potato picker. I just couldn't imagine how those people could stand the cold but it didn't seem to bother them at all. I just loved the sound of the potatoes hitting the bottom of the other barrels because it sounded like fifty cannons firing at once.

From the knot hole I could see the sun coming over the horizon when my cousin came up and shoved the barrel from over me and invited me in his truck. He told me it was to help him out and there once again I felt grown up. But I also knew it was warm in the truck. This was also a new experience for me because I had never ridden in the cab of a truck before.

I was soon ready to run around so I went to see my mother and helped her pick potatoes. I would pick one potato at a time; that was once in a while. For the rest of the time I either watched mom pick or I'd run errands for her such as getting the barrels which I rolled all the way to her then stood them upright for her to fill up.

I went through that over and over again until lunch time. By that time the sun had heated up the earth and I was warm. But I was already tired of potatoes by then and I expected to stay home in the afternoon but I found out different.

Mom said, "Don't forget that next year you'll be picking with us full time. You're a big boy now."

I nodded in agreement. I would stay and help again this afternoon. Maybe I *was* a big boy now.

WALT WHITMAN

The great nineteenth-century American poet, Walt Whitman, was born in 1819 in Huntington, Long Island, and moved soon afterwards with his family to Brooklyn. At thirteen he began a long career in newspapers with a job as a "printer's devil." In 1855 he published his first edition of *Leaves of Grass,* the book he would spend the rest of his life revising and expanding. Although Ralph Waldo Emerson said, "I greet you at the beginning of a great career" (a greeting which Whitman promptly put on the cover of his next edition), his work met with extremely unfavorable criticism, largely because his frankness about sex shocked Victorian America—an America where the legs of a piano were referred to as limbs and had modest skirts around them. The Civil War and the death of Lincoln affected him profoundly, and perhaps his greatest poem is the elegy "When Lilacs Last in the Dooryard Bloomed," on the death of Lincoln. His prose writings include *Specimen Days,* from which the following excerpt comes. His fame grew in later years; he died in Camden, New Jersey, in 1892.

Paumanok, and My Life on It as a Child and Young Man

Worth fully and particularly investigating, indeed, this Paumanok (to give the spot its aboriginal name,)[1] stretching east through Kings, Queens and Suffolk counties, 120 miles altogether—on the north Long Island sound, a beautiful, varied and picturesque series of inlets, "necks" and sea-like expansions, for a hundred miles to Orient point. On the ocean side the great south bay, dotted with countless hummocks, mostly small, some quite large, occasionally long bars of sand out two hundred rods to a mile and a half from the shore. While now and then, as at Rockaway and far east along the Hamptons, the beach makes right on the island, the sea dashing up without intervention. Several lighthouses on the shores east; a long history of wrecks' tragedies, some even of late years. As a youngster, I was in the atmosphere and traditions of many of these wrecks—of one or two almost an observer. Off Hempstead beach, for example, was the loss of the ship *Mexico* in 1840, (alluded to in "The Sleepers" in *Leaves of Grass).* And at Hampton, some years later, the destruction of the brig *Elizabeth,* a fearful affair, in one of the worst winter gales, where Margaret Fuller went down, with her husband and child.

---

[1] "Paumanok, (or Paumanake, or Paumanack, the Indian name of Long Island,) over a hundred miles long; shaped like a fish—plenty of sea shore, sandy, stormy, uninviting, the horizon boundless, the air too strong for invalids, the bays a wonderful resort for aquatic birds, the south-side meadows cover'd with salt hay, the soil of the island generally tough, but good for the locust-tree, the apple orchard, and the blackberry, and with numberless springs of the sweetest water in the world. Years ago, among the bay-men—a strong, wild race, extinct, or rather entirely changed—a native of Long Island was called a Paumanacker, or Creole-Paumanacker."—John Burroughs.

Inside the outer bars or beach this south bay is everywhere comparatively shallow; of cold winters all thick ice on the surface. As a boy I often went forth with a chum or two, on those frozen fields, with hand-sled, ax and eel-spear, after messes of eels. We would cut holes in the ice, sometimes striking quite an eel-bonanza, and filling our baskets with great, fat, sweet, white-meated fellows. The scenes, the ice, drawing the hand-sled, cutting holes, spearing the eels, etc., were of course just such fun as is dearest to boyhood. The shores of this bay, winter and summer, and my doings there in early life, are woven all through *L. of G.* One sport I was very fond of was to go on a bay-party in summer to gather seagulls' eggs. (The gulls lay two or three eggs, more than half the size of hens' eggs, right on the sand, and leave the sun's heat to hatch them.)

The eastern end of Long Island, the Peconic bay region, I knew quite well too—sail'd more than once round Shelter island, and down to Montauk—spent many an hour on Turtle hill by the old lighthouse, on the extreme point, looking out over the ceaseless roll of the Atlantic. I used to like to go down there and fraternize with the blue-fishers, or the annual squads of sea-bass takers. Sometimes, along Montauk peninsula, (it is some 15 miles long, and good grazing,) met the strange, unkempt, half-barbarous herdsmen, at that time living there entirely aloof from society or civilization, in charge, on those rich pasturages, of vast droves of horses, kine or sheep, own'd by farmers of the eastern towns. Sometimes, too, the few remaining Indians, or half-breeds, at that period left on Montauk peninsula, but now I believe altogether extinct.

More in the middle of the island were the spreading Hempstead plains, then (1830-'40) quite prairie-like, open, uninhabited, rather sterile, cover'd with kill-calf and huckleberry bushes, yet plenty of fair pasture for the cattle, mostly milch cows, which fed there by hundreds, even thousands, and at evening, (the plains too were own'd by the towns, and this was the use of them in common,) might be seen taking their way home, branching off regularly in the right places. I have often been out on the edges of these plains toward sundown, and can yet recall in fancy the interminable cow processions, and hear the music of the tin or copper bells, clanking far or near, and breathe the cool of the sweet and slightly aromatic evening air, and note the sunset.

Through the same region of the island, but farther east, extended wide central tracts of pine and scrub oak, (charcoal was largely made here,) monotonous and sterile. But many a good day or half-day did I have, wandering through those solitary crossroads, inhaling the peculiar and wild aroma. Here, and all along the island and its shores, I spent intervals many years, all seasons, sometimes riding, sometimes boating, but generally afoot, (I was always then a good walker,) absorbing fields, shores, marine incidents, characters, the bay-men, farmers, pilots—always had a plentiful acquaintance with the latter, and with fishermen—went every summer on sailing trips—always liked the bare sea-beach, south side, and have some of my happiest hours on it to this day.

As I write, the whole experience comes back to me after the lapse of forty and more years—the soothing rustle of the waves, and the saline smell—boyhood's times, the clam-digging, barefoot, and with trousers roll'd up—hauling down the creek—the perfume of the sedge meadows—the hay boat, and the chowder and fishing excursions;—or, of later years, little voyages down and out New York bay, in the pilot boats. Those same later years, also, while living in Brooklyn (1836-'50,) I went regularly every week in the mild seasons down to Coney Island, at that time a long, bare, unfrequented shore, which I had all to myself, and where I loved, after bathing, to race up and down the hard sand, and declaim Homer or Shakespeare to the surf and seagulls by the hour.

WALLACE STEGNER

Wallace Stegner was born in Lake Mills, Iowa, in 1909. He graduated from the University of Utah in 1930 and received advanced degrees from the University of Iowa. He has written eight novels, two books of short stories *(The City of the Living,* 1956, and *The Women on the Wall,* 1950), and four nonfiction works, including *Wolf Willow* (1963), from which the following excerpt comes. He has taught at several American universities and is currently Director of the Creative Writing Program at Stanford.

The Dump Ground

One aspect of Whitemud's history, and only one, and a fragmentary one, we knew: the town dump. It lay in a draw at the southeast corner of town, just where the river left the Hills and where the old Mounted Police patrol trail (I did not know that that was what it was) made a long, easy, willow-fringed traverse across the bottoms. That stretch of the river was a favorite campsite for passing teamsters, gypsies, sometimes Indians. The very straw scattered around those camps, the ashes of those strangers' campfires, the manure of their teams and saddle horses, were hot with adventurous possibilities. The camps made an extension, a living suburb, of the dump ground itself, and it was for this that we valued them. We scoured them for artifacts of their migrant tenants as if they had been archaeological sites potent with the secrets of ancient civilizations. I remember toting around for weeks a broken harness strap a few inches long. Somehow or other its buckle looked as if it had been fashioned in a far place, a place where they were accustomed to flatten the tongues of buckles for reasons that could only be exciting, and where they had a habit of plating the metal with some valuable alloy, probably silver. In places where the silver was worn away, the buckle underneath shone dull yellow: probably gold.

Excitement liked that end of town better than our end. Old Mrs. Gustafson, deeply religious and a little raddled in the head, went over there once with a buckboard full of trash, and as she was driving home along the river she saw a spent catfish, washed in from the Swift Current or some other part of the watershed in the spring flood. He was two feet long, his whiskers hung down, his fins and tail were limp—a kind of fish no one had seen in the Whitemud in the three or four years of the town's life, and a kind that none of us children had ever seen anywhere. Mrs. Gustafson had never seen one like him, either. She perceived at once that he was the devil, and she whipped up the team and reported him, pretty loudly, at Hoffman's elevator.

We could still hear her screeching as we legged it for the river to see for ourselves. Sure enough, there he was, drifting slowly on the surface. He looked very tired, and he made no great effort to get away when we rushed to get an old rowboat, and rowed it frantically down to where our scouts eased along shore beckoning and ducking willows, and sank the boat under him and brought him ashore in it. When he died we fed him experimentally to two half-wild cats, who seemed to suffer no ill effects.

Upstream from the draw that held the dump, the irrigation flume crossed the river. It always seemed to me giddily high when I hung my chin over its plank edge and looked down, but it probably walked no more than twenty feet above the water on its spidery legs. Ordinarily in summer it carried six or eight inches of smooth water, and under the glassy surface of the little boxed stream the planks were coated with deep sun-warmed moss as slick as frogs' eggs. A boy could sit in the flume with the water walling up against his back, and grab a cross-brace above him, and pull, shooting himself sledlike ahead until he could reach the next cross-brace for another pull, and so on across the river in four scoots.

After ten minutes in the flume he would come out wearing a dozen or more limber black leeches, and could sit in the green shade where darning needles flashed blue, and dragonflies hummed and stopped in the air, and skaters dimpled slack and eddy with their delicate transitory footprints, and there pull the leeches off one by one, while their sucking ends clung and clung, until at last, stretched far out, they let go with a tiny wet *puk* and snapped together like rubber bands. The smell of the flume and the low bars of that part of the river was the smell of wolf willow.

But nothing else in the east end of town was as good as the dump ground. Through a historical process that went back to the roots of community sanitation, and that in law dated from the Unincorporated Towns Ordinance of the territorial government, passed in 1888, the dump was the very first community enterprise, the town's first institution.

More than that, it contained relics of every individual who had ever lived there. The bedsprings on which Whitemud's first child was begotten might be out there; the skeleton of a boy's pet colt; books soaked with water and chemicals in a house fire, and thrown out to flap their stained eloquence in the prairie wind. Broken dishes, rusty tinware, spoons that had been used to mix paint; once a box of percussion caps, sign and symbol of the carelessness that most of us had in matters of personal or public safety. My brother and I put some of them on the railroad tracks and were anonymously denounced in the *Leader* for nearly derailing the speeder of a section crew. There were also old iron, old brass, for which we hunted assiduously, by night conning junkmen's catalogs to find out how much wartime value there might be in the geared insides of clocks or in a pound of tea lead carefully wrapped in a ball whose weight astonished and delighted us.

Sometimes the unimaginable world reached out and laid a finger on us because of our activities on the dump. I recall that, aged about seven, I wrote a Toronto junk house asking if they preferred their tea lead and tinfoil wrapped in balls, or whether they would rather have it pressed flat in sheets, and got back a typewritten letter in a window envelope advising me that they would be happy to have it in any way that was convenient to me. They added that they valued my business and were mine very truly. Dazed, I carried that windowed grandeur around in my pocket until I wore it out.

We hunted old bottles in the dump, bottles caked with filth, half buried, full of cobwebs, and we washed them out at the horse trough by the elevators, putting in a handful of shot along with the water to knock the dirt loose; and when we had shaken them until our arms were tired, we hauled them down in somebody's coaster wagon and turned them in at Bill Christenson's pool hall, where the smell of lemon pop was so sweet on the dark pool-hall air that it sometimes awakens me in the night even yet.

Smashed wheels of wagons and buggies, tangles of rusty barbed wire, the collapsed perambulator that the French wife of one of the town's doctors had once pushed proudly up the plank sidewalks and along the ditchbank paths. A welter of foul-smelling feathers and coyote-scattered carrion, that was all that remained of somebody's dream of a chicken ranch. The chickens had all got some mysterious pip at the same time, and died as one, and the dream lay out there with the rest of the town's short history to rustle to the empty sky on the border of the Hills.

There was melted glass in curious forms, and the half-melted office safe left from the burning of Joe Knight's hotel. On very lucky days we might find a piece of the lead casing that had enclosed the wires of the town's first telephone system. The casing was just the right size for rings, and so soft that it could be whittled with a jackknife. If we had been Indians of fifty years earlier, that bright soft metal could have enlisted our maximum patience and craft, and come out as ring and medal and amulet inscribed with the symbols of our observed world. Perhaps there were too many ready-made alternatives in the local drug, hardware, and general stores; in any case our artistic response was feeble, and resulted in nothing better than crude seal rings with initials or pierced hearts carved in them. They served a purpose in juvenile courtship, but they stopped a good way short of art.

The dump held very little wood, for in that country anything burnable got burned. But it had plenty of old metal, furniture, papers, mattresses that were the delight of field mice, and jugs and demijohns that were sometimes their bane, for they crawled into the necks and drowned in the rainwater or redeye that was inside.

If the history of Whitemud was not exactly written, it was at least hinted, in the dump. I think I had a pretty sound notion even at eight or nine of how significant was that first institution of our forming Canadian civilization. For rummaging through its foul purlieus I had several times been surprised and shocked to find relics of my own life tossed out there to blow away or rot.

Some of the books were volumes of the set of Shakespeare that my father had bought, or been sold, before I was born. They had been carried from Dakota to Seattle, and Seattle to Bellingham, and Bellingham to Redmond, and Redmond back to Iowa, and Iowa to Saskatchewan. One of the Cratchet girls had borrowed them, a hatchet-faced, thin, eager, transplanted Cockney girl with a frenzy for reading. Stained in a fire, they had somehow found the dump rather than come back to us. The lesson they preached was how much is lost, how much thrown aside, how much carelessly or of necessity given up, in the making of a new country. We had so few books that I knew them all; finding those thrown away was like finding my own name on a gravestone.

And yet not the blow that something else was, something that impressed me even more with how closely the dump reflected the town's intimate life. The colt whose picked skeleton lay out there was mine. He had been incurably crippled when dogs chased our mare Daisy the morning after she foaled. I had worked for months to make him well, had fed him by hand, curried him, talked my father into having iron braces made for his front legs. And I had not known that he would have to be destroyed. One weekend I turned him over to the foreman of one of the ranches, presumably so that he could be better cared for. A few days later I found his skinned body, with the braces still on his crippled front legs, lying on the dump. I think I might eventually have accepted the colt's death, and forgiven his killer, if it had not been for that dirty little two-dollar meanness that skinned him.

Not even finding his body cured me of going to the dump, though our parents all forbade us on pain of cholera or worse to do so. The place fascinated us, as it should have. For this was the kitchen midden of all the civilization we knew. It gave us the most tantalizing glimpses into our neighbors' lives and our own; it provided an aesthetic distance from which to know ourselves.

The town dump was our poetry and our history. We took it home with us by the wagonload, bringing back into town the things the town had used and thrown away. Some little part of what we gathered, mainly bottles, we managed to bring back to usefulness, but most of our gleanings we left lying around barn or attic or cellar until in some renewed fury of spring cleanup our families carted them off to the dump again, to be rescued and briefly treasured by some other boy. Occasionally something we really valued with a passion was snatched from us in horror and returned at once. That happened to the mounted head of a white mountain goat, somebody's trophy from old times and the far Rocky Mountains, that I brought home one day. My mother took one look and discovered that his beard was full of moths.

I remember that goat; I regret him yet. Poetry is seldom useful, but always memorable. If I were a sociologist anxious to study in detail the life of any community I would go very early to its refuse piles. For a community may be as well judged by what it throws away—what it has to throw away and what it chooses to—as by any other evidence. For whole civilizations we sometimes have no more of the poetry and little more of the history than this.

TWO

HAMLIN GARLAND

Hamlin Garland's father made the long trek from the woods of Maine to uninhabited Wisconsin, where Hamlin Garland was born in 1860 in a log cabin. His family moved to Iowa, and he graduated in 1881 from Cedar Valley Seminary in Osage, Iowa. His finest book, *A Son of the Middle Border*, from which the following selection comes, was published in 1917. His work reflects agrarian America attempting "to return to normal" after the shock of the Civil War. As the following excerpt suggests, movement and change, not normalcy, were to be the nation's future. Garland died in 1940 in Los Angeles.

The Last Threshing in the Coulee

Life on a Wisconsin farm, even for the women, had its compensations. There were times when the daily routine of lonely and monotonous housework gave place to an agreeable bustle, and human intercourse lightened the toil. In the midst of the slow progress of the fall's plowing, the gathering of the threshing crew was a most dramatic event to my mother, as to us, for it not only brought unwonted clamor, it fetched her brothers William and David and Frank, who owned and ran a threshing machine, and their coming gave the house an air of festivity which offset the burden of extra work which fell upon us all.

In those days the grain, after being brought in and stacked around the barn, was allowed to remain until October or November when all the other work was finished.

Of course some men got the machine earlier, for all could not thresh at the same time, and a good part of every man's fall activities consisted in "changing works" with his neighbors, thus laying up a stock of unpaid labor against the home job. Day after day, therefore, father or the hired man shouldered a fork and went to help thresh, and all through the autumn months, the ceaseless ringing hum and the *bow-ouw, ouw-woo, boo-oo-oom* of the great balance wheels on the separator and the deep bass purr of its cylinder could be heard in every valley like the droning song of some sullen and gigantic autumnal insect.

I recall with especial clearness the events of that last threshing in the coulee.—I was eight, my brother was six. For days we had looked forward to the coming of "the threshers," listening with the greatest eagerness to father's report of the crew. At last he said, "Well, Belle, get ready. The machine will be here tomorrow."

All day we hung on the gate, gazing down the road, watching, waiting for the crew, and even after supper, we stood at the windows still hoping to hear the rattle of the ponderous separator.

Father explained that the men usually worked all day at one farm and moved after dark, and we were just starting to "climb the wooden hill" when we heard a far-off faint halloo.

"There they are," shouted father, catching up his old square tin lantern and hurriedly lighting the candle within it. "That's Frank's voice."

The night air was sharp, and as we had taken off our boots we could only stand at the window and watch father as he piloted the teamsters through the gate. The light threw fantastic shadows here and there, now lighting up a face, now bringing out the separator which seemed a weary and sullen monster awaiting its den. The men's voices sounded loud in the still night, causing the roused turkeys in the oaks to peer about on their perches, uneasy silhouettes against the sky.

We would gladly have stayed awake to greet our beloved uncles, but mother said, "You must go to sleep in order to be up early in the morning," and reluctantly we turned away.

Lying thus in our cot under the sloping raftered roof we could hear the squawk of the hens as father wrung their innocent necks, and the crash of the "sweeps" being unloaded sounded loud and clear and strange. We longed to be out there, but at last the dance of lights and shadows on the plastered wall died away, and we fell into childish dreamless sleep.

We were awakened at dawn by the ringing beat of the iron mauls as Frank and David drove the stakes to hold the "power" to the ground. The rattle of trace chains, the clash of iron rods, the clang of steel bars, intermixed with the laughter of the men, came sharply through the frosty air, and the smell of sizzling sausage from the kitchen warned us that our busy mother was hurrying the breakfast forward. Knowing that it was time to get up, although it was not yet light, I had a sense of being awakened into a romantic new world, a world of heroic action.

As we stumbled down the stairs, we found the lamp-lit kitchen empty of the men. They had finished their coffee and were out in the stack-yard oiling the machine and hitching the horses to the power. Shivering yet entranced by the beauty of the frosty dawn we crept out to stand and watch the play. The frost lay white on every surface, the frozen ground rang like iron under the steel-shod feet of the horses, and the breath of the men rose up in little white puffs of steam.

Uncle David on the feeder's stand was impatiently awaiting the coming of the fifth team. The pitchers were climbing the stacks like blackbirds, and the straw-stackers were scuffling about the stable door.—Finally, just as the east began to bloom, and long streamers of red began to unroll along the vast gray dome of sky Uncle Frank, the driver, lifted his voice in a "Chippewa war-whoop."

On a still morning like this his signal could be heard for miles. Long drawn and musical, it sped away over the fields, announcing to all the world that the McClintocks were ready for the day's race. Answers came back faintly from the frosty fields where dim figures of laggard hands could be seen hurrying over the plowed ground, the last team came clattering in and was hooked into its place, David called "All right!" and the cylinder began to hum.

In those days the machine was either a "J. I. Case" or a "Buffalo Pitts," and was moved by five pairs of horses attached to a "power" staked to the ground, round which they travelled pulling at the ends of long levers or sweeps, and to me the force seemed tremendous. "Tumbling rods" with "knuckle joints" carried the motion to the cylinder, and the driver who stood upon a square platform above the huge, greasy cog-wheels (round which the horses moved) was a grand figure in my eyes.

Driving, to us, looked like a pleasant job, but Uncle Frank thought it very tiresome, and I can now see that it was. To stand on that small platform all through the long hours of a cold November day, when the cutting wind roared down the valley sweeping the dust and leaves along the road, was work. Even I perceived that it was far pleasanter to sit on the south side of the stack and watch the horses go round.

It was necessary that the "driver" should be a man of judgment, for the horses had to be kept at just the right speed, and to do this he must gauge the motion of the cylinder by the pitch of its deep bass song.

The three men in command of the machine, were set apart as "the threshers."—William and David alternately "fed" or "tended," that is, one of them "fed" the grain into the howling cylinder while the other, oilcan in hand, watched the sieves, felt of the pinions and so kept the machine in good order. The feeder's position was the high place to which all boys aspired, and on this day I stood in silent admiration of Uncle David's easy powerful attitudes as he caught each bundle in the crook of his arm and spread it out into a broad, smooth band of yellow straw on which the whirling teeth caught and tore with monstrous fury. He was the ideal man in my eyes, grander in some ways than my father, and to be able to stand where he stood was the highest honor in the world.

It was all poetry for us and we wished every day were threshing day. The wind blew cold, the clouds went flying across the bright blue sky, and the straw glistened in the sun. With jarring snarl the circling zone of cogs dipped into the sturdy greasy wheels, and the single-trees and pulley-chains chirped clear and sweet as crickets. The dust flew, the whip cracked, and the men working swiftly to get the sheaves to the feeder or to take the straw away from the tail-end of the machine, were like warriors, urged to desperate action by battle cries. The stackers wallowing to their waists in the fluffy straw-pile seemed gnomes acting for our amusement.

The straw-pile! What delight we had in that! What joy it was to go up to the top where the men were stationed, one behind the other, and to have them toss huge forkfuls of the light fragrant stalks upon us, laughing to see us emerge from our golden cover. We were especially impressed by the bravery of Ed Green who stood in the midst of the thick dust and flying chaff close to the tail of the stacker. His teeth shone like a negro's out of his dust-blackened face and his shirt was wet with sweat, but he motioned for "more straw" and David, accepting the challenge, signalled for more speed. Frank swung his lash and yelled at the straining horses, the sleepy growl of the cylinder rose to a howl and the wheat came pulsing out at the spout in such a stream that the carriers were forced to trot on their path to and from the granary in order to keep the grain from piling up around the measurer. —There was a kind of splendid rivalry in this backbreaking toil—for each sack weighed ninety pounds.

We got tired of wallowing in the straw at last, and went down to help Rover catch the rats which were being uncovered by the pitchers as they reached the stack bottom.—The horses, with their straining, outstretched necks, the loud and cheery shouts, the whistling of the driver, the roar and hum of the great wheel, the flourishing of the forks, the supple movement of brawny arms, the shouts of the men, all blended with the wild sound of the wind in the creaking branches of the oaks, forming a glorious poem in our unforgetting minds.

At last the call for dinner sounded. The driver began to call, "Whoa there, boys! Steady, Tom," and to hold his long whip before the eyes of the more spirited of the teams in order to convince them that he really meant "stop." The pitchers stuck their forks upright in the stack and leaped to the ground. Randal, the band-cutter, drew from his wrist the looped string of his big knife, the stackers slid down from the straw-pile, and a race began among the teamsters to see whose span would be first unhitched and at the watering trough. What joyous rivalry it seemed to us!—

Mother and Mrs. Randal, wife of our neighbor, who was "changing works," stood ready to serve the food as soon as the men were seated.—The table had been lengthened to its utmost and pieced out with boards, and planks had been laid on stout wooden chairs at either side.

The men came in with a rush, and took seats wherever they could find them, and their attack on the boiled potatoes and chicken should have been appalling to the women, but it was not. They enjoyed seeing them eat. Ed Green was prodigious. One cut at a big potato, followed by two stabbing motions, and it was gone.—Two bites laid a leg of chicken as bare as a slate pencil. To us standing in the corner waiting our turn, it seemed that every "smitch" of the dinner was in danger, for the others were not far behind Ed and Dan.

At last even the gauntest of them filled up and left the room and we were free to sit at "the second table" and eat, while the men rested outside. David and William, however, generally had a belt to sew or a bent tooth to take out of the "concave." This seemed of grave dignity to us and we respected their self-sacrificing labor.

Nooning was brief. As soon as the horses had finished their oats, the roar and hum of the machine began again and continued steadily all the afternoon, till by and by the sun grew big and red, the night began to fall, and the wind died out.

This was the most impressive hour of a marvellous day. Through the falling dusk, the machine boomed steadily with a new sound, a solemn roar, rising at intervals to a rattling impatient yell as the cylinder ran momentarily empty. The men moved now in silence, looming dim and gigantic in the half-light. The straw-pile mountain high, the pitchers in the chaff, the feeder on his platform, and especially the driver on his power, seemed almost super-human to my childish eyes. Gray dust covered the handsome face of David, changing it into something both sad and stern, but Frank's cheery voice rang out musically as he called to the weary horses, "Come on, Tom! Hup there, Dan!"

The track in which they walked had been worn into two deep circles and they all moved mechanically round and round, like parts of a machine, dull-eyed and covered with sweat.

At last William raised the welcome cry, "All done!"—the men threw down their forks. Uncle Frank began to call in a gentle, soothing voice, "*Whoa,* lads! *Steady,* boys! Whoa, there!"

But the horses had been going so long and so steadily that they could not at once check their speed. They kept moving, though slowly, on and on till their owners slid from the stacks and seizing the ends of the sweeps, held them. Even then, after the power was still, the cylinder kept its hum, till David throwing a last sheaf into its open maw, choked it into silence.

Now came the sound of dropping chains, the clang of iron rods, and the thud of hoofs as the horses walked with laggard gait and weary down-falling heads to the barn. The men, more subdued than at dinner, washed with greater care, and combed the chaff from their beards. The air was still and cool, and the sky a deep cloudless blue starred with faint fire.

Supper though quiet was more dramatic than dinner had been. The table lighted with kerosene lamps, the clean white linen, the fragrant dishes, the women flying about with steaming platters, all seemed very cheery and very beautiful, and the men who came into the light and warmth of the kitchen with aching muscles and empty stomachs, seemed gentler and finer than at noon. They were nearly all from neighboring farms, and my mother treated even the few hired men like visitors, and the talk was all hearty and good tempered though a little subdued.

One by one the men rose and slipped away, and father withdrew to milk the cows and bed down the horses, leaving the women and the youngsters to eat what was left and "do up the dishes."

After we had eaten our fill Frank and I also went out to the barn (all wonderfully changed now to our minds by the great stack of straw), there to listen to David and father chatting as they rubbed their tired horses.—The lantern threw a dim red light on the harness and on the rumps of the cattle, but left mysterious shadows in the corners. I could hear the mice rustling in the straw of the roof, and from the farther end of the dimly-lighted shed came the regular *strim-stram* of the streams of milk falling into the bottom of a tin pail as the hired hand milked the big roan cow.

All this was very momentous to me as I sat on the oat box, shivering in the cold air, listening with all my ears, and when we finally went toward the house, the stars were big and sparkling. The frost had already begun to glisten on the fences and well-curb, and high in the air, dark against the sky, the turkeys were roosting uneasily, as if disturbed by premonitions of approaching Thanksgiving. Rover pattered along by my side on the crisp grass and my brother clung to my hand.

How bright and warm it was in the kitchen with mother putting things to rights while father and my uncles leaned their chairs against the wall and talked of the west and of moving. "I can't get away till after New Year's," father said. "But I'm going. I'll never put in another crop on these hills."

With speechless content I listened to Uncle William's stories of bears and Indians, and other episodes of frontier life, until at last we were ordered to bed and the glorious day was done.

Oh, those blessed days, those entrancing nights! How fine they were then, and how mellow they are now, for the slow-paced years have dropped nearly fifty other golden mists upon that far-off valley. From this distance I cannot understand how my father brought himself to leave that lovely farm and those good and noble friends.

David and His Violin

Most of the events of our last autumn in Green's Coulee have slipped into the fathomless gulf, but the experiences of Thanksgiving day, which followed closely on our threshing day, are in my treasure house. Like a canvas by Rembrandt only one side of the figures therein is defined, the other side melts away into shadow—a luminous shadow, through which faint light pulses, luring my wistful gaze on and on, back into the vanished world where the springs of my life lie hidden.

It is a raw November evening. Frank and Harriet and I are riding into a strange land in a clattering farm wagon. Father and mother are seated before us on the spring seat. The ground is frozen and the floor of the carriage pounds and jars. We cling to the iron-lined sides of the box to soften the blows. It is growing dark. Before us (in a similar vehicle) my Uncle David is leading the way. I catch momentary glimpses of him outlined against the pale yellow sky. He stands erect, holding the reins of his swiftly-moving horses in his powerful left hand. Occasionally he shouts back to my father, whose chin is buried in a thick buffalo-skin coat. Mother is only a vague mass, a figure wrapped in shawls. The wind is keen, the world gray and cheerless.

My sister is close beside me in the straw. Frank is asleep. I am on my knees looking ahead. Suddenly with rush of wind and clatter of hoofs, we enter the gloom of a forest and the road begins to climb. I see the hills on the right. I catch the sound of wheels on a bridge. I am cold. I snuggle down under the robes and the gurgle of ice-bound water is fused with my dreams.

I am roused at last by Uncle David's pleasant voice, "Wake up, boys, and pay y'r lodging!" I look out and perceive him standing beside the wheel. I see a house and I hear the sound of Deborah's voice from the warmly-lighted open door.

I climb down, heavy with cold and sleep. As I stand there my uncle reaches up his arms to take my mother down. Not knowing that she has a rheumatic elbow, he squeezes her playfully. She gives a sharp scream, and his team starts away on a swift run around the curve of the road toward the gate. Dropping my mother, he dashes across the yard to intercept the runaways. We all stand in silence, watching the flying horses and the wonderful race he is making toward the gate. He runs with magnificent action, his head thrown high. As the team dashes through the gate his outflung left hand catches the end-board of the wagon—he leaps into the box, and so passes from our sight.

We go into the cottage. It is a small building with four rooms and a kitchen on the ground floor, but in the sitting room we come upon an open fireplace,—the first I had ever seen, and in the light of it sits Grandfather McClintock, the glory of the flaming logs gilding the edges of his cloud of bushy white hair. He does not rise to greet us, but smiles and calls out, "Come in! Come in! Draw a cheer. Sit ye down."

A clamor of welcome fills the place. Harriet and I are put to warm before the blaze. Grandad takes Frank upon his knee and the cutting wind of the gray outside world is forgotten.

This house in which the McClintocks were living at this time, belonged to a rented farm. Grandad had sold the original homestead on the LaCrosse River, and David who had lately married a charming young Canadian girl, was the head of the family. Deborah, it seems, was also living with him and Frank was there—as a visitor probably.

The room in which we sat was small and bare but to me it was very beautiful, because of the fire, and by reason of the merry voices which filled my ears with music. Aunt Rebecca brought to us a handful of crackers and told us that we were to have oyster soup for supper. This gave us great pleasure even in anticipation, for oysters were a delicious treat in those days.

"Well, Dick," Grandad began, "so ye're plannin' to go west, air ye?"

"Yes, as soon as I get all my grain and hogs marketed I'm going to pull out for my new farm over in Iowa."

"Ye'd better stick to the old coulee," warned my grandfather, a touch of sadness in his voice. "Ye'll find none better."

My father was disposed to resent this. "That's all very well for the few who have the level land in the middle of the valley," he retorted, "but how about those of us who are crowded against the hills? You should see the farm I have in Winneshiek! Not a hill on it big enough for a boy to coast on. It's right on the edge of Looking Glass Prairie, and I have a spring of water, and a fine grove of trees just where I want them, not where they have to be grubbed out."

"But ye belong here," repeated Grandfather. "You were married here, your children were born here. Ye'll find no such friends in the west as you have here in Neshonoc. And Belle will miss the family."

My father laughed. "Oh, you'll all come along. Dave has the fever already. Even William is likely to catch it."

Old Hugh sighed deeply. "I hope ye're wrong," he said. "I'd like to spend me last days here with me sons and daughters around me, sich as are left to me," here his voice became sterner. "It's the curse of our country,—this constant moving, moving. I'd have been better off had I stayed in Ohio, though this valley seemed very beautiful to me the first time I saw it."

At this point David came in, and everybody shouted, "Did you stop them?" referring of course to the runaway team.

"I did," he replied with a smile. "But how about the oysters. I'm holler as a beech log."

The fragrance of the soup thoroughly awakened even little Frank, and when we drew around the table, each face shone with the light of peace and plenty, and all our elders tried to forget that this was the last Thanksgiving festival which the McClintocks and Garlands would be able to enjoy in the old valley. How good those oysters were! They made up the entire meal,—excepting mince pie which came as a closing sweet.

Slowly, one by one, the men drew back and returned to the sitting room, leaving the women to wash up the dishes and put the kitchen to rights. David seized the opportunity to ask my father to tell once again of the trip he had made, of the lands he had seen, and the farm he had purchased, for his young heart was also fired with desire of exploration. The level lands toward the sunset allured him. In his visions the wild meadows were filled with game, and the free lands needed only to be tickled with a hoe to laugh into harvest.

He said, "As soon as Dad and Frank are settled on a farm here, I'm going west also. I'm as tired of climbing these hills as you are. I want a place of my own—and besides, from all you say of that wheat country out there, a threshing machine would pay wonderfully well."

As the women came in, my father called out, "Come, Belle, sing 'O'er the Hills in Legions Boys!'—Dave get out your fiddle—and tune us all up."

David tuned up his fiddle and while he twanged on the strings mother lifted her voice in our fine old marching song.

Cheer up, brothers, as we go,
O'er the mountains, westward ho—

and we all joined in the jubilant chorus—

Then o'er the hills in legions, boys,
Fair freedom's star
Points to the sunset regions, boys,
Ha, ha, ha-ha!—

My father's face shone with the light of the explorer, the pioneer. The words of this song appealed to him as the finest poetry. It meant all that was fine and hopeful and buoyant in American life, to him—but on my mother's sweet face a wistful expression deepened and in her fine eyes a reflective shadow lay. To her this song meant not so much the acquisition of a new home as the loss of all her friends and relatives. She sang it submissively, not exultantly, and I think the other women were of the same mood though their faces were less expressive to me. To all of the pioneer wives of the past that song had meant deprivation, suffering, loneliness, heart-ache.

From this they passed to other of my father's favorite songs, and it is highly significant to note that even in this choice of songs he generally had his way. He was the dominating force. "Sing 'Nellie Wildwood,'" he said, and they sang it.—This power of getting his will respected was due partly to his military training but more to a distinctive trait in him. He was a man of power, of decision, a natural commander of men.

They sang "Minnie Minturn" to his request, and the refrain,—

I have heard the angels warning,
I have seen the golden shore—

meant much to me. So did the line,

But I only hear the drummers
As the armies march away.

Aunt Deb was also a soul of decision. She called out, "No more of these sad tones," and struck up "The Year of Jubilo," and we all shouted till the walls shook with the exultant words:

Ol' massa run—ha-ha!
De darkies stay,—ho-ho!
It must be now is the kingdom a-comin'
In the year of Jubilo.

At this point the fire suggested an old English ballad which I loved, and so I piped up, "Mother, sing, 'Pile the Wood on Higher!' and she complied with pleasure, for this was a song of home, of the unbroken fire-side circle.

Oh, the winds howl mad outdoors
The snow clouds hurry past,
The giant trees sway to and fro
Beneath the sweeping blast.

and we children joined in the chorus:

Then we'll gather round the fire
And we'll pile the wood on higher,
Let the song and jest go round;
What care we for the storm,
When the fireside is so warm,
And pleasure here is found?

Never before did this song mean so much to me as at this moment
when the winds were actually howling outdoors, and Uncle Frank was
in very truth piling the logs higher. It seemed as though my stuffed
bosom could not receive anything deeper and finer, but it did, for father
was saying, "Well, Dave, now for some *tunes.*"

This was the best part of David to me. He could make any room
mystical with the magic of his bow. True, his pieces were mainly
venerable dance tunes, cotillions, hornpipes,—melodies which had
passed from fiddler to fiddler until they had become veritable
folksongs,—pieces like "Money Musk," "Honest John," "Haste to the
Wedding," and many others whose names I have forgotten, but with a
gift of putting into even the simplest song an emotion which subdued
us and silenced us, he played on, absorbed and intent. From these
familiar pieces he passed to others for which he had no names,
melodies strangely sweet and sad, full of longing cries, voicing
something which I dimly felt but could not understand.

At the moment he was the somber Scotch Highlander, the true
Celt, and as he bent above his instrument his black eyes glowing, his
fine head drooping low, my heart bowed down in worship of his skill.
He was my hero, the handsomest, most romantic figure in all my world.

He played, "Maggie, Air Ye Sleepin'," and the wind outside went
to my soul. Voices wailed to me out of the illimitable hill-land forests,
voices that pleaded:

Oh, let me in, for loud the linn
Goes roarin' o'er the moorland craggy.

He appeared to forget us, even his young wife. His eyes looked
away into gray storms. Vague longing ached in his throat. Life was a
struggle, love a torment.

He stopped abruptly, and put the violin into its box, fumbling with
the catch to hide his emotion and my father broke the tense silence
with a prosaic word. "Well, well! Look here, it's time you youngsters
were asleep. Beckie, where are you going to put these children?"

Aunt Rebecca, a trim little woman with brown eyes, looked at us reflectively, "Well, now, I don't know. I guess we'll have to make a bed for them on the floor."

This was done, and for the first time in my life, I slept before an open fire. As I snuggled into my blankets with my face turned to the blaze, the darkness of the night and the denizens of the pineland wilderness to the north had no terrors for me.

I was awakened in the early light by Uncle David building the fire, and then came my father's call, and the hurly burly of jovial greeting from old and young. The tumult lasted till breakfast was called, and everybody who could find place sat around the table and attacked the venison and potatoes which formed the meal. I do not remember our leave-taking or the ride homeward. I bring to mind only the desolate cold of our own kitchen into which we tramped late in the afternoon, sitting in our wraps until the fire began to roar within its iron cage.

Oh, winds of the winter night! Oh, firelight and the shine of tender eyes! How far away you seem tonight!

So faint and far,
Each dear face shineth as a star.

Oh, you by the western sea, and you of the south beyond the reach of Christmas snow, do not your hearts hunger, like mine tonight for that Thanksgiving Day among the trees? For the glance of eyes undimmed of tears, for the hair untouched with gray?

It all lies in the unchanging realm of the past—this land of my childhood. Its charm, its strange dominion cannot return save in the poet's reminiscent dream. No money, no railway train can take us back to it. It did not in truth exist—it was a magical world, born of the vibrant union of youth and firelight, of music and the voice of moaning winds—a union which can never come again to you or me, father, uncle, brother, till the coulee meadows bloom again unscarred of spade or plow.

MARK SULLIVAN

Mark Sullivan, the son of Irish immigrants, was born in Avondale, Pennsylvania, in 1874. In 1893 he bought a newspaper in Phoenixville, Pennsylvania, for $300 and made sufficient profit on it for a Harvard education (B.A. 1900, LL.B. 1903). He worked for most of his life as a newspaperman in Washington and was considered the "dean and Jeremiah of Washington correspondents." He wrote the six volume *Our Times*, a series of "contemporary histories" covering the years 1900 to 1925. The following selection comes from *The Education of an American*, published in 1938. Mark Sullivan died in 1952.

The Farm

The house, and the farm on which it sits, is in a country of soft, gentle hills and little winding creeks, about fifteen miles from the Delaware River, where river widens into bay. The two small streams that flow through the farm, and one that rises on it, find their way into Delaware Bay. A few miles west of the farm is a rise in the land, a watershed, so slight as to be almost imperceptible, beyond which the streams flow into Chesapeake Bay and the Susquehanna River.

The village near by is called Avondale; some time before my father bought the farm it was called Stone Bridge. In those early days it was just a tavern and a blacksmith shop, an overnight stopping place for waggoners on the first turnpike in America, the one from Newport, Delaware, to Lancaster, Pennsylvania. When the railroad came it divided all the countryside hamlets into two classes, those which the railroad passed through—these became stations; and those which were left—phrase of doom—"off the railroad." Avondale was one of the fortunate former. It, like the railroad stations everywhere, drew into itself the little businesses and trades of the now isolated hamlets. Avondale became a village of some three or four hundred people; in eighty years it has not greatly expanded.

The country thereabouts is fertile, smiling, kind. A place name given to a township by the early settlers, expressive of their delight with the land, is New Garden. Other place names—Locust Grove, West Grove, Harmony Grove—recall the woodlands the early settlers found, of oak, hickory, beech and poplar, parts of which they preserved and which still stand as wood lots here and there among the open fields.

II

My earliest memory, that I can identify, is of a scent. It was late on a sunny September afternoon, "potato-digging time." My father was plowing up the long furrows of fresh earth in the potato field, which sloped southward from the house. Following behind him, my mother gathered the potatoes into pails which, when full, she emptied into bags set at intervals along the rows. She rarely worked in the fields—with a family of growing boys she did not need to; but potato digging coincided with the opening of school. In order that the children should go the first day, and every day, she took on herself the potato picking. Because there was no one in the house to look after me she took me to the field with her. I was not more than two or three years old; I suppose I spent the afternoon playing in the fresh earth. Here and there among the uprooted potato vines grew two herbs, pennyroyal and St-John's-wort. Both were strong-scented and were prized in our neighborhood as having medicinal value. Some wisps of these my mother gathered into a small bundle which she laid aside. In the evening, walking back to the house, she carried me, the fragrant pennyroyal and St-John's-wort in her hand brushing my face.

There this memory ends. But other memories recall the herbs tied into bundles and hung from hooks in the kitchen ceiling, against the winter weather when the children would have colds, for which "pennyrile tea" was believed to be a remedy.

All the more vivid of my early memories are of smells, farm smells: the acrid scent of burning weeds in the fall, at the end of a day of clearing the field for planting wheat; the faint fragrance of blossoms wafted down from the orchard in May, followed in midsummer by the strong, mellow odor of ripening apples, and in fall by the cidery scent of apples pared and sliced and spread in wooden racks in the sun, to provide our winter store of dried apples; the harvest smell of mown grass and of threshed straw; the barn smell of dried hay; the dank scent of the woods after a rain; the odor of bloodroot, the first spring flower, and of sassafras as the sap began to run; the pervading smell of October, which settled for weeks upon the whole countryside, so heavy it seemed almost visible, almost like a mist, a potpourri of ripening walnuts, ripening wild grapes, leaves fallen and just beginning to decay. Each season, almost each day, each spot on the farm, had its special scent. All are still vivid to me. One bred on a farm knows that

Smells are surer than sounds or sights
To make your heart-strings crack.

Next to scents, my most vivid early memories are of sounds: the whir of the mowing machine in outlying fields in June; the two-note *clunk, clank* of the whetstone against the scythe, which we kept for mowing corners of the field and bits of hillside too steep for the mowing machine. Another two-note sound was of the ax cutting down a tree in the woods, a low-pitched *chug* from the level stroke that made the bottom of the incision, a higher-pitched note made by the downward chop—both followed, after a half-hour of chopping, by a moment of silence, having the effect of suspense, by which I knew my father had stepped hurriedly back, and then the swish of the falling tree against the twigs and limbs of its neighbors, the sound gathering volume and tempo until it became a roar, climaxing in a mighty crash as the tree struck the ground. The two-pitched whine of the crosscut saw, a high note as the faster of the two sawyers drew the blade toward him, a lower note made by the slower worker.

In the fields, as the sun told us noon was near, we listened for the dinner bells. On our farm we had none—we depended on my mother's voice. But on many of the neighboring farms was a huge bell, as big as a school or church bell—indeed, I think the makers of the bells did not differentiate in size between those designed to summon to spiritual refreshment Sunday mornings and those designed to announce the noonday meal of the flesh. The dinner bell hung from a tall post, with a chain attached to it. This the housewife pulled at a moment nicely chosen to enable the men to get back from the fields just as the dishes came hot from stove to table. The bells rang about the same time, their deep-toned voices a rude neighborhood carillon.

From the swamps and bottoms in early March came the chorus of the young frogs. They sounded hurried, breathless, as if passionately eager to bring the spring, of which they were the heralds. We called them "knee-deeps." For that name we had two explanations: one that the frogs were still knee-deep in the swamp, the other that their cry sounded like *knee-deep*—the first note low in pitch, the second high, almost a whistle. The knee-deep was not musical, much less so than the bobwhite or the dove; nor is the frog a glamorous creature, whether young or full-grown. Yet of all the sounds my childhood knew, the cry of the knee-deeps remained the most vivid, the most potent to evoke the past. During all the middle years of my life, wherever I was, in cities or in distant lands, I never saw March come on the calendar without thinking of the farm and wishing I could hear the knee-deeps.

. . . .

III

The house, wooden, had four rooms downstairs, three above. Two of the rooms, one downstairs, one up, had been added by my father about the time I was born. The addition was the occasion of some confusion to me as a child, and one of my earliest intellectual illuminations was to become aware that the family's name for the southern part of the house was not one word, "newend," but two, "new end," and that the phrase was descriptive—I had supposed it to be the term for a part of every house, like "kitchen" and "shed." Building the new end strained the family finances; for several years the whole house stood unpainted. We could have whitewashed it, but my mother resisted; she, though never an optimist, felt the time might come when we could have it painted. By the law of her nature, in everything, she would have either the best or nothing. When the time did arrive when we could afford painting it, choice of a color consumed weeks of family discussion. A memento of that, a sheet of sample colors, little squares of stiff paper about an inch each way, differently colored, was one of the prized possessions of my childhood.

. . . .

IV

In the neighborhood were tree nurseries. From one of them my father got four young evergreens, firs, which he planted in a row in front of the house, to the east. There was another evergreen, a cedar, called by the family "Johnny's tree," for some association it had with one of my brothers. After I grew up and went away the cedar was removed; when I returned on visits I missed it, poignantly. But the four tall firs are still there, landmarks to the country round.

One of my serenities in recent years has been to sit on the porch on late afternoons, with the descending sun behind me, and watch the tall shadows of the firs lengthen and swing toward the right, like a four-columned army deploying. The shadows march down the slope of the field in front of the house, cross the little stream and the road and, with increasing speed as the sun goes down, march up the other hill.

Once, watching the tips of the shadows advance through the clover field an eighth of a mile away, I observed them give notice of nightfall to a hen. She had been, with the rest of the flock, catching grasshoppers in the clover. This hen was an individualist, she had enterprise and industry. After the rest of the flock had gone home she had remained busily pursuing the hoppers. She had resourcefulness, knew how to adapt herself to circumstance and make it serve her. In the pursuit of grasshoppers she had developed an individual technique. In the field was a horse, grazing. As he moved his nose forward in the grass, he stirred up hoppers. The hen placed herself a yard or so in front of the horse and facing him. As the horse stepped·forward the hen stepped backward. As each forward move of the horse's munching mouth caused a barrage of grasshoppers to leap forward, the hen kept herself at the bottom of the arc where the barrage descended. Busily clutching and gulping, she neglected the passage of time until the tip of one of the tree shadows reached and covered her. As it shut off the sun she cocked her head alertly, looked toward the sun, observed it close to setting, and at once, without another peck at a hopper or a look behind, started down the hill toward home. She was startled but not disturbed. She did not run, but walked rapidly and directly in a straight line, with a continuity of intention, a settled purposefulness, that marked her off from the race of hens as a whole. Belated but safe, she arrived at the chicken house with her craw better filled than her less assiduous sisters'.

On three sides of the yard my father planted rows of young evergreens close together, as a hedge, partly for ornament, more for utilitarian shelter against the wind. But as the trees became so tall as to shut off the sun he cut them down. On the front the yard was enclosed by a fence of upright white palings, with a red gate. When I was a boy the palings were whitewashed—that was one of my spring tasks. By the time the first fence began to decay we were, in the phrase we used, "better fixed," and the successor fences were painted white, the gate green.

Along the lane my father planted a row of pines; they are there yet, excepting four that succumbed to various disasters and have been replaced. The first that was lost came to its end through my unintentional hands. Each summer, after harvest, with a scythe we cut the weeds along the edges of the field close to the fence. I raked some of the dried weeds into a pile and set fire to them. The wind, changing direction, blew the flames close to one of the pines, the tar in the needles took fire, and in one leaping blaze the tree was stripped and gaunt. It was a tragedy, to me and to the family, for we cherished the trees, had for them some of the same feeling we had for the farm animals.

Where the lane entered the road there was, when my father came to the place, a giant old oak. It was cut down while I was still a child. I remember it only as an immense stump, over four feet in diameter, the low flat top making an excellent place to arrange the broken bits of bright-colored china which for a time were my principal playthings. To replace the oak, my father planted two maples; they remained for half a century, tall sentinels at the gate.

Back of the house, a field away, standing alone, was a tall old poplar, always referred to, almost with a manner of ritual, as "the poplar tree," as if to distinguish its age and dignity and solitariness from the scores of other poplars that were in the woods. The poplar tree—we put the emphasis on the last word—was almost one of the farm's personalities. It was a place of family council. In the house we children would notice our parents grow serious, perhaps as the result of a letter, or of information brought from a neighbor by my mother, or from the village by my father. They would move toward the door and go out and walk slowly toward the poplar tree, talking earnestly, their heads bent. After a while they would return, walking more briskly, with the manner of decision arrived at.

Always, when my parents went to the poplar tree, I felt that something serious was afoot, though not necessarily ominous. Once, when they remained at the tree for what seemed a long while, I, a little disturbed, walked out toward the tree myself, simulating what I meant to be a manner of casualness. As I got near them I heard my mother conclude the conference, saying firmly, "We'll sell the Whitie cow," by which I knew the question whether my older brother could go to boarding school another term had been settled, the funds would be provided.

As the older children grew more mature they were admitted to the poplar tree councils. On Sundays it was a place of cheerful family gathering. After church, and dinner, and a period of replete repose, as the afternoon began to wane, we would all go out to the poplar tree—it was on the highest point on the farm—to enjoy pride in the view. There was stimulus to my imagination in looking at the horizon and speculating about what was beyond it.

Back of the house, on a northward slope, my father planted an orchard of apple trees. He had selected the varieties with an eye to graduated ripening; from the middle of July until late fall there were always two or three trees in bearing. When I was a boy they were in their prime; without any spraying or other care they produced prodigious yields. I used to gather wagonloads and take them to the village to peddle. Late in the season, when the more juicy varieties were ripe, I would gather cartloads and take them, with an empty barrel, to the near-by mill, where they were ground into cider, which we drank sweet, or relatively sweet, until about Thanksgiving Day, and then rather hard until near Christmas.

The trees had charming names. The earliest-ripening one, coming to fruit in the time of wheat harvest early in July, we called simply the "harvest apple." Overeager anticipation of its ripening led to intestinal disturbance which I understood the doctor to describe, much to my mystification, as "cholera marbles." About August came the Townsends, large, mellow, mealy apples; in September the Smokehouse, of firmer flesh and more cidery. Later came the Red Romanites, the Baldwins and the Rambos (originally, I suppose, Rambeau). The Rambo was the apple of my teacher's preference; each morning I would pick the largest to take to her. The Russets, called by us "rusty coats," were not good for eating until well after frost. One immense white apple, the largest in the orchard, we called by a name which I can only reproduce phonetically as "Follow-older." One apple tree was called by a name aptly descriptive, the "Maiden's Blush"; it was cream-white with a reddish-pink glow. This tree stood on the edge of the orchard that was most distant from the house, at the top of a steep bank overlooking a ravine and a long swale of swamp. September afternoons I used to lie on the ground beneath the tree and look out across the autumn fields to the western horizon where the sun was descending. The place and the scene always stirred me to vague ambition and adventure.

HERBERT READ

Sir Herbert Edward Read was born in 1893 in Yorkshire, England, a descendant of a long line of Yorkshire farmers. He attended the University of Leeds but his studies were interrupted by World War I. He served as a captain in the Yorkshire Regiment for four years and received the Distinguished Service Order and the Military Cross. His experiences in the War are included in *The Contrary Experience* (1963). Of those who survived the War he says, "they stumbled into the post-war world like stragglers from a fallen outpost." A professor of fine arts and well-known art critic, he wrote *The Philosophy of Modern Art* and almost a dozen other books on art, in addition to work in aesthetics, literary criticism, and poetry. He died in 1968.

The Innocent Eye

The Vale

When I went to school I learned that the Vale in which we lived had once been a lake, but long ago the sea had eaten through the hills in the east and so released the fresh waters, leaving a fertile plain. But such an idea would have seemed strange to my innocent mind, so remote was this menacing sea. Our farm was towards the western end of the Vale, and because all our land was as flat as once the surface of the lake had been, we could see around us the misty hills, the Moors to the north, the Wolds to the south, meeting dimly in the east where they were more distant. This rim of hills was nearest in the south, at least in effect; for as the sun sank in the west the windows of Stamper's farm in the south caught the blazing rays and cast them back at us, continually drawing our eyes in that direction. But we never travelled so far south as those hills; for the Church and the Market, the only outer places of pilgrimage, lay to the north, five or six miles away. By habit we faced north: the south was 'behind.'

I seemed to live, therefore, in a basin, wide and shallow like the milkpans in the dairy; but the even bed of it was checkered with pastures and cornfields, and the rims were the soft blues and purples of the moorlands. This basin was my world, and I had no inkling of any larger world, for no strangers came to us out of it, and we never went into it. Very rarely my father went to York or Northallerton, to buy a piece of machinery for the farm or to serve on a jury at the Assizes; but only our vague wonder accompanied him, and the toys he brought back with him might have come, like sailors' curios, from Arabia or Cathay. The basin at times was very wide, especially in the clearness of a summer's day; but as dusk fell it would suddenly contract, the misty hills would draw near, and with night they had clasped us close: the centre of the world had become a candle shining from the kitchen window. Inside, in the sitting-room where we spent most of our life, a lamp was lit, with a round glass shade like a full yellow moon. There we were bathed before the fire, said our prayers kneeling on the hearthrug, and then disappeared up the steep stairs lighted by a candle to bed; and once there, the world was finally blotted out. I think it returned with the same suddenness, at least in summer; but the waking world was a new world, a hollow cube with light streaming in from one window across to a large bed holding, as the years went by, first one, then two, and finally three boys, overseen by two Apostles from one wall and adjured from another, above a chest of drawers, by a white pottery plaque within a pink-lustre frame, printed with a vignette of an angel blowing a trumpet and the words:

PRAISE YE THE LORD

Sometimes the child's mind went on living even during the darkness of night, listening to the velvet stillness of the fields. The stillness of a sleeping town, of a village, is nothing to the stillness of a remote farm; for the peace of day in such a place is so kindly that the ear is attuned to the subtlest sounds, and time is slow. If by chance a cow should low in the night it is like the abysmal cry of some hellish beast, bringing woe to the world. And who knows what hellish beasts might roam by night, for in the cave by the Church five miles away they once found the bones of many strange animals, wolves and hyaenas, and even the tusks of mammoths. The night-sound that still echoes in my mind, however, is not of this kind: it is gentler and more musical—the distant sound of horse-hooves on the highroad, at first dim and uncertain, but growing louder until they more suddenly cease. To that distant sound, I realized later, I must have come into the world, for the doctor arrived on horseback at four o'clock one December morning to find me uttering my first shriek.

I think I heard those hooves again the night my father died, but of this I am not certain; perhaps I shall remember when I come to relate that event, for now the memory of those years, which end shortly after my tenth birthday, comes fitfully, when the proper associations are aroused. If only I can recover the sense and uncertainty of those innocent years, years in which we seemed not so much to live as to be lived by forces outside us, by the wind and trees and moving clouds and all the mobile engines of our expanding world—then I am convinced I shall possess a key to much that has happened to me in this other world of conscious living. The echoes of my life which I find in my early childhood are too many to be dismissed as vain coincidences; but it is perhaps my conscious life which is the echo, the only real experiences in life being those lived with a virgin sensibility—so that we only hear a tone once, only see a colour once, see, hear, touch, taste and smell everything but once, the first time. All life is an echo of our first sensations, and we build up our consciousness, our whole mental life, by variations and combinations of these elementary sensations. But it is more complicated than that, for the senses apprehend not only colours and tones and shapes, but also patterns and atmospheres, and our first discovery of these determines the larger patterns and subtler atmospheres of all our subsequent existence.

The Farm

I have given the impression that the Farm was remote, but this is not strictly true. Not half a mile on each side of us was another farmhouse, and clustering near the one to the east were three or four cottages. We formed, therefore, a little community, remote as such; in 'Doomsday Book' we had been described as a hamlet. The nearest village was two or three miles away, but to the south, so that it did not count for much until we began to go to school, which was not until towards the end of the period of which I write. Northwards our farm road ran through two fields and then joined the highroad running east and west; but eastward this road soon turned into a road running north and south, down which we turned northwards again, to the Church five miles away, and to Kirby, our real metropolis, six miles away.

The farmhouse was a square stone box with a roof of vivid red tiles; its front was to the south, and warm enough to shelter some apricot trees against the wall. But there was no traffic that way: all our exits and entrances were made on the north side, through the kitchen; and I think even our grandest visitors did not disdain that approach. Why should they? On the left as they entered direct into the kitchen was an old oak dresser; on the right a large open fireplace, with a great iron kettle hanging from the reckan, and an oven to the near side of it. A long deal table, glistening with a honey gold sheen from much scrubbing, filled the far side of the room; long benches ran down each side of it. The floor was flagged with stone, each stone neatly outlined with a border of some softer yellow stone, rubbed on after every washing. Sides of bacon and plum-dusky hams hung from the beams of the wooden ceiling.

By day it was the scene of intense bustle. The kitchenmaid was down by five o'clock to light the fire; the labourers crept down in stockinged feet and drew on their heavy boots; they lit candles in their horn lanthorns and went out to the cattle. Breakfast was at seven, dinner at twelve, tea at five. Each morning of the week had its appropriate activity: Monday was washing day, Tuesday ironing, Wednesday and Saturday baking, Thursday 'turning out' upstairs and churning, Friday 'turning out' downstairs. Every day there was the milk to skim in the dairy—the dairy was to the left of the kitchen, and as big as any other room in the house. The milk was poured into large flat pans and allowed to settle; it was skimmed with horn scoops, like toothless combs.

At dinner, according to the time of the year, there would be from five to seven farm labourers, the two servant girls, and the family, with whom, for most of the time, there was a governess—a total of from ten to fifteen mouths to feed every day. The bustle reached its height about midday; the men would come in and sit on the dresser, swinging their legs impatiently; when the food was served, they sprang to the benches and ate in solid gusto, like animals. They disappeared as soon as the pudding had been served, some to smoke a pipe in the saddle room, others to do work which could not wait. Then all the clatter of washing up rose and subsided. More peaceful occupations filled the afternoon. The crickets began to sing in the hearth. The kettle boiled for tea. At nightfall a candle was lit, the foreman or the shepherd sat smoking in the armchair at the fireside end of the table. The latch clicked as the others came in one by one and went early to bed.

The kitchen was the scene of many events which afterwards flowed into my mind from the pages of books. Whenever in a tale a belated traveller saw a light and came through the darkness to ask for shelter, it was to this kitchen door. I can no longer identify the particular stories, but they do not belong to this period of childhood so much as to my later boyhood and youth, long after I had left the Farm; and even today my first memories easily usurp the function of the imagination, and clothe in familiar dimensions and patterns, exact and objective, the scenes which the romancer has purposely left vague. Perhaps the effect of all romance depends on this faculty we have of giving our own definition to the fancies of others. A mind without memories means a body without sensibility; our memories make our imaginative life, and it is only as we increase our memories, widening the imbricated shutters which divide our mind from the light, that we find with quick recognition those images of truth which the world is pleased to attribute to our creative gift.

The Green

The Green, a space of about an acre, lay in front of the kitchen door. It was square; one side, that to the left as we came out of the house, was fully taken up by a range of sheds. A shorter range of buildings continued in line with the house on the right—first the saddle-room, one of my favourite haunts, then the shed where the dog-cart and buggy were kept, and finally the blacksmith's shop. Beyond this were the grindstones and the ash-heap (in just such a heap, I imagined, Madame Curie discovered radium) and then a high hedge led to the corner of the Green, where three enormous elm-trees, the only landmark near our farm, overhung the duck-pond. On the other two sides the Green was bounded by hedges. The farm-road led past the sheds and then to the left through the stackyard; to the right there was a cart-track leading across the fields to the next farm with its cluster of cottages.

Our dominion was really four-fold: the Green I have just described, and then three other almost equal squares, the one to the left of the Green being the farm outhouses, a rectangular court of low buildings enclosing the Fodgarth, or fold-garth, and two others to the south of the house, the orchard to the east, the garden to the west. Each province was perfectly distinct, divided off by high walls or hedges; and each had its individual powers or mysteries. The Green was the province of water and of fowl, of traffic and trade, the only province familiar to strangers—to the postman and the pedlar, and the scarlet huntsmen. In winter we made the snowman there; in summer avoided its shelterless waste. On Mondays the washed clothes flapped in the wind, but for the rest of the week it was willingly resigned to hens, ducks, geese, guinea fowls, and turkeys—whose discursive habits, incidentally, made it no fit playground for children. The pond was more attractive, but because of its stagnation it could not compete with the becks not far away. I remember it best in a hot summer, when the water dried up and left a surface of shining mud, as smooth as moleskin, from which projected the rusty wrecks of old cans and discarded implements. Perhaps it was a forbidden area; it serves no purpose in my memory.

The pump was built over a deep well, in the corner of the Green near the kitchen; it was too difficult for a boy to work. One day, underneath the stones which took the drip, we discovered bright green lizards. Behind the pump, handy to the water, was the copper-house—the 'copper' being a large cauldron built in over a furnace. Here the clothes were boiled on a Monday; here, too, potatoes for the pigs were boiled in their earthy skins, and the pigs were not the only little animals who enjoyed them, for they are delicious when cooked in this way. Outside the same copper-house the pigs were killed, to be near the cauldron of boiling water with which they were scalded. The animal was drawn from its sty by a rope through the ring in its nose; its squealing filled the whole farm till it reached the copper-house, and there by the side of a trestle its throat was cut with a sharp knife and the hot blood gushed on to the ground. The carcass was then stretched on the trestle, and the whole household joined in the work of scraping the scalded hide: it was done with metal candlesticks, the hollow foot making a sharp and effective instrument for removing the bristles and outer skin. The carcass was then disembowelled and dismembered. The copper was once more requisitioned to render down the super-fluous fat, which was first cut into dice. The remnants of this process, crisp shreds known as scraps, formed our favourite food for days afterwards. In fact, pig-killing was followed by a whole orgy of good things to eat—pork-pies, sausages and pigs'-feet filling the bill for a season. But the scenes I have described, and many others of the same nature, such as the searing of horses' tails, the killing of poultry, the birth of cattle, even the lewdness of a half-witted labourer, were witnessed by us children with complete passivity—just as I have seen children of the same age watching a bull-fight in Spain quite unmoved by its horrors. Pity, and even terror, are emotions which develop when we are no longer innocent, and the sentimental adult who induces such emotions in the child is probably breaking through defences which nature has wisely put round the tender mind. The child even has a natural craving for horrors. He survives just because he is without sentiment, for only in this way can his green heart harden sufficiently to withstand the wounds that wait for it.

On the south side of the Green were two familiar shrines, each with its sacred fire. The first was the saddle-room, with its pungent clean smell of saddle-soap. It was a small white-washed room, hung with bright bits and stirrups and long loops of leather reins; the saddles were in a loft above, reached by a ladder and trap-door. In the middle was a small cylindrical stove, kept burning through the winter, and making a warm friendly shelter where we could play undisturbed. Our chief joy was to make lead shot, or bullets as we called them; and for this purpose there existed a long-handled crucible and a mould. At what now seems to me an incredibly early age we melted down the strips of lead we found in the window-sill, and poured the sullen liquid into the small aperture of the mould, which was in the form of a pair of pincers—closed whilst the pouring was in progress. When opened, the gleaming silver bullets, about the size of a pea, fell out of the matrix and rolled away to cool on the stone floor. We used the bullets in our catapults, but the joy was in the making of them, and in the sight of their shining beauty.

The blacksmith's shop was a still more magical shrine. The blacksmith came for a day periodically, to shoe or re-shoe the horses, to repair wagons and make simple implements. In his dusky cave the bellows roared, the fire was blown to a white intensity, and then suddenly the bellows-shaft was released and the soft glowing iron drawn from the heart of the fire. Then clang clang clang on the anvil, the heavenly shower of ruby and golden sparks, and our precipitate flight to a place of safety. All around us, in dark cobwebbed corners, were heaps of old iron, discarded horseshoes, hoops and pipes. Under the window was a tank of water for slaking and tempering the hot iron, and this water possessed the miraculous property of curing warts.

In these two shrines I first experienced the joy of making things. Everywhere around me the earth was stirring with growth and the beasts were propagating their kind. But these wonders passed unobserved by my childish mind, unrecorded in memory. They depended on forces beyond our control, beyond my conception. But fire was real, and so was the skill with which we shaped hard metals to our design and desire.

The Orchard

The front garden was formal, like the drawing-room; it was not part of our customary world. If we went there during the day, it was to see if the forbidden apricots were ripening, or to play for a short time round the monkey-puzzle-tree which grew in the middle of a small lawn. But a monkey-puzzle-tree is not a friendly shelter; its boughs are too near the ground, it is hirsute and prickly. The lawn was enclosed by hedges of box, through which narrow arches led to the flower garden in front, to the vegetable garden on the right, and to the orchard on the left. Again, all these provinces were rectangular, without any picturesque charm, but riotous with natural detail, with great variety of shrubs, fruit-bushes and vegetables. The Garden, too, had its shrine. The northern end, in line with the back of the house, was bounded by a high stone wall, sheltering pear-trees. Between this wall and a line of plum-trees, a path, bordered by flowering-currants and honesty, led to the ivy-clad privy. This green retreat, always in memory a place spangled in leaf-flecked sunlight, with ivy-fruit tapping against the small window-pane, has no grosser associations. Its friendliness, its invitation to sociability, was further emphasized by its furniture of two seats, and there we could sit side by side, the needs of our bodies relieved in no furtive secrecy, but in unabashed naturalness.

On the other side, through the wicket that led into the Orchard, there came first the water-trough, an immense stone tank fed from the eaves; this rain water was very precious for washing purposes, so we were forbidden to play with it. It is one of the few memories I have of the sternness of my father, that on one occasion finding me transgressing this law, he immediately picked me up by the seat and immersed me bodily in the water.

Above the trough, high up on the gable of the house, was another forbidden object: the bell which was pealed at midday to announce dinner to the scattered labourers, none of whom was likely to wear a watch.

Behind the saddle-room, in this region of the trough, was the Sand-heap, in a corner formed by a lime house and a low cow-shed. The hours we spent in this corner were too habitual to linger much in the memory. It was a generous heap, allowing an extensive system of trenches and castles; near-by was the shade of the apple-trees and the elms; our days there were timeless. Once, playing there, I slipped into the cow-shed to stroke a young calf housed there, closing the door behind me. The calf was lying in fresh clean straw, and did not stir at my approach. Hours later I was missed, and after long searching and much shouting in the farm and the fields, I was discovered sleeping with my head against the calf's warm flank.

The Orchard, like the Green, must have been about an acre in extent. I have no memory of it, except in spring and summer, when the branches, with their succession of blossom, leaf and fruit, met to form an overgrowth supported by aisles of trunks, green with moss or misty grey-blue when the lichen was dry and crusted. One old russet tree sloped up from the ground at a low angle, easy to climb; and in its boughs we shook the blossom till it fell in flakes like snow, or helped ourselves unchecked to the sweet rough-skinned apples. I think the Orchard only held two treasures besides the trees: an old disused roller about which we clambered, and in a far corner, by a bush whose hollow twigs made excellent stems for improvised pipes (in which we smoked a cunning mixture of dried clover and pear leaves), a small trough which usually held rock salt, brown and glassy. In the orchard, and in the paddock beyond, we dug up sweet pig-nuts, and ate them without much regard for the soil engrained in them.

When we emerged from the Paddock, where our pony and the mare for the dog-cart used to graze, there was a sudden sense of space. The ground sloped down gently towards our main stream, the Riccall, which formed the southern boundary of the farm. Beyond the Riccall, which flowed rather deeply in the soft earth and was quite impassable to us, lay a mysterious land we never explored: the south, with the hills rising in the distance, the farm with the fiery windows hidden in their folds.

The Church

Every Sunday the dog-cart was yoked up and the whole family climbed into the high seats, my father and mother in front with the youngest of us between them, the rest of us clinging to the precarious back-seat. When it rained an immense gingham umbrella, like the roof of a pagoda, sheltered us all. The big wheels crunched on the gritty roads. The Farm retreated from us as we trotted down the northern road to our parish Church, five miles away. The road had three points of interest: the Little Beck, the Big Beck, and the peacocks. The becks excited us because they had no bridges: they widened out into shallow fords through which the horse splashed as if born to this watery element. In spring the becks were often flooded, and sometimes the water stretched for hundreds of feet in a lake of incalculable depth. Then the excitement was intense, but my father must have known the safe limits of the flood. I remember the water coming up to the horse's belly, and our anxiety for the rug, which had a way of hanging below the footboard.

About a mile before we reached the Church we passed a small village in the middle of which was a country-house known as 'The Hall', and here, on a high wall, we sometimes saw the peacocks which inhabited the garden beyond. For us they were fabulous birds, and the glory of their plumage the most exotic sight of those days. A mile farther on, the road descended steeply into a narrow valley, and there, in complete isolation, stood our Church. First came a row of sheds and stables, where the horse was unyoked and the trap put under shelter. Then the path led a little lower down to the gate of the churchyard, where in summer a few men would be standing, enjoying the air until the last moment. The bell, or rather the clapper, clanged in the squat tower. The Church is of grey stone with a slated roof, and stands out clearly as you approach it against a dark wood of firs. Ancient tombstones lean out of the grassy mounds at all angles. We were taught that it was wicked to walk over a grave, but this graveyard is so ancient and so thickly populated, that we had to wander as if in a maze. Either before or after the service we made our way to the family graves, at the east end of the Church; but it was not until Mariana died that this duty became a melancholy one, the sight of my mother's tears communicating a wondering sense of woe.

In summer we brought flowers to this grave, and sometimes I was sent to throw away the withered remains of last week's wreath. At the end of the churchyard there was a low wall, and below this a deep ravine in which the river ran, quite overshadowed by trees. Into this gloomy cavern I threw my handfuls of wisps, glad to hide my uneasiness in this gesture.

Over the porch of the Church is a famous Saxon sundial with an inscription carved on the stone panels at each side which tells us that Orm the son of Gamal bought Saint Gregory's minster when it was all broken down and fallen, and he caused it to be made new from the ground, to Christ and Saint Gregory, in the reign of Edward the King, in the days of Tosti the Earl. Round the dial itself are the words:

THIS IS DAEGES SOL MERCA AET
ILCVMTIDE

—this is the day's sun mark at every tide; and below the dial is written: Hawarth made me and Brand the priest.

Inside, the walls are whitewashed, and an aqueous light filters through the foliage-bound windows. The nave was then filled with square box-pews, very high, so that we retired into a little private world, to pray as a family safe from the distractions of less familiar human beings. But the family included our Howkeld relations, of whom I shall soon speak; and my uncle, so patriarchal in his crisp white beard, officiated within our box. He was too stout to kneel on the hassocks which saved our knees from the cold stone floor, but the rest of us, sometimes eight or nine in number, knelt rigidly with hands pressed palm to palm.

The service was of extreme simplicity and dispatch. The sermon never lasted more than ten minutes, sometimes only five. The music came from a small harmonium, and there was a surpliced choir of perhaps two men and three boys. The congregation numbered in all not more than forty—many less when the weather was wild. In winter the Church was very cold, so we kept our overcoats on, and our breath issued in plumes as we sang the hymns. Once a month there was a Communion Service, and then for a few minutes, when our elders went to receive the Sacrament, we were left in possession of the box, at liberty to fidget and to let our eyes wander to the heraldic monsters displayed on the painted wooden hatchments, to the gallery where the servants sat, and to the trees waving across the leaded trellis of the windows.

After the service (which alternated each week between morning and afternoon, for the vicar served two parishes) the congregation gathered in groups and chatted peacefully as they walked up the path to the gate, and waited for the traps to be yoked up. The inhuman stillness of the situation aided our friendliness; our Church was still where the monks who first built it twelve centuries ago had wanted it to be, in a wild valley, near a running beck, grey like a wild hawk nesting in a shelter of dark trees.

The Mill

About half a mile above the Church the beck suddenly slackens; part of its waters (in summer all) disappear down a fissure in the rocky bed. They keep to a subterranean channel for a mile and a half and suddenly reappear, bubbling up from a great depth, at the head of a field which belonged to my uncle, whose small estate was on that account called Howkeld, which means 'springhead.' Here we came often and always with great joy, as to an enchanted kingdom. My uncle was a miller, and the mysterious water, which left its proper course and dived underground as if on very purpose to come up again in this particular spot to offer him its services, ran deep and strong in a willow-fringed bend round the large field separating the mill from the road. At the end of the field it became a walled dam, and to the right overflowed through a sluice into a round lake, which acted as a reservoir for times of drought. The private road to the mill followed the course of the stream and the dam, and then crossed by a bridge under which the water disappeared, combed by an iron grill. It emerged in a swift channel at the other side, and then sluiced in a roaring torrent over the water-wheel. The churned water fell in a dazzling white foaming cascade to a whirling pool below the wheel, and then flowed away with diminishing contortions in a stream which ran round the large gardens and through the fields until it rejoined the mother stream a mile and a half farther south.

There was so much here for childish wonder! The mill itself, with its swinging straps and flickering wheels, the bright chains that hoisted the grain to the top storey, the dusty machines in which we could see, through little windows, the grain trickling, and the general earth-shaking hum and whirr. The foreman's bright eyes twinkled from a face all powdered with flour, his clothes were like white mouse-skin, his beard hoary. His voice was piping high, from having to make himself heard in the din. On Sundays, when the mill was still, flour-dust deadened the sound of our feet on the worn wooden floors; our hands ran sweetly along smooth step-ladders and horny ropes.

Perhaps because there was always a plentiful supply of grain, my aunt kept all kinds of poultry, and in the yard round the mill the most motley assembly of fowls strutted and pecked—not only various breeds of hens, but guinea-fowl, turkeys, ducks and geese. The house was at the end of the yard, T-shaped, its leg in line with the mill. A side door led into the leg, which was a low extension of the original building and here was the Little Room where the family always lived, except on festive occasions. It was a very low room with a varnished wooden beam running across the ceiling. Most of the space was taken up by a sideboard and a large dining-table, and it is hard to think of this room without its complement of food. This was always spread in the most lavish way, with great hams and sirloins of beef, pies, pastries and puddings, and, at tea-time, cakes and tarts of the most alluring kind. My aunt was a famous cook: the mill and the gardens and the farm poured forth their plenty at the doorstep; by barter, in exchange for flour, most of the other essentials and luxuries of life were forthcoming. A deep spring of purest water flowed in the nearest field. War and famine could pass over the land and leave such bounty unaffected.

It was always peaceful here, a peace of guelder-roses and peonies, of laden fruit-trees and patient waters. Perhaps this impression means that our visits were mainly confined to the summer; in winter I only remember the frozen lake, on which we learned to skate. People came from far and near on such occasions, and the ice rang with the swift metallic strokes of the skaters' feet. In summer the lake, round which a path led among the reeds and rushes, was given over to the water-hens and wild ducks. Sometimes a flight of wild geese would come sweeping out of the sky on their way north.

I have already described my uncle as patriarchal, and this was true of him in more than appearance. My aunt was the eldest (and my mother the youngest) of the large family I have already mentioned. Some of these had married and migrated to other parts of the world, but such as remained, a goodly number, looked up to my uncle as the head of the clan into which he had married. His stout figure, his crisp white beard and twinkling eyes, his little linen bags of sample grain, his chuckle and his soft rich dialect, were familiar to the whole countryside; and at the time I speak of he was blessed with much happiness and prosperity. But during the next thirty years (he lived to be nearly ninety) he was to suffer many afflictions: the death of his favourite son, the bankruptcy of another, followed by the mortgaging of his own estate and finally a moratorium—and during all these tribulations he remained, a Lear of these Steppes, magnificent in courage and faith.

His children were contemporaries of my father and mother, and this introduced complications into our childish minds, for we called our cousins simply by their Christian names, whilst others who seemed their equals were aunts and uncles. The youngest of these cousins was not too old to despise the part of guide and initiator. One day he organized an expedition to explore the cave at Kirkdale. This famous cave extends for three hundred feet underground, and has more than one branch inside. The expedition, therefore, had to be undertaker with proper precautions. These consisted of candles, a large ball o binder-band, and the retriever, Jet. At the entry of the cave we made the end of the band secure, lit our candles, and crept forward unrolling the ball as we went. The sides of the cave glistened in the candlelight; drops of moisture fell from the stalactites above us; the air we breathed was cold and dank. I cannot remember how far we penetrated, but at one point we were terrified by the sudden appearance of two fiery eyes in the darkness confronting us. Could it be one of the ancient hyaenas, not yet a remnant of bones? But it was only Jet, who had run round some loop in the cave and come to meet us.

Once or twice we made expeditions up the dale beyond the cave and the Church. It is one of the wildest and most beautiful places in the whole country; and I still remember my father driving some fine lady from the outer world along the track that went along the ridge of the dale, and how she swore that it was more beautiful than Switzerland, a country of which we had no conception, but which we thought must be wonderful because people travelled far just to look at its hills and dales. This track up the dale ended at a house about two miles from the Church; here the dale became narrower and was filled with thick woods where lilies grew. No road led through these woods, not even a path; but an adventurous spirit could make his way along the bed of the stream, and after a mile or two he would discover that the dale opened out again, to give space to a mill and a few farms and cottages. This is Bransdale, an oasis on the Moors, which in our time only had a poor moorland track to link it with the outer world. The people who lived here were strange and dark and beautiful even to my childish eyes. For sometimes, when staying at Howkeld, I would go out for the day with the wagoners. Our load of grain and flour was drawn by great shaggy-footed cart-horses, their harness bright with brass ornaments, their manes and tails plaited with coloured ribbons—drawn over the wide purple Moors, where God seems to have left the earth clear of feature to reveal the beauty of its naked form, till we dipped down into the green dales and lifted our burden.

The Attic

The successive governesses who helped my mother with our upbringing remain utterly vague to me. They must have occupied a large place in our lives, but except for one insubstantial ghost of dark hair and spectacles, none of them can I recall. I know that they taught us to read, but I doubt if I had acquired that accomplishment before the age of seven. Then books immediately became my element. There was nothing to encourage me in this taste: there were no books in the living-rooms, and my father read little except the *Yorkshire Post* and various agricultural papers. On Sunday he would read to us the lessons of the day (perhaps this was only when it was impossible to go to Kirkdale) and he made us learn the Collect by heart. The only book of his I still possess is *The Poetical Works of Sir Walter Scott.* My mother read to us often, especially *Little Arthur's History of England, Evenings at Home, Forget-me-not,* and a tendentious story published by the Religious Tract Society called *Little Meg's Children* (by the author of *Jessica's First Prayer, The Children of Cloverley,* etc.). I still possess *Little Meg's Children,* and I see now that its grim pathos, too simple to be wholly sentimental, may have worked into the texture of my unfolding imagination, above all to prepare me for the shock of death which waited for me so near; for the first chapter describes the death of Little Meg's mother, and the plight of the orphaned children.

'She turned her face round to the wall with a deep sigh, and closed her eyelids, but her lips kept moving silently from time to time. Meg cried softly to herself in her chair before the fire, but presently she dozed a little for very heaviness of heart, and dreamed that her father's ship was come into dock, and she, and her mother, and the children, were going down the dingy streets to meet him. She awoke with a start; and creeping gently to her mother's side, laid her warm little hand upon hers. It was deadly cold with a chill such as little Meg had never before felt; and when her mother neither moved nor spoke in answer to her repeated cries, she knew that she was dead.

'For the next day, and the night following, the corpse of the mother lay silent and motionless in the room where her three children were living. Meg cried bitterly at first; but there was Robin to be comforted, and the baby to be played with when it laughed and crowed in her face. Robin was nearly six years old, and had gained a vague dim knowledge of death, by having followed, with a troop of other curious children, many a funeral that had gone out from the dense and dirty dwellings to the distant cemetery, where he had crept forward to the edge of the grave, and peeped down into what seemed to him a very dark and dreadful depth. When little Meg told him Mother was dead, and lifted him up to kneel on the bedside, and kiss her icy lips for the last time, his childish heart was filled with an awe which almost made him shrink from the sight of that familiar face, scarcely whiter or more sunken now than it had been for many a day past. . . .'

We must have wept often over the tribulations of Little Meg, and may have been duly impressed by her Christian constancy. Were we held by anything but the pathos of the story? This strange country of dingy streets and attics (an attic perhaps I could visualize), of lack of bread and clothes, of evil and misery—it was as fairy-like as any story that I had heard—as hard to realize, but just as easy to believe. The emotions were involved, and the imagination, but nothing like reflection or reasoning. We were moved in exactly the same way, and perhaps even to a greater degree, by the adventures of Little Red Riding-hood. Both she and Meg were 'Little,' and both survived the perils they encountered. When even the perils we ourselves encounter as children leave so little impression on our sensibility (just because we have no reasoning power to trace their consequences) why should the fictitious pathos of a story have more effect? The perturbations of the intellect are a danger to the instinctive basis of life; no wonder, then, that nature is wise enough to wrap us in a cocoon of insensibility, until such time as we have the power to counter intelligence with deeper intuitions.

Little Meg's attic could be visualized because we had our own attic at the top of the house. It was approached by a steep staircase just outside the nursery door. On the left, when you reached the top, were two bedrooms, partitioned off and occupied by the maids. But the rest of the space under the roof was free. One side was used for storing apples, and their musty sweetness pervaded the whole room. There were several chests and wardrobes, full of old wedding-dresses, and many other things which I do not distinctly remember. But here also was the only considerable store of books in the house, a miscellaneous collection of foxed volumes of sermons and devotional works which can have had little appeal to me, but which I pored over with an instinctive love. But two larger tomes were an inexhaustible mine of delight. They were bound volumes of the *Illustrated London News* for the year of the Great Exhibition (presumably 1850), full of the steel engravings of the period.

My lust for books was not satisfied in the attic; I soon craved for novelty. But I must have realized thus early that such a longing was a personal affair, to be fulfilled only by a personal effort. Looking round for a means to this end, I seized on the postman as the only link with the printed world. He came daily on his long pedestrian round, for if there were no letters to bring, there was always the *Yorkshire Post*. I made friends with him, and confided to him my secret desires. He was sympathetic, but his acquaintance with literature was limited. It was limited, in fact, to a lurid pink periodical called, I think, *The Police Gazette,* and this he passed on to me; but though I remember the act of reading it, it left no particular impression on me. Evidently its contents had nothing of the reality of a fairy world.

I return again and again, in retrospection, to this early untutored interest in books, for how could it have developed, in such isolation and such neglect, but for the presence of some inborn disposition. And faith in such a disposition becomes, with the growth of the personality, a controlling factor. We are only happy so long as our life expands in ever widening circles from the upward gush of our early impulses; and even love, of which the child is ignorant, is only real in so far as it is a transformation, in adolescence, of our first instinctive attachments.

The Musical Box

One day my father brought a delightful toy back from Northallerton: it was a small musical box which played 'For there's nae luck about the house.' But my mother, perhaps then, or perhaps shortly afterwards, when there was sufficient cause, thought the tune was ominous. My only sister was a baby then, between two and three years old. Our farm was called the Grange, and though it had no moat, this daughter was christened Mariana. Perhaps that too was ominous, for a sad song goes by her name. Mariana was fair as sunlight, and smiled to the tinkle of the musical box. And that is all I remember of her, for that spring I was suddenly sent away. A few days later my aunt told me that Mariana had become an angel, and the next time we went to Kirkdale I was taken to see the unmeaning mound that covered her body.

Apart from this fatal musical box, the only other music I ever heard in my childhood was Fiddler Dick's. Every year the young horses bred on the Farm had to be 'broken in,' and this was work for a specialist, who, like the blacksmith, paid us periodical visits. Fiddler Dick was a natty little man, with a hot swarthy complexion and waxed moustaches—probably he was of gipsy blood. He would stay a few days at the Farm, sleeping in the loft above the saddle-room. He always brought his fiddle with him, and after dinner, or in the evening, used to play to a wondering audience. I was fascinated by this man—fascinated when he stood in the Cow Pasture, his neat leggings winking in the sunshine, a wild young colt galloping, trotting, walking in a circle at the end of a long rope, controlled by Fiddler Dick's flicking whip—still more fascinated when the brown fiddle came out of its box and a sound, never imagined before, was conjured out of the air. Now, I had seen, in a chest in the attic, just such a brown fiddle, and one day when Fiddler Dick was at the Farm, I brought it down and asked him to teach me to make such music. But some of the strings were broken, and the bow had no horse-hair. Some untwisted binder-band served to repair the bow, and we got some cat-gut from the nearest cobbler for the strings. Fiddler Dick rejoiced in the word cat-gut, and cats took on a new significance for me. I cannot now believe that the sounds which issued from this improvised instrument bore any resemblance to the plaintive voice of a violin, but I retained my longing to play. Later, when I went away to school, I persuaded my mother to let me take music as an extra subject, and she consented. But I was put to the piano, which had no charm for me, no urgency of aspiration. I could not rival Fiddler Dick on such an instrument! Besides, instead of Fiddler Dick, I had for a teacher a fierce Dutchman, bristling with long hair and a silk bow-tie, flashing with rings. At the end of the year my enthusiasm had so waned that I could not urge my mother to pay the extra fees for music. But I still clung to the old violin, with the vague hope that I might one day learn to play it. It was still in my possession at the beginning of the war, but my mother died at this time, and in the subsequent confusion the violin disappeared. I had expected to find it among the few possessions I had stored in a cellar against my return, but it was not there. I should perhaps never have given it another thought but for an experience of several years later. I came late one evening, after a walk along a forest road in Bavaria, the moon staring at me through the cage bars of the trees, to a large castle where many guests were being entertained. Supper was finished and there was not a soul to be seen, except a porter who took my bag, and told me that everyone was in the music-room—even the servants—and that I had better make my way there and wait for the end. I was directed to a small balcony, which I could enter without disturbing the audience. The room was in darkness, except for an electric lamp at the far end of the room, above the dais where the music was being played. It was a violin sonata, and I was immediately held, not so much by the music as by the image which came into my mind as I gazed at the woman playing the violin. Her slender body was like a stem on which nodded, to the rhythm of the music, a strange exotic flower. The corolla of this flower was a human face, very white beneath an arch of raven black hair, and it seemed to brood over the coiled tawny petals of the instrument, preserving an essential stillness in the midst of the force that agitated them. The notes of the piano, to whose rise and fall it seemed bound in some inevitable way, might have been the voice of a stream urging its way past the resisting stem of the flower that swayed above its swift current.

All my early fascination for this instrument, awakened long before by Fiddler Dick and long dormant, awoke again at this moment with a glow in which there was no longer any sense of aspiration or self-directed interest, a fire of renunciation and surrender. Once more an early impulse had found its fulfilment, its transformation, to become a conscious interest in my life.

Death

These scenes of childhood end abruptly with the death of my father. In the winter of my ninth year, he was taken ill with a fever; and the house became muted and silent. Mrs. Walker, the nurse from one of the cottages by Peacock's farm, whom I have not mentioned before, but who had attended my mother in all her confinements, was called in; and our cousin the doctor came from Kirby daily. He and my father were fast friends, and when the illness became critical, all his energies were devoted to the saving of this precious life. But in vain. Rheumatic fever developed. The air of anguish in every one, my mother's tearful eyes—these were obvious even to us children. One day leeches were brought, and stood in a glass jar on a shelf in the dairy. They were black, blind and sinister. But then we were taken away. I went to Howkeld, and one night I suffered intolerable earache, so that I cried aloud, and was poulticed with onions. The pain had gone in the morning, but by my aunt's tears I knew that my father was dead. The next day I was driven back to the Farm. The blinds were drawn, everywhere it was very still, and dark. We were taken upstairs to say good-bye to my dead father. The cold wintry light came evenly through the open slats of the venetian blind. My father lay on the bed, sleeping, as he always did, with his arms on the coverlet, straight down each side of his body. His beautiful face was very white, except for the red marks on his temples, where the leeches had clung. I was told to kiss that face; it was deadly cold, like the face of Little Meg's mother.

I felt stunned, but could not comprehend my loss, nor the grief of those about me. I moved away in the unnatural stillness, walking in a living sleep. Downstairs candles were burning on a table laden with cold meat and cakes. Then we all drove to Kirkdale, slowly over the frozen flint roads, and there a grave was ready dug at the east end of the Church, by the side of Mariana's. The dark cirque of fir-trees rose in the background, sighing in the frosty wind. The bell in the grey tower clanged its toneless note. The horses were not unyoked. Six friends of my father carried his coffin into the ancient church, and then to the grave. The earth fell with a hollow sound on to the lowered coffin. My mother sobbed against my uncle's shoulder. The last amen was murmured in that immemorial stillness, and when we had taken a last look at the forlorn coffin, we drove back swiftly over the frozen flint roads, horse-hooves beating clearly in the metallic air.

A few weeks later the sheep were driven into pens, the cattle labelled, and a crowd of farmers from far and near assembled at the Farm. A wagon was drawn out on the Green, to serve as a platform for the auctioneer. Everything was sold, except a few pieces of old furniture which my mother was fond of—even the books from the attic, the sermons tied in bundles, and the two volumes of the *Illustrated London News. Little Meg, Little Arthur, Evenings at Home,* and *Forget-me-not* alone were left for me.

We went to stay with a cousin at the other end of the Vale, but only for a few months. Then the elder of my two brothers and I left for a boarding-school, far away from these scenes; my childhood, the first phase of my life, was isolated: it grew detached in my memory and floated away like a leaf on a stream.But it never finally disappeared, as these pages witness. Instead, as this body of mine passes through the rays of experience, it meets bright points of ecstasy which come from the heart of this lost realm. But the realm is never wholly lost: it is reconstructed stage by stage whenever the sensibility recovers its first innocence, whenever eye and ear and touch and tongue and quivering nostril revive sensation in all its child-godly passivity.

To-day I found a withered stem of honesty, and shelled the pods between my thumb and finger; silver pennies, which grew between the fragrant currant-bushes. Their glistening surfaces, seeded, the very faint rustle they make in the wind—these sensations come direct to me from a moment thirty years ago. As they expand in my mind, they carry everything in their widening circle—the low crisp box-hedge which would be at my feet, the pear-trees on the wall behind me, the potato-flowers on the patch beyond the bushes, the ivy-clad privy at the end of the path, the cow pasture, the fairy rings—everything shimmers for a second on the expanding rim of my memory. The farthest tremor of this perturbation is lost only at the finest edge where sensation passes beyond the confines of experience; for memory is a flower which only opens fully in the kingdom of Heaven, where the eye is eternally innocent.

ANNE MOODY

Anne Moody was born in Mississippi in 1940, the daughter of sharecroppers. She attended Natchez Junior College and graduated from Tougaloo College in 1964. After graduation, she embarked on a nationwide speaking tour for the Congress of Racial Equality. She is married and lives in New York City. The following selection comes from *Coming of Age in Mississippi*, a book highly praised by many, including Senator Edward Kennedy.

Then What Was It?

Now that school was out and there was no one for us to stay with, we would sit on the porch and rock in the rocking chair most of the day. We were scared to go out and play because of the snakes. Often as we sat on the porch we saw them coming up the hill from the swamp. Sometimes they would just go to the other side of the swamp. But other times they went under the house and we didn't see them come out. When this happened, we wouldn't eat all day because we were scared to go inside. The snakes often came into the house. Once as I was putting wood in the stove for Mama, I almost put my hands on one curled up under the wood. I never touched the woodpile again.

One day we heard Mrs. Cook's dog barking down beside the swamp at the base of the cornfield. We ran out to see what had happened. When we got there, the dog was standing still with his tail straight up in the air barking hysterically. There, lying beside a log, was a big old snake with fishy scales all over his body. Adline, Junior, and I stood there in a trance looking at it, too scared to move. We had never seen one like this. It was so big it didn't even look like a snake. It looked like it was big enough to swallow us whole. Finally the snake slowly made its way back into the swamp, leaving a trail of mashed-down grass behind it.

When Mama came home that evening from the café, we told her all about the snake. At first, she didn't believe us, but we were shaking so that she had us go out back and show her where we had seen it. After she saw the place next to the log where it had been lying and the trail it left going to the swamp, she went and got Mr. Cook. For days Mr. Cook and some other men looked in the swamp for that snake, but they never did find it. After that Mama was scared for us to stay at home alone, and she began looking for a house in town closer to where she worked. "Shit, snakes that damn big might come up here and eat y'all up while I'm at work," she said.

In the meantime, she got our Uncle Ed, whom we liked so much, to come over and look after us every day. Sometimes he would take us hunting. Then we wouldn't have to sit on the porch and watch those snakes in that boiling hot summer sun. Ed made us a "niggershooter" each. This was a little slingshot made out of a piece of leather connected to a forked stick by a thin slab of rubber. We would take rocks and shoot them at birds and anything else we saw. Ed was the only one who ever killed anything. He always carried salt and matches in his pockets and whenever he'd kill a bird he'd pick and roast it right there in the woods. Sometimes Ed took us fishing too. He knew every creek in the whole area and we'd roam for miles. Whenever we caught fish we'd scrape and cook them right on the bank of the creek. On those days we didn't have to eat that hard cold pone of bread Mama left for us.

Sometimes Ed would keep us in the woods all day, and we wouldn't hunt birds or fish or anything. We just walked, listening to the birds and watching the squirrels leap from tree to tree and the rabbits jumping behind the little stumps. Ed had a way of making you feel so much a part of everything about the woods. He used to point out all the trees to us, telling us which was an oak, and which was a pine and which bore fruit. He'd even give us quizzes to see if we could remember one tree from another. I thought he was the smartest person in the whole world.

One day Ed was late coming and we had resigned ourselves to spending the whole day on the porch. We rocked for hours in the sun and finally fell asleep. Eventually Ed came. He locked the house up immediately and rushed us off the porch. He told us he was going to surprise us. I thought we were going to a new creek or something so I begged him to tell me. He saw that I was upset so finally he told me that he was taking us home with him.

As we were walking down the rock road, it occurred to me that I had never been home with Ed and I was dying to see where he lived. I could only remember seeing Grandma Winnie once, when she came to our house just after Junior was born. Mama never visited Grandma because they didn't get along that well. Grandma had talked Mama into marrying my Daddy when Mama wanted to marry someone else. Now that Mama and Daddy had separated, she didn't want anything to do with Grandma, especially when she learned that her old boyfriend was married and living in Chicago.

Ed told us that he didn't live very far from us, but walking barefooted on the rock road in the boiling hot sun, I began to wonder how far was "not very far."

"Ed, how much more longer we gotta go? These rocks is burning my foots," I said.

"Ain't much further. Just right around that bend," Ed yelled back at me. "Why didn't you put them shoes on? I told you them rocks was hot." He waited on me now. "Oughter make you go all the way back to that house and put them shoes on. You gonna be laggin' behind comin' back and we ain't never gonna make it 'fore Toosweet get off o' work!"

"Mama told us we ain't supposed to wear our shoes out round the house. You know we ain't got but one pair and them my school shoes."

"Here it is, right here," Ed said at last. "Essie Mae, run up front and open that gate." By this time he was carrying Junior on his back and Adline half asleep on his hip.

I ran to the gate and opened it and rode on it as it swung open. We entered a green pasture with lots of cows.

"Is that where you stay?" I asked Ed as I pointed to an old wooden house on the side of a hill.

"Is any more houses down there?" Ed said, laughing at me. "See that pond over there, Essie Mae!" he called as I ran down the hill. "I'm gonna bring y'all fishing over here one day. Boy, they got some big fishes in there! You shoulda seen what Sam and Walter caught yesterday."

I glanced at the pond but ran right past it. I didn't have my mind on fishing at all. I was dying to see Grandma Winnie's house and Sam and Walter, Ed's younger brothers, and his sister Alberta whom I had never met. Ed had told me that George Lee was now living with his daddy and stepmother. I was glad because I didn't want to run into him there.

Alberta was standing in the yard at the side of the house feeding the big fire around the washpot with kindling. Two white boys about my size stood at her side. I looked around for Sam and Walter. But I didn't see them.

"Ed, what took you so long? I oughta made you tote that water fo' you left here," Alberta shouted at Ed as she turned and saw us.

"I had to tote Adline and Junior all the way here. You must think um superman or something," Ed answered angrily.

"I ain't asked you what you is! You just git that bucket and fill that rinse tub up fulla water!" Alberta shouted. "Sam, yo'n Essie Mae help Ed with that water. And, Walter, take Adline and Junior on that porch outta the way."

I stood dead in my tracks with my mouth wide open as the two white boys jumped when Alberta yelled Sam's and Walter's names. One boy ran to the wash bench against the house and got a bucket and the other picked up Junior, took Adline by the hand, and carried them on the porch.

"Essie Mae! Didn't I tell you to help Sam and Ed with that water?" Alberta yelled at me.

"Where is Sam and Walter?" I asked with my eyes focused on the white boy on the porch with Adline and Junior.

"Is you blind or somethin'? Get that bucket and help tote that water," Alberta yelled.

I turned my head to look for Ed. He was headed for the pond in front of the house with a bucket in his hand. "Ed!" I shouted, still in a state of shock. He turned and looked at me. I stood there looking from Ed to the white boys and back to Ed again, without saying anything. Ed opened his mouth to speak but no words came. A deep expression of hurt crossed his face. For a second he dropped his head to avoid my eyes. Then he walked toward me. He picked up another bucket and handed it to me. Then he took me by the hand and led me to the pond.

As we walked toward the pond, one of the white boys ran ahead of us. He climbed through the barbed-wire fence right below the levee of the pond. Then he turned and pushed the bottom strand of the wire down to the ground with his foot and held the middle strand up with his hands, so Ed and I could walk through. I began to pull back from Ed but he clutched my hand even harder and led me toward the fence. As we ducked under, I brushed against the white boy. Jerking back, I caught my hair in the barbed-wire overhead.

"Essie Mae, watch yo' head 'fore you git cut! Wait, wait, you got your hair caught," the white boy said as he quickly and gently untangled my hair from the wire. Then he picked up the bucket I had dropped and handed it to me. Ed didn't say one word as he stood beside the fence watching us.

The white boy caught me by the hand and attempted to pull me up the levee of the pond. I pulled back. Still holding my hand, he stopped and stared at me puzzled. "Come on, Essie Mae!" yelled Ed, giving me an "it's O.K., stupid" look as he ran up the levee past us. Then the white boy and I followed Ed up the hill holding hands.

As we toted water from the pond, I kept watching the white boys and listening to Alberta and Ed call them Sam and Walter. I noticed that they treated them just like they treated me, and the white boy called Sam was nice to me just like Ed. He kept telling me about the fish he and Walter had caught and that I should come and fish with them sometimes.

After we finished toting the water, we went on the porch where Adline, Junior, and Walter sat. Adline had a funny look on her face. I could tell that she was thinking about Sam and Walter too. Before the evening was over, I finally realized that the two boys actually were Ed's brothers. But how Ed got two white brothers worried me.

On our way back home, Ed carried us through the woods. As we walked, he talked and talked about the birds, the trees, and everything else he could think of, without letting me say a word. I knew he didn't want to talk about Sam and Walter, so I didn't say anything. I just walked and listened.

I thought about Sam and Walter so much that night, it gave me a headache. Then I finally asked Mama:

"Mama, them two boys over at Winnie's. Ed say they is his brothers. Is they your brothers?"

"What boys?" Mama asked.

"Over at Winnie's. They got two boys living with her about my size and they is the same color as Miss Cook. . . ."

"What did y'all do over at Winnie's today? Was Winnie home?" Mama asked as if she hadn't heard me.

"No, she was at work. Wasn't nobody there but Alberta and those two boys. . . ."

"What was Alberta doing?" Mama asked.

"She was washing and we toted water from the pond for her. Them boys is some nice and they say they is kin to us. Ain't they your brothers, Mama?"

"Look, don't you be so stupid! If they's Winnie's children and I'm Winnie's too, don't that make us sisters and brothers?" Mama shouted at me.

"But how come they look like Miss Cook and Winnie ain't that color and Alberta ain't that color and you . . ."

"'Cause us daddy ain't that color! Now you shut up! Why you gotta know so much all the time? I told Ed not to take y'all to Winnie's," she shouted.

Mama was so mad that I was scared if I asked her anything else she might hit me, so I shut up. But she hadn't nearly satisfied my curiosity at all.

While Mama was working at the café in town, she began to get fat. She often told us how much she could eat while she was working. So I didn't think anything of her slowly growing "little pot." But one day after taking a good look, I noticed it wasn't a little pot any more. And I knew she was going to have a baby. She cried just about every night, then she would get up sick every morning. She didn't stop working until a week before the baby was born, and she was out of work only three weeks. She went right back to the café.

Mama called the baby James. His daddy was a soldier. One day the soldier and his mother came to get him. They were real yellow people. The only Negro near their color I had ever seen was Florence, the lady my daddy was now living with. The soldier's mother was a stout lady with long thin straight black hair and very thin lips. She looked like a slightly tanned white woman. Mama called her "Miss Pearl." All the time they were in our house, Mama acted as though she was scared of them. She smiled a couple of times when they made general comments about the baby. But I could tell she didn't mean it.

Just before the soldier and Miss Pearl left, Miss Pearl turned to Mama and said, "You can't work and feed them other children and keep this baby too." I guess Mama did want to keep the little boy. She looked so sad I thought she was going to cry, but she didn't say anything. Miss Pearl must have seen how Mama looked too. "You can stop in to see the baby when you are in town sometimes," she said. Then she and the soldier took him and drove away in their car. Mama cried all night. And she kept saying bad things about some Raymond. I figured that was the name of the soldier who gave her the baby.

At the end of that summer Mama found it necessary for us to move into town, in Centreville, where she worked. This time we moved into a two-room house that was twice the size of the other one. It was next to where a very poor white family lived in a large green frame house. It was also located on one of the main roads branching off Highway 24 running into Centreville. We were now a little less than a mile from the school that I was to attend, which was on the same road as our house. Here we had a sidewalk for the first time. It extended from town all the way to school where it ended. I was glad we lived on the sidewalk side of the road. Between the sidewalk and our house the top soil was sand about two feet deep. We were the only ones with clean white sand in our yard and it seemed beautiful and special. There was even more sand for us to play in in a large vacant lot on the other side of our house. The white people living next to us only had green grass in their yard just like everybody else.

A few weeks after we moved there, I was in school again. I was now six years old and in the second grade. At first, it was like being in heaven to have less than a mile to walk to school. And having a sidewalk from our house all the way there made things even better.

I was going to Willis High, the only Negro school in Centreville. It was named for Mr. C. H. Willis, its principal and founder, and had only been expanded into a high school the year before I started there. Before Mr. Willis came to town, the eighth grade had been the limit of schooling for Negro children in Centreville.

For the first month that I was in school a Negro family across the street kept Adline and Junior. But after that Mama had them stay at home alone and, every hour or so until I came home, the lady across the street would come down and look in on them. One day when I came home from school, Adline and Junior were naked playing in the sand in front of our house. All the children who lived in town used that sidewalk that passed our house. When they saw Adline and Junior sitting in the sand naked they started laughing and making fun of them. I was ashamed to go in the house or recognize Adline and Junior as my little sister and brother. I had never felt that way before. I got mad at Mama because she had to work and couldn't take care of Adline and Junior herself. Every day after that I hated the sand in front of the house.

Before school was out we moved again and I was glad. It seemed as though we were always moving. Every time it was to a house on some white man's place and every time it was a room and a kitchen. The new place was much smaller than the last one, but it was nicer. Here we had a large pasture to play in that was dry, flat, and always closely cropped because of the cattle. Mama still worked at the café. But now she had someone to keep Adline and Junior until I came home from school.

One day shortly after Christmas, Junior set the house on fire. He was playing in the front room. We had a small round tin heater in there and Junior raked red-hot coals out of it onto the floor and pushed them against the wall. I was washing dishes in the kitchen when I looked up and saw flames leaping toward the ceiling. I ran to get Junior. The house had loose newspaper tacked to the walls and was built out of old dry lumber. It was burning fast.

After I had carried Junior outside, I took him and Adline up on a hill a little distance away. The whole house was blazing now. I stood there with Junior on my hip and holding Adline by the hand and suddenly I thought about the new clothes Mama had bought us for Christmas. These were the first she had ever bought us. All our other clothes had been given to us. I had to get them. I left Adline and Junior on the hill and ran back to the house. I opened the kitchen door and was about to crawl into the flames and smoke when a neighbor grabbed me and jerked me out. Just as she pulled me away, the roof fell in. I stood there beside her with tears running down my face and watched the house burn to the ground. All our new Christmas clothes were gone, burned to ashes.

We had only lived there for a few months and now we moved again to another two-room house off a long rock road. This time Mama quit the job at the cafe to do domestic work for a white family. We lived in their maid's quarters. Since Mama made only five dollars a week, the white woman she worked for let us live in the house free. Mama's job was now close to home and she could watch Adline and Junior herself.

Sometimes Mama would bring us the white family's leftovers. It was the best food I had ever eaten. That was when I discovered that white folks ate different from us. They had all kinds of different food with meat and all. We always had just beans and bread. One Saturday the white lady let Mama bring us to her house. We sat on the back porch until the white family finished eating. Then Mama brought us in the house and sat us at the table and we finished up the food. It was the first time I had seen the inside of a white family's kitchen. That kitchen was pretty, all white and shiny. Mama had cooked that food we were eating too. "If Mama only had a kitchen like this of her own," I thought, "she would cook better food for us."

Mama was still seeing Raymond, the soldier she had the baby for. Now we were living right up the road, about a mile from Miss Pearl. Raymond started coming to our house every weekend. Often he would bring us candy or something to eat when he came. Some Sundays, Mama would take us out to his house to see the baby, James, who was now two years old and looked a lot like his daddy. Mama seemed to like the baby very much. But she was always so uncomfortable around Miss Pearl and the rest of Raymond's people. They didn't like Mama at all. Sometimes when Mama was there she looked as if she would cry any minute. After we had come home from their place, she would cry and fuss all evening. She would say things like, "They can't keep me from seeing my baby. They must be crazy. If I can't go see him there I'll bring him home." But she only said those things. She knew she couldn't possibly take the baby home and work and take care of the four of us. Once when we went out there to see the baby, he was filthy from head to toe. Mama gave him a bath and washed all of his clothes. Then every Sunday after that Mama would go there just to wash his clothes and bathe him.

Raymond was going with a yellow woman at the same time he was going with Mama. All of his people wanted him to marry her. They didn't want him to marry Mama, who wasn't yellow and who was stuck with the three of us. Things began to get so tense when we would go to see the baby that we'd only stay long enough for Mama to give him a bath. Then one day Raymond went back to the service and that ended some of the tension. But Mama got scared to go to Miss Pearl's without Raymond there, so she stopped going and we didn't see the baby for a long time.

That white lady Mama was working for worked her so hard that she always came home griping about backaches. Every night she'd have to put a red rubber bottle filled with hot water under her back. It got so bad that she finally quit. The white lady was so mad she couldn't get

Mama to stay that the next day she told Mama to leave to make room for the new maid.

This time we moved two miles up the same road. Mama had another domestic job. Now she worked from breakfast to supper and still made five dollars a week. But these people didn't work Mama too hard and she wasn't as tired as before when she came home. The people she worked for were nice to us. Mrs. Johnson was a schoolteacher. Mr. Johnson was a rancher who bought and sold cattle. Mr. Johnson's mother, an old lady named Miss Ola, lived with them.

Our house, which was separated from the Johnsons' by a field of clover, was the best two-room house we had been in yet. It was made out of big new planks and it even had a new toilet. We were also once again on paved streets. We just did make those paved streets, though. A few yards past the Johnsons' house was the beginning of the old rock road we had just moved off.

We were the only Negroes in that section, which seemed like some sort of honor. All the whites living around there were well-to-do. They ranged from schoolteachers to doctors and prosperous businessmen. The white family living across the street from us owned a funeral home and the only furniture store in Centreville. They had two children, a boy and a girl. There was another white family living about a quarter of a mile in back of the Johnsons who also had a boy and a girl. The two white girls were about my age and the boys a bit younger. They often rode their bikes or skated down the little hill just in front of our house. Adline, Junior and I would sit and watch them. How we wished Mama could buy us a bike or even a pair of skates to share.

There was a wide trench running from the street alongside our house. It separated our house and the Johnsons' place from a big two-story house up on the hill. A big pecan tree grew on our side of the trench, and we made our playhouse under it so we could sit in the trench and watch those white children without their knowing we were actually out there staring at them. Our playhouse consisted of two apple crates and a tin can that we sat on.

One day when the white children were riding up and down the street on their bikes, we were sitting on the apple crates making Indian noises and beating the tin can with sticks. We sounded so much like Indians that they came over to ask if that was what we were. This was the beginning of our friendship. We taught them how to make sounds and dance like Indians and they showed us how to ride their bikes and skate. Actually, I was the only one who learned. Adline and Junior were too small and too scared, although they got a kick out of watching us. I was seven, Adline five, and Junior three, and this was the first time we had ever had other children to play with. Sometimes, they would take us over to their playhouse. Katie and Bill, the children of the whites that owned the furniture store, had a model playhouse at the side of their parents' house. That little house was just like the big house, painted snow white on the outside, with real furniture in it. I envied their playhouse more than I did their bikes and skates. Here they were playing in a house that was nicer than any house I could have dreamed of living in. They had all this to offer me and I had nothing to offer them but the field of clover in summer and the apple crates under the pecan tree.

The Christmas after we moved there, I thought sure Mama would get us some skates. But she didn't. We didn't get anything but a couple of apples and oranges. I cried a week for those skates, I remember.

Every Saturday evening Mama would take us to the movies. The Negroes sat upstairs in the balcony and the whites sat downstairs. One Saturday we arrived at the movies at the same time as the white children. When we saw each other, we ran and met. Katie walked straight into the downstairs lobby and Adline, Junior, and I followed. Mama was talking to one of the white women and didn't notice that we had walked into the white lobby. I think she thought we were at the side entrance we had always used which led to the balcony. We were standing in the white lobby with our friends, when Mama came in and saw us. "C'mon! C'mon!" she yelled, pushing Adline face on into the door. "Essie Mae, um gonna try my best to kill you when I get you home. I told you 'bout running up in these stores and things like you own 'em!" she shouted, dragging me through the door. When we got outside, we stood there crying, and we could hear the white children crying inside the white lobby. After that, Mama didn't even let us stay at the movies. She carried us right home.

All the way back to our house, Mama kept telling us that we couldn't sit downstairs, we couldn't do this or that with white children. Up until that time I had never really thought about it. After all, we were playing together. I knew that we were going to separate schools and all, but I never knew why.

After the movie incident, the white children stopped playing in front of our house. For about two weeks we didn't see them at all. Then one day they were there again and we started playing. But things were not the same. I had never really thought of them as white before. Now all of a sudden they were white, and their whiteness made them better than me. I now realized that not only were they better than me because they were white, but everything they owned and everything connected with them was better than what was available to me. I hadn't realized before that downstairs in the movies was any better than upstairs. But now I saw that it was. Their whiteness provided them with a pass to downstairs in that nice section and my blackness sent me to the balcony.

Now that I was thinking about it, their schools, homes, and streets were better than mine. They had a large red brick school with nice sidewalks connecting the buildings. Their homes were large and beautiful with indoor toilets and every other convenience that I knew of at the time. Every house I had ever lived in was a one- or two-room shack with an outdoor toilet. It really bothered me that they had all these nice things and we had nothing. "There is a secret to it besides being white," I thought. Then my mind got all wrapped up in trying to uncover that secret.

One day when we were all playing in our playhouse in the ditch under the pecan tree, I got a crazy idea. I thought the secret was their "privates." I had seen everything they had but their privates and it wasn't any different than mine. So I made up a game called "The Doctor." I had never been to a doctor myself. However, Mama had told us that a doctor was the only person that could look at children's naked bodies besides their parents. Then I remembered the time my Grandma Winnie was sick. When I asked her what the doctor had done to her she said, "He examined me." Then I asked her about "examined" and she told me he looked at her teeth, in hear ears, checked her heart, blood and privates. Now I was going to be the doctor. I had all of them, Katie, Bill, Sandra, and Paul plus Adline and Junior take off their clothes and stand in line as I sat on one of the apple crates and examined them. I looked in their mouths and ears, put my ear to their hearts to listen for their heartbeats. Then I had them lie down on the leaves and I looked at their privates. I examined each of them about three times, but I didn't see any differences. I still hadn't found that secret.

That night when I was taking my bath, soaping myself all over, I thought about it again. I remembered the day I had seen my two uncles Sam and Walter. They were just as white as Katie them. But Grandma Winnie was darker than Mama, so how could Sam and Walter be white? I must have been thinking about it for a long time because Mama finally called out, "Essie Mae! Stop using up all that soap! And hurry up so Adline and Junior can bathe 'fore that water gits cold."

"Mama," I said, "why ain't Sam and Walter white?"

"'Cause they mama ain't white," she answered.

"But you say a long time ago they daddy is white."

"If the daddy is white and the mama is colored, then that don't make the children white."

"But they got the same hair and color like Bill and Katie them got," I said.

"That still don't make them white! Now git out of that tub!" she snapped.

Every time I tried to talk to Mama about white people she got mad. Now I was more confused than before. If it wasn't the straight hair and the white skin that made you white, then what was it?

ROBERT P. T. COFFIN

Descendant of a famous whaling family, Robert P. T. Coffin was born in 1892. He graduated *summa cum laude* from Bowdoin College in 1915 and received a Rhodes Scholarship to Oxford, where he was awarded a B. Litt. in 1921. He returned to Bowdoin where he taught for the rest of his life. He won the Pulitzer Prize in poetry in 1936 for *Strange Holiness*. He died in 1955.

Christmas in Maine

If you want to have a Christmas like the one we had on Paradise Farm when I was a boy, you will have to hunt up a salt-water farm on the Maine coast, with bays on both sides of it, and a road that goes around all sorts of bays, up over Misery Hill and down, and through the fir trees so close together that they brush you and your horse on both cheeks. That is the only kind of place a Christmas like that grows. You must have a clear December night, with blue Maine stars snapping like sapphires with the cold, and the big moon flooding full over Misery, and lighting up the snowy spruce boughs like crushed diamonds. You ought to be wrapped in a buffalo robe to your nose, and be sitting in a family pung, and have your breath trailing along with you as you slide over the dry, whistling snow. You will have to sing the songs we sang, "God Rest You Merry, Gentlemen" and "Joy to the World," and you will be able to see your songs around you in the air like blue smoke. That's the only way to come to a Paradise Christmas.

And you really should cross over at least one broad bay on the ice, and feel the tide rifts bounce you as the runners slide over them. And if the whole bay booms out, every now and then, and the sound echoes around the wooded islands for miles, you will be having the sort of ride we loved to take from town, the night before Christmas.

I won't insist on your having a father like ours to drive you home to your Christmas. One with a wide moustache full of icicles, and eyes like the stars of the morning. That would be impossible, anyway, for there has been only one of him in the world. But it is too bad, just the same. For you won't have the stories we had by the fireplace. You won't hear about Kitty Wells who died beautifully in song just as the sun came over the tops of the eastern mountains and just after her lover had named the wedding day.

But you will be able to have the rooms of the farmhouse banked with emerald jewels clustered on bayberry boughs, clumps of everlasting roses with gold spots in the middle of them, tree evergreens, and the evergreen that runs all over the Maine woods and every so often puts on a bunch of palm leaves. And there will be rose-hips stuck in pine boughs. And caraway seeds in every crust and cookie in the place.

An aunt should be on hand, an aunt who believes in yarrow tea and the Bible as the two things needed to keep children well. She will read the Nativity story aloud to the family, hurrying over the really exciting parts that happened at the stable, and bearing down hard on what the angels had to say and the more edifying points that might be supposed to improve small boys who like to lie too long abed in the mornings. She will put a moral even into Christmas greens, and she will serve well as a counterirritant to the over-eating of mince pies. She will insist on all boys washing behind their ears, and that will keep her days full to the brim.

The Christmas tree will be there, and it will have a top so high that it will have to be bent over and run along the ceiling of the sitting room. It will be the best fir tree of the Paradise forests, picked from ten thousand almost perfect ones, and every bough on it will be old-fashioned fans wide open. You will have brought it home that very morning, on the sled, from Dragonfly Spring.

Dragonfly Spring was frozen solid to the bottom, and you could look down into it and see the rainbows where you dented it with your coppertoed boots, see whole ferns caught motionless in the crystal deeps, and a frog, too, down there, with hands just like a baby's on him. Your small sister—the one with hair like new honey laid open in the middle of a honeycomb—had cried out, "Let's dig him up and take him home and warm his feet!" Your dog, Snoozer, who is a curious and intricate combination of many merry pugs and many mournful hound-dogs, was snuffling all the time, hot on the feather-stitching the mice had made from bush to bush while you were felling the Christmas tree. A red squirrel was taking a white-pine cone apart on a hemlock bough, and telling Snoozer what he thought of him and all other dogs, the hour or so you were there.

There will be a lot of aunts in the house besides the Biblical one. Aunts of every complexion and cut. Christmas is the one time that even the most dubious of aunts take on value. One of them can make up wreaths, another can make rock candy that puts a tremble on the heart, and still another can steer your twelve-seater bobsled—and turn it over, bottom up, with you all in just the right place for a fine spill.

There will be uncles, too, to hold one end of the molasses taffy you will pull sooner or later, yanking it out till it flashes and turns into cornsilk that almost floats in the air, tossing your end of it back and probably lassoing your uncle around his neck as you do it, and pulling out a new rope of solid honey.

There will be cousins by the cart load. He-ones and she-ones. The size you can sit on, and the size that can sit on you. Enough for two armies, on Little Round Top and on Big, up in the haymow. You will play Gettysburg there till your heads are full of hay chaff that will keep six aunts busy cleaning it out.

Every holiday that came along, in my father's house, was the gathering of an Anglo-Saxon clan. My father was built for lots of people 'round him. But Christmas was a whole assembly of the West Saxons! My father wanted people in squads. There were men with wide moustaches and men with smooth places on top of their heads, women wide and narrow. Cousins of the second and third water, even, were there. Hired men, too. Babies were underfoot in full cry. The older children hunted in packs. The table had to be pieced out with flour barrels and bread boards and ironing boards. It was a house's length from the head of the table, where your father sat and manufactured the roast up into slivers, to your mother dishing out the pork gravy. Whole geese disappeared on the way down. The Christmas cake, which had been left sweetly to itself for a month to age into a miracle, was a narrow isthmus when it got to Mother. But Mother always said that Christmas, to her, was watching other people eat. She was the kind of mother who claimed that the neck and the back of the chicken were the tastiest parts.

The prize goose, whom you had brought up by hand and called Oliver Cromwell, Old Ironsides, or some such distinguished title, was duly carved. And Father found his wishbone snow-white and you all applauded, for that meant lots of snow and two more months of coasting on your sleds. There were mince pies by the legion. And if Uncle Tom was there, a whole raccoon baked just for him and girt around with browned sweet potatoes. Mother's wild strawberry jam was there on deck, winking at you like rubies from the holes in tarts that melted away like bubbles in the mouth. That dinner was three hours in Beulah Land!

The whole nation of you in the house will go from one thing to another. The secret of the best Christmases is everybody doing the same things all at the same time. You will all fall to and string cranberries and popcorn for the tree, and the bright lines each of you has a hold on will radiate from the tree like ribbons on a maypole. Everybody will have needles and thread in the mouth, you will all get in each other's way, but that is the art of doing Christmas right. You will all bundle up together for a ride in the afternoon. You had better take the horsesled, as the pung will not begin to hold you. And even then a dozen or so of assorted uncles and aunts and cousins will have to come trooping after through the deep snow, and wait for their turn on the straw in the sled. Smaller cousins will fall off over the sides in great knots and never be missed, and the hullabaloo will roar on and send the rabbits flying away through the woods, showing their bobbing scuts.

Everybody will hang presents on the tree at once, when the sun has dipped down into the spruces in the west and you are back home in the sitting-room. There will be no nonsense of tip-toeing up and edging a package on when nobody is looking. Everybody knows who is giving him what. There is no mystery about it. And then you will turn right around and take the presents off again, the minute you have got them all on and have lighted the candles up.

There will be boughten presents, to be sure—a turtle of cardboard in a glassed, dainty box, hung on springs and swimming for dear life with all four feet, and popguns with their barrels ringed and streaked with red and yellow lines. Somebody will probably get one of those Swiss music-boxes that will eke out a ghostly "Last Rose of Summer," if tenderly cranked. There should be those little bottles of transparent candies, with real syrup in them, which I used to live for through the years. And there must be a German doll for every last girl, with mountains of yellow hair and cheeks looking as if life were a continuous blowing of bubbles. Boughten things are all right.

But if it is going to be our kind of Christmas, most of the presents will be home-made. Socks knit by the aunt who swears only by useful gifts. You have seen those socks growing up from their white toes for the last two weeks. Wristers, always red. A box of Aunt Louise's candied orange peel that she will never let on to anybody how she makes. Your father will have made a sled for every mother's son and daughter of you, with a bluebird, or robin redbreast, more real than life, painted on each one and your name underneath. You will never have another present to match that, though you grow up and become Midases. Popcorn balls, big as muskmelons, will be common ware. They will be dripping with molasses, and will stick your wristers and socks and other treasures together.

But the pith of the party is not reached until the whole nation of you sits down in rocking chairs, or lies down on their bellies in front of the six-foot gulf of the fireplace. The presents are all stowed, heaped and tucked away, stuck fast with cornballs. The last lamps are out. The firelight dances on the ceiling. It lights up the steel engraving of Major McCullock leaping from Kentucky to Ohio, with ten thousand mounted redskins yelling and reining in their steeds behind him. It lights up Daniel Boone's daughters as they lean away towards their boat's end and scream their silent screams and drop their lilies, while

Indian head after Indian head grins up at them from the river of the Dark and Bloody Ground.

Then you had best find a fair substitute for my father. Give him the best chair in the house—and the way to find *that* is to push the cat out of it—and let him tear! He will begin by telling you about such people as the brilliant young ladies of Philadelphia who had a piano too big to fit their house, so they put it on the porch and played on it through the open window. Then he will sit back and work his way to the Caliph of Bagdad, who had a daughter so homely that she had to wear a sack on her head when her suitors came a-wooing, and how she fell down a well and made herself a great fortune, and won the handsomest husband that ever wore a turban. That story, by the way, you will not find in the *Arabian Nights* even though you look for it, as I have done, till you have gray hairs in your head.

The firelight will get into your father's eyes and on his hair. He will move on from Bagdad to Big Bethel, and tell you all how the Yankee campfires looked like the high Milky Way itself, all night long before the battle; how the dew silvered every sleeping soldier's face and the stacked rifles, as the dawn came up with the new day and death. And you will hug your knees and hear the wind outside going its rounds among the snowy pines, and you will listen on till the story you are hearing becomes a part of the old winds of the world and the motion of the bright stars. And probably it will take two uncles at least to carry you to bed.

SHERWOOD ANDERSON

Sherwood Anderson, American storyteller, was born in Camden, Ohio, in 1876. His first experience in fiction came from his father, a teller of tall stories who was the model for his fictional "Windy" McPherson. After service in Cuba during the Spanish-American War, he became manager of a paint factory in Elyria, Ohio. One day he simply walked out and went to Chicago to write (an event brutally satirized by Ernest Hemingway in *The Torrents of Spring*). He struggled to find publishers, but was helped by other writers in Chicago (Theodore Dreiser, Floyd Dell, Carl Sandburg) and was finally able to publish his masterpiece, *Winesburg, Ohio*, a series of stories transformed into a kind of novel by a common observer (George Willard), by the themes of isolation and loneliness, and by the characters' groping inability to communicate. Malcolm Cowley suggests that the generation of American writers which came after Anderson, "Hemingway,

Faulkner, Wolfe, Steinbeck, Caldwell, Saroyan, Henry Miller . . . each of these owes him an unmistakable debt." Faulkner and Wolfe acknowledged this debt freely. The following excerpt comes from Anderson's *Memoirs*. He died in 1941.

A Small-Town Street

The street grew longer. On Sundays, horses hitched to buggies, phaetons, and even to farm wagons, stood tied at sheds back of the two churches and in the street before the churches. Neither our father nor our mother went to church and I do not remember any of us children going to Sunday School while we lived in that street. We were perhaps too poor and had no fit clothes. Mother's pride would have kept us at home.

But we had begun to prosper a little. Now father had become a house painter. He had begun to speak a new language. There was much talk of the fine art of mixing house paint, of how the brush should be held in the hand. At that time there was a great passion for what was called "graining." The trick was to make pine look like oak, oak like cherry, cherry like walnut. Father had acquired an outfit of graining tools and practiced on the doors and walls of our house. He spread a dirty brown mixture over a panel of one of the doors and got out his tools. He advanced upon the door, made certain flourishes with his hand. The point was to imitate the grain of some particular wood.

"You see, it is pine, it will become oak. See how perfectly the grain of oak is reproduced. There is not another man in Ohio could do so perfect or beautiful a job of graining."

Now father was always coming home covered with paint. I was also, when later he sometimes took me with him to help paint some farmer's barn. There was paint in his hair, on his eyebrows and mustache. It was on his hands, on his face. His clothes were yellow, then brown, then green, then red.

It must have been about this time that our mother began her career as a washwoman. She had worked all of her life, even from childhood, for others, a childhood and young girlhood of washing dishes, milking cows, waiting on tables, a kind of half servant in a house of strangers to her own blood, only, after marriage and the coming of her children, to become a washwoman. And I remember keenly a kind of shame that began to grow in the breasts of us children when we were sent off to bear home baskets of dirty clothes or to return them washed and ironed.

We did not go, on these trips, through the streets but kept as far as possible to the alleyways. If we went through the streets and heard someone coming we quickly turned into a yard before some house and set the basket down. We tried to pretend we had nothing to do with it. It was shame to us that mother should have to do such work. She was no longer strong and she coughed a good deal.

Of course it is possible that the feeling of shame in us that our mother should be brought down to so low a position in the town life was due to remarks made by other children on our street. The same may have come at first into the minds of the two older children, Karl and Stella, and may have been transmitted to us younger ones through them. At any rate, it was there and I am sure that even then we had begun asking ourselves the unanswerable question:

"Why is it that this one is born into life in a big house, with a carriage at the door, with no thought of where food comes from, with warm clothes to wear, all of life to be lived in luxury, while we others, outside in the cold, often in ragged clothes, like little animals, are compelled to hunt our food from day to day? Why is it? Why is it?

"Why does our mother have to wash the dirty clothes soiled by other people?"

It was not, I am sure, hatred of seemingly more fortunate ones that was growing in us. It was not even envy. It was a kind of shame, and I am quite sure that at a very early age it took the form (at least it did in me) of despising our father.

It was a feeling that was to stay in me, as the hardship of our mother's life continued, down to the very day of her death, and to grow into a kind of hatred. Our mother, I felt, was not made for the life she was compelled to live. She was a woman delicately built and whom I thought beautiful and I am quite sure that, even as a child, I began to want for her the things in life she was never to have.

Am I running too far ahead now? I do not know. I do know that it was only after I had become a mature man, long after our mother's death, that I began to appreciate our father and to understand somewhat his eternal boyishness, his lack of the feeling of responsibility to others, his passion for always playing with life, qualities which, I have no doubt, our mother saw in him and which enabled her, in spite of the long hardship of her life with him, to remain always a faithful, and for anything I ever heard her say, a devoted wife.

And if in my own life, after many attempts at living as laborer, soldier, follower of race horses, factory hand, and business man, I became at last a writer, a writer whose sympathy went out most to the little frame houses, on often mean enough streets in American towns, to defeated people, often with thwarted lives, it is, I am sure, all due to this feeling toward our mother that had begun to grow in me as a small child.

Frances Fowler's "The Day We Flew the Kites" first appeared in *Parent's Magazine* in May 1949.

The Day We Flew the Kites

"String!" shouted Brother, bursting into the kitchen. "We need lots more string."

It was Saturday. As always, it was a busy one, for "Six days shalt thou labor and do all thy work" was taken seriously in those days. My father and Mr. Patrick next door were doing chores about their large yards. March was a busy time.

Indoors, Mother and Mrs. Patrick were running around in their usual Saturday marathon, complicated by spring cleaning. Such a windy day was ideal for "turning out" clothes closets. Already woolens flapped on clotheslines which snaked across the adjoining back yards.

Somehow the boys had slipped away to the back lot with their kites. Now, even at the risk of having Brother impounded for beating carpets or washing windows, they had sent him to the house for more string. All of theirs had played out—heaven knows how many yards! Apparently there was no limit to the heights to which kites would soar today.

My mother looked out the window. The sky was piercingly blue; the breeze fresh and infinitely exciting. Up in all that blueness sailed great puffy billows of clouds. It had been a long, hard winter, but today was Spring.

My mother looked from the pie-baking clutter on the kitchen table to the disordered sitting room, its furniture all moved out of line for a really Spartan sweeping. Again her eyes wavered toward the window. "Come on, girls!" She fumbled in the kitchen-table drawer for a new roll of twine. "Let's take string to the boys and watch them fly the kites a minute."

On the way we met our neighbor, Mrs. Patrick, laughing guiltily, escorted by her girls.

There never was such a day for flying kites! God doesn't make two such days in a century. We played all our fresh twine into the boys' kites, and still they soared. We could hardly distinguish the tiny, orange-colored specks. Now and then we slowly reeled one in, finally bringing it, dipping and tugging, to earth, for the sheer joy of sending it up again, feeling its vibrant tug against the twine as it sought the sky. What a thrill to run with them, to the right, to the left, and see our poor, earth-bound movements reflected minutes later, in the majestic sky-dance of the kites! We wrote "wishes" on slips of paper, punched holes in them, and slipped them over the string. Slowly, irresistibly, they climbed up until they reached the kites. Surely all such wishes would be granted!

Even our fathers dropped hoe and hammer and joined us. Our mothers took their turn, laughing like schoolgirls. Their hair blew out of their decorous pompadours and curled loose about their cheeks, their gingham aprons whipped about their legs. Mingled with our puppyish delight was a feeling akin to awe. These adults were playing with us, really playing! The gulf between parent and child was greater then than now. Once I looked at Mother and thought she looked actually pretty! And her over forty!

We never knew where the hours went on that hilltop day. There were no hours, just a golden, breezy Now. I think we were all a little beyond ourselves. Parents forgot their duty and their dignity; children forgot the combativeness and small spites. "Perhaps it's like this in the Kingdom of Heaven," I thought confusedly. All our personalities stood out clearer, more individual than ever, and yet there was no sense of separateness.

It was growing dark before, drunk with sun and air, we all stumbled sleepily back to the houses. Things were just as we had left them, but Mother looked as if she hardly saw the half-rolled pastry, the stripped sitting room. I suppose we had some sort of supper. I suppose there must have been a surface tidying-up, for the house on Sunday looked decorous enough, or do I remember?

The strange thing was, we didn't mention that day, afterward. I felt a little embarrassed. Surely none of those other sensible, balanced people had thrilled to it as deeply as I; none had had ridiculous, sacrilegious thoughts about comparing flying kites with the Kingdom of Heaven. I locked the memory up in that deepest part of me where we keep "the things that cannot be and yet are" . . . and the years went on.

A good many years had passed, and one day I was flying about a kitchen of my own in a city apartment. I was trying to get some work out of the way while my three-year-old insistently whined her desire to "go park and see ducks."

"I can't go!" (My reasonableness was wearing thin.) "I have this and this and this to do first, and when I'm through I'll be too tired to walk that far."

My mother, who was visiting us, looked up from the peas she was shelling. "It's a wonderful day," she offered, "really warm, yet there's a fine, fresh breeze. It reminds me of that day we flew the kites." I stopped in my dash between stove and sink. So she remembered! The locked door flew open, and with it a gush of memories, and the application of her little parable. There had been much to do on that long-ago Saturday.

I pulled off my apron. "Come on," I told my little girl. "You're right, it's too good a day to miss."

Another decade passed. We were in the uneasy aftermath of a great war. All evening we had been asking our returned soldier, the youngest Patrick boy, about his experiences as a prisoner of war. He had talked freely, but now for a long time he had been silent, watching his cigarette smoke curl upward into the summer darkness. The silence seemed suddenly to throb. What was he thinking of . . . what dark and dreadful things? What was he going to tell?

"Say!" A smile twitched his lips. He looked like the little boy he used to be, the very little boy always tagging behind us others. "Say, do you remember . . . no, of course you wouldn't. It probably didn't make the impression on you it did on me. It was the first time I'd seen them."

I hardly dared speak. "Remember what?"

"I used to think of that day a lot in P.W. camp, when things weren't too good. Do you remember the day we flew the kites?"

Winter came, and the sad duty of a call of condolence on Mrs. Patrick, recently widowed. Her family had moved away many years before, but she had brought back her husband's body to our town for burial. I dreaded the call. I couldn't imagine how Mrs. Patrick would face life alone.

I found her quite gray, a little stooped, much thinner than in her vigorous, maternal middle years. But she still had those warm, brown eyes, that low, caressing voice. We talked a little of my family and her grandchildren and the changes in our town. Then she was silent, looking down at her lap. I cleared my throat. Now I must say something about her loss, and she would begin to cry.

When I looked up, I was dumbfounded. Mrs. Patrick was smiling. "I was just sitting here thinking," she said. "Henry had such fun that day. Frances, do you remember the day we flew the kites?"

LILLIAN SMITH

Lillian Smith was born in 1897 in Jasper, Florida. Her first two novels were not published, but *Strange Fruit* (1944) sold three million copies and was translated into fifteen languages. *Killers of the Dream,* from which the following selection comes, is an experiment—an attempt to write an autobiography of a person *and* her region. Her work has dealt largely with race; *Strange Fruit* tells of the love of a Negro girl for a white man, *Killers of the Dream* explores the psychological bases of prejudice. She died in 1966 after a fourteen-year battle with cancer. Her last book was *The Journey,* which ends with these words: "To believe in something not yet proved and to underwrite it with our lives; it is the only way we can leave the future open. Man, surrounded by facts, permitting himself no surmise, no intuitive flash, no great hypothesis, no risk is in a locked cell. Ignorance cannot seal the mind and imagination more surely. To find the point where hypothesis and fact meet; the delicate equilibrium between dream and reality; the place where fantasy and earthy things are metamorphosed into a work of art; to lay down one's powers for others in need; to shake off the old ordeal and get ready for the new; to question, knowing that never can the full answer be found; to accept uncertainties quietly, even our incomplete knowledge of God: This is what man's journey is about, I think."

When I Was a Child

Even its children know that the South is in trouble. No one has to tell them; no words said aloud. To them, it is a vague thing weaving in and out of their play, like a ghost haunting an old graveyard or whispers after the household sleeps—fleeting mystery, vague menace, to which each responds in his own way. Some learn to screen out all except the soft and the soothing; others deny even as they see plainly, and hear. But all know that under quiet words and warmth and laughter, under the slow ease and tender concern about small matters, there is a heavy burden on all of us and as heavy a refusal to confess it. The children know this "trouble" is bigger than they, bigger than their family, bigger than their church, so big that people turn away from its size. They have seen it flash out like lightning and shatter a town's peace, have felt it tear up all they believe in. They have measured its giant strength and they feel weak when they remember.

This haunted childhood belongs to every southerner. Many of us run away from it but we come back like a hurt animal to its wound, or a murderer to the scene of his sin. The human heart dares not stay away too long from that which hurt it most. There is a return journey to anguish that few of us are released from making.

We who were born in the South call this mesh of feeling and memory "loyalty." We think of it sometimes as "love." We identify with the South's trouble as if we, individually, were responsible for all of it. We defend the sins and sorrows of three hundred years as if each sin had been committed by us alone and each sorrow had cut across our heart. We are as hurt at criticism of our region as if our own name were called aloud by the critic. We have known guilt without understanding it, and there is no tie that binds men closer to the past and each other than that.

It is a strange thing, this umbilical cord uncut. In times of ease, we do not feel its pull, but when we are threatened with change, suddenly it draws the whole white South together in a collective fear and fury that wipe our minds clear of reason and we are blocked off from sensible contact with the world we live in.

To keep this resistance strong, wall after wall has been thrown up in the southern mind against criticism from without and within. Imaginations close tight against the hurt of others; a regional armoring takes place to keep out the "enemies" who would make our trouble different—or maybe rid us of it completely. For it is a trouble that we do not want to give up. We are as involved with it as a child who cannot be happy at home and cannot bear to tear himself away, or as a grown-up who has fallen in love with his own disease. We southerners have identified with the long sorrowful past on such deep levels of love and hate and guilt that we do not know how to break old bonds without pulling our lives down. *Change* is the evil word, a shrill clanking that makes us know too well our servitude. *Change* means leaving one's memories, one's sins, one's ancient prison, the room where one was born. How can we do this when we are tied fast!

The white man's burden is his own childhood. Every southerner knows this. Though he may deny it even to himself, yet he drags through life with him the heavy weight of a past that never eases and is rarely understood, of desire never appeased, of dreams that died in his heart.

In this South I was born and now live. Here it was that I began to grow, seeking my way, as do all children, through the honeycomb cells of our life to the bright reality outside. Sometimes it was as if all doors opened inward. . . . Sometimes we children lost even the desire to get outside and tried only to make a comfortable home of the trap of swinging doors that history and religion and a war, man's greed and his guilt had placed us in at birth.

It is not easy to pick out of such a life those strands that have to do only with color, only with Negro-white relationships, only with religion or sex, for they are knit of the same fibers that have gone into the making of the whole fabric, woven into its basic patterns and designs. Religion . . . sex . . . race . . . money . . . avoidance rites . . . malnutrition . . . dreams—no part of these can be looked at and clearly seen without looking at the whole of them. For, as a painter mixes colors and makes of them new colors, so religion is turned into something different by race, and segregation is colored as much by sex as by skin pigment, and money is no longer a coin but a lost wish wandering through a man's whole life.

A child's lessons are blended of these strands however dissonant a design they make. The mother who taught me what I know of tenderness and love and compassion taught me also the bleak rituals of keeping Negroes in their place. The father who rebuked me for an air of superiority toward schoolmates from the mill and rounded out his rebuke by gravely reminding me that "all men are brothers," trained me in the steel-rigid decorums I must demand of every colored male. They who so gravely taught me to split my body from my feelings and both from my "soul," taught me also to split my conscience from my acts and Christianity from southern tradition.

Neither the Negro nor sex was often discussed at length in our home. We were given no formal instruction in these difficult matters but we learned our lessons well. We learned the intricate system of taboos, of renunciations and compensations, of manners, voice modulations, words, feelings, along with our prayers, our toilet habits, and our games. I do not remember how or when, but by the time I had learned that God is love, that Jesus is His Son and came to give us more abundant life, that all men are brothers with a common Father, I also knew that I was better than a Negro, that all black folks have their place and must be kept in it, that sex has its place and must be kept in it, that a terrifying disaster would befall the South if ever I treated a Negro as my social equal and as terrifying a disaster would befall my family if ever I were to have a baby outside of marriage. I had learned that God so loved the world that He gave His only begotten Son so that we might have segregated churches in which it was my duty to worship each Sunday and on Wednesday at evening prayers. I had learned that white southerners are a hospitable, courteous, tactful people who treat those of their own group with consideration and who as carefully segregate from all the richness of life "for their own good and welfare" thirteen million people whose skin is colored a little differently from my own.

I knew by the time I was twelve that a member of my family would always shake hands with old Negro friends, would speak gently and graciously to members of the Negro race unless they forgot their place, in which event icy peremptory tones would draw lines beyond which only the desperate would dare take one step. I knew that to use the word "nigger" was unpardonable and no well-bred southerner was quite so crude as to do so; nor would a well-bred southerner call a Negro "mister" or invite him into the living room or eat with him or sit by him in public places.

I knew that my old nurse who had patiently cared for me through long months of illness, who had given me refuge when a little sister took my place as the baby of the family, who comforted me, soothed, fed me, delighted me with her stories and games, let me fall asleep on her deep warm breast, was not worthy of the passionate love I felt for her but must be given instead a half-smiled-at affection similar to that which one feels for one's dog. I knew but I never believed it, that the deep respect I felt for her, the tenderness, the love, was a childish thing which every normal child outgrows, that such love begins with one's toys and is discarded with them, and that somehow—though it seemed impossible to my agonized heart—I too, must outgrow these feelings. I learned to give presents to this woman I loved, instead of esteem and honor. I learned to use a soft voice to oil my words of superiority. I learned to cheapen with tears and sentimental talk of "my old mammy" one of the profound relationships of my life. I learned the bitterest thing a child can learn: that the human relations I valued most were held cheap by the world I lived in.

From the day I was born, I began to learn my lessons. I was put in a rigid frame too intricate, too complex, too twisting to describe here so briefly, but I learned to conform to its slide-rule measurements. I learned that it is possible to be a Christian and a white southerner simultaneously; to be a gentlewoman and an arrogant callous creature in the same moment; to pray at night and ride a Jim Crow car the next morning and to feel comfortable in doing both. I learned to believe in freedom, to glow when the word *democracy* is used, and to practice slavery from morning to night. I learned it the way all of my southern people learn it: by closing door after door until one's mind and heart and conscience are blocked off from each other and from reality.

I closed the doors. Or perhaps they were closed for me. Then one day they began to open again. Why I had the desire or the strength to open them or what strange accident or circumstance opened them for me would require in the answering an account too long, too particular, too stark to make here. And perhaps I should not have the insight or wisdom that such an analysis would demand of me, nor the will to make it. I know only that the doors opened, a little; that somewhere along that iron corridor we travel from babyhood to maturity, doors swinging inward began to swing outward, showing glimpses of the world beyond, of that clear bright thing we call "reality."

I believe there is one experience in my childhood which pushed these doors open, a little. And I am going to tell it here, although I know well that to excerpt from a life and family background one incident and name it as a "cause" of a change in one's life direction is a distortion and often an irrelevance. The profound hungers of a child and how they are filled have too much to do with the way in which experiences are assimilated to tear an incident out of a life and look at it in isolation. Yet, with these reservations, I shall tell it, not because it was in itself so severe a trauma, but because it became for me a symbol of buried experiences that I did not have access to. It is an incident that has rarely happened to other southern children. In a sense, it is unique. But it was an acting-out, a special private production of a little script that is written on the lives of most southern children before they know words. Though they may not have seen it staged this way, each southerner has had his own dramatization of the theme.

I should like to preface the account by giving a brief glimpse of my family and background, hoping that the reader, entering my home with me, will be able to blend the ragged edges of this isolated experience into a more full life picture and in doing so will see that it is, in a sense, everybody's story.

I was born and reared in a small Deep South town whose population was about equally Negro and white. There were nine of us who grew up freely in a rambling house of many rooms, surrounded by big lawn, back yard, gardens, fields, and barn. It was the kind of home that gathers memories like dust, a place filled with laughter and play and pain and hurt and ghosts and games. We were given such advantages of schooling, music, and art as were available in the South, and our world was not limited to the South, for travel to far places seemed a simple, natural thing to us, and usually there was one of the family in a remote part of the earth.

We knew we were a respected and important family of this small town but beyond this knowledge we gave little thought to status. Our father made money in lumber and naval stores for the excitement of making and losing it—not for what money can buy nor the security which it sometimes gives. I do not remember at any time wanting "to be rich" nor do I remember that thrift and saving were ideals which our parents considered important enough to urge upon us. Always in the family there was an acceptance of risk, a mild delight even in burning bridges, an expectant "what will happen now!" We were not irre-sponsible; living according to the pleasure principle was by no means our way of life. On the contrary we were trained to think that each of us should do something that would be of genuine usefulness to the world, and the family thought it right to make sacrifices if necessary, to give each child adequate preparation for this life's work. We were also trained to think learning important, and books, but "bad" books our mother burned. We valued music and art and craftsmanship but it was people and their welfare and religion that were the foci around which our lives seemed naturally to move. Above all else, the important thing was what we "planned to do with our lives." That each of us must do something was as inevitable as breathing for we owed a "debt to society which must be paid." This was a family commandment.

While many of our neighbors spent their energies in counting limbs on the family tree and grafting some on now and then to give symmetry to it, or in reliving the old bitter days of Reconstruction licking scars to cure their vague malaise, or in fighting each battle and turn of battle of that Civil War which has haunted the southern conscience so long, my father was pushing his nine children straight into the future. "You have your heritage," he used to say, "some of it good, some not so good; and as far as I know you had the usual number of grandmothers and grandfathers. Yes, there were slaves, far too many of them in the family, but that was your grandfather's mistake, not yours. The past has been lived. It is gone. The future is yours. What are you going to do with it?" Always he asked this question of his children and sometimes one knew it was but an echo of the old question he had spent his life trying to answer for himself. For always the future held my father's dreams; always there, not in the past, did he expect to find what he had spent his life searching for.

We lived the same segregated life as did other southerners but our parents talked in excessively Christian and democratic terms. We were told ten thousand times that status and money are unimportant (though we were well supplied with both); we were told that "all men are brothers," that we are part of a democracy and must act like democrats. We were told that the teachings of Jesus are real and important and could be practiced if we tried. We were told also that to be "radical" is bad, silly too; and that one must always conform to the "best behavior" of one's community and make it better if one can. We were taught that we were superior not to people but to hate and resentment, and that no member of the Smith family could stoop so low as to have an enemy. No matter what injury was done us, we must not injure ourselves further by retaliating. That was a family commandment too.

We had family prayers once each day. All of us as children read the Bible in its entirety each year. We memorized hundreds of Bible verses and repeated them at breakfast, and said "sentence prayers" around the family table. God was not someone we met on Sunday but a permanent member of our household. It never occurred to me until I was fourteen or fifteen years old that He did not see every act and thought and chalk up the daily score on eternity's tablets.

Despite the strain of living so intimately with God, the nine of us were strong, healthy, energetic youngsters who filled our days with play and sports and music and books and managed to live much of our lives on the careless level at which young lives should be lived. We had our times of profound anxiety of course, for there were hard lessons to be learned about the body and "bad things" to be learned about sex. Sometimes I have wondered how we ever learned them with a mother so shy with words.

She was a wistful creature who loved beautiful things like lace and sunsets and flowers in a vague inarticulate way, and took good care of her children. We always knew this was not her world but one she accepted under duress. Her private world we rarely entered, though the shadow of it lay at times heavily on our hearts.

Our father owned large business interests, employed hundreds of colored and white laborers, paid them the prevailing low wages, worked them the prevailing long hours, built for them mill towns (Negro and white), built for each group a church, saw to it that religion was supplied free, saw to it that a commissary supplied commodities at a high price, and in general managed his affairs much as ten thousand other southern businessmen manage theirs.

Even now, I can hear him chuckling as he told my mother how he won his fight for Prohibition. The high point of the campaign was election afternoon, when he lined up the entire mill force of several hundred (white and black), passed out a shining silver dollar to each one of them, marched them in and voted liquor out of our county. It was a great day in his life. He had won the Big Game, a game he was always playing with himself against all kinds of evil. It did not occur to him to scrutinize the methods he used. Evil was a word written in capitals; the devil was smart; if you wanted to win you outsmarted him. It was as simple as that.

He was a practical, hardheaded, warmhearted, high-spirited man born during the Civil War, earning his living at twelve, struggling through bitter decades of Reconstruction and post-Reconstruction, through populist movement, through the panic of 1893, the panic of 1907, on into the twentieth century accepting his region as he found it, accepting its morals and its mores as he accepted its climate, with only scorn for those who held grudges against the North or pitied themselves or the South; scheming, dreaming, expanding his business, making and losing money, making friends whom he did not lose, with never a doubt that God was always by his side whispering hunches as to how to pull off successful deals. When he lost, it was his own fault. When he won, God had helped him.

Once while we were kneeling at family prayers the fire siren at the mill sounded the alarm that the mill was on fire. My father did not falter from his prayer. The alarm sounded again and again—which signified that the fire was big. With quiet dignity he continued his talk with God while his children sweated and wriggled and hearts beat out of their chests in excitement. He was talking to God—how could he hurry out of the presence of the Most High to save his mills! When he finished his prayer, he quietly stood up, laid the Bible carefully on the table. Then, and only then, did he show an interest in what was happening in Mill Town. . . . When the telegram was placed in his hands telling of the death of his beloved favorite son, he gathered his children together, knelt down, and in a steady voice which contained no hint of his shattered heart, loyally repeated, "God is our refuge and strength, a very present help in trouble. Therefore will we not fear, though the earth be removed, and though the mountains be carried into the midst of the sea." On his deathbed, he whispered to his old Business Partner in Heaven: "I have fought the fight; I have kept the faith."

Against this backdrop the drama of the South was played out one day in my life:

A little white girl was found in the colored section of our town, living with a Negro family in a broken-down shack. This family had moved in only a few weeks before and little was known of them. One of the ladies in my mother's club, while driving over to her washerwoman's, saw the child swinging on a gate. The shack, as she said, was hardly more than a pigsty and this white child was living with ignorant and dirty and sick-looking colored folks. "They must have kidnapped her," she told her friends. Genuinely shocked, the clubwomen busied themselves in an attempt to do something, for the child was very white indeed. The strange Negroes were subjected to a grueling questioning and finally grew frightened and evasive and refused to talk at all. This only increased the suspicion of the white group, and the next day the clubwomen, escorted by the town marshal, took the child from her adopted family despite their tears.

She was brought to our home. I do not know why my mother consented to this plan. Perhaps because she loved children and always showed tenderness and concern for them. It was easy for one more to fit into our ample household and Janie was soon at home there. She roomed with me, sat next to me at the table; I found Bible verses for her to say at breakfast; she wore my clothes, played with my dolls and followed me around from morning to night. She was dazed by her new comforts and by the interesting activities of this big lively family; and I was as happily dazed, for her adoration was a new thing to me; and as time passed a quick, childish, and deeply felt bond grew up between us.

But a day came when a telephone message was received from a colored orphanage. There was a meeting at our home, whispers, shocked exclamations. All afternoon the ladies went in and out of our house talking to Mother in tones too low for children to hear. And as they passed us at play, most of them looked quickly at Janie and quickly looked away again, though a few stopped and stared at her as if they could not tear their eyes from her face. When my father came home in the evening Mother closed her door against our young ears and talked a long time with him. I heard him laugh, heard Mother say, "But Papa, this is no laughing matter!" And then they were back in the living room with us and my mother was pale and my father was saying, "Well, work it out, honey, as best you can. After all, now that you know, it is pretty simple."

In a little while my mother called my sister and me into her bedroom and told us that in the morning Janie would return to Colored Town. She said Janie was to have the dresses the ladies had given her and a few of my own, and the toys we had shared with her. She asked me if I would like to give Janie one of my dolls. She seemed hurried, though Janie was not to leave until next day. She said, "Why not select it now?" And in dreamlike stiffness I brought in my dolls and chose one for Janie. And then I found it possible to say, "Why? Why is she leaving? She likes us, she hardly knows them. She told me she had been with them only a month."

"Because," Mother said gently, "Janie is a little colored girl."

"But she can't be. She's white!"

"We were mistaken. She is colored."

"But she looks——"

"She is colored. Please don't argue!"

"What does it mean?" I whispered.

"It means," Mother said slowly, "that she has to live in Colored Town with colored people."

"But why? She lived here three weeks and she doesn't belong to them, she told me she didn't."

"She is a little colored girl."

"But you said yourself that she has nice manners. You said that," I persisted.

"Yes, she is a nice child. But a colored child cannot live in our home. '

"Why?"

"You know, dear! You have always known that white and colored people do not live together."

"Can she come over to play?"

"No."

"I don't understand."

"I don't either," my young sister quavered.

"You're too young to understand. And don't ask me again, ever again, about this!" Mother's voice was sharp but her face was sad and there was no certainty left there. She hurried out and busied herself in the kitchen and I wandered through that room where I had been born, touching the old familiar things in it, looking at them, trying to find the answer to a question that moaned in my mind like a hurt thing. . . .

And then I went out to Janie, who was waiting, knowing things were happening that concerned her but waiting until they were spoken aloud.

I do not know quite how the words were said but I told her that she was to return in the morning to the little place where she had lived because she was colored and colored children could not live with white children.

"Are you white?" she said.

"I'm white," I replied, "and my sister is white. And you're colored. And white and colored can't live together because my mother says so."

"Why?" Janie whispered.

"Because they can't," I said. But I knew, though I said it firmly, that something was wrong. I knew my father and mother whom I passionately admired had done that which did not fit in with their teachings. I knew they had betrayed something which they held dear. And I was shamed by their failure and frightened, for I felt that they were no longer as powerful as I had thought. There was something Out There that was stronger than they and I could not bear to believe it. I could not confess that my father, who had always solved the family dilemmas easily and with laughter, could not solve this. I knew that my mother who was so good to children did not believe in her heart that she was being good to this child. There was not a word in my mind that said it but my body knew and my glands, and I was filled with anxiety.

But I felt compelled to believe they were right. It was the only way my world could be held together. And, like a slow poison, it began to seep through me: *I was white. She was colored. We must not be together. It was bad to be together. Though you ate with your nurse when you were little, it was bad to eat with any colored person after that. It was bad just as other things were bad that your mother had told you. It was bad that she was to sleep in the room with me that night. It was bad. . . .*

I was suddenly full of guilt. For three weeks I had done things that white children are not supposed to do. And now I knew these things had been wrong.

I went to the piano and began to play, as I had always done when I was in trouble. I tried to play Paderewski's *Minuet* and as I stumbled through it, the little girl came over and sat on the bench with me. Feeling lonely, lost in these deep currents that were sweeping through our house that night, she crept closer and put her arms around me and I shrank away as if my body had been uncovered. I had not said a word, I did not say one, but she knew, and tears slowly rolled down her little white face. . . .

And then I forgot it. For more than thirty years the experience was wiped out of my memory. But that night, and the weeks it was tied to, worked its way like a splinter, bit by bit down to the hurt places in my memory and festered there. And as I grew older, as more experiences collected around that faithless time, as memories of earlier, more profound hurts crept closer and closer drawn to that night as if to a magnet, I began to know that people who talked of love and Christianity and democracy did not mean it. That is a hard thing for a child to learn. I still admired my parents, there was so much that was strong and vital and sane and good about them and I never forgot this; I stubbornly believed in their sincerity, as I do to this day, and I loved them. Yet in my heart they were under suspicion. Something was wrong.

Something was wrong with a world that tells you that love is good and people are important and then forces you to deny love and to humiliate people. I knew, though I would not for years confess it aloud, that in trying to shut the Negro race away from us, we have shut ourselves away from so many good, creative, honest, deeply human things in life. I began to understand so slowly at first but more and more clearly as the years passed, that the warped, distorted frame we have put around every Negro child from birth is around every white child also. Each is on a different side of the frame but each is pinioned there. And I knew that what cruelly shapes and cripples the personality of one is as cruelly shaping and crippling the personality of the other. I began to see that though we may, as we acquire new knowledge, live through new experiences, examine old memories, gain the strength to tear the frame from us, yet we are stunted and warped and in our lifetime cannot grow straight again any more than can a tree, put in a steel-like twisting frame when young, grow tall and straight when the frame is torn away at maturity.

As I sit here writing, I can almost touch that little town, so close is the memory of it. There it lies, its main street lined with great oaks, heavy with matted moss that swings softly even now as I remember. A little white town rimmed with Negroes, making a deep shadow on the whiteness. There it lies, broken in two by one strange idea. Minds broken in two. Hearts broken. Conscience torn from acts. A culture split in a thousand pieces. That is segregation. I am remembering: a woman in a mental hospital walking four steps out, four steps in, unable to go further because she has drawn an invisible line around her small world and is terrified to take one step beyond it. . . . A man in a Disturbed Ward assigning "places" to the other patients and violently insisting that each stay in his place. . . . A Negro woman saying to me so quietly, "We cannot ride together on the bus, you know. It is not legal to be human in Georgia."

Memory, walking the streets of one's childhood . . . of the town where one was born.

THREE

DYLAN THOMAS

The magnificent Welsh poet, Dylan Thomas, was born in 1914. He published his first small volume of poetry when he was nineteen. Among his finest poems are "A Refusal to Mourn the Death, by Fire, of a Child in London," "Fern Hill," "The Force that Through the Green Fuse Drives the Flower," "Poem in October," "Do Not Go Gentle into that Good Night," and "And Death Shall Have No Dominion." His autobiographical work is included in *Quite Early One Morning* and *Portrait of the Artist as a Young Dog,* his short stories in *Adventures in the Skin Trade.* Although he wrote only six poems in the last six years of his life, death has had no dominion over him or his work; his superb voice lives on through the many recordings he made of his poetry and stories. He wrote a wonderful verse-play, *Under Milk Wood,* produced with great critical acclaim in the United States, where he was celebrated much as London is said to have celebrated Robert Burns. He died, at thirty-nine, in New York City. His last days are described in John Malcolm Brinnin's *Dylan Thomas in America* and in his wife Caitlin's *Leftover Life to Kill.*

Reminiscences of Childhood

I like very much people telling me about their childhood, but they'll have to be quick or else I'll be telling them about mine.

I was born in a large Welsh town at the beginning of the Great War—an ugly, lovely town (or so it was and is to me), crawling, sprawling by a long and splendid curving shore where truant boys and sandfield boys and old men from nowhere, beachcombed, idled and paddled, watched the dockbound ships or the ships steaming away into wonder and India, magic and China, countries bright with oranges and loud with lions; threw stones into the sea for the barking outcast dogs; made castles and forts and harbours and race tracks in the sand; and on Saturday summer afternoons listened to the brass band, watched the Punch and Judy, or hung about on the fringes of the crowd to hear the fierce religious speakers who shouted at the sea, as though it were wicked and wrong to roll in and out like that, white-horsed and full of fishes.

One man, I remember, used to take off his hat and set fire to his hair every now and then, but I do not remember what it proved, if it proved anything at all, except that he was a very interesting man.

This sea-town was my world; outside a strange Wales, coal-pitted, mountained, river-run, full, so far as I knew, of choirs and football teams and sheep and storybook tall hats and red flannel petticoats, moved about its business which was none of mine.

Beyond that unknown Wales with its wild names like peals of bells in the darkness, and its mountain men clothed in the skins of animals perhaps and always singing, lay England which was London and the country called the Front, from which many of our neighbours never came back. It was a country to which only young men travelled.

At the beginning, the only "front" I knew was the little lobby before our front door. I could not understand how so many people never returned from there, but later I grew to know more, though still without understanding, and carried a wooden rifle in the park and shot down the invisible unknown enemy like a flock of wild birds. And the park itself was a world within the world of the sea-town. Quite near where I lived, so near that on summer evenings I could listen in my bed to the voices of older children playing ball on the sloping paper-littered bank, the park was full of terrors and treasures. Though it was only a little park, it held within its borders of old tall trees, notched with our names and shabby from our climbing, as many secret places, caverns and forests, prairies and deserts, as a country somewhere at the end of the sea.

And though we would explore it one day, armed and desperate, from end to end, from the robbers' den to the pirates' cabin, the highwayman's inn to the cattle ranch, or the hidden room in the undergrowth, where we held beetle races, and lit the wood fires and roasted potatoes and talked about Africa, and the makes of motor cars, yet still the next day, it remained as unexplored as the Poles—a country just born and always changing.

There were many secret societies but you could belong only to one; and in blood or red ink, and a rusty pocketknife, with, of course, an instrument to remove stones from horses' feet, you signed your name at the foot of a terrible document, swore death to all the other societies, crossed your heart that you would divulge no secret and that if you did, you would consent to torture by slow fire, and undertook to carry out by yourself a feat of either daring or endurance. You could take your choice: would you climb to the top of the tallest and most dangerous tree, and from there hurl stones and insults at grown-up passers-by, especially postmen, or any other men in uniform? Or would you ring every doorbell in the terrace, not forgetting the doorbell of the man with the red face who kept dogs and ran fast? Or would you swim in the reservoir, which was forbidden and had angry swans, or would you eat a whole old jam jar full of mud?

There were many more alternatives. I chose one of endurance and for half an hour, it may have been longer or shorter, held up off the ground a very heavy broken pram we had found in a bush. I thought my back would break and the half hour felt like a day, but I preferred it to braving the red face and the dogs, or to swallowing tadpoles.

We knew every inhabitant of the park, every regular visitor, every nursemaid, every gardener, every old man. We knew the hour when the alarming retired policeman came in to look at the dahlias and the hour when the old lady arrived in the Bath chair with six Pekinese, and a pale girl to read aloud to her. I think she read the newspaper, but we always said she read the *Wizard.* The face of the old man who sat summer and winter on the bench looking over the reservoir, I can see clearly now and I wrote a poem long long after I'd left the park and the sea-town called:

THE HUNCHBACK IN THE PARK

The hunchback in the park
A solitary mister
Propped between trees and water
From the opening of the garden lock
That lets the trees and water enter
Until the Sunday sombre ball at dark

Eating bread from a newspaper
Drinking water from the chained cup
That the children filled with gravel
In the fountain basin where I sailed my ship
Slept at night in a dog kennel
But nobody chained him up.

Like the park birds he came early
Like the water he sat down
And Mister they called Hey mister
The truant boys from the town
Running when he had heard them clearly
On out of sound

Past lake and rockery
Laughing when he shook his paper
Hunchbacked in mockery
Through the loud zoo of the willow groves
Dodging the park-keeper
With his stick that picked up leaves.

And the old dog sleeper
Alone between nurses and swans
While the boys among willows
Made the tigers jump out of their eyes
To roar on the rockery stones
And the groves were blue with sailors

Made all day until bell-time
A woman figure without fault
Straight as a young elm
Straight and tall from his crooked bones
That she might stand in the night
After the locks and the chains

All night in the unmade park
After the railings and shrubberies
The birds the grass the trees and the lake
And the wild boys innocent as strawberries
Had followed the hunchback
To his kennel in the dark.

And that park grew up with me; that small world widened as I learned its secrets and boundaries, as I discovered new refuges and ambushes in its woods and jungles; hidden homes and lairs for the multitudes of imagination, for cowboys and Indians, and the tall terrible half-people who rode on nightmares through my bedroom. But it was not the only world—that world of rockery, gravel path, playbank, bowling green, bandstands, reservoir, dahlia garden, where an ancient keeper, known as Smoky, was the whiskered snake in the grass one must keep off. There was another world where with my friends I used to dawdle on half holidays along the bent and Devon-facing seashore, hoping for gold watches or the skull of a sheep or a message in a bottle to be washed up with the tide; and another where we used to wander whistling through the packed streets, stale as station sandwiches, round the impressive gasworks and the slaughter house, past by the blackened monuments and the museum that should have been in a museum. Or we scratched at a kind of cricket on the bald and cindery surface of the recreation ground, or we took a tram that shook like an iron jelly down to the gaunt pier, there to clamber under the pier, hanging perilously on to its skeleton legs or to run along to the end where patient men with the seaward eyes of the dockside unemployed capped and muffled, dangling from their mouths pipes that had long gone out, angled over the edge for unpleasant tasting fish.

Never was there such a town as ours, I thought, as we fought on the sandhills with rough boys or dared each other to climb up the scaffolding of half-built houses soon to be called Laburnum Beaches. Never was there such a town, I thought, for the smell of fish and chips on Saturday evenings; for the Saturday afternoon cinema matinees where we shouted and hissed our threepences away; for the crowds in the streets with leeks in their hats on international nights; for the park, the inexhaustible and mysterious, bushy red-Indian hiding park where the hunchback sat alone and the groves were blue with sailors. The memories of childhood have no order, and so I remember that never was there such a dame school as ours, so firm and kind and smelling of galoshes, with the sweet and fumbled music of the piano lessons drifting down from upstairs to the lonely schoolroom, where only the sometimes tearful wicked sat over undone sums, or to repeat a little crime—the pulling of a girl's hair during geography, the sly shin kick under the table during English literature. Behind the school was a narrow lane where only the oldest and boldest threw pebbles at windows, scuffled and boasted, fibbed about their relations—

"My father's got a chauffeur."

"What's he want a chauffeur for? He hasn't got a car."

"My father's the richest man in the town."

"My father's the richest man in Wales."

"My father owns the world."

And swapped gob-stoppers for slings, old knives for marbles, kite strings for foreign stamps.

The lane was always the place to tell your secrets; if you did not have any, you invented them. Occasionally now I dream that I am turning out of school into the lane of confidences when I say to the boys of my class, "At last, I have a real secret."

"What is it—what is it?"

"I can fly."

And when they do not believe me, I flap my arms and slowly leave the ground only a few inches at first, then gaining air until I fly waving my cap level with the upper windows of the school, peering in until the mistress at the piano screams and the metronome falls to the ground and stops, and there is no more time.

And I fly over the trees and chimneys of my town, over the dockyards skimming the masts and funnels, over Inkerman Street, Sebastopol Street, and the street where all the women wear men's caps, over the trees of the everlasting park, where a brass band shakes the leaves and sends them showering down on to the nurses and the children, the cripples and the idlers, and the gardeners, and the shouting boys: over the yellow seashore, and the stone-chasing dogs, and the old men, and the singing sea.

The memories of childhood have no order, and no end.

John Updike was born in Shillington, Pennsylvania, in 1932. He graduated from Harvard *(summa cum laude)* in 1954. He contributes regularly to *The New Yorker,* and his poetry also appears in *The New Republic.* His most recent novel is *Couples,* though his best novel is perhaps *Rabbit Run* (1960) which, though uneven and imperfectly planned, has some brilliant moments. The following selection is from "The Dogwood Tree: A Boyhood," included in *Five Boyhoods* (1962), edited by Martin Levin, and in Updike's *Assorted Prose* (1965).

The Dogwood Tree: A Boyhood

When I was born, my parents and my mother's parents planted a dogwood tree in the side yard of the large white house in which we lived throughout my boyhood. This tree, I learned quite early, was exactly my age, was, in a sense, me. But I never observed it closely, am not now sure what color its petals were; its presence was no more distinct than that of my shadow. The tree was my shadow, and had it died, had it ceased to occupy, each year with increasing volume and brilliance, its place in the side yard, I would have felt that a blessing like the blessing of light had been withdrawn from my life.

Though I cannot ask you to see it more clearly than I myself saw it, yet mentioning it seems to open the possibility of my boyhood home coming again to life. With a sweet damp rush the grass of our yard seems to breathe again on me. It is just cut. My mother is pushing the mower, to which a canvas catch is attached. My grandmother is raking up the loose grass in thick heaps, small green haystacks impregnated with dew, and my grandfather stands off to one side, smoking a cigar, elegantly holding the elbow of his right arm in the palm of his left hand while the blue smoke twists from under his mustache and dissolves in the heavy evening air—that misted, too-rich Pennsylvania air. My father is off, doing some duty in the town; he is a conscientious man, a schoolteacher and deacon, and also, somehow, a man of the streets.

In remembering the dogwood tree I remember the faintly speckled asbestos shingles of the chicken house at the bottom of our yard, fronting on the alley. We had a barn as well, which we rented as a garage, having no car of our own, and between the chicken house and the barn there was a narrow space where my grandfather, with his sly country ways, would urinate. I, a child, did also, passing through this narrow, hidden-feeling passage to the school grounds beyond our property; the fibrous tan-gray of the shingles would leap up dark, silky and almost black, when wetted.

The ground in this little passage seems a mysterious trough of pebbles of all colors and bits of paper and broken glass. A few weeds managed to grow in the perpetual shadow. All the ground at the lower end of the yard had an ungrateful quality; we had an ash heap on which we used to burn, in an extravagant ceremony that the war's thrift ended, the preceding day's newspaper. The earth for yards around the ashpile was colored gray. Chickens clucked in their wire pen. My grandmother tended them, and when the time came, beheaded them with an archaic efficiency that I don't recall ever witnessing, though I often studied the heavy log whose butt was ornamented with fine white neck-feathers pasted to the wood with blood.

A cat crosses our lawn, treading hastily on the damp grass, crouching low with distaste. Tommy is the cat's name; he lives in our chicken house but is not a pet. He is perfectly black; a rarity, he has no white dab on his chest. The birds scold out of the walnut tree and the apple and cherry trees. We have a large grape-arbor, and a stone birdbath, and a brick walk, and a privet hedge the height of a child and many bushes behind which my playmates hide. There is a pansy bed that in winter we cover with straw. The air is green, and heavy, and flavored with the smell of turned earth; in our garden grows, among other vegetables, a bland, turniplike cabbage called kohlrabi, which I have never seen, or eaten, since the days when, for a snack, I would tear one from its row with my hands.

History

My boyhood was spent in a world made tranquil by two invisible catastrophes: the Depression and World War II. Between 1932, when I was born, and 1945, when we moved away, the town Shillington changed, as far as I could see, very little. The vacant lot beside our home on Philadelphia Avenue remained vacant. The houses along the street were neither altered nor replaced. The high-school grounds, season after season, continued to make a placid plain visible from our rear windows. The softball field, with its triptych backstop, was nearest us. A little beyond, on the left, were the school and its boilerhouse, built in the late 1920s of the same ochre brick. In the middle distance a cinder track circumscribed the football field. At a greater distance there were the tennis courts and the poor farm fields and the tall double rows of trees marking the Poorhouse Lane. The horizon was the blue cloud, scarred by a gravel pit's orange slash, of Mount Penn, which overlooked the city of Reading.

A little gravel alley, too small to be marked with a street sign but known in the neighborhood as Shilling Alley, wound hazardously around our property and on down, past an untidy sequence of back buildings (chicken houses, barns out of plumb, a gunshop, a small lumber mill, a shack where a blind man lived, and the enchanted grotto of a garage whose cement floors had been waxed to the lustre of ebony by oil drippings and in whose greasy-black depths a silver drinking fountain spurted the coldest water in the world, silver water so cold it made your front teeth throb) on down to Lancaster Avenue, the main street, where the trolley cars ran. All through those years, Pappy Shilling, the surviving son of the landowner after whom the town was named, walked up and down Philadelphia Avenue with his thin black cane and his snow-white bangs; a vibrating chain of perfect-Sunday-school-attendance pins dangled from his lapel. Each autumn the horse-chestnut trees dropped their useless, treasurable nuts; each spring the dogwood tree put forth a slightly larger spread of blossoms; always the leaning walnut tree in our back yard fretted with the same tracery of branches the view we had.

Within our house, too, there was little change. My grandparents did not die, though they seemed very old. My father continued to teach at the high school; he had secured the job shortly after I was born. No one else was born. I was an only child. A great many only children were born in 1932; I make no apologies. I do not remember ever feeling the space for a competitor within the house. The five of us already there locked into a star that would have shattered like crystal at the admission of a sixth. We had no pets. We fed Tommy on the porch, but he was too wild to set foot in the kitchen, and only my grandmother, in a way wild herself, could touch him. Tommy came to us increasingly battered and once did not come at all. As if he had never existed: that was death. And then there was a squirrel, Tilly, that we fed peanuts to; she became very tame, and under the grape arbor would take them from our hands. The excitement of those tiny brown teeth shivering against my fingertips: that was life. But she, too, came from the outside, and returned to her tree, and did not dare intrude in our house.

The arrangement inside, which seemed to me so absolute, had been achieved, beyond the peripheries of my vision, drastically and accidentally. It may, at first, have been meant to be temporary. My father and grandfather were casualties of the early thirties. My father lost his job as a cable splicer with the telephone company; he and my mother had been living—for how long I have never understood—in boarding-houses and hotels throughout western Pennsylvania, in towns whose names (Hazelton, Altoona) even now make their faces light up with youth, a glow flowing out of the darkness preceding my birth.

They lived through this darkness, and the details of the adventure that my mother recalls—her lonely closeted days, the games of solitaire, the novels by Turgenev, the prostitutes downstairs, the men sleeping and starving in the parks of Pittsburgh—seem to waken in her an unjust and unreasonable happiness that used to rouse jealousy in my childish heart. I remember waiting with her by a window for my father to return from weeks on the road. It is in the Shillington living room. My hands are on the radiator ridges, I can see my father striding through the hedge toward the grape arbor, I feel my mother's excitement beside me mingle with mine. But she says this cannot be; he had lost his job before I was born.

My grandfather came from farming people in the south of the county. He prospered, and prematurely retired; the large suburban house he bought to house his good fortune became his fortune's shell, the one fragment of it left him. The two men pooled their diminished resources of strength and property and, with their women, came to live together. I do not believe they expected this arrangement to last long. For all of them—for all four of my adult guardians—Shillington was a snag, a halt in a journey that had begun elsewhere. Only I belonged to the town. The accidents that had planted me here made uneasy echoes in the house, but, like Tilly and Tommy, their source was beyond my vision.

Geography

As in time, so it was in space. The town was fringed with things that appeared awesome and ominous and fantastic to a boy. At the end of our street there was the County Home—an immense yellow poorhouse, set among the wide orchards and lawns, surrounded by a sandstone wall that was low enough on one side for a child to climb easily, but that on the other side offered a drop of twenty or thirty feet, enough to kill you if you fell. Why this should have been, why the poorhouse grounds should have been so deeply recessed on the Philadelphia Avenue side, puzzles me now. What machinery, then, could have executed such a massive job of grading I don't know. But at the time it seemed perfectly natural, a dreadful pit of space congruent with the pit of time into which the old people (who could be seen circling silently in the shade of the trees whose very tops were below my feet) had been plunged by some mystery that would never touch me. That I too would come to their condition was as unbelievable as that I would really fall and break my neck. Even so, I never acquired the daring that some boys had in racing along the top of the wall. In fact—let it be said now—I was not a very daring boy.

The poorhouse impinged on us in many ways. For one thing, my father, whose favorite nightmare was poverty, often said that he liked living so close to a poorhouse; if worse came to worse, he could walk there. For another, the stench of the poorhouse pigs, when the wind was from the east, drifted well down Philadelphia Avenue. Indeed, early in my life the poorhouse livestock were still herded down the street on their way to the slaughterhouse on the other side of town. Twice, in my childhood, the poorhouse barn burnt, and I remember my father (he loved crowds) rushing out of the house in the middle of one night, and my begging to go and my mother keeping me with her, and the luckier, less sheltered children the next day telling me horrific tales of cooked cows and screaming horses. All I saw were the charred ruins, still smoldering, settling here and there with an unexpected crackle, like the underbrush the morning after an ice storm.

Most whiffs of tragedy came, strangely, from the east end of the street. I remember two, both of them associated with the early morning and with the same house a few doors away in the neighborhood. When I was a baby, a man was run over and crushed by a milk wagon—a horse-drawn milk wagon. It had happened within sight of our windows, and I grew to know the exact patch of asphalt, but could never picture it. I believed all horse-drawn milk wagons were as light as the toy one I had; by the time I understood about this accident they had vanished from the streets. No matter how many times I visited the patch of asphalt, I could not understand how it had happened. And then, the family that succeeded the widow in her house—or it may have been in the other side; it was a brick semi-detached, set back and beclouded by several tall fir or cedar trees—contained a young man who, while being a counsellor at a summer camp, had had one of his boys dive into shallow water and, neck broken, die in his arms. The young counsellor at dawn one day many months later put a bullet through his head. I seem to remember hearing the shot; certainly I remember hearing my parents bumping around in their bedroom, trying to locate what had wakened them.

Beyond the poorhouse, where Philadelphia Avenue became a country lane, and crossed a little brook where water cress grew, there was a path on the right that led to the poorhouse dam. It was a sizable lake, where people fished and swam. Its mud bottom bristled with broken bottles and jagged cans. A little up from one of its shores, the yellow walls and rotten floor of the old pesthouse survived. Beyond the lake was a woods that extended along the south of the town. Here my parents often took me on walks. Every Sunday afternoon that was fair, we would set out. Sun, birds, and treetops rotated above us as we made our way. There were many routes. Farther down the road, toward Grille, another road led off, and went past a gravel cliff and sad little composition-shingled farmhouses whose invisible inhabitants I imagined as gravel-colored skeletons. By way of a lane we could leave this road and walk down toward the dam. Or we could walk up by the dam until we struck this road, and walk on until we came to a road that took us back into the town by way of the cemetery. I disliked these walks. I would lag farther and farther behind, until my father would retrace his steps and mount me on his shoulders. Upon this giddy, swaying perch—I hesitated to grip his ears and hair as tightly as I needed to—I felt as frightened as exultant, and soon confusedly struggled to be put down. In the woods I would hurl myself against dead branches for the pleasure of feeling them shatter and of disturbing whatever peace and solace my parents were managing to gather. If, at moments, I felt what they wanted me to feel—the sweet moist breath of mulching leaves, the delicate scratch of some bird in the living silence, the benevolent intricacy of moss and rocks and roots and ferns all interlocked on some bank torn by an old logging trail—I did not tell them. I was a small-town child. Cracked pavements and packed dirt were my ground.

This broad crescent of woods is threaded with our walks and suffused with images of love. For it was here, on the beds of needles under the canopies of low pine boughs, that our girls—and this is later, not boyhood at all, but the two have become entangled—were rumored to give themselves. Indeed, I was told that one of the girls in our class, when we were in the ninth grade, had boasted that she liked nothing so much as skinny-dipping in the dam and then making love under the pines. As for myself, this was beyond me, and may be myth, but I do remember, when I was seventeen, taking a girl on one of those walks from my childhood so (then) long ago. We had moved from town, but only ten miles, and my father and I drove in to the high school every day. We walked, the girl and I, down the path where I had smashed so many branches, and sat down on a damp broad log—it was early spring, chilly, a timid froth of leaves overhead—and I dared lightly embrace her from behind and cup my hands over her breasts, small and shallow within the stiffness of her coat, and she closed her eyes and tipped her head back, and an adequate apology seemed delivered for the irritable innocence of these almost forgotten hikes with my parents.

The road that came down into Shillington by way of the cemetery led past the Dives estate, another ominous place. It was guarded by a wall topped with spiky stones. The wall must have been a half-mile long. It was so high my father had to hold me up so I could look in. There were so many buildings and greenhouses I couldn't identify the house. All the buildings were locked and boarded up; there was never anybody there. But in the summer the lawns were mowed; it seemed by ghosts. There were tennis courts, and even—can it be?—a few golf flags. In any case there was a great deal of cut lawn, and gray driveway, and ordered bushes; I got the impression of wealth as a vast brooding absence, like God Himself. The road here was especially over-shadowed by trees, so a humid, stale, cloistered smell flavored my glimpses over the wall.

The cemetery was on the side of a hill, bare to the sun, which quickly faded the little American flags and killed the potted geraniums. It was a holiday place; on Memorial Day the parade, in which the boys participated mounted on bicycles whose wheels were threaded with tricolor crêpe paper, ended here, in a picnic of speeches and bugle music and leapfrog over the tombstones. From here you had a perfect view of the town, spread out in the valley between this hill and Slate Hill, the chimneys smoking like just-snuffed cigarettes, the cars twinkling down on Lancaster Avenue, the trolleys moving with the dreamlike slow motion distance imposes.

A little to one side of the cemetery, just below the last trees of the love-making woods, was a small gravel pit where, during the war, we played at being guerrillas. Our leader was a sickly and shy boy whose mother made him wear rubbers whenever there was dew on the grass. His parents bought him a helmet and khaki jacket and even leggings, and he brought great enthusiasm to the imitation of war. G.I.'s and Japs, shouting "Geronimo!" and "Banzai!," we leaped and scrambled over boulders and cliffs in one of whose clefts I always imagined, for some reason, I was going to discover a great deal of money, in a tan cloth bag tied with a leather thong. Though I visualized the bag very clearly, I never found it.

Between this pit and the great quarry on the far edge of town, I lose track of Shillington's boundaries. I believe it was just fields, in which a few things were still farmed. The great quarry was immense, and had a cave, and an unused construction covered with fine gray dust and filled with mysterious gears, levers, scoops, and stairs. The quarry was a mile from my home; I seldom went there. It wears in memory a gritty film. The tougher section of town was nearby. Older boys with .22s used the quarry as a rifle range, and occasionally wounded each other, or smaller children. To scale its sides was even more dangerous than walking along the top of the poorhouse wall. The legends of love that scattered condums along its grassy edges seemed to be of a coarser love than that which perfumed the woods. Its cave was short, and stumpy, yet long enough to let you envision a collapse blocking the mouth of light and sealing you in; the walls were of a greasy golden clay that seemed likely to collapse. The one pure, lovely thing about the quarry, besides its grand size, was the frozen water that appeared on its floor in the winter, and where you could skate sheltered from the wind, and without the fear of drowning that haunted the other skating place, the deep dam. Though the area of ice was smaller, the skaters seemed more skillful down at the quarry: girls in red tights and bouncy short skirts that gave their fannies the effect of a pompon turned and swirled and braked backward to a stop on their points, sparkling ice chips sprinkling in twin fans of spray.

Near the quarry was the Shillington Friday Market, where the sight of so many naked vegetables depressed me, and the Wyomissing Creek, a muddy little thing to skip pebbles in, and the hilly terrain where, in those unbuilding years, a few new houses were built. The best section of town, called Lynoak, was farther on, more toward Reading, around the base of Slate Hill, where I sometimes sledded. It was a long walk back through the streets, under the cold street lights, the sled runners rattling on the frozen ruts, my calves aching with the snow that always filtered through my galoshes. This hill in summer was another place my parents hiked to. The homes of the well-off (including an amazingly modern house, of white brick, with a flat roof, and blue trim, like something assembled from the two dimensions of a Holly-wood movie) could be seen climbing its sides, but there was still plenty of room for, during the war, Victory gardens, and above that, steep wilderness. The top was a bare, windy, primeval place. Looking north, you saw the roofs of Shillington merge with the roofs of other suburbs in a torn carpet that went right into the bristling center of Reading, under the blue silhouette of Mount Penn. As Shillington on the south faced the country, northward it faced the city.

Reading: a very powerful and fragrant and obscure city—who has ever heard of it? Wallace Stevens was born there, and John Philip Sousa died there. For a generation it had a Socialist mayor. Its railroad is on the Monopoly Board. It is rumored to be endeared to gangsters, for its citizens make the most tolerant juries in the East. Unexpectedly, a pagoda overlooks it from the top of Mount Penn. This is the meagre list of its singularities as I know them. Larger than Harrisburg and Wilkes-Barre and Lancaster, it is less well known. Yet to me Reading is the master of cities, the one at the center that all others echo. How rich it smelled! Kresge's swimming in milk chocolate and violet-scented toilet water, Grant's barricaded with coconut cookies, the vast vel-veted movie theatres dusted with popcorn and a cold whiff of leather, the bakeshops exhaling hearty brown drafts of molasses and damp dough and crisp grease and hot sugar, the beauty parlors with their gingerly stink of singeing, the bookstores glistening with fresh paper and bubbles of hardened glue, the shoe-repair nooks blackened by Kiwi Wax and aromatic shavings, the public lavatory with its emphatic veil of soap, the hushed, brick-red side streets spiced with grit and the moist seeds of maples and ginkgos, the goblin stench of the trolley car that made each return to Shillington a race with nausea—Reading's smells were most of what my boyhood knew of the Great World that was suspended, at a small but sufficient distance, beyond my world.

For the city and the woods and the ominous places were

peripheral; their glamour and menace did not intrude into the sunny area where I lived, where the seasons arrived like issues of a magazine and I moved upward from grade to grade and birthday to birthday on a notched stick that itself was held perfectly steady. There was the movie house, and the playground, and the schools, and the grocery stores, and our yard, and my friends, and the horse-chestnut trees. My geography went like this: in the center of the world lay our neighborhood of Shillington. Around it there was greater Shillington, and around that, Berks County. Around Berks County there was the State of Pennsylvania, the best, the least eccentric, state in the Union. Around Pennsylvania, there was the United States, with a greater weight of people on the right and a greater weight of land on the left. For clear geometrical reasons, not all children could be born, like me, at the center of the nation. But that some children chose to be born in other countries and even continents seemed sad and fantastic. There was only one possible nation: mine. Above this vast, rectangular, slightly (the schoolteachers insisted) curved field of the blessed, there was the sky, and the flag, and, mixed up with both, Roosevelt.

Democrats

We were Democrats. My grandfather lived for ninety years, and always voted, and always voted straight Democrat. A marvellous chain of votes, as marvellous as the chain of Sunday-school-attendance pins that vibrated from Pappy Shilling's lapel. The political tradition that shaped his so incorruptible prejudice I am not historian enough to understand; it had something to do with Lincoln's determination to drive all the cattle out of this section of Pennsylvania if Lee won the Battle of Gettysburg.

My parents are closer to me. The events that shaped their views are in my bones. At the time when I was conceived and born, they felt in themselves a whole nation stunned, frightened, despairing. With Roosevelt, hope returned. This simple impression of salvation is my political inheritance. That this impression is not universally shared amazes me. It is as if there existed a class of people who deny that the sun is bright. To me as a child Republicans seemed blind dragons; their prototype was my barber—an artist, a charmer, the only man, my mother insists, who ever cut my hair properly. Nimble and bald, he used to execute little tap-dance figures on the linoleum floor of his shop, and with engaging loyalty he always had the games of Philadelphia's two eighth-place teams tuned in on the radio. But on one subject he was rabid; the last time he cut my hair he positively asserted that our President had died of syphilis. I cannot to this day hear a

Republican put forth his philosophy without hearing the snip of scissors above my ears and feeling the little ends of hair crawling across my hot face, reddened by shame and the choking pressure of the paper collar.

Now

Roosevelt was for me the cap on a steadfast world, its emblem and crown. He was always there. Now he is a weakening memory, a semi-legend; it has begun to seem fabulous—like an episode in a medieval chronicle—that the greatest nation in the world was led through the world's greatest war by a man who could not walk. Now, my barber has retired, my hair is a wretched thatch grizzled with gray, and, of the two Philadelphia ball clubs, one has left Philadelphia and one is not always in last place. Now the brick home of my boyhood is owned by a doctor, who has added an annex to the front, to contain his offices. The house was too narrow for its lot and its height; it had a pinched look from the front that used to annoy my mother. But that thin white front with its eyes of green window sash and its mouth of striped awning had been a face to me; it has vanished. My dogwood tree still stands in the side yard, taller than ever, but the walnut tree out back has been cut down. My grandparents are dead. Pappy Shilling is dead. Shilling Alley has been straightened, and hardtopped, and rechristened Brobst Street. The trolley cars no longer run. The vacant lots across the town have been filled with new houses and stores. New homes have been built far out Philadelphia Avenue and all over the poorhouse property. The poorhouse has been demolished. The poorhouse dam and its aphrodisiac groves have been trimmed into a town park and a chlorinated pool where all females must sheathe their hair in prophylactic bathing caps. If I could go again into 117 Philadelphia Avenue and look out the rear windows, I would see, beyond the football field and the cinder track, a new, two-million-dollar high school, and beyond it, where still stands one row of the double line of trees that marked the Poorhouse Lane, a gaudy depth of postwar housing and a Food Fair like a hideous ark breasting an ocean of parked cars. Here, where wheat grew, loudspeakers unremittingly vomit commercials. It has taken me the shocks of many returnings, more and more widely spaced now, to learn, what seems simple enough, that change is the order of things. The immutability, the steadfastness, of the site of my boyhood was an exceptional effect, purchased for me at unimaginable cost by the paralyzing calamity of the Depression and the heroic external effort of the Second World War.

Environment

The difference between a childhood and a boyhood must be this: our childhood is what we alone have had; our boyhood is what any boy in our environment would have had. My environment was a straight street about three city blocks long, with a slight slope that was most noticeable when you were on a bicycle. Though many of its residents commuted to Reading factories and offices, the neighborhood retained a rural flavor. Corn grew in the strip of land between the alley and the school grounds. We ourselves had a large vegetable garden, which we tended not as a hobby but in earnest, to get food to eat. We sold asparagus and eggs to our neighbors. Our peddling things humiliated me, but then I was a new generation. The bulk of the people in the neighborhood were not long off the farm. One old lady down the street, with an immense throat goiter, still wore a bonnet. The most aristocratic people in the block were the full-fashioned knitters; Reading's textile industry prospered in the Depression. I felt neither prosperous nor poor. We kept the food money in a little recipe box on top of the icebox, and there were nearly always a few bills and coins in it. My father's job paid him poorly but me well; it gave me a sense of, not prestige, but *place.* As a schoolteacher's son, I was assigned a role; people knew me. When I walked down the street to school, the houses called, "Chonny." I had a place to be.

Schools

The elementary school was a big brick cube set in a square of black surfacing chalked and painted with the diagrams and runes of children's games. Wire fences guarded the neighboring homes from the playground. Whoever, at soccer, kicked the ball over the fence into Snitzy's yard had to bring it back. It was very terrible to have to go into Snitzy's yard, but there was only one ball for each grade. Snitzy was a large dark old German who might give you the ball or lock you up in his garage, depending upon his mood. He did not move like other men; suddenly the air near your head condensed, and his heavy hands were on you.

On the way to school, walking down Lancaster Avenue, we passed Henry's, a variety store where we bought punch-out licorice belts and tablets with Edward G. Robinson and Hedy Lamarr smiling on the cover. In October, Halloween masks appeared, hung on wire clotheslines. Hanging limp, these faces of Chinamen and pirates and witches were distorted, and, thickly clustered and rustling against each other, they seemed more frightening masking empty air than they did mounted on the heads of my friends—which was frightening enough. It is strange how fear resists the attacks of reason, how you can know with absolute certainty that it is only Mark Wenrich or Jimmy Trexler whose eyes are moving so weirdly in those almond-shaped holes, and yet still be frightened. I abhorred that effect of double eyes a mask gives; it was as bad as seeing a person's mouth move upside down.

I was a Crow. That is my chief memory of what went on inside the elementary school. In music class the singers were divided into three groups: Nightingales, Robins, and Crows. From year to year the names changed. Sometimes the Crows were Parrots. When visitors from the high school, or elsewhere "outside," came to hear us sing, the Crows were taken out of the room and sent upstairs to watch with the fifth grade an educational film about salmon fishing in the Columbia River. Usually there were only two of us, me and a girl from Philadelphia Avenue whose voice was in truth very husky. I never understood why I was a Crow, though it gave me a certain derisive distinction. As I heard it, I sang rather well.

The other Crow was the first girl I kissed. I just did it, one day, walking back from school along the gutter where the water from the ice plant ran down, because somebody dared me to. And I continued to do it every day, when we reached that spot on the pavement, until a neighbor told my mother, and she, with a solemn weight that seemed unrelated to the airy act, forbade it.

I walked to school mostly with girls. It happened that the mothers of Philadelphia Avenue and, a block up, of Second Street had borne females babies in 1932. These babies now teased me, the lone boy in their pack, by singing the new song, "Oh, Johnny, oh Johnny, how you can love!" and stealing my precious rubber-lined bookbag. The queen of these girls later became the May Queen of our senior class. She had freckles and thick pigtails and green eyes and her mother made her wear high-top shoes long after the rest of us had switched to low ones. She had so much vitality that on the way back from school her nose would start bleeding for no reason. We would be walking along over the wings of the maple seeds and suddenly she would tip her head back and rest it on a wall while someone ran and soaked a handkerchief in the ice-plant water and applied it to her streaming, narrow, crimson-shining nostrils. She was a Nightingale. I loved her deeply, and ineffectually.

My love for that girl carries through all those elementary-school cloakrooms; they always smelled of wet raincoats and rubbers. That tangy, thinly resonant, lonely smell: can love have a better envelope? Everything I did in grammar school was meant to catch her attention. I had a daydream wherein the stars of the music class were asked to pick partners and she, a Nightingale, picked me, a Crow. The teacher was shocked; the class buzzed. To their amazement I sang superbly; my voice, thought to be so ugly, in duet with hers was beautiful. Still singing, we led some sort of parade.

In the world of reality, my triumph was getting her to slap me once, in the third grade. She was always slapping boys in those years; I could not quite figure out what they did. Pull her pigtails, untie her shoes, snatch at her dress, tease her (they called her "Pug")—this much I could see. But somehow there seemed to be under these offensive acts a current running the opposite way; for it was precisely the boys who behaved worst to her that she talked to solemnly at recess, and walked with after school, and whose names she wrote on the sides of her books. Without seeing this current, but deducing its presence, I tried to jump in; I entered a tussle she was having with a boy in homeroom before the bell. I pulled the bow at the back of her dress, and was slapped so hard that children at the other end of the hall heard the crack. I was overjoyed; the stain and pain on my face seemed a badge of initiation. But it was not. The distance between us remained as it was. I did not really want to tease her, I wanted to rescue her, and to be rescued by her. I lacked—and perhaps here the only child suffers a certain deprivation—that kink in the instincts on which childish courtship turns. He lacks a certain easy roughness with other children.

All the years I was at the elementary school the high school loomed large in my mind. Its students—tall, hairy, smoke-breathing—paced the streets seemingly equal with adults. I could see part of its immensity from our rear windows. It was there that my father performed his mysteries every day, striding off from breakfast, down through the grape arbor, his coat pocket bristling with defective pens. He now and then took me over there; the incorruptible smell of varnish and red sweeping wax, the size of the desks, the height of the drinking fountains, the fantastic dimensions of the combination gymnasium-auditorium made me feel that these were halls in which a race of giants had ages ago labored through lives of colossal bliss. At the end of each summer, usually on Labor Day Monday, he and I went into his classroom, Room 201, and unpacked the books and arranged the tablets and the pencils on the desks of his homeroom pupils. Sharpening forty pencils was a chore, sharing it with him a solemn pleasure. To this day I look up at my father through the cedar smell of pencil shavings. To see his key open the front portals of oak, to share alone with him for an hour the pirate hoard of uncracked books and golden pencils, to switch off the lights and leave the room and walk down the darkly lustrous perspective of the corridor and perhaps halt for a few words by an open door that revealed another teacher, like a sorcerer in his sanctum, inscribing forms beside a huge polished globe of the Earth—such territories of wonder boyhood alone can acquire.

The Playground

The periphery I have traced; the center of my boyhood held a calm collection of kind places that are almost impossible to describe, because they are so fundamental to me, they enclosed so many of my hours, that they have the neutral color of my own soul, which I have always imagined as a pale oblong just under my ribs. In the town where I now live, and where I am writing this, seagulls weep overhead on a rainy day. No seagulls found their way inland to Shillington; there were sparrows, and starlings, and cowbirds, and robins, and occasionally a buzzard floating high overhead on immobile wings like a kite on a string too high to be seen.

The playground: up from the hardball diamond, on a plateau bounded on three sides by cornfields, a pavilion contained some tables and a shed for equipment. I spent my summer weekdays there from the age when I was so small that the dust stirred by the feet of roof-ball players got into my eyes. Roof ball was the favorite game. It was played with a red rubber ball smaller than a basketball. The object was to hit it back up on the roof of the pavilion, the whole line of children in succession. Those who failed dropped out. When there was just one person left, a new game began with the cry "*Noo*-oo *gay*-ame," and we lined up in the order in which we had gone out, so that the lines began with the strongest and tallest and ended with the weakest and youngest. But there was never any doubt that everybody could play; it was perfect democracy. Often the line contained as many as thirty pairs of legs, arranged chronologically. By the time we moved away, I had become a regular front-runner; I knew how to flick the ball to give it spin, how to leap up and send the ball skimming the length of the roof edge, how to plump it with my knuckles when there was a high bounce. Somehow the game never palled. The sight of the ball bouncing along the tarpaper of the foreshortened roof was always important. Many days I was at the playground from nine o'clock, when they ran up the American flag, until four, when they called the equipment in, and played nothing else.

If you hit the ball too hard, and it went over the peak of the roof, you were out, and you had to retrieve the ball, going down a steep bank into a field where the poorhouse men had stopped planting corn because it all got mashed down. If the person ahead of you hit the ball into the air without touching the roof, or missed it entirely, you had the option of "saving," by hitting the ball onto the roof before it struck the ground; this created complex opportunities for strategy and gallantry. I would always try to save the Nightingale, for instance, and there was a girl who came from Louisiana with a French name whom everybody wanted to save. At twelve, she seemed already mature, and I can remember standing with a pack of other boys under the swings looking up at the undersides of her long tense dark-skinned legs as she kicked into the air to give herself more height, the tendons on the underside of her smooth knees jumping, her sneakered feet pointing like a ballerina's shoes.

The walls of the pavilion shed were scribbled all over with dirty drawings and words and detailed slanders on the prettier girls. After hours, when the supervisors were gone, if you were tall enough you could grab hold of a crossbeam and get on top of the shed, where there was an intimate wedge of space under the slanting roof; here no adult ever bothered to scrub away the pencillings, and the wood fairly breathed of the forbidden. The very silence of the pavilion, after the day-long click of checkers and *pokabok* of ping-pong, was like a love-choked hush.

Reality seemed more intense at the playground. There was a dust, a daring. It was a children's world; nowhere else did we gather in such numbers with so few adults over us. The playground occupied a platform of earth; we were exposed, it seems now, to the sun and sky. Looking up, one might see a buzzard or witness a portent.

. . . .

End of Boyhood

I was walking down this Philadelphia Avenue one April and was just stepping over the shallow little rain gutter in the pavement that could throw you if you were on roller skates—though it had been years since I had been on roller skates—when from the semidetached house across the street a boy broke and ran. He was the youngest of six sons. All of his brothers were in the armed services, and five blue stars hung in his home's front window. He was several years older than I, and used to annoy my grandparents by walking through our yard, down past the grape arbor, on his way to high school. Long-legged, he was now running diagonally across the high-crowned street. I was the only other person out in the air. "Chonny!" he called. I was flattered to have him, so tall and grown, speak to me. "Did you hear?"

"No. What?"

"On the radio. The President is dead."

That summer the war ended, and that fall, suddenly mobile, we moved away from the big white house. We moved on Halloween night. As the movers were fitting the last pieces of furniture, furniture that had not moved since I was born, into their truck, little figures dressed as ghosts and cats flitted in and out of the shadows of the street. A few rang our bell, and when my mother opened the door they were frightened by the empty rooms they saw behind her, and went away without begging. When the last things had been packed, and the kitchen light turned off, and the doors locked, the three of us—my grandparents were already at the new house—got into the old Buick my father had bought—in Shillington we had never had a car, for we could walk everywhere—and drove up the street, east, toward the poorhouse and beyond. Somewhat self-consciously and cruelly dramatizing my grief, for I was thirteen and beginning to be cunning, I twisted and watched our house recede through the rear window. Moonlight momentarily caught in an upper pane; then the reflection passed, and the brightest thing was the white brick wall itself. Against the broad blank part where I used to bat a tennis ball for hours at a time, the silhouette of the dogwood tree stood confused with the shapes of the other bushes in our side yard, but taller. I turned away before it would have disappeared from sight; and so it is that my shadow has always remained in one place.

WILLIAM GIBSON

William Gibson was born in New York City in 1914. To support himself during his early writing days he taught piano. He won the Harriet Monroe Prize for poetry in 1945, published the best-selling novel *The Cobweb* in 1954, and wrote the plays *Two for the Seesaw* and *The Miracle Worker*. The following selection comes from his autobiography, *A Mass for the Dead*.

The Plot Where the Garden Lived

The neighborhood to which we had gone back was a part of the city not easily come to, moated by the Harlem River along the west and unentered by the el to the east; between them it rose like some backward green garden of hills, original rocks, grass, trees, small cornfields. It was known as Highbridge, after a footbridge high over the sewery river. In its midst was a broad barren of hill, which went rollicking down to a tar road under a rank of old trees, and in their shade stood a handful of narrow wooden houses yoked together, three families high, each house with its grace note of picket fence. In one of these we had the middle floor of five rooms, and it was from this flat that my father was soon to claim at the city morgue the body of his other brother.

I had been born on this street six years before in a better tenement with steam heat, from which my mother's quest for justice had unhoused us; she was dissatisfied in the four rooms with the el, they shrank as my sister grew, and my parents were eager to move back to the old neighborhood into "any kind of a dump" with a fifth room. The postwar pinch in housing had brought my mother low, she was gratified that the landlord charged nothing to let her rehabilitate this flat with her own hands. She, my father, and his brother Will worked nights on it together, peeling off eight layers of wallpaper, scrubbing floors, patching plaster, painting; only the ceilings cowed them, so a cousin-in-law who was a fireman painted the five ceilings, earning twenty-five dollars and a familial acknowledgment from Will, who called him a "cheap sonofabitch."

Family and craft both mattered to my namesake uncle, who had little of one and a good deal of the other. Will was the child begotten a few nights before the death of his father, and not until weeks after the funeral did his mother, Katherine Gollan, widowed at twenty-three with two girls and her little hunchback, discover she was pregnant; though she swallowed irritants and jumped from the bureau to bring on a miscarriage, the boy clung to his twig of life, and would eat his portion. Helped by her mother, Katherine kept the family together, but the hunchback died, and the mother died, and Katherine then boarded the children out so she could work, the girls in one institution and Will in another. Her second marriage reunited them, and Pop Gibson taught the boy his trade of cratemaking. Will grew into an excellent cabinet-maker, and it was about the time he was reclaiming our flat that he studied with a craftsman's eye the disappearing feats of an international celebrity, Houdini, who allowed several carpenters to erect a massive box around him onstage and then materialized in the theatre aisle; Will wrote Houdini a letter promising to build him singlehandedly on any stage a box he would never get out of, meaning never, and understandably received no reply; it was a famous if somewhat unclimactic incident in the family. But the furniture Will fashioned as gifts for every relative was still in daily use half a century later, and the white table at which I ate ten thousand meals survived in my mother's kitchen after her death, unshakable as iron.

So in the new flat I think it was not his plastering but the boy that was imperfect: I soon had an excavation in a wall which was my "telephone" to a crony in the next house, and privacy was insured by a cushion. We had no other telephone, but in time several other holes, debouches for squads of cockroaches that my mother drove back with squirts of green powder and rats in for potluck whom my father pursued around the furniture with a broom, until he packed every crevice in the flat with broken glass; and one day my crony and I overturned all the rocks in the fields roundabout, loaded two cigar-boxes to the brim with petite snakes, and stored them in the earthen cellar, whence they vanished, only to reappear peeking spitefully out of rotted floorboards and riding up and down in the dumbwaiter. "Snakes now," my mother said brightly, but nervous, "rats, roaches, snakes, my goodness, this house is a regular menagerie." It had no electricity, we read by gaslight, but its chief lack was heat; with the first huff of cold weather we set out the kerosene heaters to taint the air of the flat, sealed off its front half with newspaper wads around the doors, and saw we had enlarged our lot down to three rooms. In these we huddled each winter for the next three years, burgeoning into the front rooms every spring. It was low point in the climb to our middle-class lodestar, we never again lived in so primitive or infested a house, and thirty years later my mother still spoke of "the old days in Highbridge, when we were all so happy."

The garden was not of local earth, of course, the clemency of its climate was off the flesh of my parents; some loving touch of their courtship was upon them always. Afternoons when my father left the flat for work my mother would be half out the window to watch him walk down the road to the corner rocks, where before disappearing he waved back and cried, "I, L, Y!" and she waved out and cried to him, "I, L, Y!"—their unbreakable code for the three bedrock words in the language—and the climate between them filled the block. It was more than figurative. At Christmas my father would bring home a bonus, a sum varying with the bank's profits but usually a couple of hundred dollars; he spent it to the last penny on gifts, and a generation later I was reminded by a girl who "never forgot it, there wasn't a kid on the block who didn't get a present." Children not his would run to meet him when he came home from work. In the summer nights half the block would gather under our streetlight while upstairs my father, having pushed the piano to the bay window, banged out tune after tune for the roadful to sing and dance to. The neighborhood was itself a family, a skein of friendships that tied school, church, street games, holidays, into one knot of living.

It was here my mother first led me to school by the hand, two blocks around the hilltop and across a cobblestone street, where the iron-barred yard and graystone walls engulfed me instantly in a slumber; I see no detail of three years within it except a classroom storybook and a twisted ear, two hypnotizing pities. My parents lurk in both. The twisted ear was on a boy otherwise hale and hearty whom I saw only in the schoolyard, but at each encounter I delivered to him like an automaton whatever I had on me, pennies, candies, my lunch, a little ape of my father. The fat print of the storybook told the adventures of the gingerbread boy, run, run, you can't catch me, a gleeful rebel whose tragic end, to be eaten up, was inexorable once he had run away from his matronly maker, who wished only to eat him up. I had no outer eye then for the small tyrannies of my matron, and I did her proud in school; I was twice "skipped" into higher grades of slumber.

It was a public school because my mother was convinced, by ample evidence in the Dore family, that Catholic schooling resulted in illiteracy. On weekdays she ascribed this to "too much time spent on religion," though her folk were not notable for saintliness either; on the Sabbath however she pointed me forth through hailstorms to nine o'clock mass and Sundayschool. Here with gummy eye I sat in a candle-lit dungeon through years of total gibberish. The priest wandered before the altar muttering in Latin to himself, now and then turning to lift a bored hand in blessing, and at long last ascended the pulpit to announce in unmistakable English that my stingy offerings had caused a shortage of coal in the church; two altarboys in skirts rang bells, genuflected, and decanted wine for the priest, a pair of angels, tarnished only by my knowing I would soon be shooting immies with them and hearing of their struggle to free the decanter from the priest's inebriated clutch; I sat, stood, knelt each time enough of the congregation sat, stood, knelt, all of us erratic and at the mercy of some confident soul in the front pew, until that late moment when it was not quite sinful to leave—perceived by all with infallible unison—and whatever prayers remained were drowned out by hundreds of hasty feet, mine among the first. The interlude of fact in the daylight was shortlived. A herd of children soon trudged up the cobbled alley that led to the Sundayschool shed of corrugated tin that sat dark green on the rocks above our backyard; inside a multitude of folding wooden chairs was grouped for buttocks according to age, but even the youngest now much the worse for wear, under the tutelage of unmarried ladies of the parish with no duties in their kitchens; they drilled us for another hour in our catechism, and rewarded the diligent with picturecards of the saints in sepia. The hailstorms were real enough, cackling on the tin overhead, and it seemed a fit setting for the odd chant with which we concluded, "Hail, Mary, full of grapes"; it was the grapes that seemed irrelevant.

Every seventh day my head was stuffed to the ears with this quaint cosmology, and my mother was happy. Its reward was not in the hereafter, but in the here: I was at one in tedium with the neighborhood gang, all named Murphy and O'Brien, and every grown-up I knew on our block I saw in the church, except my mother and father. Home at last, I would find them still living in sin, with my sister at her doll cut-outs, my father at ease behind the sports page in his pajama tops and the pants he had worn downstairs to buy the newspaper, while my mother in a crisp housedress darted about the kitchen in the midst of the roast with four vegetables which was her Sunday act of devotion. And instantly I was on my belly with the gaudy funny-pages, for my delight in which that particular newspaper was chosen by my father, and I would inveigle him into joining heads with me over the "red magic"—tricks with matchsticks and cards and tumblers of water, all printed in diabolic red—which never quite worked, but cleared my brain of other devils until the next Sunday.

My father's indifference to the deity was a male prerogative in his family; the womenfolk were all strict churchgoers, but Pop Gibson had preferred saloons. And Will in his youth was "full of fun" with his pious sisters. Much embarrassed by their stepfather, they were dismayed one night to overhear Will stagger in muttering to himself, and spied upon him trying to hang his clothes on a non-existent nail in the wall; after he was snoring Milly stole in to smell his breath, but in the dark her nose inhaled only his whisper of glee, "Go to bed, you nut." Ada's churchgoing was a profession, which presently took her off to Africa as a missionary, and always she sat discoursing of the word in a rapture, with gestures; when Will put a book in her hand it would end unnoticed in her lap, and she preached on while Will in passing handed her a towel, a sewing basket, a pipe and pouch, a shoe, until coming out of her sermon with a broom in her glorifying hands, her broad lap brimful of junk, Ada cried in exasperation, "Will, you fool!" At his jauntiest twenty my father was the recipient of a Bible inscribed to *George Irv Gibson from Sister Ada,* not with love, only an admonitory *John 3–16* if he wished not to perish, but he steered a steady course between church and saloon behind the Sunday sports page. The one time I provoked him to a statement of faith was on the question of where all our rats came from; I said they came "from the Protestant church" on the hill, and he said irritatedly, "What's Protestant got to do with it? I'm a Protestant myself!"

In fact the Catholic church was nearer, its green shed almost touchable from our kitchen window, and much in our family life was implicated with it. Once a year the tin hall blossomed into a weeklong bazaar, whereby the church augmented its coalpile. Here, at a booth with a variety of prizes and a wheel of chance, my sister fell in love with a china doll as big as herself; it was not for sale, but all that week my father led us up the path among the rocks to the shed, where night after night he played against the wheel for the doll and never won, dollar after dollar coming out of his pocket, the week dwindling, the coalpile growing, the doll paid for several times over out of my father's three-o'clock-in-the-morning labors; on the last night he put his money down until they dismantled the booth, and then sought out the priest, laid upon him the tale of his tot's love, waited while the arrangements committee dug among invoices for the cost of the doll, paid it, and brought the doll home to my sister. The day came when she dropped it, and half the night lay moaning—"Daddy: I broke my dollie, Daddy: I broke my dollie: Daddy, I broke my dollie"—while my parents in their bed listened in that grief for a child's grief which the child cannot suspect; love like water tumbles downhill between generations.

It was this tin hall which also bred the minstrel show, a yearly venture by parishioners, at which my father played piano for any neighbor with a voice or a delusion. When my sister was a plump four my parents rehearsed her in the words and gestures of a song about a little red schoolhouse, my mother attired her in a brief red frock and hair ribbon, and with my father at the piano our sprite topped the show; I had promised her a dime if she sang without mistakes, but on our arrival home I presented her with my entire bank, and was also applauded. My parents had made a point subtler than they knew, that generosity was the gayest conqueror of envy. And it was from this tin shed that I took home as a Sundayschool prize the first book I owned, its jacket overcome by a young daredevil in goggles riding a motor-cycle straight at me; I thought it a dud of a prize, books having no value in our house, but I gave the motorcycle a try and on it rode into all literature, and out of my family's arms.

But most haunting was a summer afternoon, queer as a twisted mirror, in the parish house. It was a weekday tea of the Sundayschool teachers, with my mother and me prim in our good clothes, and hovering at a piano a favorite male countenance, my uncle Will, out of work for reasons of health and brought along because he had dropped in on us in the midst of a lonely walk. A fine tenor, he seated one of the teachers at the keyboard and entertained the tea party with a ballad, which all the ladies enjoyed, so he sang another, his eyes closed in his good face with its pitted chin and boyish spill of gray hair, and all praised his third song, so he sang a fifth, and the ladies were more than satisfied, so he sang a seventh, and his grim hand would not let the lady pianist escape, and they rollicked into a ninth, and the tea broke up in a scurry of purse gathering and bobs of terrified hats with Will chanting at the top of his voice and "talking queer"; and my mother, though mortified, waited to guide him home. This was the summer I first spied the snake in the garden—when on my belly beneath a communal oak I feasted upon a bared inch of knee, the property of an adolescent girl who sat above me in a nest of baby carriages and mothers, and I lay all the idle afternoon adoring it, bland under my mother's distrustful eye—and unknown to me its venom was then writhing in the limbs of my uncle, forking into his skull.

In happier days he and his wife would stand singing to my father's jangbangling piano, two of the dozens of relatives, friends, neighbors who "loved to visit," as one recalled, because my parents were "so cheerful." My mother had a gift for hospitality which was radiantly semisuicidal. She had entered upon marriage able to cook only toast—which went unnoticed for a while, since my father's invariable meal was a charred slab of round steak—and the first dinner they gave saw her in a panic in the kitchen, beset by mutinous potfuls of unknown matter, until one husband venturing in hastily donned an apron, asked only that she "keep the guys out of here," and subdued the entire meal for her. But panic was an old acquaintance, the motor of my mother's soul, and her genius was for turning it into useful activity; she soon became an extraordinary housekeeper, studying the households of my father's sisters, and so outdoing them that he said teasingly he expected her next to "wash the coal before using it." It was literally so that visitors could have dined off her kitchen floor, and their numbers made it imminent, anyone dropping in at once found himself captive at the table to too much good food, and Sunday nights were festive with gossip and music in a resurrection of Mary Dore's parties, with ten or twelve in for an improvised supper. The wives helped clean up and put away the dishes, each couple left the flat feeling like the choice light of our world, and my mother and father sat in exhaustion, pondering how to keep from being eaten out of house and home.

All dead, the faces of those grown-ups return to me quite unlike ghosts, laughing and boisterous, full of news of my parents, but under the fixative of time, deaf to my questions. The neighbors ambled in from upstairs, downstairs, adjoining houses—lettercarrier, printer, el gateman, each with his missus—into friendships that were joined for life; their aging faces reappeared at my father's wake. Other friends were inseparables out of his youth, my mock uncles and aunts, all with their troubles. The most successful was a man who had entered the postoffice with my father a dozen years earlier; authoritative as a hammer, he rose in his official career to the postmastership of the city, but his unofficial career was wandering indecisively with his household from neighborhood to neighborhood, some thirty moves in a decade; his wife was so sickly my mother would routinely visit her to do her housework. Two of my father's buddies were musicmakers like him, a pair of bricklayers, one a dapper johnny with fingers so nimble on the keyboard my father acknowledged him as "a star," the other a giant with a baritone roar that he loosed at the ceiling, one hand cupped for amplification behind his ear; in picnic snapshots the three stand with interlocked arms, their straw-hatted faces majestic with cigars, captioned by my father as "we smoke but we don't buy," and again with their young wives, six grinning heads together, "married but happy"; one buried his wife and took to drink, the other lost his life-savings in a lapidary shop he bought into a day before the great depression. My mother's own pal from schooldays—"my oldest and dearest friend, Nelie"—was a placid spinster in an auburn wig worn since a childhood fever, who dwelt at her elbow, loyalty incarnate, and outlived her like a severed shadow. I brought her my questions, but in old age she had no memories other than my mother's, eerily echoed in my mother's very words, so vicarious her life; she summoned up the young Flo as vaguely—though emphatically—"lovely, like she always was"; then I asked if among the seventeen brothers she had any recollection of Alfred, dead at twenty-six, dead for more than half a century, and she said, "I was engaged to Alfred." Others from the old postoffice gang straggled into the flat, on shore leave from the navy or back from drifting in the west, wistful fellows who had also missed the turn into family life. And we had a breadline of unmarried clerks from the bank, the most memorable of them a piano-playing cockney, a tippler who composed hundreds of popular songs, though not popular enough; he spent much of his week at the heels of music publishers and songpluggers, his life going to seed for the "break" that was never to come, while over the years he appeared with each fresh manuscript to sing it at our piano for his only public, my father, who admired him. My mother admired his accent, she thought it English and refined. My parents' capacity for friendliness was exhausted only by one avuncular character who, together with his wife, was banished from our flat. A curly-haired runt with a missing finger, he was an heirloom from my father's bachelor days and that rarest of souls, a person my mother disliked, though he was widely travelled, shipping out as a strikebreaker to scattered cities, and clever, talking compensation boards out of sum after sum for his finger lost in honest labor ten different times, and devoted as a tick to my father, who in periods between strikes and prestidigital amputations kept him in handouts; my mother tolerated him for the sake of his wife, a fruity woman, childless, who was genuinely fond of my sister and me and often cared for us when my mother was sick in bed, at which times the household money, in saucer and pennybank, showed an odd tendency to evaporate. But it was not until the winter that Will's widow after one gathering reclaimed her purse from the bedroom where coats were heaped and missed sixty dollars out of it that heads were put together, and tales, of other shortages graced by the presence of the couple. My father that week led a few complainants to a shabby flat in Harlem, where his unemployed pal, coming home warm at last in a new overcoat, and his wife, pale in the cheer of a new floorlamp, said their purchases were nobody's business; and my father invited them not to visit us again.

Thirty years later the woman, dying in a county hospital where a cousin of ours worked, still asked how my sister and I had fared. Dead with her, all dead, that phantasmagoria of grown-ups whom I could not wait to be like, rich, wise, lucky, they seem so to me yet; they lie coffined in possession of a treasure I can never come by, in their earfuls of the small talk of my parents, and their eyefuls of those two ordinary faces in the years when I was too busy with my tops and marbles to look at them.

Yet even around our street games the figures of all the parents, looked at or not, lent a benevolence to the neighborhood. Its heart was the hill, and our games came up with its seasonal changes from outbreak of weed grass to burial drifts of snow; but it was one changeless flock of families upon the hillside in summer and winter, and time hardly moved, the children grew no older, the parents were as durable as the big trees of the street.

In spring, when we were digging dirtholes with our heels for immies—marbles, imitations—our fathers were in view digging with spades, until the field next to the end house was a crazy quilt of little vegetable gardens; here in the evenings the grown-ups would cluster in twos and threes, the mothers in aprons talking, the men on their knees in old pants coaxing along their tomatoes and stringbeans. In the untended afternoons these garden squares, staked and roped off, made ideal sites for their sons to stage mock prizefights in, a sport which resulted in some baffling crop failures. The true sport was baseball on the plateau of our hill, a trodden diamond in the rough, alive all day with a scatter of players, the gang I was in and the teen-age giants who chased us off and after supper the young fathers in collarless shirts, home from the bondage of offices. At a bottom corner of the hill was a dell with the communal oak, where in late spring the "strawberry festival" with its free ice cream was sponsored by our wardheelers for a pandemonium of neighborhood children and our mothers, who had recently received the vote; their purity was expected to redeem the world, a hope which was not quite realized, it succumbed under my eyes to free strawberry ice cream.

Summer opened officially the day my mother let me out barefoot —my soles gingerly among the fallen catkins of the poplars, so like the caterpillars of her terror—and was a long contentment of dirty toes. Out of our parents' eyes we cavorted on imaginary steeds over the hillside, vying in death leaps from its ledgerocks, elevation three feet; we bellycrawled to its far side in high weeds, to spy on the walrus-faced caretaker of the Protestant church, and sprang in the air with cries of "Kaiser Bill! Kaiser Bill!" until in frenzy he lumbered after us halfway down to our road; we scavenged for the stubs of holy candles dumped back of the true church, and bore them away to the hut of slats and cardboard which was our unfinished lifework; we watched the iceman stagger under his load into our cellars, and then clambered over his horse-drawn wagon to pilfer ice for sucking, cautious not to swallow the cloudy "pneumonia" it was made with; we trekked down to the sunken Harlem, and watched the older boys dive bare-assed among a drift of feces and mystifying number of white balloons, and charged up to the footbridge above, climbing outside its iron railings to execute skips which, elevation one hundred feet, would have given my mother a heart attack to witness; we knuckled our immies along miles of gutter, and gambled on curbstone and stoop with picturecards of leaping ballplayers and menacing prizefighters that came one with each penny's worth of gum; and gum lacking, we waited by the fire barrel of the roadworkers and chewed the ebony nuggets of tar leavings, which were "good for" the teeth they did not pull out. And under my father's eye I feasted on hot dogs and sodapop in the grandstand at the big-league ballgames he took me to. Once he instructed me to "never forget" I had seen a no-hitter, so I never did, and another time at the players' gate I shook hands with a second baseman beloved by him for sliding into base head first, a practice I thereafter followed, luckily without serious brain damage, and one dawn we stood together in line for half the day to get into a World Series game, which canonized me in the gang.

But that was in autumn, when my mother had shod me again for school. To the sill outside our kitchen window my father now wired the orange crate that was to be our winter icebox, and my mother encased it prettily in figured oilcloth, which would keep the snow out. All along the block the front rooms were abandoned, and children slept in kitchens, dining rooms, parental beds. Up from the cellar bin came our kerosene heaters, stovepipes on squat legs, glowing in the dark with sizzly pans of water set on top to replenish the oxygen; and when in the morning I scrambled from the sofa I found my schoolclothes on a chair at the lively coalstove in the kitchen, hung there by my mother to make them inhabitable.

It was the season for fire. On the hill each night the kids with permission to "sneak out" congregated at cookfires of scrap boards borrowed from buildings in construction, and crammed a few brands into tin cans punched with nail holes and reined with wire, to whip them round and round as personal ovens. In them we roasted mickies —potatoes, stolen on the gallop past the sidewalk displays of grocery stores—until they were as inedible as charcoal, when we ate them. Potato thieving was only an exercise of neighborly rights, but one night I and another fire worshipper climbed a fence into a "dago" contractor's backyard, toted bundle after bundle of his laths over the hill, and cooked our two mickies in a ten-foot conflagration of the neatest firewood ever. The irate contractor next day tracked our fathers down; mine, the other being needier, paid for all the laths, and punished me only by convoying me to apologize to the foreigner and advising me next time to "use my head," at which I felt more stupid than piratical. And each fall there was a towering bonfire which belonged to the grown-ups. For a week the neighborhood contributed to it, piling on the hillside the unwanted articles from every household, bundles of newspapers, cartons and crates, seatless chairs, wobbly tables and bureaus, disgraceful mattresses, until on Election Day night two or three of the fathers climbing over the edifice sprinkled it with kerosene; when they touched a match to it, every family on the block was present to cheer this gotterdammerung in honor of our brand-new leaders with the same old strawberry ice cream.

Winter came with the first snow in the night that stuck—the trolley cars stuck on the bridges with it, and in one blizzard my father labored home with me in his arms for better than an hour—until in the sunlit morning the hill was transubstantiated. It was heaven, a whiteness of packed slope trafficked by hollering boys, girls, young parents, and a host of sleds tugged by figures uphill, tots on wee sleds inching down, youngsters streaking past on slim racers, big sleds loaded with families spilling into the road, and battles of snowballs flying between the igloo forts. Here I charged with my racer in a bellywhopping delight while below a moving-van rolled toward us, and I shot out into the white road; a fingersnap earlier and my sled would have been under its doublewheel, but I struck the tire and was thrown back into my life, and tugged my sled uphill again into a company of merrymakers intact in our magic skins.

And the earth emerged as always, into Easter; another year of holidays was begun. Holidays were the hinges of the seasons, remote from their origins, and Easter signified only the terminus of the six-week lenten fast during which, for some adult kink of reason, we had survived without candy. It collapsed in an orgy of jellybeans and chocolate bunnies, hidden by my mother in odd nooks of the flat, where after church my sister and I hunted them out; they baptized gummily the pockets of our new "good" apparel, good for nothing but to stand around in on our sidewalk all the holy afternoon like awkward manikins in a storewindow, stuffed with jellybeans.

The holy day of summer was the Fourth of July. Miniature explosives had been accumulating throughout the week in every household, but none to equal ours; my father would bear home from a store downtown some twenty or twenty-five dollars' worth, half a week's pay, which bought a great deal of noise. It took me from breakfast to dusk, and fifty trips up and down our stairs after fresh pocketfuls, to exhaust this arsenal. There were baby firecrackers, wads of a hundred fused together, which were detached and lit singly by me, though in a royal gesture my father would set a wad off in one wild spitting mass; and torpedoes, which exploded when hurled onto the sidewalk, preferably at somebody's heel; and pellets called snakes, which if touched with a match gave birth to a writhing gray serpent that strove along the ground and perished at last in a crumble of ash; and sulfuric patties which were ground underheel till they crackled away to a smoking scab; and the larger firecrackers, the two-inchers I lit with my stick of punk and fled from, and the six-inchers I was not allowed to play with alone, but watched my father ignite under tin cans, which flew up over our heads; and pinwheels, nailed to a tree in twilight to whiz their colorful life away, and sparklers, the dipped wires that hissed a thousand white sparks, desirable only after dark came to the hill; and into the night my father launched our showering rocket, price one dollar, the climax of the day. Only our sparklers then, glittering in all hands, were left to star the hillside with constellations of families, until at the last quarter-inch we slung them skywards to die out like falling souls.

Autumn came with two holidays, minor and major. Though decorum was her staff, my mother was a gay participant in disorder that was institutional, and on Halloween she prepared for my sister and me the socks full of flour with which the neighborhood smallfry belabored one another, until by suppertime we ourselves looked ready for the oven; and in the evening her laugh shrilled like a bird above the shenanigans in our flat, where neighbors and their offspring joined us with hands behind backs to tongue pennies out of her platterfuls of flour, spewing, and over a washtub we stalked with dribbling noses the apples my father had turned into treasure islands, tipsy with buried silver. And on Thanksgiving Day it was my mother who with a burnt bottlecork dirtied up my sister's face and mine, and sent us downstairs in rags. Our lives that day were inverted like the jackets we wore inside out, whites turned black, boys in their mothers' skirts and girls in their fathers' pants, cherubs in false-faces with depraved noses, and all, in a travesty of that poverty our families were two jumps ahead of, begging alms, swarming in threes and fours like a plague of mad dwarfs through the houses to every doorbell—"Anything for Thanksgiving, mister?" —and choiring in the courtyards until the coins in newspaper twists came plummeting through the clotheslines, and voices pled with us to sing no more. Late in the day my sister and I would straggle home, our pockets burdened down with the neighbors' fruit, candies, and loose change, to find my father at the door handing out to the neighbors' kids a countersupply of fruit, candies, and loose change, the flat made aromatic by the pipe of my uncle Will and genial with other relatives, my mother in command of too many cooks in the kitchen, and her silverware impeccably laid out for the turkey dinner all had come to share.

And at last the earth turned toward the holiday for which the year existed. The month that intervened was somehow lived through, with its character-building threats in Santa's name, its letters mailed confidently to the North Pole, its visits to the lanky geezers with slack beards in department stores and my suspicion that something was much amiss, perhaps with my mother's eyes; and one evening my father took us all to pick our Christmas tree out of the mass on a sidewalk rope at the grocery. I helped him lug it home, and it slept that week on our fire escape. It was not set up till the night before Christmas, after my sister and I were tucked in but hardly asleep, and that Santa himself ornamented it was the first fact to crumble, for we could hear our parents long at it in the frigid parlor, wrapped in their overcoats, hissing instructions at each other. Quiet then took over the darkened flat, and my sister and I lay awake with all our senses alert for Santa's entry through our coalstove. It was an endless night, when every rat scratching in the walls promised to be him, and we started up fearful that we had missed him or he us, calling was it time to get up, and our parents fumbling for the alarm clock groaned it was two o'clock, go back to sleep, and so with every half-hour as the night wore miserably on; and before dawn they staggered out of bed, my father to light the gas mantles and plant a kerosene heater in the parlor, my mother to bundle us up in sweaters and bathrobes and bring hot cocoa to us all where, in a tiny cheap cold room, we sat again under the tree of paradise. It was broken out in a winter bloom of jubilant fruits, angels, birds, stars, and around the cotton snowscape under its branches all the floor was a windfall of riches that dizzied our eyes, the big gifts standing bare amid a mob of brilliant packages that we tore apart, crawling and yelping and backtracking from tricycle to doll carriage, from trains to scooter, from baseball mitt and toy house to sewing machine and soldiers, to sled, to dolls, to trucks, to games, to books, all of my father's bonus lavished in an unthinking lesson that, in its wink of light, the time of man was a horn of plenty.

But in the new year the tree was stripped of its miracle. My father forced it out the bay window to drop into the tiny snowyard, and I dragged it across the road to the hill, where in time some hand set fire to it; half out of the snow, its charred skeleton pointed to something. High above it the misshapen snowman with coal hunks for eyes saw nothing of his drippage in the raids of the sun, time and the hill melting away. For now, like the clock that ticked in the night at my parents' skulls, the charm was running down; in the new year my uncle Will lay dying, and I was sprouting into myself.

It was evident the summer I pondered not only a girl's knee, but two lessons about money. I sold a half-dollar's worth of my fireworks to another boy for a penny or two, and sat on the curbstone happy with myself as an enterprising fellow; my father said nothing, but when my mother told me how I had hurt his feelings an utter desolation overtook me, I was an eight-year-old miser, I had violated his work, his code, his love, and that two-cent transaction would always seem one of the worst mistakes of my life. My father observed that when he was dead they might say he "spent a lot of money, but he had a heck of a good time," and the pursuit of this ideal took me into the second lesson. When his own uncle slipped a dollar into my palm I treated myself to some penny candy, and, with a vision of buying up the world, hid my handful of change on the darksome sill of a window high in our hallway which let neither light nor air into our bathroom; I had to leap to it from the banister, it was out of reach of all normal life, but my mother was led by her angel of cleanliness even to that altitude, with chair and dustrag, to discover my crime; and my vision and coins ended up permanently out of reach in my piggybank. The first lesson taught me not to live for money, and the second to put it in a safer hiding-place.

The crime was secretiveness. It is the first evidence I see that I was finding my mother's hand steely upon me; in my father's laxities of live and let live the chores of disciplining us fell to her, though in any circumstances she could not but invite them; matter not in her control made her nervous. It was by reflex that, when my sister in her baby carriage had bitten somebody's finger, my mother bit hers back. I came home sooty-faced from a mickie roast on the hill and my father said I "looked like a real boy," but my mother flew for the soap, her amulet against the devil. One afternoon a pubescent boy from upstairs backed me against our picket fence and fed me nonsense syllables; he said, "Say shit," and I obliged, and he said, "Say fuck," and I obliged, and he then stopped in to tell my mother the words his devout ear had been shocked to hear me utter; that evening I came home for supper and found my mouth being scrubbed out with soap instead, frothing with human justice. Much of my mother's energy was devoted to contesting nature on the battlefield of my scalp. My hair grew forward, but she soused and combed it back in a pompadour which, though it brought out a certain bulgy-browed idiocy in her child, she was fond of and determined to "train it" to; for years her hands drove at it pistonlike, with water, brushes, vaseline, combs, lard, nightcaps, until when I was graduated from elementary school not a hair in that pompadour was rebellious; she could not see my soul.

It sprouted, though the days in the garden were growing chill; it was that autumn my father's brother disappeared. Much of Will—his humor, his skill with his hands—had in any case been fading into his past, and his renewal in the flesh of four children had disappeared more than a decade before. The twins his wife conceived first had died in the womb, and were removed surgically; in her second pregnancy she bore a daughter who a few hours later died; the following year she gave Will a son, christened after him, and in his fifth autumn the boy died of a brain infection. It was not mischance, the children could not survive the inheritance of the syphilis that commingled in their parents' flesh.

When it was contracted, nobody knew. But Will was little more than twenty when he began marriage, on his fourteen dollars a week in that room furnished with hope, and before he was thirty the four children were dead. Much later the surgeon who excised the twins told Will's mother the disease was "of long standing" in the girl, but misdoer or dupe, it hardly mattered, two creatures were caught in the coils of the snake, and wherever his finger of lust had appointed him, to whorehouse or peccant bride, Will held his tongue; though he and his wife were to separate more than once, he "never said a word against her." Will was something of the family intellectual, a voting socialist, reading man, owner of a few operatic records. His tenor joined with my father's piano at many a church or bank supper, and the two half-brothers were "very close"; the married sisters had moved out into New Jersey towns, taking the old folks along, and with only the brothers left in the Bronx our flat often echoed with my uncle's voice. The lonely walk that brought him to our door the afternoon of the parish-house tea was not unusual, after a quarrel at home, but his breakup of the tea was the flare of disaster: the illness exploded in him that summer.

Taken in by his mother and half-sister Ethel in Jersey, he found work as a carpenter on rooftops. The sun beating on his head was "the worst thing for him," he was moody and would not join company at the table, but chiefly his head was "burning," and he bent by the quarter-hour soaking it under the coldwater tap; when the fright of an imminent "spell" was on him he would ask his mother to pray with him, and they knelt in a locked bedroom together, my whitehaired grandmother of sixty-five and her son with the boyish spill of gray hair, praying for the help that could not stay the microscopic worms now festive in the brain. Its signallings were awry, he "made the screens wrong" that he planned as a gift for Ethel's new house, and they were left unfinished. One autumnal morning he climbed down from his roof, and at noon turned up at his flat in the Bronx looking for his wife, who was not at home, and he distractedly made his way on foot north to Mt. Vernon, where he arrived by evening at the house of an uncle dishevelled and wild with inarticulate talk "about everybody, not like him"; the next day he was taken in custody to the penal hospital in the East River then known as Blackwells Island.

My father visiting him there would come home shaken with the sight of his brother in a straitjacket. It was not long since I had bought myself a pencilbox for school, my father with one glance at its underside said, "There'll be nothing in this house made in Germany," and escorted me and it down to the store to get my money back; now the death of a brother was in his nostrils again. He was ravaged by the bruises he saw on Will's face, which the burly guards blamed on falls, but in our kitchen my father demanded of my mother, "Why did he flinch? He flinched from me!" All winter in the violent ward Will lay in the bonds of worse than death, but before the first leaf of spring he was unsouled of that straitjacket of flesh, his lungs filled with pneumonia and he died. His body, delivered to the city morgue, was spoken for by my father and removed to a mortuary in Harlem; in a coffin it reposed in familiar clothes again and a new necktie of dark blue with white dots, his favorite pattern; my father had hunted the city for it, and said to a sister, "I bought the tie, and I tied it on him." The body was buried in a grave with the children, the one-day-old girl, the five-year-old boy, the forty-two-year-old man.

So went out that light, unwanted in birth and in death, the boy who never knew his father's face, grew in no garden, and for half his years had lived with the taste of himself as his children's killer. His sister Milly was haunted by one memory of him, peering from behind a fence along the road on which she and Ada, eleven and nine, trotted from school to lunch at the home where they were boarded out; the fence was around the other institution that held Will, then four, and each noontime without fail the diminutive boy was there, waiting in silence, his face between the white slats, to see his sisters come and go; that face through the fence peered after her for seventy-five years.

In the summer after his death we moved out of the flat that his hands had helped make livable. My mother's goiter again was thickening in her throat, the doctor told my father she must have rest, and the throngs of company that dropped in for a cheerful evening with my parents drove us half into bankruptcy and altogether out of the state; we followed the van filled with our furniture across the river into Jersey. We were the last of the family to leave the Bronx, and though we were to come back to it, my childhood was no longer there.

We could not find the garden again. In better neighborhoods our life was enriched by radiators, electricity, radio, telephone, refrigerator, car: but we had no hill. And of all the sounds in the world, none was to fill any other room so plangently as the music I ignored in that parlor, evenings, when I lay on the floor teaching my sister the rules of parchesi, at which she cheated, while my mother in the scrollwork chair with her mandolin and my father in his collarless shirt at the piano, both playing, gaily sang out "their" song of first encounter, "Oh by the Golden Gate, that's where I first met Kate, she stole my heart away: on San Francisco, oh you Frisco, San Francisco Baaay—" Even in manhood, when I stood again before the house and saw it ugly, cramped, defeated, and the rollicking green country gone, carted away with the poplars and the hill, and everything around me bronxed over with cement sidewalks and brick apartment houses, it could not touch my image of a half-wild garden in which I still spied the bay-window house as it was, the bellybutton of a world to come, and its tar road under a hanging mercy of trees, and its hill populous with knots of kids and parents, seated, standing, in the calm of the summer evenings: we were happy as the day was long.

That time, that neighborhood, thousands of miles ago and thirty-odd years behind me, scattered with its folk, was to live only in me, a green haven I could never find my way home to, until by the grace which is in our bowels I crossed a threshold, in the night around me all the house again was safe, and slept, and checking the beds of my unwitting boys I perceived I was back in the garden.

MARY ELLEN CHASE

Mary Ellen Chase was born in 1887 in Blue Hill, Maine, one of eight children. She attended Blue Hill Academy, graduated from the University of Maine in 1909, and received her Ph.D. from the University of Minnesota. She has taught at the University of Minnesota and at Smith College. She inherits the regional tradition of Sarah Orne Jewett, evident in her best-known novel, *Mary Peters*. The following selections come from *The White Gate* and *A Goodly Heritage*, vividly recalled stories of her Maine childhood.

The White Gate

Many years ago, when I was a child in Maine, our large and rambling white house was surrounded by a long white picket fence, which enclosed our apple orchard on one side and, on the other, set us apart from the field and apple orchard of our next-door neighbor. At the entrance to our driveway the fence was broken by a white gate, which swung inward or outward as necessary to allow for our comings-in or goings-out. The pickets of this gate were nailed firmly to sturdy cross-timbers, the lower one wide enough for us children to stand on, the upper one just high enough for our elbows or our fingers, depending on our ages. On either side stood a stout white post, that on the right holding the hinges of the gate and that on the left, its strong iron hook.

The most clear and lasting impressions of my childhood are related to this gate, which both sheltered and extended the small, tight world in which we lived. Behind it, our driveway moved past our house and toward the barn, also large and white, filled with the smells of hay and of kindly animals in their stalls and with the sound of pigeons, which swept in blue and white flocks to and from their dovecote high in the loft. Before it lay the country road, which ran downhill toward the village and the sea and uphill toward the sky. Dusty in the summer, muddy in the spring rains, cut into frozen ruts in the late autumn, and buried beneath snow in the winter, this road was, to me as a child standing on the white gate, next to the weather the most thrilling thing I knew.

If I looked behind me, there was the sureness of my home, a safety which lay warm and comfortable somewhere deep inside my pinafore. There was my bed with its bright patchwork quilts; there were my first books, my doll, my mother and father, my amusing grandmother, the warm kitchen with its black cookstove, the fire in the library, mugs of milk, and lamplight against the shadowy corners of our big rooms. But if I stared before me, beyond the pickets of the white gate, what excitement might not be coming or going along that road between the sky and the sea?

Tim Finn, the blind man, might suddenly cut the bright space between the hilltop and the sky and come down the road, tap-tap-tapping with his stick, which told him where the road gave way to the deep ditch on either side. He was coming for his mail, which someone else must read for him, and for his food at the store, which somehow, my mother said, he could cook himself, though he could not see either the food or his pots and pans.

"Be polite to him," my father said. "Were it not for the Grace of God, you might be blind yourselves."

But in spite of the Grace of God, which we did not at all understand, we were frightened of Tim Finn, especially of the black patch which he wore over his eyes and which made my brother Edward think darkly of pirates.

"Hush!" Edward would whisper from his place on the gate when the tapping came closer and the black patch was more clearly visible. "Be still. He can't see us, remember!"

Tim Finn usually tapped his way past us as we perched on the gate, red-cheeked and breathless from fear; but on one awful morning he stopped in front of us all. He raised his stick high in the air. He said: "Do I, or do I not, smell the four Chase children on that gate?"

My sister Mildred, who was eleven when I was nine, was the only one of us who behaved well under these terrifying circumstances. She remained on the gate while my sister Edith, who was eight, and Edward, who was five, and I ran for the orchard and began to clamber each into an apple tree. She remembered even at that moment what she had often been told—that she, being the eldest, was *responsible* for the rest of us.

"Good morning, Mr. Tim Finn," she said politely, though her voice was small and weak. "Can we do anything for you?"

"No, my dear," said Tim Finn, beginning to tap the road again with his stick, "though I thank you kindly. There's nothing anyone can do for me but to pray that some day I'll see Our Lord face to face, for once He made the blind to see."

Edith, Edward, and I were too far up our trees at this moment to hear Tim Finn's odd request, but Mildred repeated it to us when we had at last come down and were on the gate once more. Before she told it, she exacted the promise of a penny from each of us (once each should have one to give to her) in return for *her* promise not to tell our mother of our rudeness. We were all puzzled by what the blind man had asked, for although we said our prayers every night, we were not used to people who spoke so openly about either prayers or Our Lord. Later on, after we had turned our pennies over to her and she had kept her promise, she asked our father about what Tim Finn had said. He explained that Tim Finn was an Irishman who had wandered into our village from God knew where in the days when he was not quite blind, and that he belonged to a church which was different from our own and used far different language. After that, I prayed for Tim Finn now and then, though I did not tell anyone, and I lost my fear of him, his black patch, and his tapping stick. Edward still believed him a pirate, whose eyes had been put out by his fellow pirates because he had discovered more gold than they on a desert island; and he also got the odd notion into his head that all Irishmen were pirates, though such a silly fancy was in no way my father's fault.

But Tim Finn was by no means the only source of excitement on our country road. Peddlers might and, indeed, did come down the hill once the road was dried of spring mud—dark women in queer, bright clothes with gold rings in their ears, who carried on their hips great oilcloth bags stuffed with household wares, trinkets, laces, shawls, and odd toys. These women came from far-off countries, Syria or Armenia, my father said, and we must always be kind to them as they were *footsore and weary* and *strangers in a strange land.* It was not difficult to be kind to them as we were rarely the losers by such behavior.

In early summer when school was over, the organ-grinder came either down the hill or up from the village. His name was Lorenzo. He said he had no other name. He ground out quick and merry tunes from his faded green organ, which he carried strapped around his shoulders, and introduced us quite formally each year to his monkey, Jock, who wore a green suit and a red hat with a green feather and shook hands with us all. My mother invited Lorenzo to come through the gate into the driveway, whereupon all the neighborhood children came running in from the board sidewalk outside our fence to dance in squealing circles through our orchard grass. When we presented our pennies to Jock, placing them in his small yellow hand, he took off his hat with a sweeping gesture and jumped to his master's shoulder or to the organ top between each offering. My mother gave Lorenzo a cup of coffee or a glass of lemonade before they went away; and Lorenzo never failed to remove his tattered straw hat and say, "Thank you, good madam," which impressed us deeply. Then with a strong shrug of his left shoulder which moved the heavy organ-strap nearer to his neck, he would set forth on his way, with Jock on his right shoulder and a crowd of us following, for his yearly coming was a mighty event in our lives.

Sometimes, but rarely, a cloud of dust at the top of the hill with a clatter of swaying pots and pans announced the dreaded but delightful advent of gypsies. Of all wayfarers on our road they were the most unwelcome, at least to all village parents, who hated their filthiness and feared them as thieves and, perhaps, even kidnappers. Once their dirty covered wagon and its approaching din were unmistakable, we fled in terror from the gate and up the driveway to inform our mother of their arrival, whereupon she quickly locked all our doors and allowed us only to peer with her from the front windows of our house. Down the hill their wagon rumbled and rocked, driven by a dark, evil-looking man with a black pipe in his mouth and drawn by tired, shaggy horses with faded red tassels above their ears. Two or three equally evil-looking dogs usually trotted beside it, and always barefoot, ragged children with long, untidy hair ran about in the dust. The terror which shook us all was wonderful as we saw from the window the iron pots swinging from beneath the wagon and watched the children performing rude antics in the road beside it. Once, the terror amounted to panic when the wagon halted and a small, slight gypsy woman in a long red dress and a red scarf over her head swung open the gate and came sidling up our driveway to the door. She was shaking a drumlike object surrounded by tiny bells, and she moved her feet gracefully in worn red carpet slippers as though in tune with the bells.

"Keep back!" my mother said to us in a hoarse whisper; but since at that awful moment she was too agitated to command our obedience, we slunk behind her to the dining-room window, which she opened before the gypsy woman had quite reached our porch.

"Go away!" she cried to the gypsy woman. "Go right away!"

The woman tossed her head then and laughed, showing even, white teeth against her dark face. And somehow her ringing, careless laughter there in our driveway made my mother seem, even in her fierce protection of us all, the loser in an odd battle between what was respectable and clean and safe and what was free and wild and exciting, even though dirty, shiftless, and dangerous.

"Your fortune, lady," the gypsy said in a high, whining voice, "for only a dime, dear lady. And don't be afraid, dear little ones. I've children of my own."

We stood transfixed at the open window, peering around my mother until the gypsy had laughed again and shaken her bells high in the air before she turned and danced down our driveway toward the waiting wagon and her filthy children by our white gate. Then they all laughed and screamed together, and one little boy about Edward's age put his thumb to his nose, waggled his fingers, and then turned a beautiful somersault in the dust, before the wagon creaked and clattered away down the road. I never forgot his rude gesture or the sight of his brown feet waving in the air.

My mother sank into a chair then, for her knees quite failed her, and we stood about her, safe but regretful. Danger was past, to be sure, but at what a loss!

"What's in their wagon?" Edward whispered, though how he dared to speak with my mother so unlike herself was a mystery.

"Dirt," she said briefly, now suddenly herself again. "Dirt and lice."

"What's lice?" Edward persisted, as we watched the disappearing cloud of dust.

"Something you will never know," my mother said.

Secretly we adored the coming of the gypsies, not only because of its immediate excitement, but because of the talk among our elders for days afterward, in the store, after church, and when callers came. Everyone always wondered why they chose to traverse our particular countryside, where cleanliness was the first of the cardinal virtues and where only the most outlying field or pasture could afford them a camping-place. We loved the thought of their fire at night with the children sprawling about it and some stew cooking in one of their iron pots, even more savory because it was made of stolen chickens or a stolen lamb. I loved, too, the odd knowledge, proffered by my father, that they wandered because they could not help it, because the necessity for wandering was placed inside them all when they were born and had lain inside them for centuries, *from generation to generation,* as he said. This idea was far more pleasing to me than my mother's almost angry opinion that they had taken to ranging about because their own faraway country could not tolerate their dirt and dishonesty, and so had most justly turned them out.

I used to ask myself in what far countries I would wander if only I had been made that way, and settled on several—Spain, and Italy, and California, and the Land of the Midnight Sun. And as I wandered, I wore a red dress, danced about with utmost grace, and swung a drum with tiny silver bells high into the air.

Indians often came down or up our road, usually singly and always on foot. These were mostly men, with small, long black eyes and high cheekbones; and since they were slung about with baskets and with long strands of withes, reeds, and grasses, sometimes plain but more often colored, they, too, lent brightness as well as excitement. Although they also were usually not overclean, they were not looked upon with the suspicion accorded to gypsies. My father insisted that they be made welcome because, he said, their race had been treated unjustly by our forefathers and we must make up for such injustice, late as it was to do so. Therefore, much to our delight, my mother always bought a basket from them for her sewing or for a Christmas gift. The scent of these baskets tantalized me since I could never, to my own satisfaction, discover its source. There seemed to be trailing arbutus (which we called *mayflowers*) in it, and apple blossoms, though clearly neither could have been woven into mere reeds and grass. Once, when I had the measles and lay in bed itching and burning, my mother allowed me to hold one of her baskets and smell it all I liked; and since it gave me great comfort and pleasure, I decided that in some strange way the Indians knew about things and even thoughts which would heal sickness and had somehow imprisoned these in strands of grass.

My father lent authority to this fancy by his confidence in the mysterious medicines which they sold, salves and ointments, and bottles of dark liquids with enticing names, Kickapoo Indian Sagwaw and Passamaquoddy Painkiller. He said that since they lived so close to Nature, they understood her secrets as we could not. This remark my mother treated with disdain, which mounted to scorn when my father claimed that both the Sagwaw and the Painkiller had cured him of many a cold and stomach upset. She said he knew very well that they were not concocted of innocent herbs and roots, and she always insisted that the bottles stand in a dark corner of one of our cellar shelves, away from the sight of anyone who might come in.

I would not give the impression that only foreigners, or *outlanders,* as our alien wayfarers were locally termed, lent drama to our road and to us children watching from the white gate. They were, of course, the unusual, the new, and the strange, and as such they severed the bonds and widened the boundaries of our snug existence; yet even in the ordinary and customary travelers on the road there was always interest for us. The scissors-grinder came two or three times a year, ringing his bell and calling out: "Bring out your knives and your scissors"; the meat peddler in his white-covered cart made his weekly round of calls, his joints and sides of beef and lamb and his wooden pails of livers and kidneys kept clean from the dust by the tight back doors on his wagon, which he opened when my mother came through the gate to inspect his wares; the fish peddler came, too, but except in the winter months when ice closed our harbor, we preferred to buy from the fish-boat, manned by Captain Andrew Cole, which moored at the town wharf three mornings each week and carried tubs of black-striped haddock at three cents a pound, clams and scallops at ten cents a quart, and, in the spring, alewives and tinker mackerel, which Captain Cole often threw in for goodwill only.

And always there was the passing up and down of our neighbors and our friends, bound for their mail or their groceries and stopping for some welcome words with us. There were laden hayracks drawn by slow, stumbling oxen; blue dumpcarts filled with straw-strewn manure for village gardens; and, in winter, sledges piled high with blocks of ice which, catching the sunlight, held quivering rainbows inside their pale blue transparency.

Even if there was nothing except the empty road itself, it never seemed empty to me. If I looked across it from the gate, there was a wide field with the wind tossing the grass, and beyond the field, tall trees and the white steeple of the church with its gilded weathercock. If I looked downward, there was the distant blue of the harbor water, coming from who knew where. If I looked upward, there was the top of the hill with the sky above and nothing beyond, at least nothing which I could see. I knew, of course, precisely what lay beyond, but I loved to pretend that I knew nothing at all—that the line of the horizon and the great half-circle of the sky above, blue, or gray with storm clouds, or red with sunset, held only mysteries quite unknown to me and waiting to be discovered in some strange time which people called the future.

Aunt Mi

My aunt Mi differed from my other so-called "aunts" in being, I often thought, *unfortunately* bound to me by ties of blood relationship, for I liked her the least of them; in fact, neither I nor any of us liked her at all. Still, there she was, old, querulous, fussy, and demanding, bone of our bone and flesh of our flesh, and we had to put up with her. I must say in fairness to Aunt Mi that she did not often exact the costly price of our tolerance and charity; but the rare occasions when she did are stamped indelibly upon my memory.

She was (if I have our family tree straight after all these years) an aunt of my mother's, and, therefore, our great-aunt. Her real name was Almira, although she was never called by it, and her maiden name had been Hinckley, a surname widely, well, and favorably known in our community. She had been married once upon a time to a man named Scammon, who came "from away" and whom we had never known, save to pity. Since his death, for he presumably had died, she lived with some forbearing relatives in an outlying district some five miles distant from our home.

On her infrequent visits to the village Aunt Mi spent a few days with her sister, Miss Lizzie Hinckley, also old and querulous, who "kept" for a time our Ladies' Social Library in one room of her beautiful old house. Her house, much extended and remodeled, is now the Blue Hill Memorial Hospital; and I never enter its front door facing the sea but that I am again in the room on the left of the entrance as it used to be when it housed the Ladies' Social Library, open one afternoon and one evening a week throughout the year. This name in Miss Lizzie's day (we never called her *aunt*), was a misnomer, for not only was the library skimpy in the extreme, but it was hardly *social* with Miss Lizzie in charge and with Aunt Mi occasionally in the warmest corner next the stove.

Miss Lizzie wore eyeglasses, which quivered constantly, and a black "hug-me-tight" over her black dress. She sat bolt upright at a table with a large blank-book upon which she entered books returned or withdrawn. She was very thin and of a pale blue color, with cold, pale eyes. I remember once, when I asked her feebly for *Twenty Thousand Leagues under the Sea*, she tried to give me *The Wide, Wide World* instead, as "better for you." I had read *The Wide, Wide World* several times for want of more nourishing fare, although I did not like it overmuch, and I politely declined her suggestion. Luckily, for her,

Twenty Thousand Leagues was out, so that I left with nothing but relief.

At those times, usually in the winter, when Aunt Mi visited Miss Lizzie and increased the depression of the Ladies' Social Library, she always came either for dinner with us or to spend the night. When she chose to come for dinner, my father said she was *the destruction that wasteth at noonday;* when she came for overnight, he called her *the pestilence that walketh in darkness.* Although he made these remarks to my mother, the older of us knew quite well what he meant, since we had to memorize psalms early both in school and Sunday school; and though the humor and aptness of his comments were doubtless lost upon us then, they have remained a cheering legacy.

Aunt Mi was small, thin, and pale blue like her sister; and she was always cold. Her hair was very thin also, crimped in front and of a yellowish hue, probably the result of overhot curling tongs. I do not now recall much about her dinners with us except that they were distinctly subdued meals given over mostly to Aunt Mi's catalogue of all the things which were wrong with her: her digestion (though she ate extremely well); her existence far from the center of things; her rheumatism; her lack of children; her fading bank account; and the *cold.* I do remember, however, with complete clarity her nights with us, largely, I suppose, because at least one of them filled me with a haunting dread which lasted long after Aunt Mi had returned to her isolated existence, far from the center.

Aunt Mi always spent her one night with us in a small bedroom off our dining-room. This room was not only the warmest bedroom in the house, but, since it demanded no stairs, coddled her rheumatism. The preparation for her retiring began early, for she insisted upon hot rocks in her bed. A soapstone was far too heavy and unwieldy, she said, and a flatiron was little better than nothing since it had to be moved so often from place to place. Moreover, in her opinion, rocks, if thoroughly heated, held their warmth longest.

The rocks were not hard to find even if there was snow when she came, as there usually was, since there were plenty of them under our barn, left there, I suppose, years ago when the foundations were laid. Aunt Mi had to have six sizable ones, and these had to be well heated in my mother's oven for some hours before bedtime. My mother's face as she moved Aunt Mi's rocks to make room for Johnny-cake, pot roast, or potatoes, revealed her state of mind, though unlike my father she used no words to describe it.

At precisely eight o'clock, which was Aunt Mi's bedtime, the six rocks, done up in pieces of old blankets, were placed in her bed, two at the foot, and two on either side, in the proximity of her hips and shoulders. Then a lighted lamp was placed on her bureau; and after a doleful goodnight to all and the prophecy that the cold was steadily increasing, Aunt Mi went to her room. How she managed to circumvent the rocks on the outside of her bed, I do not know, but she did; and, once within it, she called to someone to blow out her lamp.

I suppose it must have been in the discharge of this duty that I once saw her in bed and felt creeping over me the terror which this sight engendered; or I may have gone into her room with my mother. At all events, I saw her there. She wore a tight black woolen cap over her head, and as I looked upon her among her hot rocks, her blue, shrunken face against the white pillow, even more shrunken because her teeth were out and in a saucer on her stand by the bed, I was overwhelmed, stricken by a sudden and dreadful understanding.

I knew, of course, with the unfamiliar, remote, unreal acquiescence of childhood, that everyone must sometime grow old; but the recognition, the cruel confirmation of this certainty, had never before wrapped me in its chill. Someday, I realized standing there in Aunt Mi's shadowy room, after long years had passed, to be sure, but *someday*, I, too, would be old. I do not think I saw myself as Aunt Mi, wizened, and unwanted, and disliked. Those were minor fears, lost in this strange new burden of time, this stealthy creeping on of days, against which no one, try as one might, could do anything at all.

Coast Children of the Nineties

1

The heavy toll which change and progress inevitably take as they make their inroads is today nowhere more evident than along the coast of Maine. In the smaller towns and villages even the grass-grown ruins of docks have been destroyed; in the larger, shipbuilding except for the construction of pleasure craft or of an occasional steamship, has virtually ceased. The five- and six-masted schooners, which add a touch of romance to populous harbours like Portland, have floated, rotting, untenanted, and useless, for more than several years. Square-riggers are no more. The lithe and beautiful yachts, which cruise idly from Kittery to Eastport or catch the sun on their brass and mahogany as they lie at anchor about Mount Desert or in Camden harbour, speak all too eloquently of the new industry which feeds and clothes the coast. Maine, once secure in her integrity, depends largely for her livelihood, at least so far as her coast life is concerned, upon the capital of those who seek her shores during the summer months.

In the nineties this was not yet so. True, the tide of the new prosperity had already crept into the spacious harbours about Mount Desert and Casco. Bar Harbor already knew its millionaires and Old Orchard its many sojourners. But the smaller, more land-locked villages still kept much to themselves, their carpenters building only an occasional cottage for strangers, their small hotels, boarding-houses, and homes entertaining only a few "rusticators." Blue Hill, now deservedly one of the most notable resorts of the coast, knew then neither golf-links nor club-house, neither estates whose clipped lawns sloped to the shore nor Chicago and Cleveland financiers who had money in plenty to spend. And Blue Hill children, although they were occasionally shy before city boys and girls with more stylish clothes and more urbane speech, had the village and the coast for their own.

We knew the manifold excitements of coast life, major and minor. We knew even then the drama of incoming vessels, waiting beyond the Narrows in the outer bay for the tides, tacking up the snug inner channel to anchor just off the harbour island or to tie up at the wharf to unload their provisions for the village stores and to load the staves and larger lumber for their outgoing. The names and the rigging of these craft were as familiar as the words in our spelling-books and far more welcome: *The Gold Hunter,* the *Mildred May,* the *John W. Stetson.* We knew, occasionally, the inexpressible excitement of the arrival of a "foreign ship" from Barbados, manned by strange, swarthy men with bright handkerchiefs around their necks, and in their mouths unintelligible sounds. Once, indeed, as we of our family sat one September evening with our lessons around the dining-room table, such a dark face above such a handkerchief appeared in our open window, its owner muttering outlandish words and gesticulating with tattooed arms and hands. My mother in her perturbation and terror well-nigh threw the lighted lamp at our caller, who, as we discovered upon the hurried arrival of my father, wanted only to know the way to the "medicine house." It was days before we recovered from our fright and more days before we ceased to be the centre of an envious group at school.

We knew and cherished with no little covetousness the stories of the "traders," which had gladdened the hearts of children of an earlier generation. A trader was a vessel from Boston or New York which earned the livelihood of its captain, or perchance of its owner, by carrying annually into the smaller harbours of the coast every kind of ware imaginable and selling its multifarious cargo at prices which the village stores could not meet. Blue Hill children of the sixties and seventies had waited months for the arrival of this floating junk-shop, scanning the sea from every hill and headland for an unfamiliar sail. According to the older people among us, its captain was invariably an accommodating soul, who was not in the least averse to interpreting as coin of the realm any stray bits of old iron, in exchange for which he would proffer oranges and great Boston apples, gorgeously striped candies, dates, figs, and nuts. Moreover, he carried in his hold, for those who had been most thrifty and parsimonious of their small savings, doll buggies and pop-guns, and for the despair of fathers and mothers, who could be lured to the wharf, bolts of cloth and shiny new shoes with voluptuous and alluring tassels.

Sometimes in those days, we understood, still with envy that progress had cheated us of so much greater excitement, Blue Hill had supplied her own traders. An obliging captain, with a weather eye out for his own pocket, sailing light from Boston or New York, Philadelphia or Norfolk, would gladly undertake the filling of commissions in those centres and bring home a sundry cargo. My aunt, a child of the sixties, told us on her infrequent visits the engrossing tale of a new bureau which she procured in this romantic fashion. At the age of six she had pieced together a bed-quilt by the "over and over" method, sewing together innumerable squares and triangles of calico, keeping as she did so the reward for her enterprise and perseverance ever before her eyes. Scanning critically for weeks each distant sail, she at last espied the *Merchant* ploughing through the waters of the outer bay. For hours she waited at the wharf until the tide should be sufficiently favourable for a landing and saw at last her bureau ready for unloading on the quarter-deck. Once again as a reward for industry or virtue (perhaps for both, for in those days, as in our own, they were well-nigh inseparable) she was allowed the fulfillment of great longing. This time, impelled no doubt by her seafaring heritage, she made the choice of a trunk which came after long weeks of waiting by way of another ship, *The Python.*

These shopping sea-captains must, indeed, have been men of gregarious instincts and of great good nature. A slip of paper much torn and obviously incomplete, dated in 1859, gives a partial list of commissions to be fulfilled and suggests the arduous undertaking of the purchaser:

For J. Candage, a hoss harness
For Messrs. Holt, Horton, Candage, & 3 Hinckleys tobaco, both
    chewing & smoking
For J. C.—a new hat, my own size with 2 cravats & ties
For the minister, one cane, snake's head prefered, not to cost over $1
For Silvester C., a good quantity nails, all sizes, & 12 brass handles
For Coggin family, to invest $20 in white flour & raisins, also nuts of
    sorts, also toys such as marbles, tops, & a book of pictures
For Miss Clara Wood, stuff for weding dress with threads & silks for
    sewing same & white lace for triming

For Mrs. Duffy, 1 bolt flowered calico at lowest price, blue & white
prefered, also buttons, also wools for kniting socks in bright
shades, also pink roses for bonet brims
For Horton boys, 2 large pocket knives
For H. Henderson, 6 steel traps suitable for rabits or foxes
For litle Osgood girl, a doll with black hair, blue eyes, big as possible
for $1
For Mrs. Grindle, one singing bird in cage, for the church gift.

Even we in the nineties knew at first hand something of this sort of
supply and demand. When I was in the neighbourhood of twelve, my
father, together with three other men of the village, bought a quarter
share in a two-masted schooner called *The Gold Hunter.* Rumour had it
that their act was largely one of charity since the captain and owner
had fallen on evil days by the decline of the coast trade. But whatever
its cause, the effect brought delighted satisfaction to four large
families. *The Gold Hunter* was summarily dispatched to Boston with
divers commissions to be accomplished by her relieved captain, and we
waited with atavistic feverishness for her return.

Perhaps her cargo, when after a fortnight she again drew to the
wharf, was less romantic than those of former days. I am sure,
however, that it gave no less thrill. We children of the four families
concerned, and we were many, watched with fascination the unloading
of barrels of flour, sacks of grain, kegs of molasses and vinegar, cans of
pilot bread (that invincible cracker!), bags of oatmeal—all the manifold
sorts of provender which were to prove the staples for the men and
beasts of our large and respective households during a long winter. We
watched, too, the wet line on the black hull of *The Gold Hunter* as it
increased in width from her steady rising out of the water during the
steady disembowelling of her dark, musty hold.

Most remarkable of all her goods in those relatively fruitless days
were crates of oranges, two kegs of white grapes, packed in sawdust,
and—most wonderful to relate!—a huge bunch of bananas in a long,
slatted frame. It may seem impossible today to wax romantic over a
bunch of bananas! But in that huge frame standing on *The Gold
Hunter's* deck, behind those masses of brown, tropical grass, were
concealed far more than bananas, delectable and desirable as they
were in themselves. Therein among those unripe, green protuberances,
of whose snug members we caught now and then a baffling glimpse, lay
a prestige and a pre-eminence among our fellows which in all the years
that have passed I have never been able to recapture. My father had
bought the bananas as a surprise. We were all excessively fond of
them, but since they were tacitly recognized as an indulgence and since
the price of them in the village store, at least of enough to supply our

family, was prohibitive, we had never completely satisfied our desire. The acknowledgment of our supremacy over all the other children in town began as soon as the bananas had been lifted from their frame, cleared of their wiry grass, and hung from a beam in our cellar. Visible from the entrance of our bulkhead, they immediately attracted a crowd of spectators. There was hardly a school-less hour, indeed, for a space of three days, when half a dozen pairs of eyes were not gazing in wonder and envy down those stone stairs. We children meanwhile managed our exhibition by sitting on the open bulkhead doors, swinging our legs and dilating upon our possession with suitable and, I fear, complacent comments.

The culminating moment in this daily-enacted drama occurred one noon when my father, upon inspection of the great ungainly bunch, suggested that we cut the yellowest. That he contemplated any distribution never once occurred to any of us, neither to exhibitors nor to spectators. We watched him procure a box, mount it, and draw his jack-knife from his pocket. I can yet feel the stilling of my heart when he handed down to me, who waited below with outstretched apron, five, six, eight, twelve bananas, when he proposed that we should treat our friends. From that day to this I have never been able to regard a banana with the supercilious stare of the cultivated mind and eye. The munificence and magnanimity of my father, the opulence and distinction of us as a family, remain, always to be evoked by any chance sight of that humblest and ugliest of fruits.

2

The minor and usual excitements of coast life were legion. In the nineties there were still among us old sea-captains, barometers of sky and sea, who, in addition to telling us chimerical tales, instructed us in the mysterious ways of weather. We learned to predict the ominous secrets of winds that backed, of restless gulls flying inland, of mare's-tails swishing their milky white across the heavens, of still, cloudless days. We knew what to expect of spring tides, always cherishing the hope that on a March full moon boats would be torn from moorings and lumber floated from the town wharves. We knew when smelts were most likely to "run," coming in great shoals from the outer ocean on night tides in April and May and seeking the tidal streams for spawning. On such nights we went to bed at sundown to be called at three o'clock by my father. Armed with all the pails and baskets of the house, we walked a mile through the darkness to the most favoured brook. The tide was out, and the smelts were foiled and trapped in their tardy return to wider water. Their silver backs and white bellies, as in thousands they hurried pell-mell down the shallow stream, gleamed in the light of our lanterns; and we gathered them in our cold hands by hundreds, filling great baskets full and perhaps, when the miracle was accomplished and we gazed upon our catch, feeling a surprise and exhilaration not unlike that of the boy of the Galilean picnic who began his exciting day with but three small fishes.

The offerings of the sea in the ebb of springs were always more momentous than those of ordinary tides. Shells were more plentiful and often more rare. Wreckage strewed the shores of the outer bay, logs and beams which not infrequently held within their golden brown sides bolts of iron caked with salt. These meant inimitable driftwood fires and were always carried high up the beach and left to dry among the vetches and the lavender. After a spring tide there was also much high talk of treasure and no little search for it. We lived, indeed, on a coast that at once invited and nurtured such fancies. Not far from us lay the very island which was rumoured to hide within its sands the bulk of Captain Kidd's ill-gotten gains. Moreover, not so many years past, two boys who lived near us had been granted an experience, the equal of which few boys of any time or place could boast. Following an old foot-path through the woods during a storm, they had rested against a small boulder beneath a pine tree. One of them, idly kicking the soft mould at the base of the rock, caught the glint of metal, tarnished yet still bright enough to be distinguished against the black earth. They dug farther, with feet and with hands alike, to discover at last an iron pot half filled with gold coins—coins marked by strange designs and a stranger language. They proved to be French pieces of the seventeenth century, probably buried there, so the learned of our coast surmised, by escaping French traders and settlers of the nearby town of Castine when their fort was surprised and captured by the Dutch. What wonder that we scrutinized the wreckage of spring tides and dug now and again in likely coves or beneath giant boulders!

Yet another tale encouraged us to hope for dramatic possibilities even in the ploughing of a spring field. A fisherman not many miles distant had unearthed one May morning, while attempting to cultivate a hitherto barren half-acre, a large piece of copper, marked with unintelligible characters. Seeing in it a remedy for a leaking boat, he tacked it securely to the hull, to be told a few weeks later by summer visitors whom he took out for mackerel, that he had utilized for most practical purposes the corner-stone of a Jesuit chapel, dedicated to Our Lady of Holy Hope in the year 1609!

There was hardly a winter in the nineties when the ocean remained open. By January, sometimes even by Christmas, a great steel-like sheet of ice began to creep farther and farther out toward open sea. Then one cold morning we woke to find no water at all between our shores and those of Long Island, seven miles distant. This meant skating in plenty on the inner bay, and on the outer, once the cold had continued a full week, the laying out of a great track and horse-racing in open sleighs. Not even a launching, which we alas! had been born just too late to see from our own shores, could have been much more thrilling than these village gatherings on certain clear cold afternoons, the participants drawn from village barns, the bells jingling, a blazing fire at the starting-point by which we could warm ourselves with much laughter and many wagers on the horses of our choice.

Those long stretches of ice meant, too, the cutting and hauling of island wood. Oxen drew the creaking sledges which smelled of pine and fir, and obliging farmers encouraged us, once we had obtained our parents' consent, to ride out empty and to return on the top of the load or clinging to the broad runners. The white expanse stretched far and wide beneath a clear, cold sky. The islands were surrounded by rough, uneven boundaries where the tide had cracked and broken the ice, throwing up jagged slabs and cakes around their edges. Wraiths of blue mist rose from the muzzles of the oxen above the icicles clinging to their hairy throats; the creaking of the sledges was now and then supplemented by the booming of the ice as the moving water far beneath it raised or lowered the great solid mass. The climatic changes, even of thirty years, have robbed the coast children of today of no higher adventure.

More suddenly even than it had come, the great sheet of ice broke up and moved seaward. Suspicious gleams of pale blue appeared here and there on a warm, windy morning in March or early April; sullen and explosive muttering punctuated the air. Then with the full outgoing tide the cakes of ice began to move, jamming and hurtling one another, sometimes being thrown into the air by the pressure beneath. Adventuresome boys of parents more careless than our own occasionally tried the risky experiment of crossing the inner bay by jumping from one to another if perchance the break-up occurred on a Saturday. If it happened on ordinary days, it must be intermittently watched from the schoolhouse windows, which on one side faced the sea, but which were placed so high in the wall as to be barely accessible even to the most ambitious vision. The difficulty of keeping one's mind and eyes upon one's books on such a morning was intense.

Tuesdays, Thursdays, and Saturdays in spring and summer were fish-boat mornings. By seven o'clock on days when the tide served, Captain Andrew Cole had sailed from the outer bay, having far earlier hauled his trawl. The young representatives of each family table gathered at the wharf, not reluctant to wait their turn while the green water slapped at the piers and the gulls were certain of full stomachs. A five-pound haddock, cleaned and scraped, could be bought for fifteen cents, the black stripe down his silvery sides guaranteeing wary purchasers against the despised hake, which no Maine connoisseur of fish could tolerate. There were clams, too, dipped from a sodden tub at ten cents a quart measure and, upon occasion, tinker mackerel in ravishing shades of blue and green, so cheap that two dozen might be bought without greatly diminishing the family pocket-book.

There were clams to be dug from the mud flats, many bare feet spotting them by the tiny jets of water which they spouted from their hiding-places. The backaches produced by heavy clam-hoes in tough mud were always less painful than those engendered by piling wood or cultivating garden rows of potatoes or beans! We baked them by building fires of driftwood beneath flat rocks and laying the clams between layers of wet seaweed. Nearly every summer these clambakes took on a co-operative character participated in by the village at large. On these occasions our elders chartered a schooner in the harbour large enough to consider a hundred persons a mere handful. We sailed then to Long Island, laden with foodstuffs sufficient for any ordinary siege, and spent the day on wider, sandier shores. The dinner served on such village picnics tested the gastronomic capacities of the community and could hardly be excelled by any eighteenth century repast. Lobsters and clams, broiled and baked, fish in chowders, hard-boiled eggs, sandwiches and doughnuts, fresh cakes, turnovers, and tarts, blueberry and apple pies, root beer, lemonade and coffee! What wonder that the sail homeward before a southeast wind was silent and that we trudged in families, still silent, up the village street, filled, among many other things, with a sleepy content!

3

Beyond all these tangible influences, the coast itself, and the very fact that we lived upon it, placed its intangible mark upon our minds. Secure though we were in our safe haven, we knew full well that the sea was treacherous and insecure. Something of the same shrewd, patient wisdom must be the heritage of prairie children or of those dwelling by great rivers, who are born to scent disaster in rising winds and waters. Few of us of my generation will ever forget that tragic November night when the Boston boat went down with all on board. Reared on tales of shipwreck and suffering upon oceans near and far, we were not surprised by the hardships which every winter brought within our knowledge. We read or were told of lighthouse children drowned by falling into fissures of the rock, of a woman who tended a great lamp through a three days' storm while the body of her husband lay in the lighthouse sitting-room. We knew of outlying islands beset with starvation in an especially bitter winter, of mailboats foundered in high seas. Is it too much then to believe that there crept into our minds earlier than into the minds of most children a sense of the inevitability, not only of suffering but of endurance as well, that we grew, perhaps unconsciously and insensibly, to look upon sorrow not as an individual, concrete matter but rather as a mighty abstraction, necessary and common to all human life? An easier, more fortified age may well question such an assumption; but few who were born to a seafaring heritage and few who knew coast life even a quarter of a century ago will doubt it.

MARGARET LYNN

Margaret Lynn's "A Step-Daughter of the Prairie" appeared in *The Atlantic Monthly,* March 1911.

A Step-Daughter of the Prairie

Far away on the almost bare line of the prairie's horizon, a group of trees used to show. There was a tall one and a short one, and then a tallish crooked one and another short one. To my childish eyes they spelled l-i-f-e, as plainly as any word in my second reader was spelled. They were the point that most fascinated me as I knelt at the upstairs window, with my elbows on the sill and my chin on my folded arms. I don't know when I first noticed them, for they had been there always, so far as I could remember, a scanty little bit of fringe on a horizon that was generally clear and bare. There were tips of other woods farther to the south, woods that were slightly known to me; but that group of trees on the very edge seemed to lie beyond the knowledge of any one. Even on the afternoons when I was allowed to go with my father on one of his business errands, and we drove and drove, we never came in sight of it. Yet, when I next went upstairs and looked from the window, there it stood against the sky.

I had no sense of making an allegory of it. At that age, to the fairy-tale-fed child, the line between allegory and reality is scarcely perceptible anyway, and at least negligible. The word on the horizon was quite a matter of course to me. An older person, had it occurred to me to mention the matter, would perhaps have seen something significant, even worthy of sentimental remark, in the child's spelling out the life waiting for her on her far horizon. But to me, mystery as it was, it was also a matter of fact; there it stood, and that was all. Yet it was also a romance, a sort of unformulated promise. It was related to the far distant, to the remote in time, to the thing that was some day to be known. So I rested my chin on my little arms and watched.

I suppose the fact that the trees were evidently big and old—ours were still young and small—and perhaps a part of some woods, was their chief appeal to me. For no one can picture what the woods mean to the prairie child. They are a glimpse of dream-things, an illustration of poems read, a mystery of undefined possibilities. To pass through our scant bits of woods, even, was an excursion into a strange world. From places on the road to town, we could see pieces of timber. On some blessed occasions when a muddy hollow was impassable or when the Howell bridge, the impermanent structure of a prairie country, was out, we went around through the Crossley woods. That was an experience! The depth of greenness—the prairie had nothing like it.

I think my eyes were born tired of the prairie, ungrateful little soul that I was. And the summer shadows in the woods were marvelous. The shadow of the prairie was that of a passing cloud, or the square shade of some building, deepest at noon-day. But the green depths of the woods' shadows, the softly-moving light and shade, were a wonderful thing. To me these trips put all probability on a new basis. Out on the bare prairie, under the shining sun, stories were stories, the dearest of them inventions. But in these shady depths, where my little eyes were led on from green space through green space to a final dimness, anything might be true. Fiction and tradition took on a reality that the glaring openness would not allow. Things that were different might happen in a wood. I could not help expecting a new experience. But it never came: we passed out of the timber to the prairie again. But at least expectation had been stirred. The possibility that something might happen seemed nearer.

For Romance was always just around the corner, or just a little way ahead. But out on the prairie how could one overtake it? Where could the unknown lurk in that great open? The woods seemed to put me nearer to the world on whose borders I always hovered, the world of stories and poems, the world of books in general. The whole business of my life just then was to discover in the world of actual events enough that was bookish to reconcile me to being a real child and not one in a story. For the most part, aside from play, which was a thing in itself, and had a sane importance of its own, the realities of life were those that had their counterparts in books. Whatever I found in books, especially in poetry, I craved for my own experience. Only my childish secretiveness saved me from seeming an inordinate little prig.

For there is no bookishness like that of a childish reader; and there is no romanticism like that of a child. For good or ill, I was steeped in both. But the two things, books and the visible world that the sun shone in and the prairie spread out in, were far apart and, according to my lights, incompatible. I always had a suspicion of a distinct line between literature and life, at least life as I knew it, far out in Iowa. Who had ever read of Iowa in a novel or a poem? No essays on Literature and Life had then enlightened me as to their relation; I didn't know they had any. I wished that life could be translated into terms of literature, but so far as I could see I had to do it myself if it was to be done.

VLADIMIR NABOKOV

Vladimir Nabokov was born in St. Petersburg, Russia, in 1899, into an aristocratic family. His father was a great liberal statesman whose ideas forced the family to flee the Revolution. Nabokov went to college in England (Trinity College, Cambridge), lived for long periods in Germany and France, and, in 1940, came to the United States. He became a citizen in 1945. His most famous work is *Lolita* (1955). *Pale Fire* was published in 1962, and *The Gift* and *The Defense*, both translations from Russian, in 1963 and 1964. As well as being a renowned writer, Nabokov is an expert on butterflies. The following excerpt from his memoir, *Speak, Memory* (1960), suggests the boyhood excitement which was to develop into the scholarly zeal of the adult.

A Boy in Old Russia

The cradle rocks above an abyss, and common sense tells us that our existence is but a brief crack of light between two eternities of darkness. Although the two are identical twins, man, as a rule, views the prenatal abyss with more calm than the one he is heading for (at some forty-five hundred heartbeats an hour). I know, however, of a young chronophobiac who experienced something like panic when looking for the first time at homemade movies that had been taken a few weeks before his birth. He saw a world that was practically unchanged—the same house, the same people—and then realized that he did not exist there at all and that nobody mourned his absence. He caught a glimpse of his mother waving from an upstairs window, and that unfamiliar gesture disturbed him, as if it were some mysterious farewell. But what particularly frightened him was the sight of a brand-new baby carriage standing there on the porch, with the smug, encroaching air of a coffin; even that was empty, as if, in the reverse course of events, his very bones had disintegrated.

Such fancies are not foreign to young lives. Or, to put it otherwise, first and last things often tend to have an adolescent note—unless, possibly, they are directed by some venerable and rigid religion. Nature expects a full-grown man to accept the two black voids, fore and aft, as stolidly as he accepts the extraordinary visions in between. Imagination, the supreme delight of the immortal and the immature, should be limited. In order to enjoy life, we should not enjoy it too much.

I rebel against this state of affairs. I feel the urge to take my rebellion outside and picket nature. Over and over again, my mind has made colossal efforts to distinguish the faintest of personal glimmers in the impersonal darkness on both sides of my life. That this darkness is caused merely by the walls of time separating me and my bruised fists from the free world of timelessness is a belief I gladly share with the most gaudily painted savage. I have journeyed back in thought—with thought hopelessly tapering off as I went—to remote regions where I groped for some secret outlet only to discover that the prison of time is spherical and without exits. Short of suicide, I have tried everything. I have doffed my identity in order to pass for a conventional spook and steal into realms that existed before I was conceived. I have mentally endured the degrading company of Victorian lady novelists and retired colonels who remembered having, in former lives, been slave messengers on a Roman road or sages under the willows of Lhasa. I have ransacked my oldest dreams for keys and clues—and let me say at once that I reject completely the vulgar, shabby, fundamentally medieval world of Freud, with its crankish quest for sexual symbols (something like searching for Baconian acrostics in Shakespeare's works) and its bitter little embryos spying, from their natural nooks, upon the love life of their parents.

. . . .

On a summer morning, in the legendary Russia of my boyhood, my first glance upon awakening was for the chink between the white inner shutters. If it disclosed a watery pallor, one had better not open them at all, and so be spared the sight of a sullen day sitting for its picture in a puddle. How resentfully one would deduce, from a line of dull light, the leaden sky, the sodden sand, the gruel-like mess of broken brown blossoms under the lilacs—and that flat, fallow leaf (the first casualty of the season) pasted upon a wet garden bench!

But if the chink was a long glint of dewy brilliancy, then I made haste to have the window yield its treasure. With one blow, the room would be cleft into light and shade. The foliage of birches moving in the sun had the translucent green tone of grapes, and in contrast to this there was the dark velvet of fir trees against a blue of extraordinary intensity, the like of which I rediscovered only many years later, in the montane zone of Colorado.

From the age of seven, everything I felt in connection with a rectangle of framed sunlight was dominated by a single passion. If my first glance of the morning was for the sun, my first thought was for the butterflies it would engender. The original event had been banal enough. On the honeysuckle, overhanging the carved back of a bench just opposite the main entrance, my guiding angel (whose wings, except for the absence of a Florentine limbus, resemble those of Fra Angelico's Gabriel) pointed out to me a rare visitor, a splendid, pale-yellow creature with black blotches, blue crenels, and a cinnabar eyespot above each chrome-rimmed black tail. As it probed the inclined flower from which it hung, its powdery body slightly bent, it kept restlessly jerking its great wings, and my desire for it was one of the most intense I have ever experienced. Agile Ustin, our town-house janitor, who for a comic reason (explained elsewhere) happened to be that summer in the country with us, somehow managed to catch it in my cap, after which it was transferred, cap and all, to a wardrobe, where domestic naphthalene was fondly expected by Mademoiselle to kill it overnight. On the following morning, however, when she unlocked the wardrobe to take something out, my Swallowtail, with a mighty rustle, flew into her face, then made for the open window, and presently was but a golden fleck dipping and dodging and soaring eastward, over timber and tundra, to Vologda, Viatka and Perm, and beyond the gaunt Ural range to Yakutsk and Verkhne Kolymsk, and from Verkhne Kolymsk, where it lost a tail, to the fair Island of St. Lawrence, and across Alaska to Dawson, and southward along the Rocky Mountains—to be finally overtaken and captured, after a forty-year race, on an immigrant dandelion under an endemic aspen near Boulder. In a letter from Mr. Brune to Mr. Rawlins, June 14, 1735, in the Bodleian collection, he states that one Mr. Vernon followed a butterfly nine miles before he could catch him (*The Recreative Review or Eccentricities of Literature and Life,* Vol. 1, p. 144, London, 1821).

Soon after the wardrobe affair I found a spectacular moth, marooned in a corner of a vestibule window, and my mother dispatched it with ether. In later years, I used many killing agents, but the least contact with the initial stuff would always cause the porch of the past to light up and attract that blundering beauty. Once, as a grown man, I was under ether during appendectomy, and with the vividness of a decalcomania picture I saw my own self in a sailor suit mounting a freshly emerged Emperor moth under the guidance of a Chinese lady who I knew was my mother. It was all there, brilliantly reproduced in my dream, while my own vitals were being exposed: the soaking, ice-cold absorbent cotton pressed to the insect's lemurian head; the subsiding spasms of its body; the satisfying crackle produced by the pin penetrating the hard crust of its thorax; the careful insertion of the point of the pin in the cork-bottomed groove of the spreading board; the symmetrical adjustment of the thick, strong-veined wings under neatly affixed strips of semitransparent paper.

I must have been eight when, in a storeroom of our country house, among all kinds of dusty objects, I discovered some wonderful books acquired in the days when my mother's mother had been interested in natural science and had had a famous university professor of zoology (Shimkevich) give private lessons to her daughter. Some of these books were mere curios, such as the four huge brown folios of Albertus Seba's work *(Locupletissimi Rerum Naturalium Thesauri Accurata Descriptio . . .),* printed in Amsterdam around 1750. On their coarse-grained pages I found woodcuts of serpents and butterflies and embryos. The fetus of an Ethiopian female child hanging by the neck in a glass jar used to give me a nasty shock every time I came across it; nor did I much care for the stuffed hydra on plate CII, with its seven lion-toothed turtleheads on seven serpentine necks and its strange, bloated body which bore buttonlike tubercules along the sides and ended in a knotted tail.

Other books I found in that attic, among herbariums full of alpine columbines, and blue palemoniums, and Jove's campions, and orange-red lilies, and other Davos flowers, came closer to my subject. I took in my arms and carried downstairs glorious loads of fantastically attractive volumes: Maria Sibylla Merian's (1647-1717) lovely plates of Surinam insects, and Esper's noble *Die Schmetterlinge* (Erlangen, 1777), and Boisduval's *Icones Historiques de Lépidoptères Nouveaux ou Peu Connus* (Paris, begun in 1832). Still more exciting were the products of the latter half of the century—Newman's *Natural History of British Butterflies and Moths,* Hofmann's *Die Gross-Schmetterlinge Europas,* the Grand Duke Nikolay Mihailovich's *Mémoires* on Asiatic lepidoptera (with incomparably beautiful figures painted by Kavrigin, Rybakov, Lang), Scudder's stupendous work on the *Butterflies of New England.*

Retrospectively, the summer of 1905, though quite vivid in many ways, is not animated yet by a single bit of quick flutter or colored fluff around or across the walks with the village schoolmaster: the Swallowtail of June, 1906, was still in the larval stage on a roadside umbellifer; but in the course of that month I became acquainted with a score or so of common things, and Mademoiselle was already referring to a certain forest road that culminated in a marshy meadow full of Small Pearl-bordered Fritillaries (thus called in my first unforgettable and unfadingly magical little manual, Richard South's *The Butterflies of the British Isles* which had just come out at the time) as *le chemin des papillons bruns.* The following year I became aware that many of our butterflies and moths did not occur in England or Central Europe, and more complete atlases helped me to determine them. A severe illness (pneumonia, with fever up to 41° centigrade), in the beginning of 1907, mysteriously abolished the rather monstrous gift of numbers that had made of me a child prodigy during a few months (today I cannot multiply 13 by 17 without pencil and paper; I can add them up, though, in a trice, the teeth of the three fitting in neatly); but the butterflies survived. My mother accumulated a library and a museum around my bed, and the longing to describe a new species completely replaced that of discovering a new prime number. A trip to Biarritz, in August 1907, added new wonders (though not as lucid and numerous as they were to be in 1909). By 1908, I had gained absolute control over the European lepidoptera as known to Hofmann. By 1910, I had dreamed my way through the first volumes of Seitz's prodigious picture book *Die Gross-Schmetterlinge der Erde,* had purchased a number of rarities recently described, and was voraciously reading entomological periodicals, especially English and Russian ones. Great upheavals were taking place in the development of systematics. Since the middle of the century, Continental lepidopterology had been, on the whole, a simple and stable affair, smoothly run by the Germans. Its high priest, Dr. Staudinger, was also the head of the largest firm of insect dealers. Even now, half a century after his death, German lepidopterists have not quite managed to shake off the hypnotic spell occasioned by his authority. He was still alive when his school began to lose ground as a scientific force in the world. While he and his followers stuck to specific and generic names sanctioned by long usage and were content to classify butterflies by characters visible to the naked eye, English-speaking authors were introducing nomenclatorial changes as a result of a strict application of the law of priority and taxonomic changes based on the microscopic study of organs. The Germans did their best to ignore the new trends and continued to cherish the philately-like side of entomology. Their solicitude for the "average collector who should not be made to dissect" is comparable to the way nervous publishers of popular novels pamper the "average reader"—who should not be made to think.

There was another more general change, which coincided with my ardent adolescent interest in butterflies and moths. The Victorian and Staudingerian kind of species, hermetic and homogeneous, with sundry (alpine, polar, insular, etc.) "varieties" affixed to it from the outside, as it were, like incidental appendages, was replaced by a new, multiform and fluid kind of species, organically *consisting* of geographical races or subspecies. The evolutionary aspects of the case were thus brought out more clearly, by means of more flexible methods of classification, and further links between butterflies and the central problems of nature were provided by biological investigations.

The mysteries of mimicry had a special attraction for me. Its phenomena showed an artistic perfection usually associated with man-wrought things. Consider the imitation of oozing poison by bubblelike macules on a wing (complete with pseudo-refraction) or by glossy yellow knobs on a chrysalis ("Don't eat me—I have already been squashed, sampled and rejected"). Consider the tricks of an acrobatic caterpillar (of the Lobster Moth) which in infancy looks like bird's dung, but after molting develops scrabbly hymenopteroid append-ages and baroque characteristics, allowing the extraordinary fellow to play two parts at once (like the actor in Oriental shows who *becomes* a pair of intertwisted wrestlers): that of a writhing larva and that of a big ant seemingly harrowing it. When a certain moth resembles a certain wasp in shape and color, it also walks and moves its antennae in a waspish, unmothlike manner. When a butterfly has to look like a leaf, not only are all the details of a leaf beautifully rendered but markings mimicking grub-bored holes are generously thrown in. "Natural selec-tion," in the Darwinian sense, could not explain the miraculous coincidence of imitative aspect and imitative behavior, nor could one appeal to the theory of "the struggle for life" when a protective device was carried to a point of mimetic subtlety, exuberance, and luxury far in excess of a predator's power of appreciation. I discovered in nature the nonutilitarian delights that I sought in art. Both were a form of magic, both were a game of intricate enchantment and deception.

TRUMAN CAPOTE

Truman Capote, an American writer of the postwar Southern Renaissance, was born in New Orleans in 1924. In 1946 he won the O. Henry Short Story Award for "Shut a Final Door." In 1954 he wrote the book for the Broadway play *House of Flowers. Breakfast at Tiffany's* (1958) was made into a popular movie. His most recent full-length work, *In Cold Blood* (1965), a "nonfiction novel," has also been transformed into an effective film.

A Christmas Memory

Imagine a morning in late November. A coming of winter morning more than twenty years ago. Consider the kitchen of a spreading old house in a country town. A great black stove is its main feature; but there is also a big round table and a fireplace with two rocking chairs placed in front of it. Just today the fireplace commenced its seasonal roar.

A woman with shorn white hair is standing at the kitchen window. She is wearing tennis shoes and a shapeless gray sweater over a summery calico dress. She is small and sprightly, like a bantam hen; but, due to a long youthful illness, her shoulders are pitifully hunched. Her face is remarkable—craggy and tinted by sun and wind; but it is delicate too, finely boned, and her eyes are sherry-colored and timid. "Oh, my," she exclaims, her breath smoking the windowpane, "it's fruitcake weather!"

The person to whom she is speaking is myself. I am seven; she is sixty-something. We are cousins, very distant ones, and we have lived together as long as I can remember. Other people inhabit the house, relatives; and though they have power over us, and frequently make us cry, we are not, on the whole, too much aware of them. We are each other's best friend. She calls me Buddy, in memory of a boy who was formerly her best friend. The other Buddy died when she was still a child. She is still a child.

"I knew it before I got out of bed," she says, turning away from the window with a purposeful excitement in her eyes. "The courthouse bell sounded so cold and clear. And there were no birds singing; they've gone to warmer country. Oh, Buddy, stop stuffing biscuit and fetch our buggy. Help me find my hat. We've thirty cakes to bake."

It's always the same: a morning arrives in November, and my

friend, as though officially inaugurating the Christmas time of year that exhilarates her imagination and fuels the blaze of heart, announces: "It's fruitcake weather! Fetch our buggy. Help me find my hat."

The hat is found, a straw cartwheel, corsaged with velvet roses, has faded: it once belonged to a more fashionable relative. Together, we guide our buggy, a dilapidated baby carriage, out to the garden and into a grove of pecan trees. The buggy is mine; that is, it was bought for me when I was born. It is made of wicker, rather unraveled, and the wheels wobble like a drunkard's legs. But it is a faithful object; springtimes, we take it to the woods and fill it with flowers, herbs, wild fern for our porch; in the summer, we pile it with picnic paraphernalia and sugar-cane fishing poles and roll it down to the edge of a creek; it has its winter uses, too: as a truck for hauling firewood from the yard to the kitchen, as a warm bed for Queenie, our tough little orange and white rat-terrier who has survived distemper and two rattlesnake bites. Queenie is trotting beside it now.

Three hours later we are back in the kitchen hulling a buggy-load of windfall pecans. Our backs hurt from gathering them: how hard they were to find (the main crop having been shaken off the trees and sold by the orchard's owners) among the concealing leaves, the frosted, deceiving grass. Caarackle! A cheery crunch, scraps of miniature thunder sound as the shells collapse and the golden mound of sweet oily ivory meat mounts in a milk glass bowl. Queenie begs to taste, and now and again my friend sneaks her a mite, though insisting we deprive ourselves. "We mustn't, Buddy. If we start, we won't stop. And there's scarcely enough as there is. For thirty cakes." The kitchen is growing dark. Dusk turns the window into a mirror: our reflections mingle with the rising moon as we work by the fireside in the firelight. At last, when the moon is quite high, we toss the final hull into the fire, with joined sighs, watch it catch flame. The buggy is empty, the bowl is brimful.

We eat our supper (cold biscuits, bacon, blackberry jam) and discuss tomorrow. Tomorrow the kind of work I like best begins: buying. Cherries and citron, ginger and vanilla, canned pineapple, raisins and walnuts and whisky and oh, so much flour, butter, many eggs, spices: we'll need a pony to pull the buggy home.

But before these purchases can be made, there is the question of money. Neither of us has any. Except for skinflint sums persons in the house occasionally provide (a dime is considered very big money); or what we earn ourselves from various activities: holding rummage sales, selling buckets of hand-picked blackberries, jars of homemade jam and apple jelly and peach preserves, rounding up flowers for funerals and weddings. Once we won seventy-ninth prize, five dollars, in a national football contest. Not that we know a fool-thing about football. It's just that we enter any contest we hear about: at the moment our hopes are on the fifty-thousand dollar Grand Prize being offered to name a new brand of coffee. To tell the truth, our only *really* profitable enterprise was the Fun and Freak Museum we conducted in a back-yard woodshed two summers ago. The Fun was a stereopticon with slide views of Washington and New York lent us by a relative who had been to those places (she was furious when she discovered why we'd borrowed it); the Freak was a three-legged biddy-chicken hatched by one of our own hens. Everybody hereabouts wanted to see that biddy: we charged grownups a nickel, kids two cents. And took in a good twenty dollars before the museum shut down due to the decease of the main attraction.

But one way and another each year we accumulate Christmas savings, a Fruitcake Fund. These moneys we keep hidden in an ancient bead purse under a loose board under the floor under my friend's bed. The purse is seldom removed from this safe location except to make a deposit, or, as happens every Saturday, a withdrawal; for on Saturdays I am allowed ten cents to go to the picture show. My friend has never been to a picture show, nor does she intend to: "I'd rather hear you tell the story, Buddy. That way I can imagine it more. Besides, a person my age shouldn't squander their eyes. When the Lord comes, let me see him clear." In addition to never having seen a movie, she has never: eaten in a restaurant, traveled more than five miles from home, received or sent a telegram, read anything except funny papers and the Bible, worn cosmetics, cursed, wished someone harm, told a lie on purpose, let a hungry dog go hungry. Here are a few things she has done and does do: killed with a hoe the biggest rattlesnake ever seen in this country (sixteen rattles), dip snuff (secretly), tame hummingbirds (just try it) till they balance on her finger, tell ghost stories (we both believe in ghosts) so tingling they chill you in July, talk to herself, take walks in the rain, grow the prettiest japonicas in town, know the recipe for every sort of old-time Indian cure, including a magical wart-remover.

Now, with supper finished, we retire to the room in a faraway part of the house where my friend sleeps in a scrap-quilt-covered iron bed painted rose pink, her favorite color. Silently, wallowing in the pleasures of conspiracy, we take the bead purse from its secret place and spill the contents on the scrap quilt. Dollar bills, tightly rolled and green as May Buds. Somber fifty-cent pieces, heavy enough to weight a dead man's eyes. Lovely dimes, the liveliest coin, the one that really jingles. Nickels and quarters, worn smooth as creek pebbles. But mostly a hateful heap of bitter-odored pennies. Last summer others in the house contracted to pay us a penny for every twenty-five flies we killed.

Oh, the carnage of August: the flies that flew to heaven! Yet it was not work in which we took pride. And, as we sit counting pennies, it is as though we were back tabulating dead flies. Neither of us has a head for figures; we count slowly, lose track, start again. According to her calculations, we have $12.73. According to mine, exactly $13. "I do hope you're wrong, Buddy. We can't mess around with thirteen. The cakes will fall. Or put somebody in the cemetery. Why I wouldn't dream of getting out of bed on the thirteenth." This is true: she always spends thirteens in bed. So, to be on the safe side, we subtract a penny and toss it out the window.

Of the ingredients that go into our fruitcakes, whisky is the most expensive, as well as the hardest to obtain: State laws (at that time) forbid its sale. But everybody knows you can buy a bottle from Mr. Haha Jones. And the next day, having completed our more prosaic shopping, we set out for Mr. Haha's business address, a "sinful" (to quote public opinion) fish-fry and dancing café down by the river. We've been there before, and on the same errand; but in previous years our dealings have been with Haha's wife, an iodine-dark Indian woman with brassy peroxide hair and a dead-tired disposition. Actually, we've never laid eyes on her husband, though we've heard that he's an Indian too. A giant with razor scars across his cheeks. They call him Haha because he's so gloomy, a man who never laughs. As we approach his café (a large log cabin festooned inside and out with chains of garish-gay naked light bulbs and standing by the river's muddy edge under the shade of river trees where moss drifts through the branches like gray mist) our steps slow down. Even Queenie stops prancing and sticks close by. People have been murdered in Haha's café. Cut up. Hit on the head. There's a case coming up in court next month. Naturally these goings-on happen at night when the colored lights cast crazy patterns and the victrola wails. In the daytime Haha's is shabby and deserted. I knock at the door, Queenie barks, my friend calls: "Mrs. Haha, ma'am? Anyone to home?"

Footsteps. The door opens. Our hearts overturn. It's Mr. Haha Jones himself! And he *is* a giant; he *does* have scars; he *doesn't* smile. No, he glowers at us through Satan-tilted eyes and demands to know: "What you want with Haha?"

For a moment we are too paralyzed to tell. Presently my friend half-finds her voice, a whispery voice at best: "If you please, Mr. Haha, we'd like a quart of your finest whisky."

His eyes tilt more. Would you believe it? Haha is smiling! Laughing, too. "Which one of you is a drinkin' man?"

"It's for making fruitcakes, Mr. Haha. Cooking."

This sobers him. He frowns. "That's no way to waste good whisky." Nevertheless, he retreats into the shadowed café and seconds later appears carrying a bottle of daisy yellow unlabeled liquor. He demonstrates its sparkle in the sunlight and says: "Two dollars."

We pay him with nickels and dimes and pennies. Suddenly, jangling the coins in his hand like a fistful of dice, his face softens. "Tell you what," he proposes, pouring the money back into our bead purse, "just send me one of them fruitcakes instead."

"Well," my friend remarks on our way home, "there's a lovely man. We'll put an extra cup of raisins in *his* cake."

The black stove, stoked with coal and firewood, glows like a lighted pumpkin. Eggbeaters whirl, spoons spin round in bowls of butter and sugar, vanilla sweetens the air, ginger spices it; melting, nose-tingling odors saturate the kitchen, suffuse the house, drift out to the world on puffs of chimney smoke. In four days our work is done. Thirty-one cakes, dampened with whiskey, bask on window sills and shelves.

Who are they for?

Friends. Not necessarily neighbor friends: indeed, the larger share are intended for persons we've met maybe once, perhaps not at all. People who've struck our fancy. Like President Roosevelt. Like the Reverend and Mrs. J. C. Lucey, Baptist missionaries to Borneo who lectured here last winter. Or the little knife grinder who comes through town twice a year. Or Abner Packer, the driver of the six o'clock bus from Mobile, who exchanges waves with us every day as he passes in a dust-cloud whoosh. Or the young Wistons, a California couple whose car one afternoon broke down outside the house and who spent a pleasant hour chatting with us on the porch (young Mr. Wiston snapped our picture, the only we've ever had taken).

Is it because my friend is shy with everyone *except* strangers that these strangers, and merest acquaintances, seem to us our truest friends? I think yes. Also, the scrapbooks we keep of thank-you's on White House stationery, time to time communications from California and Borneo, the knife grinder's penny post cards, make us feel connected to eventful worlds beyond the kitchen with its view of a sky that stops.

Now a nude December fig branch grates against the window. The kitchen is empty, the cakes are gone; yesterday we carted the last of them to the post office, where the cost of stamps turned our purse inside out. We're broke. That rather depresses me, but my friend insists on celebrating—with two inches of whisky left in Haha's bottle. Queenie has a spoonful in a bowl of coffee (she likes her coffee chicory-flavored and strong). The rest we divide between a pair of jelly glasses. We're both quite awed at the prospect of drinking straight whisky; the taste of it brings screwed-up expressions and sour shudders. But by-and-by we begin to sing, the two of us singing different songs simultaneously. I don't know the words to mine, just: *Come on along, come on along, to the darktown strutters' ball.* But I can dance: that's what I mean to be, a tap dancer in the movies.

My dancing shadow rollicks on the walls; our voices rock ·the chinaware; we giggle: as if unseen hands were tickling us. Queenie rolls on her back, her paws plow the air, something like a grin stretches her black lips. Inside myself, I feel warm and sparky as those crumbling logs, carefree as the wind in the chimney. My friend waltzes round the stove, the hem of her poor calico skirt pinched between her fingers as though it were a party dress: *Show me the way to go home,* she sings, her tennis shoes squeaking on the floor, *Show me the way to go home.*

Enter: two relatives. Very angry. Potent with eyes that scold, tongues that scald. Listen to what they have to say, the words tumbling together into a wrathful tune: "A child of seven! whisky on his breath! are you out of your mind? must be loony! road to ruination! remember Cousin Kate? Uncle Charlie? Uncle Charlie's brother-in-law? shame! scandal! humiliation! kneel, pray, beg the Lord!"

Queenie sneaks under the stove. My friend gazes at her shoes, her chin quivers, she lifts her skirt and blows her nose and runs to her room. Long after the town has gone to sleep and the house is silent except for the chimings of clocks and the sputter of fading fires, she is weeping into a pillow already as wet as a widow's handkerchief.

"Don't cry," I say, sitting at the bottom of her bed and shivering despite my flannel nightgown that smells of last winter's cough sirup. "Don't cry," I beg, teasing her toes, tickling her feet, "you're too old for that."

"It's because," she hiccups, "I *am* too old. Old and funny."

"Not funny. Fun. More fun than anybody. Listen. If you don't stop crying you'll be so tired tomorrow we can't go cut a tree."

She straightens up. Queenie jumps on the bed (where Queenie is not allowed) to lick her cheeks. "I know where we'll find real pretty trees, Buddy. And holly, too. With berries big as your eyes. It's way off in the woods. Farther than we've ever been. Papa used to bring us Christmas trees from there: carry them on his shoulder. That's fifty years ago. Well, now: I can't wait for morning."

Morning. Rime lusters the grass; the sun, round as an orange and orange as hot-weather moons, balances on the horizon, burnishes the silvered winter woods. A wild turkey calls. A renegade hog grunts in the undergrowth. Soon, by the edge of knee-deep, rapid-running water, we have to abandon the buggy. Queenie wades the stream first, paddles

across, barking complaints at the swiftness of the current, the pneumo-
nia-making coldness of it. We follow, holding our shoes and equipment
(a hatchet, a burlap sack) above our heads. A mile more: of chastising
thorns, burrs and briars that catch at our clothes; of rusty pine needles
brilliant with gaudy fungus and molted feathers. Here, there, a flash, a
flutter, an ecstasy of shrillings remind us that not all the birds have
flown south. Always, the path unwinds through lemony sun pools and
pitch vine tunnels. Another creek to cross: a disturbed armada of
speckled trout froths the water round us, and frogs the size of plates
practice belly flops; beaver workmen are building a dam. On the farther
shore, Queenie shakes herself and trembles. My friend shivers, too:
not with cold but enthusiasm. One of her hat's ragged roses sheds a
petal as she lifts her head and inhales the pine-heavy air. "We're almost
there; can you smell it, Buddy?" she says, as though we were
approaching an ocean.

And, indeed, it is a kind of ocean. Scented acres of holiday trees,
prickly-leafed holly. Red berries shiny as Chinese bells: black crows
swoop upon them screaming. Having stuffed our burlap sack with
enough greenery and crimson to garland a dozen windows, we set
about choosing a tree. "It should be," muses my friend, "twice as tall
as a boy. So a boy can't steal the star." The one we pick is twice as tall
as me. A brave, handsome brute that survives thirty hatchet strokes
before it keels with a creaking, rending cry. Lugging it like a kill, we
commence the long trek out. Every few yards we abandon the struggle,
sit down and pant. But we have the strength of triumphant huntsmen;
that and the tree's virile, icy perfume revive us, goad us on. Many
compliments accompany our sunset return along the red clay road to
town; but my friend is sly and noncommittal when passersby praise the
treasure perched in our buggy: what a fine tree and where did it come
from? "Yonderways," she murmurs vaguely. Once a car stops and the
rich mill owner's lazy wife leans out and whines: "Giveya two-bits
cash for that ol tree." Ordinarily my friend is afraid of saying no; but
on this occasion she promptly shakes her head: "We wouldn't take a
dollar." The mill owner's wife persists. "A dollar, my foot! Fifty cents.
That's my last offer. Goodness, woman, you can get another one." In
answer, my friend gently reflects: "I doubt it. There's never two of
anything."

Home: Queenie slumps by the fire and sleeps till tomorrow,
snoring loud as a human.

A trunk in the attic contains: a shoe box of ermine tails (off the
opera cape of a curious lady who once rented a room in the house),
coils of frazzled tinsel gone gold with age, one silver star, a brief rope

of dilapidated, undoubtedly dangerous candy-like light bulbs. Excellent decorations, as far as they go, which isn't far enough: my friend wants our tree to blaze "like a Baptist window," droop with weighty snows of ornament. But we can't afford the made-in-Japan splendors at the five-and-dime. So we do what we've always done: sit for days at the kitchen table with scissors and crayons and stacks of colored paper. I make sketches and my friend cuts them out: lots of cats, fish too (because they're easy to draw), some apples, some watermelons, a few winged angels devised from saved-up sheets of candy-bar tin foil. We use safety pins to attach these creations to the tree; as a final touch, we sprinkle the branches with shredded cotton (picked in August for this purpose). My friend, surveying the effect, clasps her hands together. "Now honest, Buddy. Doesn't it look good enough to eat?" Queenie tries to eat an angel.

After weaving and ribboning holly wreaths for all the front windows, our next project is the fashioning of family gifts. Tie-dye scarves for the ladies, for the men a home-brewed lemon and licorice and aspirin sirup to be taken "at the first Symptoms of a Cold and after Hunting." But when it comes time for making each other's gift, my friend and I separate to work secretly. I would like to buy her a pearl-handled knife, a radio, a whole pound of chocolate-covered cherries (we tasted some once, and she always claims, "I could live on them, Buddy, Lord yes I could—and that's not taking His name in vain"). Instead, I am building her a kite. She would like to give me a bicycle (she's said so on several million occasions: "If only I could, Buddy. It's bad enough in life to do without something *you* want; but confound it, what gets my goat is not being able to give somebody something you want *them* to have. Only one of these days, I will, Buddy. Locate you a bike. Don't ask how. Steal it, maybe"). Instead, I'm fairly certain that she is building me a kite—the same as last year, and the year before: the year before that we exchanged slingshots. All of which is fine by me. For we are champion kite-fliers who study the wind like sailors; my friend, more accomplished than I, can get a kite aloft when there isn't enough breeze to carry clouds.

Christmas Eve afternoon we scrape together a nickel and go to the butcher's to buy Queenie's traditional gift, a good, gnawable beef bone. The bone, wrapped in funny paper, is placed high in the tree near the silver star. Queenie knows it's there. She squats at the foot of the tree staring up in a trance of greed: when bedtime arrives she refuses to budge. Her excitement is equaled by my own. I kick the covers and turn my pillow as though it were a scorching summer's night. Somewhere a rooster crows falsely, for the sun is still on the other side of the world.

"Buddy, are you awake?" It is my friend, calling from her room, which is next to mine; and an instant later she is sitting on my bed holding a candle. "Well, I can't sleep a hoot," she declares. "My mind's jumping like a jack rabbit. Buddy, do you think Mrs. Roosevelt will serve our cake at dinner?" We huddle in the bed, and she squeezes my hand I-love-you. "Seems like your hand used to be so much smaller. I guess I hate to see you grow up. When you're grown up, will we still be friends?" I say always. "But I feel so bad, Buddy. I wanted so bad to give you a bike. I tried to sell my cameo Papa gave me. Buddy," she hesitates, as though embarrassed, "—I made you another kite." Then I confess that I made her one, too; and we laugh. The candle burns too short to hold. Out it goes, exposing the starlight, the stars spinning at the window like a visible caroling that slowly, slowly daybreak silences. Possibly we doze; but the beginnings of dawn splash us like cold water: we're up, wide-eyed and wandering while we wait for others to waken. Quite deliberately my friend drops a kettle on the kitchen floor. I tap-dance in front of closed doors. One by one the household emerges, looking as though they'd like to kill us both; but it's Christmas, so they can't. First, a gorgeous breakfast: just everything you can imagine—from flapjacks and fried squirrel to hominy grits and honey-in-the-comb. Which puts everyone in a good humor except my friend and I. Frankly, we're so impatient to get at the presents we can't eat a mouthful.

Well, I'm disappointed. Who wouldn't be? With socks, a Sunday school shirt, some handkerchiefs, a hand-me-down sweater and a year's subscription to a religious magazine for children, *The Little Shepherd*. It makes me boil. It really does.

My friend has a better haul. A sack of Satsumas, that's her best present. She is proudest, however, of a white wool shawl knitted by her married sister. But she *says* her favorite gift is the kite I built. And it *is* very beautiful; though not as beautiful as the one she made me, which is blue and scattered with gold and green Good Conduct stars; moreover, my name is painted on it, "Buddy."

"Buddy, the wind is blowing."

The wind is blowing, and nothing will do till we've run to a pasture below the house where Queenie has scooted to bury her bone (and where, a winter hence, Queenie will be buried, too). There, plunging through the healthy waisthigh grass, we unreel our kites, feel them twitching at the string like sky fish as they swim into the wind. Satisfied, sunwarmed, we sprawl in the grass and peel Satsumas and watch our kites cavort. Soon I forget the socks and hand-me-down sweater. I'm as happy as if we'd already won the fifty-thousand-dollar Grand Prize in that coffee-naming contest.

"My, how foolish I am!" my friend cries, suddenly alert, like a woman remembering too late she has biscuits in the oven. "You know what I've always thought?" she asks in a tone of discovery, and not smiling at me but a point beyond. "I've always thought a body would have to be sick and dying before they saw the Lord. And I imagined that when he came it would be like looking at the Baptist window: pretty as colored glass with the sun pouring through, such a shine you don't know it's getting dark. And it's been a comfort: to think of that shine taking away all the spooky feeling. But I'll wager it never happens. I'll wager at the very end a body realizes the Lord has already shown himself. That things as they are," her hand circles in a gesture that gathers clouds and kites and grass and Queenie pawing earth over her bone, "just what they've always been, was seeing Him. As for me, I could leave the world with today in my eyes."

This is our last Christmas together.

Life separates us. Those who Know Best decide that I belong in a military school. And so follows a miserable succession of bugle-blowing prisons, grim, reveille-ridden summer camps. I have a new home, too. But it doesn't count. Home is where my friend is, and there I never go.

And there she remains, puttering around the kitchen. Alone with Queenie. Then alone. ("Buddy," she writes in her wild, hard-to-read script, "yesterday Jim Macy's horse kicked Queenie bad. Be thankful she didn't feel much. I wrapped her in a Fine Linen sheet and rode her in the buggy down to Simpson's pasture where she can be with all her Bones. . . .") For a few Novembers she continues to bake her fruitcakes singlehanded; not as many, but some: and, of course, she always sends me "the best of the batch." Also, in every letter she encloses a dime wadded in toilet paper: "See a picture show and write me the story." But gradually in her letters she tends to confuse me with her other friend, the Buddy who died so long ago; more and more, thirteenths are not the only days she stays in bed: a morning arrives in November, a leafless, birdless coming of winter morning, when she cannot rouse herself to exclaim: "Oh, my, it's fruitcake weather!"

And when that happens, I know it. A message saying so merely confirms a piece of news some secret vein had already received, severing from me an irreplaceable part of myself, letting it loose like a kite on a broken string. That is why, walking across a school campus on this particular December morning, I keep searching the sky. As if I expected to see, rather like hearts, a lost pair of kites hurrying toward heaven.

ALFRED KAZIN

Alfred Kazin, prominent writer, critic, and teacher, was born in the Brownsville section of Brooklyn in 1915. He went to C.C.N.Y. during the Depression, an education he recently described in *Coming of Age in the Thirties*. His books include *On Native Grounds*, a study of modern American prose literature, and *A Walker in the City*, from which the following selections are taken. In addition, he has edited *The Portable Blake*, *F. Scott Fitzgerald: The Man and His Work*, and *Moby Dick*. Writing recently of Thoreau, Kazin said, "If we have any moral heroes and imminent martyrs today, it is not men of violence, no matter how holy it seems to them, but Russian writers and poets who are locked up for years in Arctic camps for sending their manuscripts out of the country; American scientists who refuse to aid in the destruction of Viet-Nam and its people; young students who believe in peace, live by peace, and act for peace."

Brownsville

When I was a child I thought we lived at the end of the world. It was the eternity of the subway ride into the city that first gave me this idea. It took a long time getting to "New York"; it seemed longer getting back. Even the I.R.T. got tired by the time it came to us, and ran up into the open for a breath of air before it got locked into its terminus at New Lots. As the train left the tunnel to rattle along the elevated tracks, I felt I was being jostled on a camel past the last way stations in the desert. Oh that ride from New York! Light came only at Sutter Avenue. First across the many stations of the Gentiles to the East River. Then clear across Brooklyn, almost to the brink of the ocean all our fathers crossed. All those first stations in Brooklyn—Clark, Borough Hall, Hoyt, Nevins, the junction of the East and West Side express lines—told me only that I was on the last leg home, though there was always a stirring of my heart at Hoyt, where the grimy subway platform was suddenly enlivened by Abraham and Straus's windows of ladies' wear. Atlantic Avenue was vaguely exciting, a crossroads, the Long Island railroad; I never saw a soul get in or out at Bergen Street; the Grand Army Plaza, with its great empty caverns smoky with dust and chewing-gum wrappers, meant Prospect Park and that stone path beside a meadow where as a child I ran off from my father one summer twilight just in time to see the lamplighter go up the

path lighting from the end of his pole each gas mantle suddenly flaring
within its corolla of pleated paper—then, that summer I first strayed off
the block for myself, the steps leading up from the boathouse, the long
stalks of grass wound between the steps thick with the dust and smell
of summer—then, that great summer at sixteen, my discovery in the
Brooklyn Museum of Albert Pinkham Ryder's cracked oily fishing
boats drifting under the moon. Franklin Avenue was where the Jews
began—but all middle-class Jews, *alrightniks,* making out "all right" in
the New World, they were still Gentiles to me as they went out into the
wide and tree-lined Eastern Parkway. For us the journey went on and
on—past Nostrand, past Kingston, past Utica, and only then out into
the open at Sutter, overlooking Lincoln Terrace Park, "Tickle-Her"
Park, the zoo of our adolescence, through which no girl could pass on a
summer evening without its being understood forever after that she
was "in"; past the rickety "two-family" private houses built in the
fever of Brownsville's last real-estate boom; and then into Brownsville
itself—Saratoga, Rockaway, and home. For those who lived still
beyond, in East New York, there was Junius, there was Pennsylvania,
there was Van Siclen, and so at last into New Lots, where the city goes
back to the marsh, and even the subway ends.

Yet it was not just the long pent-up subway ride that led me to
think of Brownsville as the margin of the city, the last place, the car
barns where they locked up the subway and the trolley cars at night.
There were always raw patches of unused city land all around us filled
with "monument works" where they cut and stored tombstones, as
there were still on our street farmhouses and the remains of old
cobbled driveways down which chickens came squealing into our
punchball games—but most of it dead land, neither country nor city,
with that look of prairie waste I have so often seen on my walks along
the fringes of American cities near the freight yards. We were nearer
the ocean than the city, but our front on the ocean was Canarsie—in
those days the great refuse dump through which I made my first and
grimmest walks into the city—a place so celebrated in New York
vaudeville houses for its squalor that the very sound of the word was
always good for a laugh. CAN-NARR-SIE! They fell into the aisles. But
that was the way to the ocean we always took summer evenings—
through silent streets of old broken houses whose smoky red Victorian
fronts looked as if the paint had clotted like blood and had then been
mixed with soot—past infinite weedy lots, the smell of freshly cut
boards in the lumber yards, the junk yards, the marshland eating the
pavement, the truck farms, the bungalows that had lost a window or a
door as they tottered on their poles against the damp and the ocean
winds. The place as I have it in my mind still reeks of the fires burning
in the refuse dumps. Farms that had once been the outposts of settlers

in Revolutionary days had crumbled and sunk like wet sand. Canarsie was where they opened the sluice gates to let the city's muck out into the ocean. But at the end was the roar of the Atlantic and the summer house where we stood outside watching through lattices the sports being served with great pitchers of beer foaming onto the red-checked tablecloths. Summer, my summer! Summer!

We were of the city, but somehow not in it. Whenever I went off on my favorite walk to Highland Park in the "American" district to the north, on the border of Queens, and climbed the hill to the old reservoir from which I could look straight across to the skyscrapers of Manhattan, I saw New York as a foreign city. There, brilliant and unreal, the city had its life, as Brownsville was ours. That the two were joined in me I never knew then—not even on those glorious summer nights of my last weeks in high school when, with what an ache, I would come back into Brownsville along Liberty Avenue, and, as soon as I could see blocks ahead of me the Labor Lyceum, the malted milk and Fatima signs over the candy stores, the old women in their housedresses sitting in front of the tenements like priestesses of an ancient cult, knew I was home.

We were the end of the line. We were the children of the immigrants who had camped at the city's back door, in New York's rawest, remotest, cheapest ghetto, enclosed on one side by the Canarsie flats and on the other by the hallowed middle-class districts that showed the way to New York. "New York" was what we put last on our address, but first in thinking of the others around us. *They* were New York, the Gentiles, America; we were Brownsville—*Brunzvil*, as the old folks said—the dust of the earth to all Jews with money, and notoriously a place that measured all success by our skill in getting away from it. So that when poor Jews left, *even* Negroes, as we said, found it easy to settle on the margins of Brownsville, and with the coming of spring, bands of Gypsies, who would rent empty stores, hang their rugs around them like a desert tent, and bring a dusty and faintly sinister air of carnival into our neighborhood.

They have built a housing project deep down the center of Brownsville, from Rockaway to Stone, cutting clean diagonal forms within the onlooking streets, and leaving at one end only the public school I attended as a boy. As I walked past those indistinguishable red prisms of city houses, I kept remembering what they had pulled down to make this *project*—and despite my pleasure in all this space and light in Brownsville, despite even my envious wonder what our own life would have been if *we* had lived, as soon all of New York's masses will live, just like everybody else, still, I could not quite believe that what I saw before me was real. Brownsville in that model quarter looks like an old crone who has had a plastic operation, and to my amazement I miss her old, sly, and withered face. I miss all those ratty little wooden tenements, born with the smell of damp in them, in which there grew up how many schoolteachers, city accountants, rabbis, cancer specialists, functionaries of the revolution, and strong-arm men for Murder, Inc.; I miss that affected squirt who always wore a paste diamond on his left pinky and one unforgotten day, taught me to say *children* for *kids;* I miss the sinister "Coney Island" dives where before, during, and after the school day we all anxiously gobbled down hot dogs soggy in sauerkraut and mustard, and I slid along the sawdust floor fighting to get back the violin the tough guys always stole from my locker for a joke; I miss the poisonous sweetness I used to breathe in from the caramels melting inside the paper cartons every time I passed the candy wholesaler's on my way back from school; I miss the liturgical refrain *Kosher-Bosher* lettered on the windows of the butcher shops; the ducks at Thanksgiving hanging down the doorways of the chicken store; the clouds of white dust that rose up behind the windows of the mattress factory. Above all I miss the fence to the junk yard where I would wait with my store of little red volumes, THE WORLD'S GREATEST SELECTED SHORT STORIES, given us gratis by the *Literary Digest,* hoping for a glimpse of a girl named Deborah. At eleven or twelve I was so agonizedly in love with her, not least because she had been named after a prophetess in Israel, that I would stand at the fence for hours, even creep through the junk yard to be near her windows, with those little red books always in my hand. At home I would recite to myself in triumph the great lines from Judges: *Desolate were the open towns in Israel, they were desolate, until that I arose, Deborah. . . .* But near her I was afraid, and always took along volumes of THE WORLD'S GREATEST SELECTED SHORT STORIES as a gift, to ease my way into her house. She had five sisters, and every one of them always seemed to be home whenever I called. They would look up at me standing in their kitchen with the books in my hand, and laugh. "Look, boychik," the eldest once said to me in a kindly way, "you don't have to *buy* your way in here every time with those damned books just to see Deborah! Come on your own!"

There is something uncanny now about seeing the old vistas rear up at each end of that housing project. Despite those fresh diagonal walks, with their trees and children's sandboxes and Negro faces calmly at home with the white, so many of the old tenements have been left undisturbed on every side of the project, the streets beyond are so obviously just as they were when I grew up in them, that it is as if they had been ripped out of their original pattern and then pasted back again behind the unbelievable miniatures of the future.

To make that housing project they have torn away the lumber yard; the wholesale drygoods store where my dressmaker mother bought the first shirts I ever wore that she did not make herself; how many poolrooms; and that to me sinister shed that was so long a garage, but before that, in the days of the silents, a movie house where every week, while peddlers went up and down the aisles hawking ice-cream bricks and orange squeeze, I feasted in my terror and joy on the "episodes." It was there one afternoon, between the damp coldness in the movie house and the covetous cries of the peddlers, that I was first seized by that bitter guilt I always felt in the movies whenever there was still daylight outside. As I saw Monte Blue being locked into an Iron Maiden, it suddenly came on me that the penalty for my delicious reveries might be just such a death—a death as lonely, as sickeningly remote from all human aid, as the one I saw my hero calmly prepare to face against the yellow shadows of deepest Asia. Though that long-forgotten movie house now comes back on me as a primitive, folksy place—every time the main door was opened to let in peddlers with fresh goods, a hostile mocking wave of daylight fell against the screen, and in the lip-reading silence of the movies I could hear the steady whir and clacking of the machine and the screech of the trolley cars on Rockaway Avenue—I instantly saw in that ominous patch of light the torture box of life-in-death, some reproach calling out the punishment for my sin.

A sin, perhaps, only of my own devising; the sin I recorded against all idle enjoyment, looking on for its own sake alone; but a sin. The daylight was for grimness and labor.

I see that they have also torn out that little clapboard Protestant church that stood so long near the corner of Blake Avenue. It was the only church I ever saw in our neighborhood—the others were the Russian Orthodox meeting-house in East New York, and the Catholic church on East New York Avenue that marked the boundary, as I used to think of it, between us and the Italians stretching down Rockaway and Saratoga to Fulton. That little clapboard church must have been the last of its kind surviving from the days when all that land was owned by Scottish farmers. I remember the hymns that rolled out of the church on Sunday mornings, and how we sniffed as we went by. All those earnest, faded-looking people in their carefully brushed and strangely old-fashioned clothes must have come down there from a long way off. I never saw any of them except on Sunday mornings—the women often surprisingly quite fat, if not so fat as ours, and looking rather timid in their severe dresses and great straw hats with clusters of artificial flowers and wax berries along the brim as they waited for each other on the steps after the service; the men very stiff in their long four-buttoned jackets. They did not belong with us at all; I could never entirely believe that they were really there. One afternoon on my way back from school my curiosity got the better of me despite all my fear of Gentiles, and I stealthily crept in, never having entered a church in my life before, to examine what I was sure would be an exotic and idolatrous horror. It was the plainest thing I had ever seen—not, of course, homey, lived-in, and smelling of sour wine, snuff, and old prayer books, like our little wooden synagogue on Chester Street, but so varnished-clean and empty and austere, like our school auditorium, and so severely reserved above the altar and in the set rows of wooden pews to the service of an enigmatic cult, that the chief impression it made on me, who expected all Christians to be as fantastic as albinos, was that these people were not, apparently, so completely different from us as I had imagined. I was bewildered. What really held me there was the number of things written in English. I had associated God only with a foreign language. Suspended from the ceiling over the altar was a great gold-wood sign on which the black Gothic letters read: I AM THE RESURRECTION AND THE LIFE. I remember standing in the doorway, longing to go all the way up the aisle, then suddenly running away. The distance from that doorway to the altar was the longest gap in space I had ever seen.

. . . .

In Brownsville tenements the kitchen is always the largest room and the center of the household. As a child I felt that we lived in a kitchen to which four other rooms were annexed. My mother, a "home" dressmaker, had her workshop in the kitchen. She told me once that she had begun dressmaking in Poland at thirteen; as far back as I can remember, she was always making dresses for the local women. She had an innate sense of design, a quick eye for all the subtleties in the latest fashions, even when she despised them, and great boldness. For three or four dollars she would study the fashion magazines with a customer, go with the customer to the remnants store on Belmont Avenue to pick out the material, argue the owner down— all remnants stores, for some reason, were supposed to be shady, as if the owners dealt in stolen goods—and then for days would patiently fit and baste and sew and fit again. Our apartment was always full of women in their housedresses sitting around the kitchen table waiting for a fitting. My little bedroom next to the kitchen was the fitting room. The sewing machine, an old nut-brown Singer with golden scrolls painted along the black arm and engraved along the two tiers of little drawers massed with needles and thread on each side of the treadle, stood next to the window and the great coal-black stove which up to my last year in college was our main source of heat. By December the two outer bedrooms were closed off, and used to chill bottles of milk and cream, cold borscht and jellied calves' feet.

The kitchen held our lives together. My mother worked in it all day long, we ate in it almost all meals except the Passover *seder*, I did my homework and first writing at the kitchen table, and in winter I often had a bed made up for me on three kitchen chairs near the stove. On the wall just over the table hung a long horizontal mirror that sloped to a ship's prow at each end and was lined in cherry wood. It took up the whole wall, and drew every object in the kitchen to itself. The walls were a fiercely stippled whitewash, so often rewhitened by my father in slack seasons that the paint looked as if it had been squeezed and cracked into the walls. A large electric bulb hung down the center of the kitchen at the end of a chain that had been hooked into the ceiling; the old gas ring and key still jutted out of the wall like antlers. In the corner next to the toilet was the sink at which we washed, and the square tub in which my mother did our clothes. Above it, tacked to the shelf on which were pleasantly ranged square, blue-bordered white sugar and spice jars, hung calendars from the Public National Bank on Pitkin Avenue and the Minsker Progressive Branch of the Workman's Circle; receipts for the payment of insurance premiums, and household bills on a spindle; two little boxes engraved with Hebrew letters. One of these was for the poor, the other to buy back the Land of Israel. Each spring a bearded little man would suddenly appear in our kitchen, salute us with a hurried Hebrew blessing, empty the boxes (sometimes with a sidelong look of disdain if they were not full), hurriedly bless us again for remembering our less fortunate Jewish brothers and sisters, and so take his departure until the next spring, after vainly trying to persuade my mother to take still another box. We did occasionally remember to drop coins in the boxes, but this was usually only on the dreaded morning of "midterms" and final examinations, because my mother thought it would bring me luck. She was extremely superstitious, but embarrassed about it, and always laughed at herself, whenever, on the morning of an examination, she counseled me to leave the house on my right foot. "I know it's silly," her smile seemed to say, "but what harm can it do? It may calm God down."

The kitchen gave a special character to our lives; my mother's character. All my memories of that kitchen are dominated by the nearness of my mother sitting all day long at her sewing machine, by the clacking of the treadle against the linoleum floor, by the patient twist of her right shoulder as she automatically pushed at the wheel with one hand or lifted the foot to free the needle where it had got stuck in a thick piece of material. The kitchen was her life. Year by year, as I began to take in her fantastic capacity for labor and her anxious zeal, I realized it was ourselves she kept stitched together. I can never remember a time when she was not working. She worked because the law of her life was work, work and anxiety; she worked because she would have found life meaningless without work. She read almost no English; she could read the Yiddish paper, but never felt she had time to. We were always talking of a time when I would teach her how to read, but somehow there was never time. When I awoke in the morning she was already at her machine, or in the great morning crowd of housewives at the grocery getting fresh rolls for breakfast. When I returned from school she was at her machine, or conferring over *McCall's* with some neighborhood woman who had come in pointing hopefully to an illustration—"Mrs. Kazin! Mrs. Kazin! Make me a dress like it shows here in the picture!" When my father came home from work she had somehow mysteriously interrupted herself to make supper for us, and the dishes cleared and washed, was back at her machine. When I went to bed at night, often she was still there, pounding away at the treadle, hunched over the wheel, her hands steering a piece of gauze under the needle with a finesse that always contrasted sharply with her swollen hands and broken nails. Her left hand had been pierced through when as a girl she had worked in the infamous Triangle Shirtwaist Factory on the East Side. A needle had gone straight through the palm, severing a large vein. They had sewn it up for her so clumsily that a tuft of flesh always lay folded over the palm.

The kitchen was the great machine that set our lives running; it whirred down a little only on Saturdays and holy days. From my mother's kitchen I gained my first picture of life as a white, overheated, starkly lit workshop redolent with Jewish cooking, crowded with women in housedresses, strewn with fashion magazines, patterns, dress material, spools of thread—and at whose center, so lashed to her machine that bolts of energy seemed to dance out of her hands and feet as she worked, my mother stamped the treadle hard against the floor, hard, hard, and silently, grimly at war, beat out the first rhythm of the world for me.

FOUR

DAVID IRISH

David Irish was born in 1950 in Island Falls, Maine. He graduated from Katahdin High School and attends Bates College. His essay first appeared in *Growing Up in Maine*, a collection of essays by Bowdoin College Upward Bound Students in 1968.

Barn

My father leads a very strange life. In some ways it is very interesting and fun, and in other ways it is a very hard life.

On the days when he has to work in the barn, he has to get up at a most beautiful hour, three o'clock in the morning. The air is extremely cold, crisp, and fresh. There is usually a sort of dim light outside due to the attempts of the sun to come up. There is almost always a hazy mist there, which makes the cold even colder.

Dad always gets up at just the right time, and he never uses an alarm clock. After long years of working like this, he has sort of developed his own alarm clock. He gets up immediately, without stretching, and his eyes are already wide open and his mind is as keen as ever. He pulls on the smelly, dirty, faded pants and colored plaid workshirt. He keeps his shoes downstairs, so he tiptoes in his stockinged feet so as not to wake us up. I would feel extremely guilty if I let him know I was awake. It is as if this were his own private world, and no one should ever intrude, except maybe my mother.

I can hear him moving around downstairs, picking up clothes for Mom so that she won't have to work so hard during the day. He goes out and splits a pile of wood, making sharp cracking echoes that reverberate through the trees. I can almost see him smiling because his muscles are just waking up and he feels better. He picks up a whole pile at once, rearranging them with his right hand while holding them with his left arm. The snow crunches and the door squeaks on his way in. He drops the wood on the mat by the stove, making a clunking noise. The old stove bangs a lot while he is arranging paper, putting in kindling wood, and then putting in the heater wood. As soon as he lights it, I can hear the crackling of kindling and can smell the pungent odor of wood smoke. After he has finished he sits at the table and has some coffee and toast. When I smell that buttered toast, my stomach suddenly feels empty and I feel obliged to turn over and try to ignore it.

He'll have a real breakfast later on, so he's just filling up what he calls the 'lower cavity.' Now Dad takes the kettle of hot water, no longer making any attempt to be quiet because, to him, his world has come alive; the sun is breaking up the mist and glaring off the crusted snow. He walks out to the car and pours the water on the ice on the windshield, using the windshield wiper to help clear it off. Now he starts up the car so that it will be nice and warm when he gets ready to leave.

If it wasn't for the fact that he sometimes gets me up to go to the barn to help him, I would probably never get to know any more about his morning. He comes in on these mornings and comes to the bottom of the stairs and says my name. "Come on Dave, y' gotta get up if you want to go with me." He says it so softly that I feel almost obliged to get up, so I just jump right up, "Comin,' Dad, just get me some of that toast and coffee, huh?"

We drive off and head for the barn. He drives very slowly, and he even gets angry if I'm driving and I'm driving with any speed. It kind of startled me at first, but I soon found out why. I never knew before that there were so many small creatures still moving in the winter, but at this time in the morning they are active because they are trying to store up food for the day. We would pass by several creatures, each seeming to disregard us and just walking along beside us. They were so dulled by winter sleepiness that they were incapable of scurrying away. We saw animals like porcupine, muskrat, and others. Dad kept talking to me and pointing out little things about the animals he thought I should know. He'd point out their size to indicate how they were faring the winter or maybe if they were just collecting food for their families. He'd point out where they came out of the woods and where they went back in so that we would know where they lived when we needed to know. He'd also see how often a certain species appeared so that we would know how plentiful they were, in preparation for the hunting and trapping seasons, and he'd describe the tracks in detail and their habits in detail so that someday I'd be a competent hunter and trapper myself. He often lapses into verbal remembrances of times when he hunted such an animal and just what trick he used to catch it. He often likes to go off hunting, but Mom protests because there is always lots of work to do around the house. Dad says, "Women just don't know what it means to a man just to get away by himself in the woods." He is quite frank like that with my older brother and me. He is only brought back to immediate reality if he sees another animal or we reach the barn.

The barn is big and white, but always friendly at any time, night or day. It seems friendlier now because I know of the lighthearted talk, the great jokes, and the cursing of equipment and cattle that goes on inside. It was nice stepping from the frigidity of the outside world into the comfortable warmth of the inside created by the body heat of the cattle. Though my eyes are hardly ever fully awake at this time, or my stomach filled, it is a comforting feeling knowing that when we leave, we will have an hour to rest and plenty of food to eat.

Now the day is in full swing. I do the odd chores while Dad cleans the cows off and milks. I climb the mow, feeling like a little kid up there pushing bales of hay down with my feet. It is often damp and musty and so is repulsive, so I hurry with the chore and get down. I hay up the calves, playing with the smaller ones and just pushing the big ones around. It is about the only excuse they have during the winter months to use their leg muscles. Their legs act like rigor mortis has set in on a living creature. If they feel they're not getting enough attention while I'm shoveling the manure, they'll come up to my backside and gingerly nose me so that I will have to turn around and push them out of the way. About the only way I ever could get the chore done was to simply ignore them. They are visibly hurt after a while; the nosing becomes feeble, and they clumsily wander off, sniffing at the walls. Often they'll visit another stall and smell the nails. It is a strange thing to do, but they always end up there, smelling the nails.

Of all the jobs I do in the barn, the one I dislike most is putting the calves back in their dark, lonely stalls. I encourage us both by talking to them about the nice, fresh hay there, and how nice it will be to lie down in a dry bed, all the while aiming their noses at the entrance and pushing them from behind. They bawl and kick a lot, openly protesting the idea.

Sometimes, when I'm here alone with the calves enjoying these simplest of conversations, I lean ahead of the fork and think just how quiet and peaceful it is. I even wonder if maybe I'd like to live a life on the farm myself. But then I hear the milking machines Dad is handling, I hear the cows bellowing, I remember how heavy those machines are, I can visualize Dad's muscles flexing as he lifts them, the same way they've flexed and strained all of his life, and I remember what he's always told me, "You're goin' to school and make a better life for yourself." Suddenly the farm seems like a jail with its door all triggered and waiting for me. I can come to visit but I can never let the door close, because if it does I'll never have a chance to get out.

I drive out the manure-spreader and empty it down by the woods. The cold air refreshes me and I forget about my thoughts, imagining now a life of ease wherein I could maybe come and help Dad like now.

I have a special job to do. I milk the newly-freshened cows and feed their milk to the newly born calves. I take the pail of milk to the calves, which wriggle and jump and bawl with anticipation. The only way they can drink is for me to sort of simulate their mother by inserting my hand into their mouths. They suck on the hand like they would their mother, and I shove their noses into the milk. When they have begun to drink without this aid, I take my hand out and let them finish drinking. I feel satisfied and proud as if I have just finished a parental task.

Usually, by the time I finish all my chores, Dad has finished milking, so we wash out the dishes and machines, putting them neatly on the racks when we're finished. Dad dips our milk jugs into the fresh milk, which has been cooled off by the cooler, and I go to say a temporary good-bye to the cows by turning off the barn lights.

"Are you hungry now?" Those are Dad's customary words, indicating that the work is finished and it's time to go home and have a good, hearty meal. We each pick up a jug of milk and head for the car.

JESSE STUART

Jesse Stuart was born in 1907 near Riverton, Kentucky. He attended a one-room school and began working for neighboring farmers when he was nine; he later worked as a concrete mixer and as a blacksmith. He was the first in his family to attend high school and went on to Vanderbilt University, where he survived on one meal a day to become a schoolteacher and writer. Among his many books are the autobiographical *The Thread That Runs So True* and *My Land Has a Voice,* from which the following selection comes. Jesse Stuart lives in the house where he was born.

Lady

The sawmill had moved in to cut the giant trees on the farm we had rented; we were moving out. As we moved down the hollow with the last load, Pa sat on the express-wagon seat with Mom. They looked for the last time at the land they had cleared and farmed. I sat on the end of the express wagon and led Gypsy, our cow, with a long rope. Raggs and Scout, our hounds, followed the wagon.

When we reached the sawmill Pa stopped the mule, climbed from the wagon, and helped Mom down. They walked over to see the sawmill. I tied Gypsy's rope to the rim of the muddy wheel, then slid

off the back end of the wagon and hurried down to the dam where
several men were standing around the hole of water, a few of them
sighing, others laughing.

"I tell ye hit's jist hard to drown a pup," an old man with a
coal-black mustache was saying. "I've tried hit. Ye ought to put hit in a
coffee sack and put a big rock in th' sack and throw hit in."

"Jist keep throwin hit in the water," said a cleanshaven young
man. "Hit'll drown in a minute."

I saw the helpless pup working its front paws in the bottom of the
deep hole of mountain water. It worked its way to the top. When it
stuck its nose above the water, two tiny streams of water came from its
nostrils, shooting a few inches into the air.

"Jist keep shovin hit back," the young man said to the short man
with a beardy face. He pushed the pup back to the bottom with a long
pole.

"Don't shove it back any more!" I screamed. "*I want it!*"

Mom and Pa walked over to the water hole.

"What kind of a pup is it?" Pa asked.

"It's a lady pup," the old man with the black mustache said right in
front of Mom.

"Let 'im have it, Mick," Mom said. "Don't drown it."

"No she-dogs around my place," Pa said firmly.

"But remember, part of the place is mine," Mom said.

As Mom and Pa argued, the men looked at each other. And while
they argued, I hurried to the express wagon with the shivering, whining
pup in my arms. I pulled my cap off and put the pup in it.

Soon as we reached the house I carried my pup in one hand and
led Gypsy to the barn lot with the other. Pa and Mom carried house
plunder from the express wagon to the house. "We're in fer a lot o'
trouble with that she-dog," I heard Pa tell Mom. And Mom didn't try to
answer him.

That evening Mom fixed a bottle for my pup. She put a stopper in a
bottle and then put a goose quill through the stopper.

"Poor little pup," Mom said. "She's without a mother."

We filled the bottle soon as we'd milked Gypsy. Then I fed my pup
before I carried in wood, got in kindling, and drew water from the well.
All the time I worked I thought about a name for her. The name that
stuck in my mind was the name that the old man with the black
mustache called her when he told Mom and Pa what kind of dog she
was. He said she was a "lady dog." So I called her Lady Dog. But that
name was a little long when I talked to her and petted her. I started
calling her Lady.

The next morning, soon as I got out of bed and dressed, I hurried
downstairs to get Lady from her box. She was whining but stopped as

soon as I took her in my arms. Now her hair was dry and fluffy. There was a white wisp of hairs on the end of her tail. She was the prettiest pup I'd ever seen.

Mom helped me feed her. She even warmed milk for Lady before she put it in the bottle. And it wasn't long until Lady's eyes opened. She wouldn't stay in the box. She'd jump out and follow me about the house, biting at my overall legs like I was her mother. But the house wasn't a world big enough for Lady. She was soon going to the barn with me. When I started to cut cornstalks and sprouts on the steep hill slopes, Lady followed me. Soon this was not enough world for her; she went into the woods alone.

It was that summer when we were hoeing corn, I heard Lady bark after a rabbit. She ran the rabbit past me—I knew it was a she-rabbit, for most of her soft hair had been pulled out. And I knew just why, too. She had pulled it from her own body to make a bed for her little rabbits. But Lady was too young to catch her.

She often ran after rabbits. I knew her bark when she was running—little fast yelps. But on this day she barked in one place. It was a long bark. It was a sweet bark; it was music to my ears. I dropped my bean basket and took off to see why she was barking. When I found her she was barking up a hickory tree. I saw a gray squirrel right in the top, sticking to a wind-bent limb. I patted Lady on the head. "Stay, Lady," I said.

Lady stayed, too, until I got back with the gun. I laid the gun barrel across a little limb, for it was too heavy for me to hold in the air. I leveled across the barrel at the squirrel. I'd never shot a gun before. I almost closed my eyes when I pulled the trigger . . . then a great sound and a cloud of smoke—and something came tumbling down, hitting the green leaves as it fell. It was the squirrel. Lady grabbed it as soon as it hit.

One day in September when I was cutting corn, I killed seven squirrels that Lady treed on one hill slope. I couldn't cut corn for taking my gun to the hill to kill a squirrel. She smelled in a hollow beech log and barked. I cut the log with my corn knife and there was a big possum. I let Lady fight it—petted her when she did. I knew that after this she'd know I'd want her to catch a possum, and she would go after them. I'd have a possum dog as well as a squirrel dog.

When I carried my game home Pa looked at me and asked, "Where did you get all that game?"

"Caught it with Lady," I said proudly.

"You didn't cut much corn, did you?"

Pa wouldn't admit it, but he was proud of me and my dog.

When October came Lady and I spent nights in the woods together. She would tree possums like she had treed squirrels. Some nights we'd hunt all night. I'd get home at daylight, do my work around the house, then go to school. And I told the boys at school about my dog. Soon everybody was talking about the good dog I had.

"You've sold possum hides and bought your clothes and school-books," Pa said. "If you don't tag her the sheriff will kill her."

I knew Pa wanted me to ask him for the two dollars so he could refuse me. I lay in bed that night and thought about how I'd tag her. I couldn't sell more hides. It was out of season. I told Mom about it. She gave me all the money she had—a one-dollar bill. I sold my marbles to a boy at Plum Grove school for a dime; I cut stovewood one Saturday for Mr. Daugherty for fifty cents; I borrowed a quarter from my sister with a promise of ten cents interest; I borrowed a dime from my cousin, Glenn Hilton. Even then I lacked five cents—but the time was up and I hurried to the county clerk's office to get Lady a tag.

"We won't kill your dog," the clerk said gently. "And I'm not going to charge you that extra nickel."

Lady was a year old when she started having boy friends. It was June when I found her under the crib floor with a family of four. And they were all ladies.

"You'll have to drown 'em," Pa commanded.

"But I can't."

"You will 'r I'll kill her and the pups," Pa stormed at me. "Son, I ain't standing this foolishness no longer. I'm going to town this morning and I want 'em drowned by the time I'm back. Put 'em in a coffee sack with rocks and throw 'em in a hole of water."

After Pa left I put Lady in the corncrib. I took the four pups to a hole of water. But I didn't put the pups in a coffee sack with rocks. I couldn't do that. When I threw the little blind pups in the water, they slowly came to the top. I'd throw them in again like I'd seen the man do at the sawmill. Then Lady passed me like a flash. How she'd ever got between the corncrib logs I don't know. I watched her jump into the water—carry each struggling pup by the back of the neck to the bed under the corncrib floor.

"Did you kill th' pups?" Pa asked soon as he returned.

"I couldn't. Give me a chance to give 'em away."

"I'll give you a chance," Pa said.

I had a time giving her pups away. Everybody wanted a male pup—just like Pa. They said the she-dogs were so much trouble. But I told them what a tree-dog their mother was. I told them the amount of game I'd caught with Lady; I finally gave her pups away.

Winter ran into another spring. Then Lady's lovers came again. This time Pa was furious. He quarreled violently with Mom about my dog.

"I'm going to kill Lady, Mom," I finally said.

Mom wiped her eyes with her apron. She didn't say a word.

I wouldn't shoot her with the gun she loved to hear bark when it rolled the squirrels from the tall trees, I thought. I would kill her with my club.

I went to the corncrib to get her. Lady followed me up on the hill where I was going to get a club. Lady watched me cut it. Tears blinded my eyes until I couldn't see my dog. When I wiped the tears away, Lady stood before me looking straight at me with her keen vixen-eyes. Her little ears stood straight as if she were listening for me to say a kind word to her—but I held death in the club for my dog. I looked at her and didn't speak. Then, like the puppy she once was, she pulled at my overall leg and whined. *I just couldn't kill her.*

"Did you kill her?" Pa asked me soon as I reached the house.

"No, I didn't," I said.

"What are you going to do with her?" Pa asked.

"I'm going to give her away," I answered.

I told the boys near home I wanted to give Lady away. I begged them to help me find a person to take her. My cousin, Glenn Hilton, found a man that would take her, since she was a good tree-dog. Ronald Jenkins, an old hunter with a long beard, came and got Lady.

Another season passed and I didn't hunt. And another season passed and I never took a gun into the woods. We had rented another farm now, and we moved to new hunting grounds.

One day in June I followed my father up the path. We were going to the field to hoe corn. We had to pass the deserted log shack where we used to live when we had Lady.

"Can't believe it," Pa said, as he stopped and turned to look at me.

It was Lady! She ran around him to me. She greeted me by kissing my hands and face. Then she ran toward the corncrib. We hurried after her and looked under the floor. There we found four pups.

"Can't she have but four pups?" Pa asked. Then he smiled at me. "Shan, if that dog thinks that much of us, she'll never leave again."

I didn't hoe corn that afternoon. I took Lady to the new place where we had moved and fixed a bed for her puppies while she greeted Mom and my brother and sisters.

Each season I hunted with her while I went to Plum Grove school. Each spring she had four pups. But her reputation grew. When I went to high school I hunted less with Lady. When I finished high school Lady was getting gray around the mouth. She was eleven years old.

After I'd gone four years to college Lady was a little slower about greeting me.

When I started teaching school Lady was fifteen. Now she was going blind. She grew so deaf she couldn't hear me speak to her, but she could see my lips work and she knew I was talking to her. When I came home she slowly walked to greet me. She'd kiss my hands and face. She had a time getting up in a chair where she slept on the back porch. We sawed the legs from the chair and put a cushion on it for a bed. At sixteen she had two pups; at seventeen she had one puppy, though she was totally blind, totally deaf, and her hair was white as sheep's wool.

One morning I went out to wake Lady where she was sleeping in her chair. Her head was erect, her white ears pointing upward like she always looked when I spoke to her. But she stared with sightless eyes. Lady was dead. I carried her to a high hill overlooking our farm and buried her. And I put a fieldstone at the head of her grave and carved LADY on it.

HERBERT R. COURSEN, JR.

Herbert R. Coursen, Jr., was born in Newark, New Jersey, in 1932, and grew up in the New Jersey suburb of Short Hills. He graduated from Amherst College in 1954, where he edited the humor magazine, Sabrina. He has received advanced degrees from Wesleyan University and the University of Connecticut. He served for four years in the United States Air Force as a fighter pilot. He now teaches English at Bowdoin College.

The Son of Nick Massimo

Autumn, 1939, the suburbs of New Jersey—America drifts in a dream towards war with jag-helmeted Nazis, jack-booted Italians, and bandy-legged Japanese. They flicker at us from newsreels, these menacing foreigners. The grey domes of sky fill with the drone of bombers. People stand stock-still, look up, then scurry off, flicking glances over shoulders. Refugees flee from pillars of smoke, plodding and heavy beneath bundles and children, thick in peasant garments, huddled and ducking, as if avoiding invisible blows, behind crude wagons, moving too slowly, piled with bedding and other refuse that once had known a home. Hostages die with contemptuous stares, their women wringing hands and wailing. Children stare up at men swinging slowly—like dolls—from gallows. Cities crumble like castles of sand.

We play under the blue bowl of an almost endless August and

return to school through crackle-leaf streets as our suburb dozes in the bask of Indian Summer, curls cozily into wrappings of pipe-smelling smoke woven from countless bonfires licking leaves in our cobbled gutters. Munich is far away and Japan appears only on the bottoms of the cheap toys cluttering the counters of the Five and Ten.

My brother and I have a few busy-work chores each Saturday morning—rubbing wax on the floors in the spaces between the oriental rugs, emptying the wastebaskets—chores which take time only because we evade them until a motherly voice grows peremptory. By 10:30 we are bounding from the house to trot the half mile to the grammar-school field, an eroding plain rutted like a miniature Colorado by the rains coursing from the hills above to the clogged sewer below. There we play baseball until September, football until snow. Or we may dash the 100 yards to the woods around the corner, filling now with urgency as darkening skies appear earlier and grow larger through the thinning trees. Hurry, snow is coming and the woods will close. Autumn is urgent.

Spring had been eager. We had run to the woods after school, long before the mud began to parch and crumble, early ferns tracing along our bare legs, low mounds of grey snow lurking like animals in the shadows of evergreens, eager we had run into the damp scented woods to play hide-and-seek. I lie in a trench, absorbed in the smell of generations of leaves layered beneath me, watching the boy who is "it" pass by. I am warm with the knowledge that he will not find me. I rise to all fours, push off like a sprinter, and rush towards the big tree which is "home" and shout "homefree!" an instant before my fingers touch the veins of bark. The woods have a stream with a rough planked bridge over it—it had all been a farm once before trees stepped back across its acres. One day I pick out the brightest pebbles in the stream to take home to my mother. In a half hour they are uniformly dull-brown. The next day I sprinkle them back into the stream where they are bright again. The woods of spring say that something good is coming. They sing of my immortality. But the fall woods are not the same, and usually my brother and I go to the field for football.

One day we do something mean. A boy named Brian, new to the neighborhood, joins our game.

"You're the ball carrier, Brian," I say, winking at everyone else.

"Great!" he says.

The ball is centered. Brian wraps his arms around its bulk and charges forward. He is hit by everyone in the game—the three people on his team and the four on the other. Down he goes beneath 400 pounds of little boys. His ancient leather helmet spins sideways on his head, so that his nose protrudes from an ear-hole. We unpile. He sits up and twists his helmet back in place and looks at us groggily.

"Great!" I say. "Brian, that was great!" The others join in.
"Gee, was it?" We tell him how great it was and he carries the ball
again. And again. Finally Brian decides that someone else should carry
the ball. In a little while it is time for him to go home. He never plays
with us again.

Every Saturday in the fall, "Nick Massimo—Landscape Arche-
tect" (so says the sign on his old pick-up truck) works over the leaves
on the McKell's lawn across the street, never looking up as we sprint
past. With him works his son, raking steadily towards the huge piece of
canvas in which Nick will bundle the leaves. The fathers of the
neighborhood burn their leaves in the gutters. Nick carries his off to
some unknown place. One day Nick takes a mattress we have left for
the garbage men and ties it to the back of his truck. I report this theft
excitedly to my mother.

"Well, I'm glad *someone* can use that old thing," she says.
"You mean someone's going to *sleep* on it?"
"Of course. You did, didn't you?"

The son of Nick Massimo is my age—eight or nine—but smaller,
with black hair that shines in the slanting light of autumn, wearing
always the same black sweater cut short at elbows and the same
dungarees faded pale and patched in red. His lustrous eyes follow us
even as his olive forearms move the rake. We know that he watches us.

One day as we issue forth, virtuous for the completion of our
chores, I say "Hi" to Nick Massimo's son. Soon we are exchanging a
few words at the end of the McKell's lawn—tentatively, because he
doesn't go to our school, doesn't play on our field or in our woods,
doesn't, we guess, collect baseball cards or listen to "Your Hit Parade"
on Saturday nights. But soon he has convinced us that we should spend
Saturday morning helping *him* on the lawn. He hints at the money his
father will pay us.

"You get *money* for this work," he says.

We rake furiously, hoping to gain the approving eye of the elder
Massimo working stolidly far across the expansive lawn. We move the
old rakes the boy has given us and envision the jovial noon—Nick,
smiling, with thick hands full of gleaming quarters, pressing one or two
into our rake-roughened palms. We pile the pungent leaves onto the
huge canvas and curry the lawn as if we are preening a prize stallion for
a show. On we toil, perspiring now in the direct sight of the sun, until
the lawn shines. We wait politely for our pay while Nick ties the
corners of the leaf bundle and plods bent-backed to his truck, looking
like a nightmare of St. Nicholas. Finally, he approaches, grasping a
new wooden rake by the throat and pointing at it with the jab of a blunt
finger.

"Looka dis," he cries. "Looka dis!" His grainy thumb points at a missing tooth in the rake. "How you expec me to pay for dis? My new raka ruin!"

We cower before his invincible foreignness. My brother's white face reflects back my own. I hadn't used that rake. Had he? Will Nick Massimo charge across the street brandishing the rake and demanding payment from our parents? No—he moves his free hand up and down the air and across the shattered implement, then turns towards his leaf-burdened Chevrolet, where his dark-eyed son stares straight ahead and waits to go home.

War comes. Nick and his son are seen no more.

"Probably got a job in a defense plant," my mother says. Our maid, Sally, and, in fact, the entire colony of maids which had inhabited the neighborhood and which had trooped down the streets on Thursday mornings to take the train to Newark, had left for good—to take jobs in defense plants.

My brother and I play on in the woods which change only with the seasons. We play war games—always against the Japanese, who fall obligingly before our voiced gun-shots. We charge forward invulnerable and, tree by tree, reclaim our sacred woods from the invader.

But one spring our woods are full of real men, swart, with strange sounds on their tongues, carrying milk bottles full of water and eating dripping, dark sandwiches, the bread looking as if it encloses something alive. The men ride roaring machines and strew grainy sewer pipes over the ruined fields that had been our woods. And I am afraid of the men and do not know why.

SAMUEL HOPKINS ADAMS

Samuel Hopkins Adams was born in Dunkirk, New York, in 1871 and grew up along the Erie Canal, vividly described in his autobiographical work, *Grandfather Stories* (1955), from which the following selection has been taken. After graduation from Hamilton College he became a journalist, later concentrating on fiction and biography. Adams' best-known novel, *Revelry* (1926), was based on the scandals of the Harding administration and was banned in Washington. Its dramatization was banned in Philadelphia. Another of his works, *It Happened One Night* (1934), was turned into one of the great movies of the 1930's, with Clark Gable and Claudette Colbert. Since Gable did not wear an undershirt in that movie, it was blamed for ruining the "undershirt industry," but Adams disavowed any such intention. He died in 1958.

Marcia and the Celebrity

Only the rigorous family rule constrained the four of us to attendance upon our grandfather, that September Saturday. Our hearts were downtown where scandalous proceedings impended. The outcaste Dr. Mary Walker, in PANTS, if the capitals in the morning paper were to be believed, supported by Rochester's own revolutionary daughter, Susan B. Anthony, was to deliver an inflammatory address in favor of that devil's doctrine, Female Suffrage.

We were four, not five, because young Charlie had played hooky and headed for Corinthian Hall with his putty-blower up his trouser leg. As the rest of us climbed the cottage steps, Grandfather's formidable voice met us halfway.

"Why shouldn't she wear 'em if she's a mind to?"

Dr. Ely, our family physician, appeared in the partly opened door. He turned to issue a warning.

"Stop waggling that foot or I'll come back and amputate it."

We entered, Jenny in the lead. "What ails your foot, Grandpa?" she asked politely.

"Poor man's gout," he snapped. By this he meant an ingrown toenail.

He tossed aside the issue of the *Democrat & Chronicle* over which he and Dr. Ely had been holding high debate. Jenny peeked at a crumpled headline.

"Does she really wear you-know-whats?" she inquired decorously.

"What if she does?" the old gentleman retorted.

"It isn't very ladylike," Jenny said.

"Why should it be? There never yet was a women's rights speechifier that wasn't more cock than hen. Let 'em dress accordingly." He shifted his leg to a more comfortable position. "Except one," he added in a milder tone. His eyes strayed to the secretary desk against the wall.

"Who was she, sir?" Jenny asked.

"None of you has so much as heard of that brilliant, if wrongheaded exponent of Equality for the Sexes, Miss Frances Wright, I suppose," he replied.

"Did she wear 'em, sir?" Reno asked.

"She did *not*," was the emphatic answer.

"Anyway, I've heard of her," Jenny said brightly. "I've heard Grandma say that she was not a nice person."

"Then you had better not remain to hear more about her," the old gentleman growled in a tone that he seldom employed toward his favorite. "Go out to the kitchen and help your grandmother with her pin-money pickles." The spicy odor was oozing through the crack of the door. "And close the door after you."

"Oh, *Grand*-pa!" Jenny wailed, and withdrew, close to tears.

"Miss Frances Wright," said the scholarly John in a musing tone. "Didn't she write a book?"

"She did. Several. One of them is on the second shelf yonder. At the right end. You may fetch it."

He handed John the key. John opened the glass doors and took down the volume. A twinge in the afflicted toe distracted Grandfather's attention so that he failed to notice his grandson opening to the fly-leaf and holding it up for our inspection. There was an inscription in spidery handwriting.

To an Impudent Young Yankee Blade,
whom may Heaven undeservedly pardon,
this Memorial, with the Obliged
Recognizances of the Author.
                              F.W.
        London, England. Oct. 26, 1821.

We stared at one another. Our austere and dignified forebear thus characterized!

John said hesitantly, "Is the book yours, sir?"

"A gift from the gifted authoress, as you see."

"Then you're the imp—the young blade?" I ventured.

"Eh? What? Give me that book, John." A slow, reminiscent smile appeared upon the bearded lips. "Ah, yes," he murmured. "A very tongue-free lady. A clement disposition. This"—he tapped the cover—"is an earnest of her lenity."

"Why did she want Heaven to pardon you, sir?" John asked.

"My conduct," said Grandfather, "was in a measure reprehensible. I cannot look back upon it without contrition." Reno winked at me. The old gentleman's expression was anything but contrite. "She brought it upon her own fair head, however," he pursued, "by an attitude which could not but be irritant to one's sentiments of patriotism as an American. We were all powerfully patriotic in those days."

John, who had been dipping into the book, looked puzzled. "She says some pretty nice things about us here," he remarked.

"Nice! Over-nice. And she was worse on the lecture platform before the book came out. Praise to the face is open disgrace, as the rhymster puts it. She dispensed encomiums until the stomach turned.

Toosey-woosey and honey-fuggle, as one might say. One might suppose that she had discovered the United States of America and could not find words fulsome enough in which to approbate her own discovery. Doubtless she meant well by us, but, for my youthful taste, she was intolerably—how shall I put it?"

"Condescending," I suggested.

He frowned at me. "You are ignorant of the meaning of the word, Samuel."

John came to the rescue. "Doesn't it mean patronizing, sir?"

"A corrupt and deteriorate attribution. When we speak of affable and condescending manners do we indicate patronage, *de haut en bas*? No; no," he answered himself. "The proper significance of condescending is the attitude of fellowship on a basis of equality."

Having thus set us aright etymologically, he took Miss Wright's opus from John's hands.

"What was it you did to her, sir?" John asked.

The smile returned to Grandfather's lips and became momentarily a grin. "I fixed *her* flint," he said. Though critical of slang in the mouths of our generation, he occasionally came out with a phrase of ancient cant. "That is," he qualified, "I would have if my better nature and Squire Grainger had not intervened. Do any of you remember your distant kinswoman, Marcia Everingham, born Dillard?"

We did. The primmest, prissiest portrait in the family connection was that of the ringletted old lady, a very pattern of piety. Grandfather's next words somewhat mitigated that impression.

"Marcia was the town terror. Not yet eleven years of age, she was already the most accomplished liar in Ontario County. She lied to everybody; to her doting parents, to her teachers, to the parson himself. And," he added, "to Miss Frances Wright." He glanced at the kitchen door to make sure of its being tight closed. "No ladies being present, I can recite to you the circumstances," he said.

Canandaigua, New York, Grandfather began, was all of a feeze over the visit of the distinguished Miss Wright. Young Myron Adams, then just past his majority, drove from his home in East Bloomfield to attend the afternoon reception given in her honor. Passing along Main Street, he caught sight of little Marcia Dillard engaged in a study of the courthouse wall. He pulled up his high-wheeled suicide gig and mounted the steps to see what was holding her attention. It was a roster of legal actions.

At his greeting, she turned with a bright and innocent smile. "Oh, how-d'ye-do, Cousin Myron! I think crime is cruel interesting, don't you?"

"That depends," said the young man.

"What's arson?"

"Never mind," Grandfather said, foreseeing that further research into the annals of malfeasance might inspire more embarrassing questions. That list was hardly appropriate reading matter for a ten-year-old female.

"People always say that when I ask questions," she complained. She shifted an all-day sucket from one cheek-pouch to the other and turned admiring eyes upon the elegance of his velvet coat, flowered waistcoat and cameo-secured neckcloth. "Where are you going, all dressed up so dicty?" she demanded.

"To the gala for Miss Frances Wright."

"I know. At Squire Grainger's. It'll be mortal bunkum, won't it, Cousin Myron?"

He replied that the Grainger entertainments were usually quite superior. "Would you like to go, Marcy?" he asked.

Her mouth drooped. "I can't. I'm disinvited." Dolorously she explained that all the other girls in the dame school which she attended were going. "It's that meanie, Miss Gillespie," she said.

"Your teacher? I suppose you have been doing or saying something specially pernickety," said Grandfather who was conversant with her reputation.

"I never," she disclaimed. With hands piously folded before her she intoned:

Pinky, pinky bow-bell.
If I should tell a lie,
I'd go down to the bad place.
Cross my heart and die!

"Now will you believe me, Cousin Myron?"

"No," said Grandfather. "But never mind that."

"She said I was an *enfant terrible* and would disgrace the school," said the afflicted Marcia in a rush of words. "*Enfant terrible* is French. It means a bad child." She brightened a little. "I'm not very apt at the Rule of Three and I'm a downright ignorama at Gains and Losses, but nobody can say that I ain't a dab at French. I suppose there'll be raspberry lemonade," she quavered, and wept.

"See here," Grandfather said, "do you very much want to go?"

"How can I? It's scambling to go where you're disinvited. I'd never be a scambler," she declared virtuously.

"It won't be scambling if I escort you," he assured her. "Wipe your nose, smooth down your frock, and disgorge that sweetmeat."

"Oh, Cousin Myron!" she cried. "I do love you. Shall I be presented to the English lady? Will she be very proud and huffish? Is it true that she's writing a book? I ambition to write a book when I grow up."

He replied that Miss Wright was gathering data for publication.

Marcia's bright eyes became dreamy. "I could tell her things," she murmured.

That was the exact moment, said Grandfather, when Satan took over the proceedings.

The fiesta was well under way when they arrived. They made their manners to the Squire and his lady-wife and were ushered into the back parlor where a representation of Canandaigua's schools was exhibiting its best behavior.

A small, pretty Englishwoman, very finified in a silk gown, a Paisley shawl, and earbobs as big as plums, sat on a dais, gazing out over the assemblage with an air of resolute amiability. The spatulate arm of her high-backed chair held a notebook, a pewter well of briar-root ink, two fresh goose-quills, a sandbox and a shot-bowl. A file of children, solemn, starched and suffering, was being conducted to the presence. Each recited a verse or exhibited a carefully memorized compliment. The lady smiled brightly.

Her wandering regard centered upon the newcomer from East Bloomfield, who must then have been a personable young man, as he stepped up to present her with a cluster of artificial flowers delicately sprayed with scent. (Natural blooms would have been inelegant for so formal an occasion.) They exchanged appropriate observations on the weather after which he introduced his young kinswoman, Marcia Happalonia Dillard.

"Marcia aspires to woo the muse of literature," he said, adding in a sharp aside, "Drop a curtsy, ninnywit!"

"Happalonia," the lady repeated. "What interesting names the North Americans choose for their children! Do they call you 'Happy' in the home circle, my dear?"

"No, ma'am," Marcia said. "I'm not."

"Not happy? Surely you should be. Why not?"

"My folks don't understand me," Marcia said sadly.

Miss Wright smiled at Grandfather. *"La femme incomprise."* She turned to the girl. "How old are you, child?"

"Fifteen."

"What! You do not look it."

Marcia reached for a long word. "I'm precocious."

Miss Wright looked skeptical. Marcia was disappointed. Had not Cousin Myron assured her that the traveling English would believe anything that was told them?

The lady asked, "Do you live here in Canandaigua?"

"No, ma'am. I just school here. We live in Palmyra."

"Palmyra? Palmyra! Classics in the wilderness."

"We aren't wilderness," the Palmyran said. Half closing her eyes, she recited: "Palmyra is destined to become the metropolis of this region. With our advantageous situation on beautiful Ganargwa Creek, we cannot fail . . ."

"Yes, yes," the lady interrupted. "Ganargwa. That is an aboriginal name, is it not? I am interested in the aborigines. Do you have Indians in Palmyra?"

"Oh, yes, ma'am. Lots."

"Are they wild?"

"Awf'ly wild. Pa shot one last week."

"Shot an aborigine? What for?"

Marcia recalled the list on the courthouse wall. Arson she rejected—Cousin Myron had refused to tell her what it meant. She passed from A to B.

"Bastardy," she said.

Miss Wright gasped. "Do you know what you are saying, my child?"

"Oh, yes, ma'am," Marcia replied. "He weltered in his gore."

The visitor turned to Grandfather. "Can this be true?" she asked.

Grandfather was saved from the necessity of thinking up a suitable reply by the arrival of the Lady President of the Hepzibah Sewing Circle, who had elbowed her way to the dais, dragging a reluctant child with her.

"Oh, Miss Wright, ma'am," she gushed. "Such an honor to our humble village! This is my little Mirabella. Make your manners, dear."

The visitor regarded the lank and simpering maiden without enthusiasm. "How do you do?" she said. "Will you excuse me if I continue my conversation with this other little girl?" Mother and daughter passed on.

"That's Mirabella Upcraft," Marcia volunteered. "She has a tetter. It wouldn't be mannerly for me to tell you where."

"Never mind her. Tell me of yourself. You attend school, one supposes."

"Yes, ma'am."

"Do you like it?"

"No, ma'am."

"Not like your school? All these other children love it."

"So they tell *you*, ma'am. They're saucy little liars," said Marcia mournfully. "If they love it so, why do they play hooky?"

"They play hooky?" said the authoress, making a note. "And you do not?"

"No, ma'am. I would not so diminish myself."

"What are your favorite amusements?"

"Attendance upon church and Sunday school," was the prim reply.

"Hunca-munca!" retorted the lady, who prided herself on her Yankee colloquialisms. "Church is a duty. I wish to know how you and your young companions disport yourselves. Do you play with dolls?"

"Not any more."

"What do you play with?"

"Oh, wildcats and foxes, and bats and snakes and owls," Marcia replied.

"Creatures of forest and darkness," the authoress commented. "Do you, then, frequent the woodland at night?"

Marcia had once made a nocturnal excursion with a bevy of her mates, and had been soundly spanked for it. She now expanded this adventure. "Yes, ma'am," she replied. "'Most every night."

"Doubtless with your parents. Supplying meat for your larder." Miss Wright had a vision of a frontier family creeping forth in the darkness to stalk a deer or a squirrel for the morning's meal.

"No, ma'am. We get our meat from the Stone Front Store."

"What, then, is the purpose of these excursions?"

"Gold," Marcia said in a whisper.

"I was not aware that the precious metal is found in this vicinity."

"Oh, yes, ma'am! Bushels and barrels of it."

Another entry went into the ledger. "Have you, yourself, discovered any?"

"Not yet, ma'am. But Tip says we will. He's got a hazel cunjur-wand."

"Indeed!" Miss Wright turned a page and took a fresh goose-quill. "And who may Tip be?"

"The gypsy boy I go gold-hunting with. He can charm birds, too."

Miss Wright's eyebrows went up. "A gypsy? You go nightfaring with a gypsy? I have already set down some reflections upon the innocent freedom enjoyed by the youth of this great nation, but really!"

At this point, Grandfather interrupted the story to read a passage aloud to us:

> The youth of both sexes enjoy a freedom of intercourse unknown in the older and more formal nations of Europe. They dance, sing and "run in sleighs" together by sunshine and moonshine, without the occurrence or even the apprehension of any impropriety.

"This was written before the encounter with my little kins-woman," Grandfather told us. "I believe that, after the interview, it was deleted from the manuscript, but later restored. However, to resume."

"Am I then to apprehend," asked Miss Wright, "that parents permit their progeny of opposite sexes to rove the forest by night?"

"They don't know," the girl said. "We lie awake and wait, and when Presbyterian time strikes the mystic hour, we make our evasion out the window."

"This is most extraordinary," the lady said. She appealed to Marcia's escort. "Is this child truly representative of American family standards?"

"Best old York State stock," Grandfather assured her.

Gratified by the impression she was making, Marcia now recited a couplet:

" 'Oft have we passed the guilty night
In revellings and frantic mirth.' "

The British authoress' stock in trade was broad-mindedness. But there were limits. This time, she was honestly shocked. Such libertinism from a maid of tender years! Such innocence of face! It was hardly credible. In the interests of truth, as embodied in her forthcoming book, she put the question direct.

"I trust that you will take my meaning, my dear. Surely you have, yourself, remained virtuous," she said.

Marcia was puzzled, but not for worlds would she have admitted it. Memory came to her aid again. In that good old household standby, *The Temperance Almanach,* under the heading "Maxims of Conduct for Young Females," she had read that "A Virtuous Child is she who is Docile and Pious and Keeps her Face and Hands as Clean as her Soul." Her soul was all right; she had no misgivings on that score. But her hands! Why had she not stopped by the town horse trough and washed? Now it was too late. She could not qualify.

"No, ma'am," she said in a shamed quaver.

Miss Wright's fashionable earbobs oscillated. "I think it is dreadful," she exclaimed. "What sort of upbringing can the unfortunate child have had!"

"I am an ex-cept-u-ally well-brought-up girl," said Marcia. "Whoever is without sin among you, let him squale the first rock at her."

Miss Wright was not too scandalized to note a new Yankeeism. "Squale?" she repeated. "Squale a rock?"

She entered it in the margin of her ledger. "This child," she said to Squire Grainger, who now came forward to suggest that the guest of honor take some refreshment, "is quite the most extraordinary ex-

ample of youth that I have yet been privileged to meet. Will you permit
me a few moments to put my notes in order?"

"Well, my dear," the host said to Marcia as his guest withdrew,
"and how did you come on with our celebrity?"

Marcia's smile was complacent. "Slick as Zollikoffer's wheel," she
said, lapsing into a vernacular which the absent note-taker would have
appreciated. "She asked a mortal lot of questions, but I answered 'em
all. Didn't I, Cousin Myron?"

"You did, indeed!" Grandfather replied.

"I'm not sure, though, that she understood everything I told her,"
she continued reflectively. "I'm not sure I understood it quite all,
myself," she added with charming candor. She turned to the Squire.
"You're a knowledgeable gentleman, Mr. Grainger,"she said. "What *is*
bastardy?"

"Great God of Israel!" Squire Grainger ejaculated.

Grandfather dandled the slight volume upon his knee. "So," he
remarked to us, "the Squire went into the inner sanctum where his
guest was busily writing up her notes. When he returned his face was
purple as a plum. Miss Wright's projected chapter on 'Morals of
Adolescence in a New York State Community' had, I fear, stirred his
bile. Marcia and I were dismissed from the premises with undeserved
contumely."

We all stared avidly at the book. "I'd like to read that chapter, sir,"
Reno said.

The old gentleman shook his head. "You never will, Sireno."

"Aren't you going to tell us what's in it?"

"I don't know. Nobody knows. It never appeared."

"Never appeared?" John repeated. "Why? What did Miss Wright
say to you?"

"I was not permitted to see the lady again. Upon Squire Grainger's
insistence I wrote her a letter of explanation, as the result of which she
deemed it advisable to elide the chapter. Rather a pity, too. It might
have relieved the cloying amenity of the treatment."

There was a sharp knock on the door and Jenny thrust her face,
still wearing an expression of lofty resentment, in from the kitchen.

"Grandma wishes her cookery book," she said, "if you have quite
finished your private conversation."

"We have," Grandfather answered, "and you may restore this to
its proper shelf." He handed her Miss Wright's *Views.*

I have always suspected that Jenny did her pin-money pickling
close to the door. It is, at least, significant that she at once opened the
book to the fly-leaf and read the inscription.

"How funny!" she commented. "Impudent young Yankee blade.
Oh, no! It couldn't possibly be." Her prim, little laugh tinkled in the air.

Grandfather frowned. "What is so risible about it?" he demanded. "An impudent young blade? You, Grandpa, dear? Nobody would ever believe it of you."

"Hm!" the old gentleman said. *"Tempora mutant et nos in illis mutantur."*

"You must have changed a lot," she said a little cruelly. Then, with sweet insinuation, "Grandpa?"

"Well?"

"Did *she* have a temptational eye?"

"That," said Grandfather, his dignity restored, "is a wholly irrelevant question."

CLARENCE DAY

Clarence Day was born in 1874, the son of a governor of the New York Stock Exchange. He was educated at St. Paul's School in Concord, New Hampshire, and at Yale University. He was in the Navy during the Spanish-American War, but later got arthritis and became a lifelong invalid. His infirmity in no way inhibited his humor, which emerges in *Life with Father* (1935), from which the following selection comes, *Life with Mother* (1937), and *God and My Father* (1932). Clarence Day died in 1935.

A Holiday with Father

Once in a long while, as a great treat, Father took me down to his office. This could happen only on a Saturday morning, when there was no school. I felt very important and grown-up on the days I went to "The Office"—not after I got there, to be sure, but as I was leaving the house, with Mother and my three little brothers respectfully seeing me off.

If it was a rainy day, Father would prepare for rough weather by wearing a derby hat and a black rubber mackintosh over his usual tailed coat. (He seldom was informal enough to wear a sack suit in town except on warm days, or when he left New York to go to the country, in summer.) If the sun was out, he wore a silk hat and carried a cane, like his friends. When he and they passed each other on the street, they raised their canes and touched the brims of their hats with them, in formal salute.

I admired this rich and splendid gesture, and wished I could imitate it, but I was too young for a cane. I was soberly dressed in a pepper-and-salt sack suit with short pants and the usual broad flat white Eton collar that boys wore in the eighties—a collar that started out very stiff and immaculate every morning and was done for by dinner time. Black laced or buttoned shoes and black stockings. We only wore brown in the country in summer.

On one of these Saturdays, although it was sunny, Father put on his derby. I didn't know why until later. I hopped along by his side as he walked through the long rows of comfortable-looking brownstone houses from Madison Avenue over to Sixth, climbed the stairs of the Elevated, and stood on the platform, chatting with one of his friends, while we waited for the next train.

Soon a stubby little steam engine, with its open coal car piled full of anthracite, and its three or four passenger cars swinging along behind, appeared round the curve. White smoke poured from the smokestack. The engineer leaned out from his window. "Too-oot, too-too-toot!" whistled the engine as it came puffing in. We got on board and walked leisurely through the cars till Father found a seat that he liked.

During the journey downtown, except when the smoke from the engine was too thick for me to see out, I stared fascinatedly into the windows of cheap red brick tenements, or at the even more interesting interiors of lodging houses for tramps. The second-floor rooms of the lodging houses were crowded, but I envied the tramps in them. They looked so easy-going. Not a thing to do; just tilt their chairs back against the wall, in comfortable old clothes, and smoke. If I were a tramp, I wouldn't have to scrub every last bit of grime out of my knuckles each Friday, and put on tight white kid gloves, and pull some unwieldy little girl around a waxed floor at dancing school. It wouldn't cost so very much, either. The lodging-house sign said in big letters, "Ten Cents a Night."

I never had a chance to see such sights except when I went downtown with Father, for Mother kept away from the Elevated. It was comparatively new, and she felt that the horsecars were better. Besides, Sixth Avenue was so cindery and sooty that ladies disliked it. They did go that far west sometimes, to shop, and they went as far east as Lexington, but in general they lived and walked in the long narrow strip between those two boundaries.

When Father and I left the train at the end of our journey, I found myself in a tangle of little streets full of men and boys but no women. If some lonely bonnet chanced to be bobbing along in the crowd, we all stared at it. Most of the business buildings were old and many of them were dirty, with steep, well-worn wooden stairways, and dark, busy basements. Exchange Place and Broad Street were full of these warrens, and there were some even on Wall Street. The southern corner of Wall Street and Broadway was one of the dingiest. Father raised his cane and said as we passed, "That's where Great-Aunt Lavinia was born."

A few doors beyond the Assay Office we came to a neat but narrow five-story building and walked up the front stoop. This was No. 38 Wall Street. Father's office occupied the ground floor, at the top of the stoop, and on the back part of the second floor he had a small storeroom.

The office was busy in what seemed to me a mysterious way. The cashier, who never would let me go inside his cage, sat in there on a stool, with a cash drawer, a safe full of books, another safe for securities, and a tin box full of postage stamps, which he doled out as needed. One or two bookkeepers were making beautifully written entries in enormous leather-bound ledgers. They had taken the stiff white detachable cuffs off their shirtsleeves and stacked them in a corner, and they had exchanged their regular jackets for black alpaca coats. Future bookkeepers or brokers who now were little office boys ran in and out. Western Union messengers rushed in with telegrams. In the front room there was a long table full of the printed reports issued by railroads about their earnings and traffic. Only twenty or thirty industrial stocks were traded in on the Exchange in those days, and Father's office ignored them. On or around the table were the *Commercial & Financial Chronicle,* the *Journal of Commerce,* a blackboard, a ticker, and four or five whiskery men. Two were arguing heatedly about Henry Ward Beecher, and the others were shaking their heads over some crazy proposal by the "Knights of Labor" to have an eight-hour day.

Father went into his private office, where a little coal fire was burning, hung his hat on a rack, and unlocked and sat down at his desk. While he opened his mail, I proudly brought in two stone jugs of ink, one of greenish black made in England, and one to use when he wrote letters of which he wished to keep copies, because with this ink impressions could be taken to put in his files. I cleaned and filled all Father's inkwells, and put fresh steel pens in his penholders. He had quill pens at home, but he used only steel pens at the office, and as he had no stenographer he wrote a good share of the firm's letters in longhand, himself.

There were lots of things to do in the office besides filling inkwells. It was fun to scamper around the streets carrying all the messages (which are telephoned nowadays), or to roll colored pencils down the clerks' slanting desks, or try to ring the bell on the typewriter. The latter was a new contraption which seldom was used except on important occasions, when the bookkeeper or one of the office boys had to stop work and pick at it.

All of a sudden it was noon. The customers left. The ticker came to a stop. At half past twelve Father called to me and we went out for lunch.

"Will you be back, Mr. Day?" the cashier asked respectfully, but eagerly too. On days when Father said yes, all the clerks looked disappointed. They bent over their desks, saying nothing, till Father went out of the door, but if I lingered behind for a moment I heard them slamming their ledgers about. Not only did they and the office boys all have to stay, but the rule was that they couldn't even smoke until Father had gone home for the day.

Today he said no, however. I saw them getting out their sulphur matches as he was crossing the threshold, and the instant he stepped into the hall they struck them on the seats of their pants.

I trotted along at Father's side down to Beaver Street, where there stood a mellow old building. It had the look of a friendly, hospitable country hotel. There were green blinds and little outside balconies on its upper floors, and windows with looped lacy curtains; and white pillars stood at the entrance, at the top of a low flight of steps.

This was Delmonico's, and the food was so good there that even I had heard it talked of, uptown. It was one of the places that just suited people like Father.

Delmonico's stood upon a triangular-shaped plot of ground, with the front doors at the apex, and when we arrived we met a bottle-necked jam at the entrance. Silk-hatted men, who had been lunching in a lingering way, had suddenly remembered apparently that they were due back in Wall Street, and they were shoving each other, politely but urgently, to force their way out.

As Father and I went in the long crowded room, the head waiter led us with a flourish to a table for two. The air was fragrant with cigar smoke and the appetizing smell of rich, greasy cooking. A stately-look-ing foreigner who was standing at the side of the room caught Father's eye and bowed to him in a dignified way.

"Lorenzo," Father said to him, as he approached us, "this is my son."

I bobbed my head at him, rather embarrassed, and Mr. Lorenzo Crist Delmonico bowed and said he was happy to meet me.

As he left us, old François, Father's regular waiter, hurried up to our table, and he and Father had a talk, in French, about the best dish to order. They spoke so rapidly that I couldn't understand a word of it, except that François kept assuring Father that we could rely on the sauce. *"Parfaitement."* It seemed that the last time that Father had relied on this sauce, an admittedly difficult kind, he had had a severe disappointment.

When anything of this sort occurred, I had noted, François had a healing way of dealing with such a catastrophe. He seemed even more shocked and perturbed at a failure than Father, and he would snatch the offending dish away and come racing back with a substitute. Usually he was accompanied at such moments by one of the Delmonico family—Lorenzo or Charles—who bent over the table to examine the new dish as it was placed before Father, murmuring most sympathetically about the unhappy misfortune.

Today the sauce and everything else was not only successful but perfect, and Father and François smiled and nodded in a congratulatory way to each other. I used to wonder why Father never got into rages at Demonico's as he did at home, but I see now that he may have felt lonely at home, where there were no brother experts.

Father was fond of French cooking and of being served by French waiters. At home he had to put up with an Irish waitress who was changed every few months, and with cooking which, though excellent of its kind, after all wasn't French. He ate it with relish and gusto, when it came up to his standards, but he did so like a city man in the country, enjoying good, simple fare.

I didn't always appreciate French cooking myself. It tasted all right, but it was dainty and there wasn't much of it. It seemed to me that Father got along with a very light lunch. When he was having his demi-tasse, however, and saw a hungry look on my face, he smiled understandingly and beckoned to François, who smiled too and presently came running back with a large chocolate éclair. The richness of its soft, thick yellow interior and the meltingness of its chocolate outside were so delicious that time stood still as I happily ate it, and I almost forgot where I was.

After lunch, instead of taking me back uptown, Father walked down to the Battery, and to my surprise we got on the boat at South Ferry. We had never done this before. I now saw why he was wearing his derby. We were going out to the country. Off we steamed across the sweet-smelling bay filled with sail-boats and four-masted schooners and tugboats and barges, and when we landed on Staten Island Father told me that we were going to see Buffalo Bill.

We got seats in a flimsy wooden stand full of splintery benches, and there was the Wild West spread out before us—dust, horses, and all. The wonderful marksmanship of riders who hit glass balls with their rifles—balls tossed into the air and shot at with careless ease as the horsemen dashed by; the herds of cattle, the lariats, the brass band, the old Deadwood Stage Coach, the thrilling attack on it by Indians, the last-minute rescue. Father dragged me out just before the rescue so that we could get seats on the ferryboat, but I caught a glimpse of it anyway as I was being hauled through the exit.

I wanted to be a cowboy, I told Father on the way home. He chuckled and said no I didn't. He said I might as well be a tramp.

I wondered if I'd better tell him that this idea, too, had occurred to me, no further back than that very morning. I decided that upon the whole it mightn't be a good day to mention it, just after Father had taken me to lunch at Delmonico's. I did venture to ask him, however, what was the matter with cowboys.

Father briefly explained that their lives, their food, and their sleeping accommodations were outlandish and "slummy." They lived in the wilds, he informed me, and they had practically gone wild themselves. "Put your cap on straight," he added. "I am trying to bring you up to be a civilized man."

I adjusted my cap and walked on, thinking over this future. The more I thought about it, the less I wanted to be a civilized man. After all, I had had a very light lunch, and I was tired and hungry. What with fingernails and improving books and dancing school, and sermons on Sundays, the few chocolate éclairs that a civilized man got to eat were not worth it.

JOE DANE

Joe Dane is a native of Brunswick, Maine, and a graduate of Bowdoin College (1969). The following essay appeared first in *Quill: The Bowdoin College Literary Magazine* for Winter 1966.

The Man

We lived in a town, on a street crowded with old proud houses, and the yards were all small, very small except for one. Across the street lived "The Man" and beside his house, where he should have had a neighbor, was an empty lot. We never knew his real name but he loved his title and was addressed in no other manner. There were furrows carved into his brow, between his graying hair and his bright, glowing eyes, and he was always smiling, at least, as far as we were concerned he was, for we were always happy then and his joy came from us. He loved us, the kids who lived on his block, and he loved to have us play in his yard. He would watch us, maybe join us, and when any of us received a phonograph record on a birthday or Christmas, we would take it to him and he would lead us to his shed and play it on an old, hand-cranked victrola. His face would bear that smile and maybe he would tell us stories of Geronimo—an old friend of his. Certainly he knew Geronimo; he said he did. Besides, the time I dressed up as an Indian and crept over to his house, he could tell right away that *I* wasn't the old chief.

And then there was baseball and football and his sacred grass yielded to our insignificant weight. But it was only for us. No one outside our block was allowed on his grass. I suppose it was inevitable that I should make my mistake. A friend of mine from a few blocks away had come over to see me. It was summer and our own lawn was too small anyway. Tommy didn't want me to, but I couldn't see any reason for not asking The Man if he could play with me on the sacred lawn. The Man wore his glowing smile as I approached him. I asked my question and that bright smile stole silently from his face. He wasn't angry; rather, his expression denoted worry and disappointment. No he'd rather not . . . Please . . . Then finally, a resigned "All right. Go ahead." He quickly turned away and I strode jubilantly back to Tommy with the triumph on my lips. But Tommy acted strangely. He decided he'd better not invade The Man's yard after all. I hadn't really understood what I had done; I couldn't understand The Man; and I couldn't understand Tommy's decision; but I never played on The Man's lawn again.

The grass is gone now—covered up by a new house, and The Man's house has long since been sold. Yet every once in a while, my sister receives a postcard from some distant place signed "The Man." No, The Man has never written me, but when he takes his pen and addresses a card to my sister maybe he thinks of me, and that expression that I remember so well returns to his wrinkled face.

FRANK CONROY

Frank Conroy was born in New York City in 1936. He graduated from Haverford College and now lives in Brooklyn Heights, New York. The following selection is from *Stop Time* (1968), a book praised by William Styron for its "almost total lack of self-pity," and by Norman Mailer for a style "dry as an etching, sparse, elegant, modest, cheerful."

White Days and Red Nights

Jean and my mother had weekend jobs as wardens at the Southbury Training School, a Connecticut state institution for the feeble-minded. Every Friday afternoon we drove out deep in the hills to an old cabin they had bought for a few hundred dollars on the installment plan.

The first dirt road was always plowed for the milk truck, but never the second, and in the snow you could see the tracks of wagon wheels and two narrow trails where the horses had walked. A mile down the road was the Greens' farm. Every morning they hauled milk to the pick-up station, a full silent load up to the hill, and then back, the empty returns from the previous day clanging raucously behind the horses as if in melancholic celebration. No one else ever used the road. If it was passable we drove to the cabin, if not, we walked, single file, in the horses' tracks, our arms full of food.

Every Friday the cheap padlock was opened, every Friday I stepped inside. A room so dim my blood turned gray, so cold I knew no human heart had ever beaten there—every line, every article of furniture, every scrap of paper on the floor, every burned-out match in a saucer filling me with desolation, depopulating me. A single room, twelve feet by eighteen. A double bed, a bureau, a round table to eat on, and against the wall a counter with a kerosene cooker. In the exact center of the room, a potbellied coal stove. All these objects had been watched by me in a state of advanced terror, watched so many long nights that even in the daytime they seemed to be whispering bad messages.

My mother would make a quick meal out of cans. Corned-beef hash or chili. Conversation was usually sparse.

"I have a good cottage tonight."

"I can't remember where I am. We'd better stop at the administration building."

Outside, the lead-gray afternoon slipped almost imperceptibly into twilight. Very gradually the earth moved toward night and as I sat eating I noted every darkening shadow. Jean sipped his coffee and lighted a Pall Mall. My mother arranged the kerosene lamp so she could see to do the dishes.

"Frank, get me some water."

Through the door and into the twilight, the bucket against my thigh. There was a path beaten through the snow, a dark line curving through the drifts to the well. The low sky was empty, uniformly leaden. Stands of trees spread pools of darkness, as if night came up from their sunken roots. At the well I tied a rope to the handle of the bucket and dropped it into the darkness upside down, holding the line. The trick was not to hit the sides. I heard a muffled splash. Leaning over the deep hole, with the faintest hint of warmer air rising against my face, I hauled the bucket hand over hand until it rose suddenly into view, the dim sky shimmering within like some luminous oil. Back to the house with the water. Absolute silence except for the sounds of my own movement, absolute stillness except for a wavering line of smoke from the stovepipe.

While Mother did the dishes Jean and I sat at the table. He sipped at his second cup of coffee. I fished a dime out of my pocket. "Could you get me a couple of Baby Ruth bars?"

Jean sucked his teeth and reached for a wooden pick. "The stuff is poison. It rots your teeth."

"Oh Jean, I know. It won't take you a second. There's a stand in the administration building."

"You're so finicky about food and you go and eat that stuff. Can you imagine the crap in those mass-produced candy bars? Dead roaches and mouse shit and somebody's nose-pickings."

"Jean, for heaven's sake!" My mother laughed.

"Well, he won't touch a piece of perfectly good meat and then he'll eat that junk."

"It'll only take you a second." I pushed the dime across the table.

"I know the trouble with you. You're too lazy to chew your food. You wash everything down with milk." He glanced at the coin, his eyes flicking away. "All right. If you want to kill yourself. Keep the dime." He finished his coffee and cigarette slowly, savoring the mixed flavors and the moment of rest. Since he'd stopped using the holder his smoking style had changed. He'd take a quick drag, blow out about a third of the smoke immediately, inhale the rest, and let it come out as he talked. I often made it a point to sit in such a way that a strong light source behind him showed up the smoke. It was amazing how long it came out, a fine, almost invisible blue stream, phrase after phrase, changing direction smoothly as he clipped off the words. For some reason I admired this phenomenon tremendously. I could sit watching for hours.

Jean pushed back his chair and stood up, stretching his arms and yawning exaggeratedly. Even this he did gracefully. Like a cat, he was incapable of making an awkward move. Looking out the window he sucked his teeth noisily. "Well," he said slowly, "the lions and tigers seem to be under control tonight."

I felt my face flush and quickly turned away. It was a complicated moment. My fear of staying alone in the house had been totally ignored for weeks. For Jean to mention it at all was somehow promising, and I was grateful despite the unfairness of his phrasing. He knew of course that it wasn't lions and tigers I was afraid of—by using that image he was attempting to simplify my fear into the realm of childishness (which he could then ignore in good conscience) as well as to shame me out of it. Jean was telling me, with a smile, that my behavior was irrational and therefore he could do nothing to help me, something I would never have expected in any case. I knew perfectly well that no one could help me. The only possible solution would have been for me to stay in the city on weekends with Alison, but that battle had been lost. Jean and Mother wanted me with them. Not because they felt they had to look after me but because I was useful. I drew the water. I tended the fire so the house would be warm in the morning when they returned.

"We'd better go," Mother said, lifting the last dripping dish from the plastic basin. "Frank, you dry the dishes and put them away."

I watched their preparations with a sense of remoteness. It was as if they were already gone. Mother dried her hands carefully and put on her heavy coat. Jean bent over the row of paperback books and pulled out an Erskine Caldwell. "I won't be able to read tonight but I'll take it anyway."

"All right?" Mother asked. They stood for a last moment, waiting, making sure they hadn't forgotten anything, sensing in each other the precise moment to leave. Then they were through the door and away. I followed a few moments later, stepping in their footprints to the road. I watched them walk into the darkness underneath the trees. My mother turned at the top of a rise and called back to me over the snow. "Don't forget to set the alarm!" She hurried to catch up with Jean. As they moved down the hill it was as if they sank deeper and deeper into the snow. Dimly I could make out the top halves of their bodies, then only their shoulders, their heads, and they were gone.

I went back to the house. After an initial surge of panic my mind turned itself off. Thinking was dangerous. By not thinking I attained a kind of inner invisibility. I knew that fear attracted evil, that the uncontrolled sound of my own mind would in some way delineate me to the forces threatening me, as the thrashing of a fish in shallow water draws the gull. I tried to keep still, but every now and then the fear escalated up into consciousness and my mind would stir, readjusting itself like the body of a man trying to sleep in an uncomfortable position. In those moments I felt most vulnerable, my eyes widening and my ears straining to catch the sound of approaching danger.

I dried the dishes slowly and put them away, attempting to do the whole job without making a sound. Occasionally a floorboard creaked under my weight, sending a long, lingering charge up my spine, a white thrill at once delicious and ominous. I approached the stove nervously. The coal rattled and the cast-iron grate invariably banged loudly despite my precautions. I had to do it quickly, holding my breath, or I wouldn't do it at all. Once finished I checked the window latches. There was nothing to be done about the door; it couldn't be locked from the inside and Mother refused to lock it from the outside because of the danger of my getting trapped in a fire.

By the yellow light of the kerosene lamp I sat on the edge of the bed and removed my shoes, placing them carefully on the floor. The Big Ben alarm clock ticked off the seconds on a shelf above my head, and every now and then a puff of coal gas popped in the stove as the fuel shifted. I got under the covers fully clothed and surveyed the stillness of the room, trying to slow my breathing. For an hour or more I lay motionless in a self-induced trance, my eyes open but seldom moving, my ears listening to the sounds of the house and the faint, inexplicable, continuous noises from outside. (In this state my ears seemed rather far away. I was burrowed somewhere deep in my skull, my ears advance outposts sending back reports to headquarters.) As I remember it the trance must have been close to the real thing. It was an attempt to reach an equipoise of fear, a state in which the incoming fear signals balanced with some internal process of dissimulation. At best it worked only temporarily, since fear held a slight edge. But for an hour or two I avoided what I hated most, the great noisy swings up and down. The panic and the hilarity.

At the first flashing thought of the Southbury Training School I sat up and took a book from the shelf. Escaped inmates were rare, and supposedly harmless, but I knew that a runaway had ripped the teats from one of the Greens' cows with a penknife, and that another had strangled four cats in a barnyard. I read quickly, skimming the pages for action and dialogue while most of my mind stood on guard. Book after book came down from the shelf, piling up on the bed beside me as I waited for sleep. I knew that if I left the lamp on I would stay awake most of the night, so when the pages began to go out of focus I set the alarm clock, cupped my hand over the mouth of the lamp chimney and blew myself into darkness.

Being sleepy and being scared do not cancel each other out. After hours of waiting the mind insists and slips under itself into unconsciousness. The sleeping body remains tense, the limbs bent as if poised for flight, adrenalin oozing steadily into the blood. Every few minutes the mind awakens, listens, and goes back to sleep. Fantastic dreams attempt to absorb the terror, explaining away the inexplicable with lunatic logic, twisting thought to a mad, private vision so that sleep can go on for another few seconds.

I wake up in the dark, a giant hand squeezing my heart. All around me a tremendous noise is splitting the air, exploding like a continuous chain of fireworks. The alarm clock! My God, the clock! Ringing all this time, calling, calling, bringing everything evil. I reach out and shut it off. The vibrations die out under my fingers and I listen to the silence, wondering if anything has approached under the cover of the ringing bell. (Remember a children's game called Giant Steps?)

I sit up cautiously. My body freezes. Rising before me over the foot of the bed is a bright, glowing, cherry-red circle in the darkness, a floating globe pulsating with energy, wavering in the air like the incandescent heart of some dissected monster, dripping sparks and blood. I throw myself backward against the wall behind the bed. Books tumble around me from the shelves, an ashtray falls and smashes on the floor. My hands go out, palms extended, towards the floating apparition, my voice whispering "Please . . ." Impossibly a voice answers, a big voice from all around me. "FRANK! FRANK!" My knees give out and I fall off the bed to the floor. I can feel the pieces of broken ashtray under my hands.

From the corner of my eye I see the red circle. I keep quite still, and the circle doesn't move. If I turn my head I seem to sense a corresponding movement, but I can't be sure. In the blackness there is nothing to relate to. Step by step I begin to understand. My body grows calmer and it's as if a series of veils were being whisked away from my eyes. I see clearly that the circle is only the red-hot bottom of the stove—a glowing bowl, its surface rippling with color changes from draughts of cool air. The last veil lifts and reveals an image of magic beauty, a sudden miracle in the night. I fall asleep watching it, my shoulder against the bed.

Hours later the cold wakes me and I climb up under the covers. When dawn comes my limbs relax. I can tell when dawn has come even though I'm asleep.

I woke up when the wagon went by, creaking like a ship, passing close, just on the other side of the wall by my head. Chip would be driving, I knew, with Toad in back watching the cans. They never spoke as they went by. Sometimes Chip would murmur to the horses, "Haw, gee-aw." The traces rang quietly and the tall iron-rimmed wheels splintered rocks under the snow.

It was hard to get out of bed. The air was cold. Water froze in the bucket and the windows were coated with ice. The light was gray, exactly the same quality as the twilight of the night before, devoid of meaning. I cleaned out the stove, laid paper, a few sticks of kindling and some coal, splashed kerosene over everything, and struck a match. With a great whoosh the stove filled with flames. My teeth chattering, I rushed back under the covers. I fell asleep waiting to get warm.

When Jean and my mother came through the door I woke up.

They seemed tremendously alive, bustling with energy, their voices strangely loud.

"It's freezing in here. What happened to the fire?" I sat up in bed. The fire had gone out, or more likely had never caught after the kerosene had burned.

"You forgot to set the alarm," my mother said.

"No I didn't."

She knelt and relit the fire. Jean stood in the open doorway, knocking snow off his galoshes. He closed the door and sat on the edge of the bed, bending over to open the buckles. "My God, it's cold. We should have stayed in Florida."

"I vote for that," I said.

"Just get your ass out of that bed." He rubbed his stocking feet and twisted up his face. "How about some coffee?"

"Just a second," my mother said, still fussing with the stove.

Jean stood up and undid his belt. "Okay. Let's go." He waited till I was out of bed, took off his trousers, and climbed in. The heavy black and red flannel shirt he wore in cold weather was left on, buttoned tight over his narrow chest. He ran a finger over his mustache and waited for his cup of coffee.

Mother made it for him while I fixed myself a bowl of cornflakes.

"It's not very much to ask to keep the stove going," my mother said. "I never ask you to do anything."

I ate my cornflakes. The stove was beginning to give off a little heat and I pulled my chair closer, arranging it so my back was to the bed. I heard Mother undressing, and then the creak of rusty springs as she got in beside Jean. From that moment on I was supposed to keep quiet so they could sleep.

There was no place else to go. Outside the land was hidden under two and a half feet of snow. The wind was sharp and bitter (I found out later that locals considered it the worst winter in forty years) and in any case I didn't have the proper clothes. Even indoors, sitting in the chair with the stove going, I kept a blanket wrapped around me Indian style. The time dragged slowly. There was nothing to do. I tried to save the few books for nighttime, when my need of them was greater. I drew things with a pencil—objects in the room, my hand, imaginary scenes —but I was no good and quickly lost interest. Usually I simply sat in the chair for six or seven hours. Jean snored softly, but after the first hour or so I stopped hearing it.

Midway through the morning I remembered the candy bars. Certain Jean had forgotten them, I looked anyway, getting up from the chair carefully, tiptoeing to his clothes and searching through the pockets. Nothing. I watched him in bed, his face gray with sleep, his open mouth twitching at the top of each gentle snore. My mother turned to the wall. Jean closed his mouth and rolled over. The room was absolutely silent. I went back to the chair.

They awoke in the early afternoon and stayed in bed. Although the small stove was working it was still the warmest place. Freed from the necessity of keeping quiet, I walked around the room aimlessly, getting a drink of water, rubbing the haze off the windows to look outside. My mother raised her voice and I realized she was talking to me.

"Take some money from my purse and go down to the Greens' and get a dozen eggs."

The trip to the Greens' would take an hour each way. Outside the temperature was five or ten degrees above zero and it was windy. I didn't want to go. My heart sank because I knew I had to.

Children are in the curious position of having to do what people tell them, whether they want to or not. A child knows that he must do what he's told. It matters little whether a command is just or unjust since the child has no confidence in his ability to distinguish the difference. Justice for children is not the same as justice for adults. In effect all commands are morally neutral to a child. Yet because almost every child is consistently bullied by older people he quickly learns that if in some higher frame of reference all commands are equally just, they are not equally easy to carry out. Some fill him with joy, others, so obviously unfair that he must paralyze himself to keep from recognizing their quality, strike him instantly deaf, blind, and dumb. Faced with an order they sense is unfair children simply stall. They wait for more information, for some elaboration that will take away the seeming unfairness. It's a stupid way of defending oneself, but children are stupid compared to adults, who know how to get what they want.

"Couldn't we wait until they come up with the wagon?"

"No. The walk will do you good. You can't sit around all day, it's unhealthy."

"Oh Mother, it'll take hours."

Suddenly Jean sat up, his voice trembling with anger. "Look, this time just go. No arguments this time."

I looked at him in amazement. He'd never even raised his voice to me before. It was against the unwritten rules—my mother was the disciplinarian. I could see he was angry and I had no idea why. Even my mother was surprised. "Take it easy," she said to him softly. "He's going."

Jean's anger should have tipped me off, but it didn't. Wearing his galoshes and his overcoat I went to the Greens' without realizing why they had sent me.

JAMES THURBER

James Thurber, one of the great American humorists of the twentieth century, showed all of us our daydreams in "The Secret Life of Walter Mitty." He was born in 1894 in Columbus, Ohio, and attended Ohio State University there. For years he was managing editor of *The New Yorker*, contributing both his writing and drawing. The following piece is from *My Life and Hard Times* (1934). Thurber died in 1961.

The Day the Dam Broke

My memories of what my family and I went through during the 1913 flood in Ohio I would gladly forget. And yet neither the hardships we endured nor the turmoil and confusion we experienced can alter my feeling toward my native state and city. I am having a fine time now and wish Columbus were here, but if anyone ever wished a city was in hell it was during that frightful and perilous afternoon in 1913 when the dam broke, or, to be more exact, when everybody in town thought that the dam broke. We were both ennobled and demoralized by the experience. Grandfather especially rose to magnificent heights which can never lose their splendor for me, even though his reactions to the flood were based upon a profound misconception; namely, that Nathan Bedford Forrest's cavalry was the menace we were called upon to face. The only possible means of escape for us was to flee the house, a step which grandfather sternly forbade, brandishing his old army saber in his hand. "Let the sons — —— come!" he roared. Meanwhile hundreds of people were streaming by our house in wild panic, screaming "Go east! Go east!" We had to stun grandfather with the ironing board. Impeded as we were by the inert form of the old gentleman—he was taller than six feet and weighed almost a hundred and seventy pounds—we were passed, in the first half-mile, by practically everybody else in the city. Had grandfather not come to, at the corner of Parsons Avenue and Town Street, we would unquestionably have been overtaken and engulfed by the roaring waters—that is, if there had *been* any roaring waters. Later, when the panic had died down and people had gone rather sheepishly back to their homes and their offices, minimizing the distances they had run and offering various reasons for running, city engineers pointed out that even if the dam had broken, the water level would not have risen more than two additional inches in the West Side. The West Side was, at the time of the dam scare, under thirty feet of water—as, indeed, were all Ohio river towns during the great spring floods of twenty years ago. The East Side (where we lived and where all the running occurred) had never been in any danger at all. Only a rise of some ninety-five feet could have caused the flood waters to flow over High Street—the thoroughfare that divided the east side of town from the west—and engulf the East Side.

The fact that we were all as safe as kittens under a cookstove did not, however, assuage in the least the fine despair and the grotesque desperation which seized upon the residents of the East Side when the cry spread like a grass fire that the dam had given way. Some of the most dignified, staid, cynical, and clear-thinking men in town abandoned their wives, stenographers, homes, and offices and ran east. There are few alarms in the world more terrifying than "The dam has broken!" There are few persons capable of stopping to reason when that clarion cry strikes upon their ears, even persons who live in towns no nearer than five hundred miles to a dam.

The Columbus, Ohio, broken-dam rumor began, as I recall it, about noon of March 12, 1913. High Street, the main canyon of trade, was loud with the placid hum of business and the buzzing of placid businessmen arguing, computing, wheedling, offering, refusing, compromising. Darius Conningway, one of the foremost corporation lawyers in the Middle-West, was telling the Public Utilities Commission in the language of Julius Caesar that they might as well try to move the Northern star as to move him. Other men were making their little boasts and their little gestures. Suddenly somebody began to run. It may be that he had simply remembered, all of a moment, an engagement to meet his wife, for which he was now frightfully late. Whatever it was, he ran east on Broad Street (probably toward the Maramor Restaurant, a favorite place for a man to meet his wife). Somebody else began to run, perhaps a newsboy in high spirits. Another man, a portly gentleman of affairs, broke into a trot. Inside of ten minutes, everybody on High Street, from the Union Depot to the Courthouse, was running. A loud mumble gradually crystallized into the dread word "dam." "The dam has broke!" The fear was put into words by a little old lady in an electric, or by a traffic cop, or by a small boy: nobody knows who, nor does it now really matter. Two thousand people were abruptly in full flight. "Go east!," was the cry that arose—east away from the river, east to safety. "Go east! Go east! Go east!"

Black streams of people flowed eastward down all the streets leading in that direction; these streams, whose headwaters were in the drygoods stores, office buildings, harness shops, movie theaters, were fed by trickles of housewives, children, cripples, servants, dogs, and cats, slipping out of the houses past which the main streams flowed, shouting and screaming. People ran out leaving fires burning and food cooking and doors wide open. I remember, however, that my mother turned out all the fires and that she took with her a dozen eggs and two loaves of bread. It was her plan to make Memorial Hall, just two blocks away, and take refuge somewhere in the top of it, in one of the dusty rooms where war veterans met and where old battle flags and stage scenery were stored. But the seething throngs, shouting "Go east!" drew her along and the rest of us with her. When grandfather regained full consciousness, at Parsons Avenue, he turned upon the retreating mob like a vengeful prophet and exhorted the men to form ranks and stand off the Rebel dogs, but at length he, too, got the idea that the dam had broken and, roaring "Go east!" in his powerful voice, he caught up in one arm a small child and in the other a slight clerkish man of perhaps forty-two and we slowly began to gain on those ahead of us.

A scattering of firemen, policemen, and army officers in dress uniforms—there had been a review at Fort Hayes, in the northern part of town—added color to the surging billows of people. "Go east!" cried a little child in a piping voice, as she ran past a porch on which drowsed a lieutenant-colonel of infantry. Used to quick decisions, trained to immediate obedience, the officer bounded off the porch and, running at full tilt, soon passed the child, bawling "Go east!" The two of them emptied rapidly the houses of the little street they were on. "What is it? What is it?" demanded a fat, waddling man who intercepted the colonel. The officer dropped behind and asked the little child what it was. "The dam has broke!" gasped the girl. "The dam has broke!" roared the colonel. "Go east! Go east! Go east!" he was soon leading, with the exhausted child in his arms, a fleeing company of three hundred persons who had gathered around him from living-rooms, shops, garages, backyards, and basements.

Nobody has ever been able to compute with any exactness how many people took part in the great rout of 1913, for the panic, which extended from the Winslow Bottling Works in the south end to Clintonville, six miles north, ended as abruptly as it began and the bobtail and ragtag and velvet-gowned groups of refugees melted away and slunk home, leaving the streets peaceful and deserted. The shouting, weeping, tangled evacuation of the city lasted not more than two hours in all. Some few people got as far east as Reynoldsburg, twelve miles away; fifty or more reached the Country Club, eight miles away; most of the others gave up, exhausted, or climbed trees in Franklin Park, four miles out. Order was restored and fear dispelled finally by means of militiamen riding about in motor lorries bawling through megaphones: "The dam has *not* broken!" At first this tended only to add to the confusion and increase the panic, for many stampeders thought the soldiers were bellowing "The dam has now broken!," thus setting an official seal of authentication on the calamity.

All the time, the sun shone quietly and there was nowhere any sign of oncoming waters. A visitor in an airplane, looking down on the straggling, agitated masses of people below, would have been hard put to it to divine a reason for the phenomenon. It must have inspired, in such an observer, a peculiar kind of terror, like the sight of the *Marie Celeste,* abandoned at sea, its galley fires peacefully burning, its tranquil decks bright in the sunlight.

An aunt of mine, Aunt Edith Taylor, was in a movie theater on High Street when, over and above the sound of the piano in the pit (a W. S. Hart picture was being shown), there rose the steadily increasing tromp of running feet. Persistent shouts rose above the tromping. An elderly man, sitting near my aunt, mumbled something, got out of his seat, and went up the aisle at a dogtrot. This started everybody. In an instant the audience was jamming the aisles. "Fire!" shouted a woman who always expected to be burned up in a theater; but now the shouts outside were louder and coherent. "The dam has broke!" cried somebody. "Go east!" screamed a small woman in front of my aunt. And east they went, pushing and shoving and clawing, knocking women and children down, emerging finally into the street, torn and sprawling. Inside the theater, Bill Hart was calmly calling some desperado's bluff and the brave girl at the piano played "Row! Row! Row!" loudly and then "In My Harem." Outside, men were streaming across the Statehouse yard, others were climbing trees, a woman managed to get up onto the "These Are My Jewels" statue, whose bronze figures of Sherman, Stanton, Grant, and Sheridan watched with cold unconcern the going to pieces of the capital city.

"I ran south to State Street, east on State to Third, south on Third to Town, and out east on Town," my Aunt Edith has written me. "A tall spare woman with grim eyes and a determined chin ran past me down the middle of the street. I was still uncertain as to what was the matter, in spite of all the shouting. I drew up alongside the woman with some effort, for although she was in her late fifties, she had a beautiful easy running form and seemed to be in excellent condition. 'What is it?' I puffed. She gave me a quick glance and then looked ahead again, stepping up her pace a trifle. 'Don't ask me, ask God!' she said.

"When I reached Grant Avenue, I was so spent that Dr. H. R. Mallory—you remember Dr. Mallory, the man with the white beard who looks like Robert Browning?—well, Dr. Mallory, whom I had drawn away from at the corner of Fifth and Town, passed me. 'It's got us!' he shouted, and I felt sure that whatever it was *did* have us, for you know what conviction Dr. Mallory's statements always carried. I didn't know at the time what he meant, but I found out later. There was a boy behind him on roller-skates, and Dr. Mallory mistook the swishing of the skates for the sound of rushing water. He eventually reached the Columbus School for Girls, at the corner of Parsons Avenue and Town Street, where he collapsed, expecting the cold frothing waters of the Scioto to sweep him into oblivion. The boy on the skates swirled past him and Dr. Mallory realized for the first time what he had been running from. Looking back up the street, he could see no signs of water, but nevertheless, after resting a few minutes, he jogged on east again. He caught up with me at Ohio Avenue, where we rested together. I should say that about seven hundred people passed us. A funny thing was that all of them were on foot. Nobody seemed to have had the courage to stop and start his car; but as I remember it, all cars had to be cranked in those days, which is probably the reason."

The next day, the city went about its business as if nothing had happened, but there was no joking. It was two years or more before you dared treat the breaking of the dam lightly. And even now, twenty years after, there are a few persons, like Dr. Mallory, who will shut up like a clam if you mention the Afternoon of the Great Run.

FIVE

NANCY HALE

Nancy Hale was born in Boston in 1908. Her mother and father were artists, and she studied art at the Boston Museum of Fine Arts in the late 1920's. Later she worked as an editor of *Vogue* and *Vanity Fair*. In 1934 she became the first woman reporter for *The New York Times*. She has lectured on the short story at the Bread Loaf Writers' Conference (at Middlebury College, Vermont) and won the O. Henry Short Story Award in 1933. The following selection is from *A New England Girlhood* (1958).

All Things Bright and Beautiful

When I wake up in the morning in this Virginia town, the children are all calling good-by to their fathers going off to work. I can hear the cars being started up—there is an old Buick next door that takes its time and makes a deep-throated, portentous coughing—and the chorus of dozens of children up and down the block calling, in their infant Southern accents, "Ba—Ba—Ba," like a flock of tiny, excited sheep.

One spicy, promising morning last September, one of the little sheep was not calling "Ba" when I awoke but, instead, a sort of chant of triumph; I lay still to hear what the words were. The child was shouting, "I'm going to school! I'm going to school! I'm—going—to—*school!*"—each reiteration growing shriller and more incredulously ecstatic. I jumped out of bed and went to the window to see. The little girl was just climbing into the car beside her father. Her brand-new tin lunch box got in the way of her knees; she was wearing a new blue coat and a blue hat to match. I think she must have been seven. As they drove off, she poked her head out of the window and proclaimed once more, like a lark rising, "I'm going to school!"

I got back in bed, thinking, I wonder how long that will last. I wondered what it is that happens, so soon, to take the bloom off that rapturous approach to education. It doesn't take long—a matter of weeks, sometimes—before the permanent slump comes, the dismay, the reluctance, the dread that I have propelled my children through during the remainder of their school careers. Of course, some children don't seem to mind, I thought, but I doubted whether they were the ones who would carol so joyfully on the first day of school.

I tried to remember what had happened to me after my own first, blissful entrance. I can remember that first day, how round the suns of the autumn dandelions shone on our front lawn; I myself was four. And yet it cannot have been much more than two years later when I used to pull on my long brown cotton stockings for school, lace up my brown leather boots, feeling such nausea that I would have to stop and lean my head against the frame of my old maple-sugar-colored bed. What happened in between?

I remember certain preliminaries to my first day of school—old Mrs. Stanford saying (when I told her as she passed our house "I'm going to school!"), "At your age? Oh, I'm sure you're going to play school." I answered indignantly, "I'm *not* going to school to play. I'm going to school to *study,*" showing I was not under any misapprehensions. And when someone else (who?) asked me, in an indulgent voice, what I was going to learn at school, I replied, "I'm going to learn sweeping and French."

And I was taken to tea beforehand with the headmistress, an English lady who had settled in New England and opened this school for boys and girls up to about fourteen. She was very British, and so, I realize now, was her school. My mother and I had tea with her in her study while, I suppose, I was looked over. The study was dim and crowded with papers and books, and made still darker by an adjoining conservatory filled with plants and vines, vivid green in the late-afternoon sun. Of the plate of cakes that had been brought in on the tea tray, there remained one cake, round, pink-frosted, glossy; my fingers stole toward it, but Miss Cavendish's voice halted me then, for the first time. She said, "Nancy! The last cake is for Miss Manners." I stared at Miss Cavendish, not entirely taken in by this anthropomorphic projection of hers. She was a big, stout woman, somewhere in middle age, with gray curly hair, who wore a black cloth shirtwaist and skirt and, over them, academic robes.

But even this warning of discipline to come did not faintly dim my bliss and pride and self-importance the day I first went off to school—on foot, in those days, holding my father's hand.

It was the only school I knew, so I took it for granted, but, looking back at it, many things strike me as extraordinary; for example, the daily assembly in the gymnasium, all shiny, varnished yellow oak, when Miss Cavendish, in her scholar's robes, read the Order for Daily Morning Prayer out of the prayer book to us little Unitarians and Congregationalists, only partly leavened by a sprinkling of Episcopalians, and when, occasionally, we small descendants of Revolutionary patriots stood up and sang "God Save the King." We sang lots of songs not, I am sure, generally sung in American schools, when we were sitting on the cold, slippery golden-oak bench that ran around three sides of the gymnasium—"John Peel" and "The British Grenadiers" and a number of instructive jingles that were supposed to teach us history the easy way. Of these, I can remember all of only one:

Little Jimmy Watt
Saw the cover of a pot
Jumping up and down like a dandy.
So he went and learned a trade,
Built the first steam engine made,
And the whole world found it very handy.

Furthermore, when Christmastime came around, the ruling spirit of the holidays was referred to as Father Christmas, and I remember sitting in the darkened gymnasium in a folding chair beside my mother, watching the older children put on the Christmas play. It concerned Saint George and the dragon, and included characters named Holly and Mistletoe, and could probably, I now realize, have been classed as a pantomime. A year or two later, I myself, dressed in pink cheesecloth, with a gold tinsel girdle, represented Discretion in a school rendering of *Everyman*.

But none of these curious phenomena had anything to do with rubbing the bloom off my glory at going to school to study. I viewed them as one views the whole unaccountable spectacle of the world at four—with phlegmatic calm. They made as much sense as anything else. Only the black-robed figure of Miss Cavendish, reading prayers in her British voice in the chilly yellow gymnasium, became daily more frightening, less human.

We, the youngest children in the school, had as our classroom a large room on the south side of the ground floor. The school had been a private mansion in which a few changes had been made. We sat on little, chunky, green-painted chairs around long, narrow tables to do our reading lesson or to sing:

All things bright and beautiful
All creatures great and small
All things wise and wonderful
The Lord God made them all.

In the middle of the morning, we went into an adjoining pantry, where we were served either cold milk or hot cocoa. The cocoa was served in tall, narrow, white china mugs with a blue pattern; I remember how the scum on top of the cocoa clung to the bowl of the spoon as one lifted it carefully off, for I had learned, listening to the others squealing or groaning, that scum is disgusting. With the drinks went Huntley & Palmers biscuits called Petits Beurres. The winter sun streaked through the southern windows to the right; the window at the left was partly blocked by the end of Miss Cavendish's conservatory. To this dark corner, we pull our green chairs in a circle to take our

French lesson from Mlle. de Mostuéjouls, who comes to the room for the purpose; other classes are going on in the rest of the room behind us. We learn phrases and sing French songs:

> Savez-vous planter les choux
> A la mode, à la mode?

I am sitting beside a little boy named Charlie Mellon. I stare at him, transfixed, for he is the most beautiful person I have ever seen—black hair, blue eyes, pink cheeks, long, sweeping eyelashes. Prompted by my delighted admiration, I lean over and kiss him on his pink cheek. Mlle. de Mostuéjouls sees me.

At once, a torrent of horrified French bursts forth, and I am snatched from my little green chair and made to sit at the farther end of the circle from Charlie. By Mademoiselle's expression—shoulders raised, nose wrinkled—and the squeals and groans of the boys and girls once she has communicated her opinion to them, I learn that I have done something as disgusting as scum on the top of cocoa is. I sit quietly at the far end of the circle of children, over where Miss Cavendish's conservatory leaves me in the shadow.

The next bad thing I remember happening was the lie I told about the cat.

I am sitting at one of the long tables, I think in a reading class. Suddenly I have a fearful urge, a need, to assert myself, and I remark that at home I have a cat who can read and write.

"Oh, Nancy!" says the teacher. "No cat can read or write. Don't tell lies."

But it has become true. I *have* got, privately, at home, a remarkable cat who actually can read and write. In my mind's eye I can see her, the book propped up before her wise and whiskered face.

"I'm not telling a lie," I say. "She really can read and write."

The trouble that came to me after that! I was called, alone, into Miss Cavendish's study, where she sat, a thoroughly terrifying object by now, at her desk, in her robes.

"Nancy, you are telling a lie."

"No, I have a cat who can read and write." I clung to it as if everything—stability itself—depended on it.

My mother was got in touch with, paid a long call shut away with Miss Cavendish in her study, and emerged with red eyes.

"Nancy, you mean you can *imagine* a cat who could read and write," my mother said.

"No, I really have—" But here something broke. It was because I was looking at my mother. Watching her handsome, distressed face, I know that in the place where she and I live, there is no cat who can read and write. It is very much of a shock to realize this.

So then there are apologies exacted, to Miss Cavendish, to the room teacher—"I'm sorry I told a lie." And after that there is a distinct difference, not only in the way I feel about school but in the way school feels about me, for I am branded as a liar, unreliable, at least for a time.

Standing up with the others in a long line in our classroom, on a day when no sun comes through the windows to the south—perhaps it is snowing—I am given a word to spell, and I spell it wrong. The girl next to me spells it right, and I exclaim spontaneously, "Oh, I knew that!"

"Don't lie, Nancy," the teacher says. "If you'd known it, you would have spelled it right."

But I *had* known it; only forgotten. It was an injustice. The next class was in singing, and I remember how the hymn we sang so often seemed now overlaid with slime, so that I felt a sort of disgust toward it. "All things bright and beautiful—aagh . . ." it sang itself in my head.

In that first year, we small children saw really very little of Miss Cavendish except in assembly. The following year was different. The following year, to get to my classroom I had to climb one of the pair of curving, formal staircases that mounted symmetrically from either side of the big hall to the upper rooms. Now Miss Cavendish herself taught us English, and we took arithmetic instead of "numbers," and in addition to learning French orally we had to read and write a little; we had the regular penmanship teacher now, who also taught sewing to the girls, and we took a course from Ambrose, the school handyman, in something called sloyd, which meant an infant version of carpentry.

Also, we were faced with the existence of the Brigade. The Brigade was a very small group of the best children in school; that is, to belong to it you had to get high marks and, in addition, you had to display characteristics like honor, trustworthiness, responsibility for the younger ones. Those who had attained membership were given pins to wear—pale-blue enamel pins in the shape of a triangular banner, with wavy undulations, which bore the motto FAIS CE QUE TU DOIS. The year that I mounted the grand staircases for the first time, all the members of the Brigade happened to be boys. No girls had been considered worthy.

I longed—we all did—to be chosen for the Brigade, but with those blots upon my record I never expected that I should be. And I was not, until late in that year, perhaps in May.

I was standing at the top of one of the staircases, preparing to descend for recess, when Miss Cavendish bore down on me like a black-sailed ship. I don't know why she didn't call me to her study, but she didn't.

"Nancy," she said, in her clipped British accent, "I hope you will make a great effort to live up to the honor which is about to be conferred on you. You're to be a member of the Brigade, my child." She put the precious pin into the palm of my limp hand, and retained my hand in hers. She was speaking quite loud, as usual, and several of my schoolmates gathered. "It's not to be taken lightly, you know. As the only girl"—she said "gel"—"you will appreciate your position. And now," she said, turning my hand over in hers, "go into the bathroom and wash those dirty fingernails and hands."

The humiliation—meted out at such a time, in such circumstances—felt for the moment greater than the honor. I walked down the long second-story corridor to the big, old-fashioned, unconverted bathroom and, with my face crimson and burning, turned the water on in the basin. I laid the badge of the Brigade on the glass shelf, which was above my head, and dipped my hands in the water. Slantwise through the glass I could read the motto on the pin—FAIS CE QUE TU DOIS—"Do what you ought to." I was longing to be at home. It was the first time I remember getting that familiar longing. I no longer wanted to be at school. I wanted to go home.

Nowadays, of course, schools are better, or at least less eccentric, than the one I first went to. But, one way or another, the same sort of disillusion befalls those who perhaps too joyfully set off for their first day of school. This February morning when I woke up, in addition to the chorus of bleating baby lambs I heard a voice raised in wails and screams of protest—"I don't want to go to school! I *won't* go to school! I hate school!" Poor, wretched child, of course those pitiful assertions of the will did her no more good than they have any other child who roars out what he will or won't do. I looked out of the window and saw my little September friend being dumped into the front seat of the car by her father, still dressed in that brave blue coat and hat, clutching automatically at the once proud lunch box. Off they went. I figured that it had taken her about five months.

Naturally, one has to go to school, and one does get something out of it. Of my own three aims, as declared at the time of starting, two seem to have been accomplished—I did study, at school, and I did learn French rather thoroughly during a total of twelve years of it. But I never learned to sweep, alas, and I can't yet.

WILLIE MORRIS

Willie Morris was born in 1934 in Jackson, Mississippi. He was a Rhodes Scholar from the University of Texas in 1956 and was awarded the M.A. from Oxford in 1963. He is editor of *Harper's Magazine.* The following is an excerpt from his autobiography, *North Towards Home* (1967).

Yazoo City

My father had met my mother in Jackson, and when I was six months old, in 1935, they moved the forty-two miles to Yazoo. My mother cried over leaving the big city for a bedraggled place like Yazoo, where most of the streets were gravel and where they still talked about the Great Flood of 1927, that catastrophic breaking out of the Mississippi which Faulkner would one day describe in *The Old Man,* when weary prisoners like the tall convict had worked desperately to bolster the inadequate levees with sandbags; the waters, muddy and infested with snakes, had inundated the houses on the street where we were to live, forty miles from the River. There would be watermarks on many of the walls of the older houses, and in one vacant field near the house we were to occupy the water moccasins, as a neighbor was to tell it, had been so thick they were wrapped around each other, and there were bloated carcasses of horses and cows, and floating dogs and telephone poles. Even the Yazoo River, in the 1930s and 1940s, would play tricks on the town, coming out of its banks almost every spring to flood part of the business section and leave the streets and roads covered in ooze and filth sent down to us from Minnesota, Illinois, and Missouri.

At first we lived in a small frame house with a front porch shaded by great oak trees, next door to a little girl who carried me around on her back and would one day be "Miss Mississippi" and runner-up for "Miss America." We lived with "Aunt Tish," not our aunt at all but an ancient old lady, born in the 1840s or 1850s, whom everyone, in the Southern fashion of that day, called "Aunt." It is Aunt Tish whom my uncertain memory tells me I saw first; back in some old mist a swing broke and crashed to the floor, an awful crying was to be heard at close range, and an old lady picked me up and started humming a tune. The night was still except for the katy-dids all around, going "katy-did, katy-didn't, katy-did, katy-didn't," and for some reason this collection of rusty molecules and second-hand corpuscles chose that instant to take notice of the planet.

I remember the cold, quiet nights and the stifling hot summers, starched summer suits and the smell of talcum, sweet-smelling black people in white dresses who could be adoring and gentle and then impatient and demanding—tugs at my hand, and a high rich voice telling me, "If you don't behave, boy, that police gonna put you *under* the jail." There were three big birddogs named Tony, Sam, and Jimbo, warm tongue-licks and rasping barks, the feel of their bodies in front of a black stove, the taste of gingerbread and hot corn on the cob, and the whispered words, "God please bless everybody and me." God blessed with affection and comfort, three birddogs, and the little girl next door.

My father had a huge green truck—so large I had to sit on a box to see out its windows—and from the back came the heady smell of Cities Service gasoline. There was a gas station to play in, and somewhere down a wide street and beyond a railroad track a place with tanks, platforms to jump from, a cool warehouse with dirt for a floor, and room for the dogs to run and bark in the tall grass on a hill.

Later there would be long rides with my father in the green truck, on hot dusty roads over rivers and creeks, out to the edge of the world: to little towns scorching in the sun, ugly unpainted houses with tanks in front and mud everywhere, and big places with white bushes and porches that ran all around the house. Colored men would pat me on the head and say, "That's enough, Mr. Ray," and my father would take the gas hose out of the tank and the man would give him money. And then the long ride back, on the quiet flat land, past the dark woods and the little shacks, up to the town where the hills started again.

One day my father said, "I'm going to take this boy on his first hunt." We started out the way we always went, down the steep hill and onto the level land; my father was dressed in khaki clothes with his gun next to him, and in the back seat the dogs whined and shivered. It started raining and my father stopped in an open place in the middle of the woods; the dogs sprang out and started running in circles. My father said, "You wait in the car, I'm going in here for a minute to see what's there, and then I'll come get you." There was something smoky in the air, a rain mist, and I was frightened. I got out of the car and looked into the woods, but no one was there. In the ditch next to the road was a big stream of muddy water; I jumped and landed in the water. Suddenly my father came out of nowhere and lifted me out, put me in the car and wrapped a blanket around me. "Now that wasn't smart, was it?" he said. The dogs gave me a lick and I clung to them for warmth. Back home they put me under some sheets, and my mother came in and said, "He's not going to take you hunting until you're *water*proof." I went to sleep with the sound of raindrops on the roof.

We moved down Grand Avenue to our own house, set in a big yard with walnut, elm, and pecan trees. Just behind it the houses were ugly and unpainted, and there was a honky-tonk with loud music every Saturday night. One day all the grass and weeds in the back yard caught fire. My father fought the fire with a blanket and water, and a colored man walking down the sidewalk saw the fire and ran back to help. When the fire was out my father paid him. I went in the house, to the dresser where I kept pennies, and rushed out and caught up with the man and gave them to him. "Thank you, boy, thank you," he said, and later I heard a neighbor tell my father, "He gave that nigger all his pennies." I would go back across the alley to the unpainted houses and play with the colored children. Their houses smelled musty and sharp, and there was always food—gingerbread, cornbread, biscuits, and buttermilk, which we all ate under a big chinaberry tree. One afternoon my mother came and got me and yanked me home. "Don't ever play back here again," she said. "But why?" I asked. "Just you hear me. Just you don't."

My mother taught older children to play the piano. It was a large black piano which took up half the space in our front room, and on late afternoons when it began to get dark, I would sit in my room and listen to the music from the front. It was not the music they played over and over, up and down the scale, that I liked, but the things my mother would play when she told the children, "Now *I'll* play your piece all the way through like Mr. Mozart would want it played." I can sometimes hear her music now, after thirty years—and remember the leaves falling on some smoky autumn afternoon, the air crisp and the sounds of dogs barking and train whistles far away.

When I was five my mother took me by the hand into the two-story brick school on Main Street and left me in the care of Miss Bass, a stern old lady who looked as if she would bite. Someone was supposed to get me after the first day was out but failed to come. Bubba Barrier, who was in my room, and I were intimidated by the prospect, but finally we walked hand-in-hand, along the "Bayou," up Grand Avenue to home. Such adventure befitted one's stature as a first-grader in the free public school system of Yazoo County, Mississippi.

The school was a graceful and imposing old structure with white columns, iron fire-escapes, and tall old-fashioned windows. It was set in a triangle plot of ground that covered three or four acres, with the public library ("the oldest in Mississippi," the teachers would tell us) at one end and at the other, in the farthest corner of the ground, the gray Confederate monument. On top of the monument, about thirty feet from the ground, were statues of a lady holding the Confederate flag in front of her and a soldier with a rifle in one hand, his other hand slightly extended to accept the flag, but a little reluctantly, as if he didn't want to go around all day holding both a flag and a gun, particularly with a ten-inch bayonet attached. The inscription on the side of the stone read:

1861-1865

As at Thermopylae, the greater glory was to the vanquished. This monument is erected to perpetuate the memory of the noble courage, constancy, and self-sacrificing devotion of the women of the Confederacy and the patriotism and heroic valor of the Confederate soldiers and all who fought on land or sea for the country and the cause they loved so well.

By
Jefferson Davis Chapter,
United Daughters of the Confederacy . . .
And the sons of the Confederate veterans and people
of Yazoo County. Dedicated July 8, 1909

Inside, the school building was all long, shadowy corridors, smelling faintly of wax and urisol. On the wall near the front entrance were portraits of George Washington and Jefferson Davis. Downstairs was a large basement, where we congregated to wait for the bell to ring on rainy days and where, at noontime, we took our lunch. It was a dark, forbidding place, symbol and apotheosis of a dismal childhood claustrophobia. I would have a recurring nightmare of those years: I am trying to climb out of this sunless basement, through a small, narrow window to the yard outside. The window is not big enough. I am caught in it, nothing can budge me. The bell rings and everyone goes upstairs, and I am left alone. Waiting on some gray morning in the autumn solstice in that concrete chamber, with the single lightbulb in the peeled ceiling casting its grotesque shadows, I could hardly bear the time until the bell rang. The room was attached to the boys' toilet, and from it came the echoes of toilets flushing and the smell of urine. Off to the side, in a kind of wired-in compound, was the lunchroom, where lunches went for a dime apiece, and where the teachers would exhort us with shouts and occasional slaps to finish all of our weiners and sauerkraut, or our bologna and blackeyed peas. It was our small contribution to the war effort, to eat everything on our plate. Once the third-grade teacher, known as the cruelest in the school, stood over me and forced me to eat a plateful of sauerkraut, which I did, gagging and in tears, wishing I could leave that crowded underground vault and never come back. When the bell rang we would march in long lines, boys and girls together, through the toilet up the stone stairs to our classrooms.

All this was in 1940, and '41 and '42, with the war on to defend democracy, as our teachers told us; they told us we were in school to help democracy, to strengthen our country and our God, and to learn enough so we could make good money for ourselves. In the assembly hall upstairs, where we marched in every Friday with the music teacher playing the March from Aida on the spinet piano, with the American flag on the right of the stage and the Stars and Bars on the left, the speaker would tell us of the man he once knew who could have been President of the United States, except that when the time came for him to be chosen, some of his friends felt honor-bound to tell the authorities he had been a lazy worker, lied a great deal, and had taken to alcohol when he was young. Or the preachers would come regularly to speak to our souls, and remind us of our obligation to the one who had died in agony for every last one of us.

Those of us from the town's middle class probably sensed we would make it through all right, and someday in the far-distant future be sturdy citizens of the place—planters or store owners or druggists or lawyers. One of the secrets was to stay on the good side of the teachers. Trapped in the same room with twenty or twenty-five other children for a whole year under your teacher's unchallenged dominion, you learned to respond to her every whim and eccentricity, laughed when she laughed, gave her something at Christmas, and had your parents invite her to supper. Your mothers phoned her to see if you were being "good" and "working hard," and paid sly compliments to her, making up nice things you had never said about her. There were six or seven of us in every room who read faster and better than the slower children of the families from "out in the country." The red stars on the bulletin board were always next to our names, we got the A's and the 1's on our conduct reports. We knew we were the teachers' favorites; we knew that the stirring challenges they laid down were secretly meant only for us.

But within our own breed of whites and Protestants (we would never have given thought to the possibility of any other variety being there with us) that school was a democracy, a seething, turbulent cross-section of rural and small-town humanity. Each day the black-and-yellow school buses, with "Yazoo County Public Schools" written on their sides, lined up on Washington Street to discharge their cargo. The daintiest daughters of prosperous plantation owners and the meanest last sons of the most downtrodden sharecroppers came in together. In the town itself the banker's boy from the big white mansion walked down along the "Bayou" to school each day with the skinny little girls who lived in the three unpainted shacks—nicknamed Faith, Hope and Charity by our elders—which sat incongruously in the middle of the "good" section of town near Lintonia Park. These girls did not salute the flag; I would see them on Main Street on Saturdays selling their religious newspapers.

And there were the "redneck" boys—not called redneck by us, and not anything at first except "the boys from Graball Hill." They were as distinct a group as any in the school. They wore faded khakis or rough blue denim and heavy torn shoes; their teeth were bad and their hair was never combed. I would notice them at lunchtime, gathered in a large group near the Confederate Monument. Some of them would go across Main Street to Spell's Grocery to buy a nickel Moonpie or a Baby Ruth bar, and wash their lunch down with water from the cool green fountain by the door; some would not eat any lunch at all. I particularly liked one of these boys, the gentlest one from Graball. His name was Bo. He was the slowest reader in the class, and he wore the same clothes every day. Once, after Christmas, when our teacher polled every child in the room about what he got for Christmas, he said: "I didn' get nuthin'. I ain't studyin' toys."

Almost all of them were rough and open, and you learned early to treat them with a diffident respect; they were bigger and often older, from failing a grade or from having to stay out of school, sometimes for days at a time, during picking season. Their habits ran to violence of a general kind, and they performed unique acts on an instant's whim. Sometimes when there was no teacher around three or four of them, in concert, would piss on the floor of the upstairs hall; one afternoon late, having missed their bus home, they crawled through the window to the principal's office and shit on the rug. Next day the teachers were looking for answers, and appealing to school pride if not school sanitation, but there were no takers.

They suffered from strange maladies, like sleeping sickness and diarrhea, which would keep them home longer than the cotton-picking. One of them almost died from having been bitten by a black-widow spider while sitting on a woodpile. They fought hard and long, especially among themselves. Pity the poor colored child who walked past the schoolhouse when they were outside. There would be cries of "coon" or "nigger baby," followed by a barrage of rocks and dirt clods. When I was a grown man, and saw the deputy sheriffs and the mobs pummeling Negro demonstrators on television, I needed no one to tell me they had been doing the same thing since the age of eight. One afternoon—I remember the terror of it as if it were yesterday—Millard Fillmore of Graball Hill beat up Erp Windley, one of the town boys, for a distance of twelve blocks; he used fists, feet, and whatever sticks and rocks were handy, and ended by stuffing a handful of cow shit down Erp's throat. A preacher lady in a car, seeing this, stopped and said, "You should be ashamed of yourself, you big bully," and Millard replied, "Go fuck yourself, you ole bitch," something that must have seldom been said to a preacher's wife, at least in anger.

We had violent games of football at recess and at noon, bone-jarring rituals where you got your first test in physical courage. Sometimes an arm was broken, and one of our friends got a brain concussion from a flying tackle that sent him almost up against the reference to Thermopylae on the monument. I still have a scar on my left ankle from the day Millard Fillmore knocked me into a fire hydrant which served as coffin-corner. After the first ten minutes of this bloodletting, however, I learned I could run circles around the Graball boys. They tired easily and began panting like hounddogs on a long hunt. Only later did I recognize that this came from a simple lack of nutrition. Only one of them, to my knowledge, "made it." He got through high school as a football star (once knocking a vertebrae in my back out of joint when we were fifteen, so that I had to see the town chiropractor for a month before I could walk without a limp) and ended up as left tackle for the Alabama Crimson Tide. But as for the others, I sometimes wonder what became of them, if they are still hoeing the impoverished red earth on some forlorn hill, or picking the same scraggly cotton deep in the Mississippi backwoods.

GERALD KAMBER

Gerald Kamber was born in Long Branch, New Jersey, in 1925. He fought with the Marines in the Pacific during World War II. He graduated from Rutgers in 1950 and received advanced degrees from Middlebury and Johns Hopkins. He has published many articles and reviews in the field of Romance Languages and is soon to publish major works on Boccaccio and the recent American novel. He teaches Romance Languages at Kent State University in Ohio.

Memories of an American Education

As I write this, I am forty-three—old or young as you see it—a native American who began kindergarten in 1930. My primary and secondary studies were completed in the public schools of a small New Jersey commuters' town, a seashore resort that had succeeded in eradicating the last traces of natural beauty about the time I started school without, however, acquiring one iota of the sophistication that could and should have accrued to it from being virtually in the shadow of New York City.

Elementary School

Thirty years have not dimmed the memory of the prurient consternation occasioned by the sixth grade teacher's announcement that she was getting married. "Married?" exclaimed parents and teachers alike, "But surely she won't try to go on teaching!" In those days only spinsters (I catch myself starting to write "sphincters") and widows were allowed to teach in the elementary schools on the psychological theory, pre-Freudian, that they were the only ones "pure" enough and on the economic theory, pre-Keynesian, the only ones inconsequential enough to deal with the young.

Some of the overripe specimens of *Virgo Innuba Americana* who ran our lives and formed our minds appear in retrospect grotesque. Miss Sampson, the principal, was so old that the grandparents of children actually in my class remembered her as already somehow elderly. Retirement was mandatory at seventy but rumor had it that Miss Sampson's birth records had been burned up in a fire and that consequently she could stay on as long as she pleased.

A lumpy octogenarian with a bustle-like protruding rear end, she would shuffle down the corridor from classroom to classroom sowing consternation. Without a knock, the door would open and a rat's nest of nondescript gray wisps bound in a black net over a deeply lined, puffy face barred at the top by hornrimmed spectacles was thrust in. Then, in a thin, icy voice (that still makes me think of a violinist bowing on the wrong side of the bridge): "Good morning, Miss Carter. Good morning, children." Her apparition was our signal to rise, the girls curtseying while the boys bowed, and all warbled: "Good morning, Miss Sampson, good morning to you."

If she called a teacher outside, that teacher, white-faced and trembling, ran, not walked, into the corridor to hear I know not what. This was the depths of the Depression and teachers, most of them elderly, all of them either spinsters or widows, were not only paid next to nothing, they were paid a fair part of it in scrip which could only be spent in our town. Losing their place meant physical hardship for them as they were perfectly aware.

An effective autocrat, Miss Sampson struck terror into the heart of the most recalcitrant lout (of which there were not a few) not to speak of the evident anguish her unannounced visits caused her little staff of cowed gentlewomen. In the corridor between the third and fourth grade classrooms was the "Special Class" of seriously retarded and/or mentally disturbed children. Mongoloids, hydrocephalics and otherwise deformed creatures, some of them dwarfed, some virtually gigantic, they squealed and shrieked, laughed and cried the day long attended by Miss Sampson's niece, Miss Barker.

A seriously disturbed person herself, Miss Barker was unable to keep even a semblance of order and spent most of her day before the blackboard weeping and wringing her hands. Miss Sampson's idea of suitable punishment was to place a non-afflicted child in that bedlam for one or more class periods where he was not infrequently attacked and often spat or snotted upon with no hope of intervention by the demoralized Miss Barker.

When Miss Sampson entered a classroom, her eye would glide from face to face and each child upon whose head that laser beam posed for an instant was filled with a sense of unexpiable guilt. Often we *were* guilty: there was much fidgeting, giggling, whispering, hitting, pinching, throwing things, inattentiveness and procrastination on the part of the younger children, while on the part of the older, there was considerable hoodlumism, exhibition of the genitals, swearing, smoking, and even in the last grades, passing around of rather good quality pornographic material: photographs, playing cards, and little cartoon books.

A boy was ultimately caught with the playing cards and the old ladies, so nonplused they couldn't handle it themselves, turned the case over to the school nurse who promptly pocketed the cards and sent the boy back to class. No further punishment was ever imposed for this most heinous of crimes. For me the talker, Miss Sampson was above all exasperatingly obtuse. She understood nothing in its true light, everything in a light that was immediately and automatically prejudicial to the petitioner. Each new, more-convincing argument, every final "clincher," only led her farther outward to yet another tangent of misunderstanding, irrelevance and injustice.

My own troubles began in the first grade, partially because I was a precocious reader, partially because I was an aggressively obnoxious child, a really upsetting combination for the old girls. They had numerous conferences about it, calling me out of class to read for several of the other teachers, for visitors, and once even for the Superintendent of Schools. None of them was the least bit pleased by my facility in reading. Instead of shouting "Prodigy!" and calling the newspapers, they decided that I might sit quietly in class and follow along, taking my turn with the others.

Unfortunately I kept getting interested in the story and reading ahead so that I never had the place when called on, a crime that was punished by poor marks in reading, by long hours of detention after school and in other subtler ways as well. The crowning irony was that my reading ability, a source of no advantage in the classroom, nevertheless acquired for me the reputation of being a "brain" for which I was regularly beaten up by certain older boys on the playground. Nothing so infuriates the common man as an arrogant display of superior intelligence.

Learning was in scarce supply among those ladies but they

dutifully went through the motions. One of them was showing us dreary brown rotogravures of world famous monuments including the Leaning Tower of Pisa when a hateful child, probably I, had the temerity to interrupt and ask in what country Pisa was. After the exasperation at the interruption had passed, the teacher archly asked us to guess, promising to tell us if we guessed right. After we had guessed everything from China to Chile, she never did tell us for a reason that is perfectly obvious to me today although it was less so then—she didn't know herself. There were many such incidents.

Nineteen thirty-six was the year of a great surrealist exposition at the Museum of Modern Art. Already an avid reader of *The New York Times,* I had read an account of the show and asked my current teacher to explain what surrealism was. "Surrealism?" she came back, a very superior smile on her lips, "there's no such thing as *sur*realism, Gerald. Your're pro*noun*cing it wrong. It's *realism.*" And as late as the seventh grade, a pillowy, snowy-haired virago was lecturing on "Martin Van Bruen." I asked: "Isn't it Martin Van Buren?" After an apoplectic second, she cawed in raucous indignation: "I *said* Martin Van Bruen and I *meant* Martin Van Bruen." It inspired in me such a hatred of ignorance and such a love of knowledge that they have not abandoned me to this day and have rather led me into the tense little ideal world of academic scholarship.

Racial and ethnic heterogeneity are still far from being a *fait accompli* but already in the twenties and thirties, America was widely pluralistic especially in and around the urban centers. Our town had—and still has, for that matter—ipso facto segregation so that there was only one Negro in our school, a mild lad. With the savagery of the young and at the instigation of a few older boys who understood the finer nuances of usage in such matters, we used to hold him down and "massage" his scalp with our knuckles through his woolly hair, "for luck," and he would weep.

Half the children were sons of immigrant Italians, Greeks, Germans, Poles, and Jews (the majority of the Irish kids went to parochial school), most of whom derived fairly substantial cultural satisfactions from being members of their in-group. There was even one slight Chinese who could fight like hell. Nobody bothered him. But unmistakably, the power elite—by ethnic background Anglo-Saxon (we give the term a breadth the English never dreamed of, extending it to include anyone of northern European or non-Irish Celtic stock), by moral code Calvinistic, by ideology capitalistic—made the rules, set the pace, imparted the tone. The slightly pejorative acronym WASP which we used to describe such a person has gained currency in the U.S. today: the English originated the type but American know-how brought it to its present state of perfected beatitude.

No member of an ethnic or national minority was ever allowed to forget what he was for one second. We may have hated one another quite cordially but it was always with the perhaps grudging fellowship of competitors in *arrivisme* who do not really believe in and desire the ultimate "good" they are striving to attain. In the eyes of the rule makers, the pacesetters, the tone imparters, we were all pretty much alike: a bit simple, coarse but crafty, dirty, and disgracefully uninhibited.

If one of us displeased a teacher, whether by an act of exuberant misconduct or by some passing inability to cope with long division, we always heard in a nose-wrinkled tone: "Why is it that *you boys...*" do this or that?—never *you* the individual. Or if one of us took an extra day off for a non-Protestant religious observance, a privilege requiring a written request from one's parents and granted only by the express permission of Miss Sampson, she invariably commented: "I'll never understand why you children have so many holidays."

One hand was held out to me in kindness, that of Mrs. Holt the fifth grade teacher. She alone attributed importance to what I did best: reading and writing and drawing and singing. She read my compositions to the amazement of her friends, teachers from out of state; she appointed me to execute painstakingly the complicated Thanksgiving and Christmas drawings in colored chalks on the blackboard (the older tough kids invariably drew a sweaty finger through them twice daily as we filed out of the classroom so that they were constantly in need of extensive "restorations"); she invited me to walk her home after school to rake the leaves or carry out the ashes, a signal honor to my mind. For these manifold bounties I salute her here. But aside from Mrs. Holt, elementary school had the effect of destroying any intellectual motivation, of stifling all creativity, of inhibiting personal relationships either with my teachers or my peers.

High School

After the fortress of Victorian middle-class conformism that was elementary school, what a relief to escape to high school. High school was vast, diversified, confused, permissive, cynical, loud, busy, and up-to-date. And although there was a sizable complement of maiden ladies, there were also women teachers who were soft and young and pretty and many who were married (a few of whom actually smelled of alcohol which I find infinitely preferable to library paste first thing in the morning).

Most of the teachers were, however, men: lower middle class *ratés* who hadn't made it through the Depression selling vacuum cleaners. They had somehow managed to acquire credit for one year in a State

Normal School. Without that year's credit, they went into the Post Office if and when there was an opening; with it, they taught the less intellectually demanding courses: business English, business math, American history, health and first aid, and civics, and coached a little on the side. They couldn't very well report us for smoking in the toilet since they themselves occasionally sneaked one between classes if they were too far from the teachers' room. Just before Christmas vacation, Mr. Young actually cautioned us in health class: "If you guys are gonna drink, for God's sake eat a little butter first." You can't hate a man who gives children advice like that.

A few of the teachers had a bona fide college diploma and one or two actually had mild intellectual pretensions. The curriculum was divided into four levels: College Prep Classical (mainly for upper-class WASPs and Jewish girls) in which one took Latin, advanced English, ancient history, math, and a modern foreign language, usually French; College Prep Technical (mainly for eager Jewish pre-meds) in which one took physics, chemistry, biology, and/or math plus German; General (for the bulk of the middle class) in which one took a little of everything; and Commercial (mainly for the disadvantaged minorities and for the most depressed stratum of WASPs) in which one took primarily practical or vocational subjects leaning heavily on "shop" for boys and secretarial or "home economics" courses for girls. Students and teachers alike were acutely conscious of the social as well as the intellectual distinctions inherent in these divisions.

I began in the classical division but almost immediately ran afoul of the Latin teacher, Miss Cutter. A sour, lipless old maid with scallops of flat hair marcelled across her forehead, she reminded me in her humorless severity of those from whom I had just escaped. On the first day, she distributed brand new Latin books prepared by her own teacher—and I can still hear her quiet, smug voice say, "Dr. Perley Oakland Place." She pursued: "Now children, place your books on the desk in front of you without opening them. Today I am going to teach you the correct way of opening them. First you raise the cover, gently; then. you take two or three pages and smooth them back like this, gently, and then you take two or three more. . . ."

Well, I didn't need that harpy to tell me how to open a book so I grabbed a cover and half the pages in each hand and broke the back with a resounding crack. That galvanized Miss Cutter. She rushed over to my desk and, livid with rage, stood trembling over me while she delivered a marvelous oration about what Dr. Place would have thought, said, etcetera, etcetera. We spent the next twenty minutes smoothing back pages, although for my book it was too late, and finally she assigned us the Introduction to read—"A Short History of Rome" by Dr. Place—and dismissed us.

Try as I would, I couldn't read the thing; it was simply meaningless, so I gave up. Next day in class, the soft voice: "Children, put up your books and papers, we're having a test." Well, everybody except one goody-goody girl flunked it cold and we were subsequently sentenced to "3:12" (a study period beginning after the usual dismissal hour of 2:30—when I failed to show up at my father's store to work, he told my mother: "He's kep' in awreddy"). I had made the acquaintance of a pleasant fellow in one of the extra periods and we got to whiling the time away by passing amusing notes back and forth with stifled guffaws at each exchange.

The minute hand on the classroom clock did not glide but jumped from minute to minute and, towards the end of the period, every eye was riveted on it. As it jerked from 3:10 to 3:11, Miss Cutter crooned: "You two may go early today and stay one extra period next Monday." "Why don't you wait another thirty seconds," I shot back, "you can make it." And that was the end of my Latin.

So I switched to civics and thus began, in my parents' minds at any rate, that long descent into sinfulness and poverty that has been my lot ever since. The classroom was jampacked except for one chair squeezed into the very last row against the blackboard. An undercurrent of suppressed hilarity reigned which I thought boded well. Two mastodon-like Italian football linemen were sitting, impassive, on either side of me. As soon as I had gotten settled, the teacher, a tall, spare man with a perfectly round little head like a baseball, took his finger out of the book and resumed reading the lecture. "Aw fellas, now listen, this is really important. 'City government. There are three types of city government: (1) mayor and council. . . .'"

One of the mastodons feinted a ham-like fist at me and, when I tried to squirm out of reach, he hissed "Two fa flinchin," and bludgeoned me twice on the upper arm, his middle knuckle protruding. First there was a stab of sick pain, then the arm went numb down to the fingertips, and then it began to throb on point of impact. Then the other mastodon began. This went on until I learned never to flinch.

My high school comrades were sanguine and unimaginative when it came to familiar epithets. It sufficed that the epithet be without a trace of subtlety or tact. Any student's physical deformity or peculiarity immediately and automatically determined the nickname they bestowed upon him. If a student had a clubfoot, he was "Da Foot," an outsized cranium, "Da Head." A skinny, swarthy girl with toothpick legs was "Da Mouse" and one of the best-endowed was "Knobs" Berman, while a minor genius at "jostling" pinball machines with the flat of his hand was "Palmy" Whitman—there were many, many more. Our High School was clearly no place for the thinskinned.

Not all male teachers were to my liking, however. Mr. Heckelbauer taught algebra and geometry and since, in order to pass them, I had to flunk a year and repeat it, I spent four years under his baleful gaze. Quite short, immensely fat—he certainly weighed no less than three hundred pounds—and bald, he would peer earnestly through round, silver-rimmed glasses (that resembled nothing so much as flashlight lenses): a malevolent Humpty Dumpty with a most disagreeable curl to his lip. He was a Pennsylvania Dutchman and a devout Lutheran, a Germanophile who actually *spoke* German.

When the mood was on him, he would quote Schiller endlessly with great bellows of dramatic emphasis. He was given to digression and in the course of one interminable political discussion, I tried to effect an ideological rapprochement between the pro-Nazi German-American Bund and the Ku Klux Klan. Incensed, he drew himself up to his full five feet five and intoned: "The two proudest days of my entire life are the day I graduated from Orchard City State Normal School and the day I was inducted into the Klu Klux Klan" (everybody, especially members, always said "Klu"). A few days afterwards, all the evening papers carried a picture of Fritz Kuhn, Fuehrer of the Bund, in a meeting with the Kleagle of the Klan, warmly congratulating one another on the soundness of their respective positions and indeed on the similarity of their attitudes.

The apocalyptic Monday after the Japanese struck Pearl Harbor, I was bounding up the west staircase, late to class as usual. There on the second-floor landing was Mr. Heckelbauer ringed by a group of awe-struck students, declaiming, with pudgy fist upraised: "We'll bawmb their matchbawx cities. . . ." I could visualize him with a Lindy-style leather aviator's hat and goggles gallantly leading his little squadron of canvas and bamboo planes in a bold sortie across the Pacific.

He was, needless to say, an arrant racist and an ardent anti-Semite. In study hall, he would team up with another teacher, whose only saving grace that I could see was that he bore a startling resemblance to W. C. Fields, and together they would do a skin-crawling imitation of Amos and Andy, or ask each other questions such as: "Why is it that all Jews are air raid wardens? How come they never have to go into the service?" A grotesquely inept mimic of a Yiddish accent would follow: "Oi, mine boy is a air raid varden."

I can honestly say that I learned a great deal in High School, none of it, however, academic. I played hookey on fine days in spring and fall mainly to go swimming off the deserted beaches. On rainy days, I spent hours in candy stores playing the pinball machines when I had the money or devouring cheap magazines. In class I met some interesting characters a few of whom have remained my friends to this day. I fell in love a couple of times, once with a peach of a girl named

Shirley. When I did come to school, it was to indulge in elaborate practical jokes, some of them dangerous, with my cronies. Often I became totally absorbed in books and magazines that had no bearing on the courses I was taking.

I got to know many Negroes and found them more congenial and more relaxed than whites. I had always loved music of all kinds but through Negroes I discovered jazz and became "hooked" on it. This induced me to frequent certain *louche* cafés across the tracks on the west side of town where jam sessions were held regularly every night and on Sunday afternoons. I managed to buy a second hand alto saxophone and eventually a clarinet and learned to play them so that I too could sit in. By dint of listening endlessly to recordings I finally learned, all by myself, to make dance band arrangements. Eventually I joined an otherwise all-Negro band and we played weekend jobs and proms as far afield as the outskirts of Philadelphia and New York. In a word, I became "hip."

I was graduated from high school in February of 1943 and departed forthwith, accompanied on the train by my grim-faced father (I had visions of the deputy in a gangster movie handcuffed to his prisoner), for a fairly large provincial university in upper New York State. There were two principal reasons, aside from anything *I* might have thought and felt, for the precipitous departure. The first was potentially professional; my father rasped: "With your mouthpiece, you're gonna be a lawyer." The second was that my mother, who had emigrated from a province of Czarist Russia (where military service meant twenty-five years in the Czar's army for the first son), came from a proud line of draft dodgers and she hoped that my going off to college might somehow result in my being deferred from military service if only for an extra month or two.

But spring semester served to disappoint both parents: it abundantly confirmed my original impression, become by now an unshakable hypothesis, that schoolmasters were by and large a mediocre lot and that I didn't want any part of them just then; and shortly after it ended I joined the Marines (which I count an educational experience since it accords one an unparalleled opportunity to study, at close quarters, one's "fellow Amurricans" from whatever region and from all walks of life).

GEORGE ORWELL

George Orwell (the pseudonym of Eric Blair) was born in 1903. He was educated at Eton and served with the Imperial Police in Burma for five years during the 1920's. His experiences in the imperial service are described in *Shooting an Elephant and Other Essays* (1945). He fought in the Spanish Civil War on the Loyalist side until badly wounded, an experience described in *Homage to Catalonia* (1938), perhaps his finest work. His more famous political satires are *Animal Farm* (1946) and *1984* (1949). While probably not as great a satirist as Swift, his uncanny understanding of modern politics can perhaps best be glimpsed in his essay, "Politics and the English Language," which, among other things, describes the rationale for America's involvement in Southeast Asia twenty years before the fact. V. S. Pritchett (also represented in this anthology) describes Orwell as "the conscience of his generation." Orwell died in 1950.

"Such, Such Were the Joys . . ."

The various codes which were presented to you at Crossgates—religious, moral, social and intellectual—contradicted one another if you worked out their implications. The essential conflict was between the tradition of nineteenth-century asceticism and the actually existing luxury and snobbery of the pre-1914 age. On the one side were low-church Bible Christianity, sex puritanism, insistence on hard work, respect for academic distinction, disapproval of self-indulgence: on the other, contempt for "braininess" and worship of games, contempt for foreigners and the working class, an almost neurotic dread of poverty, and, above all, the assumption not only that money and privilege are the things that matter, but that it is better to inherit them than to have to work for them. Broadly, you were bidden to be at once a Christian and a social success, which is impossible. At the time I did not perceive that the various ideals which were set before us cancelled out. I merely saw that they were all, or nearly all, unattainable, so far as I was concerned, since they all depended not only on what you did but on what you *were.*

Very early, at the age of only ten or eleven, I reached the conclusion—no one told me this, but on the other hand I did not simply make it up out of my own head: somehow it was in the air I breathed—that you were no good unless you had £100,000. I had perhaps fixed on this particular sum as a result of reading Thackeray. The interest on £100,000 a year (I was in favour of a safe 4 percent), would be £4,000, and this seemed to me the minimum income that you must possess if you were to belong to the real top crust, the people in the country houses. But it was clear that I could never find my way into that paradise, to which you did not really belong unless you were born into it. You could only *make* money, if at all, by a mysterious operation called "going into the City," and when you came out of the City, having won your £100,000, you were fat and old. But the truly enviable thing about the top-notchers was that they were rich while young. For people like me, the ambitious middle class, the examination passers, only a bleak, laborious kind of success was possible. You clambered upwards on a ladder of scholarships into the Home Civil Service or the Indian Civil Service, or possibly you became a barrister. And if at any point you "slacked" or "went off" and missed one of the rungs in the ladder, you became "a little office boy at forty pounds a year." But even if you climbed to the highest niche that was open to you, you could still only be an underling, a hanger-on of the people who really counted.

Even if I had not learned this from Sim and Bingo, I would have learned it from the other boys. Looking back, it is astonishing how intimately, intelligently snobbish we all were, how knowledgeable about names and addresses, how swift to detect small differences in accents and manners and the cut of clothes. There were some boys who seemed to drop money from their pores even in the bleak misery of the middle of a winter term. At the beginning and end of the term, especially, there was naively snobbish chatter about Switzerland, and Scotland with its ghillies and grouse moors, and "my uncle's yacht," and "our place in the country," and "my pony" and "my pater's touring car." There never was, I suppose, in the history of the world a time when the sheer vulgar fatness of wealth, without any kind of aristocratic elegance to redeem it, was so obtrusive as in those years before 1914. It was the age when crazy millionaires in curly top hats and lavender waistcoats gave champagne parties in rococo houseboats on the Thames, the age of diabolo and hobble skirts, the age of the "knut" in his grey bowler and cutaway coat, the age of *The Merry Widow,* Saki's novels, *Peter Pan* and *Where the Rainbow Ends,* the age when people talked about chocs and cigs and ripping and topping and heavenly, when they went for divvy weekends at Brighton and had scrumptious teas at the Troc. From the whole decade before 1914, there seems to breathe forth a smell of the more vulgar, un-grown-up kinds of luxury, a smell of brilliantine and creme de menthe and soft-centred chocolates—an atmosphere, as it were, of eating everlasting strawberry ices on green lawns to the tune of the Eton Boating Song. The extraordinary thing was the way in which everyone took it for granted that this oozing, bulging wealth of the English upper and upper-middle classes would last for ever, and was part of the order of things. After 1918 it was never quite the same again. Snobbishness and expensive habits came back, certainly, but they were self-conscious and on the defensive. Before the war the worship of money was entirely unreflecting and untroubled by any pang of conscience. The goodness of money was as unmistakable as the goodness of health or beauty, and a glittering car, a title or a horde of servants was mixed up in people's minds with the idea of actual moral virtue.

At Crossgates, in term time, the general bareness of life enforced a certain democracy, but any mention of the holidays, and the consequent competitive swanking about cars and butlers and country houses, promptly called class distinctions into being. The school was pervaded by a curious cult of Scotland, which brought out the fundamental contradiction in our standard of values. Bingo claimed Scottish ancestry, and she favoured the Scottish boys, encouraging them to wear kilts in their ancestral tartan instead of the school uniform, and even christened her youngest child by a Gaelic name. Ostensibly we were supposed to admire the Scots because they were "grim" and "dour" ("stern" was perhaps the key word), and irresistible on the field of battle. In the big schoolroom there was a steel engraving of the charge of the Scots Greys at Waterloo, all looking as though they enjoyed every moment of it. Our picture of Scotland was made up of burns, braes, kilts, sporrans, claymores, bagpipes, and the like, all somehow mixed up with the invigorating effects of porridge, Protestantism and a cold climate. But underlying this was something quite different. The real reason for the cult of Scotland was that only very rich people could spend their summers there. And the pretended belief in Scottish superiority was a cover for the bad conscience of the occupying English, who had pushed the Highland peasantry off their farms to make way for the deer forests, and then compensated them by turning them into servants. Bingo's face always beamed with innocent snobbishness when she spoke of Scotland. Occasionally she even attempted a trace of Scottish accent. Scotland was a private paradise which a few initiates could talk about and make outsiders feel small.

"You going to Scotland this hols?"

"Rather! We go every year."

"My pater's giving me a new gun for the twelfth. There's jolly good black game where we go. Get out, Smith! What are you listening for? You've never been in Scotland. I bet you don't know what a black-cock looks like."

Following on this, imitations of the cry of a black-cock, of the roaring of a stag, of the accent of "our ghillies," etc., etc.

And the questionings that new boys of doubtful social origin were sometimes put through—questionings quite surprising in their mean-minded particularity, when one reflects that the inquisitors were only twelve or thirteen!

"How much a year has your pater got? What part of London do you live in? Is that Knightsbridge or Kensington? How many bathrooms has your house got? How many servants do your people keep? Have you got a butler? Well, then, have you got a cook? Where do you get your clothes made? How many shows did you go to in the hols? How much money did you bring back with you?" etc., etc.

I have seen a little new boy, hardly older than eight, desperately lying his way through such a catechism:

"Have your people got a car?"

"Yes."

"What sort of car?"

"Daimler."

"How many horse-power?"

(Pause, and leap in the dark.) "Fifteen."

"What kind of lights?"

The little boy is bewildered.

"What kind of lights? Electric or acetylene?"

(A longer pause, and another leap in the dark.) "Acetylene."

"Coo! He says his pater's car's got acetylene lamps. They went out years ago. It must be as old as the hills."

"Rot! He's making it up. He hasn't got a car. He's just a navvy. Your pater's a navvy."

And so on.

By the social standards that prevailed about me, I was no good, and could not be any good. But all the different kinds of virtue seemed to be mysteriously interconnected and to belong to much the same people. It was not only money that mattered: there were also strength, beauty, charm, athleticism and something called "guts" or "character," which in reality meant the power to impose your will on others. I did not possess any of these qualities. At games, for instance, I was hopeless. I was a fairly good swimmer and not altogether contemptible at cricket, but these had no prestige value, because boys only attach importance to a game if it requires strength and courage. What counted was football, at which I was a funk. I loathed the game, and since I could see no pleasure or usefulness in it, it was very difficult for me to show courage at it. Football, it seemed to me, is not really played for the pleasure of kicking a ball about, but is a species of fighting. The lovers of football are large, boisterous, nobbly boys who are good at knocking down and trampling on slightly smaller boys. That was the pattern of school life—a continuous triumph of the strong over the weak. Virtue consisted in winning: it consisted in being bigger,

stronger, handsomer, richer, more popular, more elegant, more unscru-
pulous than other people—in dominating them, bullying them, making
them suffer pain, making them look foolish, getting the better of them
in every way. Life was hierarchical and whatever happened was right.
There were the strong, who deserved to win and always did win, and
there were the weak, who deserved to lose and always did lose,
ever-lastingly.

I did not question the prevailing standards, because so far as I
could see there were no others. How could the rich, the strong, the
elegant, the fashionable, the powerful, be in the wrong? It was their
world, and the rules they made for it must be the right ones. And yet
from a very early age I was aware of the impossibility of any *subjective*
conformity. Always at the centre of my heart the inner self seemed to
be awake, pointing out the difference between the moral obligation and
the psychological *fact*. It was the same in all matters, worldly or
other-worldly. Take religion, for instance. You were supposed to love
God, and I did not question this. Till the age of about fourteen I
believed in God, and believed that the accounts given of him were true.
But I was well aware that I did not love him. On the contrary, I hated
him, just as I hated Jesus and the Hebrew patriarchs. If I had
sympathetic feelings towards any character in the Old Testament, it
was towards such people as Cain, Jezebel, Haman, Agag, Sisera: in the
New Testament my friends, if any, were Ananias, Caiaphas, Judas and
Pontius Pilate. But the whole business of religion seemed to be strewn
with psychological impossibilities. The Prayer Book told you, for
example, to love God and fear him: but how could you love someone
whom you feared? With your private affections it was the same. What
you *ought* to feel was usually clear enough, but the appropriate
emotion could not be commanded. Obviously it was my duty to feel
grateful towards Bingo and Sim; but I was not grateful. It was equally
clear that one ought to love one's father, but I knew very well that I
merely disliked my own father, whom I had barely seen before I was
eight and who appeared to me simply as a gruff-voiced elderly man
forever saying "Don't." It was not that one did not want to possess the
right qualities or feel the correct emotions, but that one could not. The
good and the possible never seemed to coincide.

There was a line of verse that I came across, not actually while I
was at Crossgates, but a year or two later, and which seemed to strike a
sort of leaden echo in my heart. It was: "The armies of unalterable
law." I understood to perfection what it meant to be Lucifer, defeated
and justly defeated, with no possibility of revenge. The schoolmasters
with their canes, the millionaires with their Scottish castles, the
athletes with their curly hair—these were the armies of the unalterable
law. It was not easy, at that date, to realise that in fact it *was* alterable.

And according to that law I was damned. I had no money, I was weak, I was ugly, I was unpopular, I had a chronic cough, I was cowardly, I smelt. This picture, I should add, was not altogether fanciful. I was an unattractive boy. Crossgates soon made me so, even if I had not been so before. But a child's belief of its own shortcomings is not much influenced by facts. I believed, for example, that I "smelt," but this was based simply on general probability. It was notorious that disagreeable people smelt, and therefore presumably I did so too. Again, until after I had left school for good I continued to believe that I was preternaturally ugly. It was what my schoolfellows had told me, and I had no other authority to refer to. The conviction that it was *not possible* for me to be a success went deep enough to influence my actions till far into adult life. Until I was about thirty I always planned my life on the assumption not only that any major undertaking was bound to fail, but that I could only expect to live a few years longer.

But this sense of guilt and inevitable failure was balanced by something else: that is, the instinct to survive. Even a creature that is weak, ugly, cowardly, smelly and in no way justifiable still wants to stay alive and be happy after its own fashion. I could not invert the existing scale of values, or turn myself into a success, but I could accept my failure and make the best of it. I could resign myself to being what I was, and then endeavour to survive on those terms.

To survive, or at least to preserve any kind of independence, was essentially criminal, since it meant breaking rules which you yourself recognized. There was a boy named Johnny Hall who for some months oppressed me horribly. He was a big, powerful, coarsely handsome boy with a very red face and curly black hair, who was for ever twisting somebody's arm, wringing somebody's ear, flogging somebody with a riding crop (he was a member of the Sixth Form), or performing prodigies of activity on the football field. Bingo loved him (hence the fact that he was habitually called by his Christian name), and Sim commended him as a boy who "had character" and could "keep order." He was followed about by a group of toadies who nicknamed him Strong Man.

One day, when we were taking off our overcoats in the changing-room, Hall picked on me for some reason. I "answered him back," whereupon he gripped my wrist, twisted it round, and bent my forearm back upon itself in a hideously painful way. I remember his handsome jeering red face bearing down upon mine. He was, I think, older than I, besides being enormously stronger. As he let go of me a terrible, wicked resolve formed itself in my heart. I would get back on him by hitting him when he did not expect it. It was a strategic moment, for the master who had been "taking" the walk would be coming back almost immediately, and then there could be no fight. I let perhaps a minute go by, walked up to Hall with the most harmless air I could assume, and then, getting the weight of my body behind it, smashed my fist into his face. He was flung backwards by the blow and some blood ran out of his mouth. His always sanguine face turned almost black with rage. Then he turned away to rinse his mouth at the washing-basins.

"*All right!*" he said to me between his teeth as the master led us away.

For days after this he followed me about, challenging me to fight. Although terrified out of my wits, I steadily refused to fight. I said that the blow in the face had served him right, and there was an end of it. Curiously enough he did not simply fall upon me then and there, which public opinion would probably have supported him in doing. So gradually the matter tailed off, and there was no fight.

Now, I had behaved wrongly, by my own code no less than his. To hit him unawares was wrong. But to refuse to fight afterwards, knowing that if we fought he would beat me—that was far worse: it was cowardly. If I had refused because I disapproved of fighting, or because I genuinely felt the matter to be closed, it would have been all right; but I had refused merely because I was afraid. Even my revenge was made empty by that fact. I had struck the blow in a moment of mindless violence, deliberately not looking far ahead and merely determined to get my own back for once and damn the consequences. I had had time to realise that what I did was wrong, but it was the kind of crime from which you could get some satisfaction. Now all was nullified. There had been a sort of courage in the first act, but my subsequent cowardice had wiped it out.

The fact I hardly noticed was that although Hall formally challenged me to fight, he did not actually attack me. Indeed, after receiving that one blow he never oppressed me again. It was perhaps twenty years before I saw the significance of this. At the time I could not see beyond the moral dilemma that is presented to the weak in a world governed by the strong: Break the rules, or perish. I did not see that in that case the weak have the right to make a different set of rules for themselves; because, even if such an idea had occurred to me, there was no one in my environment who could have confirmed me in it. I lived in a world of boys, gregarious animals, questioning nothing, accepting the law of the stronger and avenging their own humiliations by passing them down to someone smaller. My situation was that of countless other boys, and if potentially I was more of a rebel than most, it was only because, by boyish standards, I was a poorer specimen. But I never did rebel intellectually, only emotionally. I had nothing to help me except my dumb selfishness, my inability—not, indeed, to despise myself, but to *dislike* myself—my instinct to survive.

It was about a year after I hit Johnny Hall in the face that I left

Crossgates for ever. It was the end of a winter term. With a sense of coming out from darkness into sunlight I put on my Old Boy's tie as we dressed for the journey. I well remember the feeling of that brand-new silk tie round my neck, a feeling of emancipation, as though the tie had been at once a badge of manhood and an amulet against Bingo's voice and Sim's cane. I was escaping from bondage. It was not that I expected, or even intended, to be any more successful at a public school than I had been at Crossgates. But still, I was escaping. I knew that at a public school there would be more privacy, more neglect, more chance to be idle and self-indulgent and degenerate. For years past I had been resolved—unconsciously at first, but consciously later on—that when once my scholarship was won I would "slack off" and cram no longer. This resolve, by the way, was so fully carried out that between the ages of thirteen and twenty-two or -three I hardly ever did a stroke of avoidable work.

Bingo shook hands to say good-bye. She even gave me my Christian name for the occasion. But there was a sort of patronage, almost a sneer, in her face and in her voice. The tone in which she said good-bye was nearly the tone in which she had been used to say *little butterflies.* I had won two scholarships, but I was a failure, because success was measured not by what you did but by what you *were.* I was "not a good type of boy and could bring no credit on the school. I did not possess character or courage or health or strength or money, or even good manners, the power to look like a gentleman."

"Good-by," Bingo's parting smile seemed to say; "it's not worth quarrelling now. You haven't made much of a success of your time at Crossgates, have you? And I don't suppose you'll get on awfully well at a public school either. We made a mistake, really, in wasting our time and money on you. This kind of education hasn't much to offer to a boy with your background and outlook. Oh, don't think we don't understand you! We know all about those ideas you have at the back of your head, we know you disbelieve in everything we've taught you, and we know you aren't in the least grateful for all we've done for you. But there's no use in bringing it all up now. We aren't responsible for you any longer, and we shan't be seeing you again. Let's just admit that you're one of our failures and part without ill-feeling. And so, good-bye."

That at least was what I read into her face. And yet how happy I was, that winter morning, as the train bore me away with the gleaming new silk tie round my neck! The world was opening before me, just a little, like a grey sky which exhibits a narrow crack of blue. A public school would be better fun than Crossgates but at bottom equally alien. In a world where the prime necessities were money, titled relatives, athleticism, tailor-made clothes, neatly brushed hair, a charming smile,

I was no good. All I had gained was a breathing-space. A little quietude, a little self-indulgence, a little respite from cramming—and then, ruin. What kind of ruin I did not know: perhaps the colonies or an office stool, perhaps prison or an early death. But first a year or two in which one could "slack off" and get the benefit of one's sins, like Doctor Faustus. It is the advantage of being thirteen that you cannot only live in the moment, but do so with full consciousness, foreseeing the future and yet not caring about it. Next term I was going to Wellington. I had also won a scholarship at Eton, but was uncertain whether there would be a vacancy, and I was going to Wellington first. At Eton you had a room to yourself—a room which might even have a fire in it. At Wellington you had your own cubicle, and could make cocoa in the evenings. The privacy of it, the grown-upness! And there would be libraries to hang about in, and summer afternoons when you could shirk games and mooch about the countryside alone, with no master driving you along. Meanwhile there were the holidays. There was the .22 rifle that I had bought the previous holidays (the Crackshot, it was called, costing twenty-two and sixpence), and Christmas was coming next week. There were also the pleasures of overeating. I thought of some particularly voluptuous cream buns which could be bought for twopence each at a shop in our town. (This was 1916, and food-rationing had not yet started.) Even the detail that my journey-money had been slightly miscalculated, leaving about a shilling over—enough for an unforeseen cup of coffee and a cake or two somewhere on the way—was enough to fill me with bliss. There was time for a bit of happiness before the future closed in upon me. But I did know that the future was dark. Failure, failure, failure—failure behind me, failure ahead of me—that was by far the deepest conviction that I carried away.

All this was thirty years ago and more. The question is: Does a child at school go through the same kind of experiences nowadays?

The only honest answer, I believe, is that we do not with certainty know. Of course it is obvious that the present-day *attitude* towards education is enormously more humane and sensible than that of the past. The snobbishness that was an integral part of my own education would be almost unthinkable today, because the society that nourished it is dead. I recall a conversation that must have taken place about a year before I left Crossgates. A Russian boy, large and fair-haired, a year older than myself, was questioning me.

"How much a-year has your father got?"

I told him what I thought it was, adding a few hundreds to make it sound better. The Russian boy, neat in his habits, produced a pencil and a small notebook and made a calculation.

"My father has over two hundred times as much money as yours," he announced with a sort of amused contempt.

That was in 1915. What happened to that money a couple of years later, I wonder? And still more I wonder, do conversations of that kind happen at preparatory schools now?

Clearly there has been a vast change of outlook, a general growth of "enlightenment," even among ordinary, unthinking middle-class people. Religious belief, for instance, has largely vanished, dragging other kinds of nonsense after it. I imagine that very few people nowadays would tell a child that if it masturbates it will end in the lunatic asylum. Beating, too, has become discredited, and has even been abandoned at many schools. Nor is the underfeeding of children looked on as a normal, almost meritorious act. No one now would openly set out to give his pupils as little food as they could do with, or tell them that it is healthy to get up from a meal as hungry as you sat down. The whole status of children has improved, partly because they have grown relatively less numerous.And the diffusion of even a little psychological knowledge has made it harder for parents and school-teachers to indulge their aberrations in the name of discipline. Here is a case, not known to me personally, but known to someone I can vouch for, and happening within my own lifetime. A small girl, daughter of a clergyman, continued wetting her bed at an age when she should have grown out of it. In order to punish her for this dreadful deed, her father took her to a large garden party and there introduced her to the whole company as a little girl who wetted her bed: and to underline her wickedness he had previously painted her face black. I do not suggest that Bingo and Sim would actually have done a thing like this, but I doubt whether it would have much surprised them. After all, things do change. And yet—!

The question is not whether boys are still buckled into Eton collars on Sunday, or told that babies are dug up under gooseberry bushes. That kind of thing is at an end, admittedly. The real question is whether it is still normal for a school child to live for years amid irrational terrors and lunatic misunderstandings. And here one is up against the very great difficulty of knowing what a child really feels and thinks. A child which appears reasonably happy may actually be suffering horrors which it cannot or will not reveal. It lives in a sort of alien under-water world which we can only penetrate by memory or divination. Our chief clue is the fact that we were once children ourselves, and many people appear to forget the atmosphere of their own childhood almost entirely. Think for instance of the unnecessary torments that people will inflict by sending a child back to school with clothes of the wrong pattern, and refusing to see that this matters! Over things of this kind a child will sometimes utter a protest, but a great deal of the time its attitude is one of simple concealment. Not to expose your true feelings to an adult seems to be instinctive from the age of seven or eight onwards. Even the affection that one feels for a child, the desire to protect and cherish it, is a cause of misunderstanding. One can love a child, perhaps, more deeply than one can love another adult, but is rash to assume that the child feels any love in return. Looking back on my own childhood, after the infant years were over, I do not believe that I ever felt love for any mature person, except my mother, and even her I did not trust, in the sense that shyness made me conceal most of my real feelings from her. Love, the spontaneous, unqualified emotion of love, was something I could only feel for people who were young. Towards people who were old—and remember that "old" to a child means over thirty, or even over twenty-five—I could feel reverence, respect, admiration or compunction, but I seemed cut off from them by a veil of fear and shyness mixed up with physical distaste. People are too ready to forget the child's *physical* shrinking from the adult. The enormous size of grownups, their ungainly, rigid bodies, their coarse wrinkled skins, their great relaxed eyelids, their yellow teeth, and the whiffs of musty clothes and beer and sweat and tobacco that disengage from them at every moment! Part of the reason for the ugliness of adults, in a child's eyes, is that the child is usually looking upwards, and few faces are at their best when seen from below. Besides, being fresh and unmarked itself, the child has impossibly high standards in the matter of skin and teeth and complexion. But the greatest barrier of all is the child's misconception about age. A child can hardly envisage life beyond thirty, and in judging people's ages it will make fantastic mistakes. It will think that a person of twenty-five is forty, that a person of forty is sixty-five, and so on. Thus, when I fell in love with Elsie I took her to be grown up. I met her again, when I was thirteen and she, I think, must have been twenty-three; she now seemed to me a middle-aged woman, somewhat past her best. And the child thinks of growing old as an almost obscene calamity, which for some mysterious reason will never happen to itself. All who have passed the age of thirty are joyless grotesques, endlessly fussing about things of no importance and staying alive without, so far as the child can see, having anything to live for. Only child life is real life. The schoolmaster who imagines he is loved and trusted by his boys is in fact mimicked and laughed at behind his back. An adult who does not seem dangerous nearly always seems ridiculous.

I base these generalisations on what I can recall of my own childhood outlook. Treacherous though memory is, it seems to me the chief means we have of discovering how a child's mind works. Only by resurrecting our own memories can we realise how incredibly distorted is the child's vision of the world. Consider this, for example. How would Crossgates appear to me now, if I could go back, at my present age, and see it as it was in 1915? What should I think of Bingo and Sim, those terrible, all-powerful monsters? I should see them as a couple of silly, shallow, ineffectual people, eagerly clambering up a social ladder which any thinking person could see to be on the point of collapse. I would be no more frightened of them than I would be frightened of a dormouse. Moreover, in those days they seemed to me fantastically old, whereas—though of this I am not certain—I imagine they must have been somewhat younger than I am now. And how would Johnny Hall appear, with his blacksmith's arms and his red, jeering face? Merely a scruffy little boy, barely distinguishable from hundreds of other scruffy little boys. The two sets of facts can lie side by side in my mind, because these happen to be my own memories. But it would be very difficult for me to see with the eyes of any other child, except by an effort of the imagination which might lead me completely astray. The child and the adult live in different worlds. If that is so, we cannot be certain that school, at any rate boarding school, is not still for many children as dreadful an experience as it used to be. Take away God, Latin, the cane, class distinctions and sexual taboos, and the fear, the hatred, the snobbery and the misunderstanding might still all be there. It will have been seen that my own main trouble was an utter lack of any sense of proportion or probability. This led me to accept outrages and believe absurdities, and to suffer torments over things which were in fact of no importance. It is not enough to say that I was "silly" and "ought to have known better." Look back into your own childhood and think of the nonsense you used to believe and the trivialities which could make you suffer. Of course my own case had its individual variations, but essentially it was that of countless other boys. The weakness of the child is that it starts with a blank sheet. It neither understands nor questions the society in which it lives, and because of its credulity other people can work upon it, infecting it with the sense of inferiority and the dread of offending against mysterious, terrible laws. It may be that everything that happened to me at Crossgates could happen in the most "enlightened" school, though perhaps in subtler forms. Of one thing, however, I do feel fairly sure, and that is that boarding schools are worse than day schools. A child has a better chance with the sanctuary of its home near at hand. And I think the characteristic faults of the English upper and middle classes may be partly due to the practice, general until recently, of sending children away from home as young as nine, eight or even seven.

I have never been back to Crossgates. In a way it is only within the last decade that I have really thought over my schooldays, vividly though their memory has haunted me. Nowadays, I believe, it would make very little impression on me to see the place again, if it still exists.

And if I went inside and smelt again the inky, dusty smell of the big schoolroom, the rosiny smell of the chapel, the stagnant smell of the swimming bath and the cold reek of the lavatories, I think I should only feel what one invariably feels in revisiting any scene of childhood: How small everything has grown, and how terrible is the deterioration in myself!

V. S. PRITCHETT

V. S. Pritchett was born in 1900 at Ipswich, England. He lived for years in France and Spain. The latter country had a "powerful effect" on him, and he describes that effect with power in *The Spanish Temper,* published in 1954. After World War II Pritchett became literary editor of the *New Statesman and Nation.* His cogent and often witty examinations of the modern novel are collected in *The Living Novel* (1947). The following selection comes from his recent autobiography, *A Cab at the Door* (1968).

An Edwardian Dropout

I was eleven. Between the ages of ten and fourteen a boy reaches a first maturity or wholeness as a person; it is broken up by adolescence and not remade until many years later. That eager period between ten and fourteen is the one in which one can learn anything. Even in the times when most children had no schooling at all, they could be experts in a trade: the children who went up chimneys, worked in cotton mills, pushed coster barrows may have been sick, exhausted, and ill-fed, but they were at a temporary height of their intelligence and powers. This is the delightful phase of boyhood, all curiosity, energy, and spirit.

I was ready for a decisive experience, if it came. It did come. My parents had always been on the move. We rarely stayed for more than a year in any district. I was pushed off to the village school in Sedbergh and to many primary schools in London. Some were pretty rough, one or two were slummy. The classes were very large, the discipline was severe, and the teaching mechanical. We sat chanting the multiplication table aloud, and went on to sing-songing lists of the rivers and capes of England. In history I never got beyond the Saxons and Danes and was stuck with unlikely kings, like Alfred the Great, Canute, and Ethelred the Unready, in confused chronology. The effect of nomadic education was to make me backward and usually older than anyone else in the class. But now the decisive experience came. We moved to Dulwich in the south of London. Once more I was sent to a state primary school, but this time although it was very "low" compared with the private and fee-paying schools, it was good. It was called Rosendale Road school. There I decided to become a writer. The decision did not drop out of the sky and was not the result of intellectual effort. It began in the classroom and was settled in the school lavatory. It came, of course, because of a personal influence: the influence of a schoolmaster called Bartlett.

There were and are good and bad elementary schools in London. They are nearly as much created by their districts and their children as by their teachers. The children at Rosendale Road, which was a large school, were a mixture of working class and lower middles with a few foreigners and colonials—Germans, Portuguese, Australians, French, and one or two Indians. It was a mixed school. We sat next to girls in class and the class was fifty or sixty strong. We had overgrown louts from Peabody's Buildings and little titches; the sons of coalmen, teachers, railwaymen, factory workers, sailors, soldiers, draughtsmen, printers, policemen, shop assistants, and clerks and salesmen. The Germans were the children of people in the pharmaceutical trades; they had been better educated than we were and had more pocket money. One dark satanically handsome boy owned a "phonograph" and claimed to be a direct descendant of Sir Francis Drake and did romantic pictures of galleons. At fourteen the girls would leave school, work in offices, in factories like my father's, or become waitresses or domestic servants.

In most schools such a crowd was kept in order by the cane. Girls got it as much as the boys and sniveled afterwards. To talk in class was a crime: to leave one's desk inconceivable. Discipline was meant to encourage subservience, and to squash rebellion—very undesirable in children who would grow up to obey orders from their betters. No child here would enter the ruling classes unless he was very gifted and won scholarship after scholarship. A great many boys from these schools did so and did rise to high places; but they had to slave and crush part of their lives, to machine themselves so that they became brain alone. They ground away at their lessons, and, for all their boyhood and youth and perhaps all their lives, they were in the ingenious torture chamber of the examination halls. They were brilliant children, of course, but some when they grew up tended to be obsequious to the ruling class and ruthless to the rest, if they were not tired out. Among them were many who were emotionally infantile.

A reaction against this fierce system of education had set in at the turn of the century. Socialism and the scientific revolution—which

Wells has described—had moved many people. New private schools for the well-off were beginning to break with the traditions of the nineteenth century and a little of the happy influence seeped down to ourselves. Mr. Bartlett represented it. The Education Officer had instructed the headmaster to give Mr. Bartlett a free hand for a year or so and to introduce something like the Dalton or tutorial system into our class. The other teachers hated him and it; we either made so much noise that the rest of the school could hardly get on with their work, or were so silent that teachers would peep over the frosted glass of the door to see if we had gone off for a holiday.

Mr. Bartlett was a stumpy, heavy-shouldered young man with a broad swarthy face, large brown eyes, and a lock of black hair wagging romantically over his forehead. He looked like a boxer, lazy in his movements, and his right arm hung back as he walked to the blackboard as though he was going to swing a blow at it. He wore a loose tweed jacket with baggy pockets in which he stuck books, chalk, and pencils and, by some magnetism, he could silence a class almost without a word. He never used the cane. Since we could make as much noise as we liked, he got silence easily when he wanted it. Manners scarcely existed among us except as a scraping and sniveling; he introduced us to refinements we had never heard of and his one punishment took the form of an additional and excruciating lesson in this subject. He would make us write a formal letter of apology. We would make a dozen attempts before he was satisfied. And when, at last, we thought it was done he would point out that it was still incomplete. It must be put in an envelope, properly addressed: not to Mr. Bartlett, not to Mr. W. W. Bartlett, not, as I did, to Mr. W. W. Bartlett Esquire, but to the esquire without the mister. It often took us a whole day, and giving up all the pleasant lessons the rest were doing, to work out the phrasing of these letters of shame.

At Rosendale Road I said goodbye to Ethelred the Unready and the capes and rivers of England, the dreary sing-song. We were no longer foredoomed servants but found our freedom. Mr. Bartlett's methods were spacious. A history lesson might go on for days; if it was about early Britain and old downland encampments he would bring us wild flowers from the Wiltshire tumuli. He set up his easel and his Whatman boards and painted pictures to illustrate his lesson. Sometimes he changed to pastels. And we could go out and watch him and talk about what he was doing. He made us illustrate our work and we were soon turning out "Bartletts" by the dozen. He set us tasks in threes or fours; we were allowed to talk to each other, to wander about for consultations: we acted short scenes from books at a sudden order.

For myself the lessons on literature and especially poetry were the revelation. No textbooks. Our first lessons were from Ford Madox

Ford's *English Review* which was publishing some of the best young writers of the time. We discussed Bridges and Masefield. Children who seemed stupid were suddenly able to detect a fine image or line and disentangle it from the ordinary. A sea poem of Davidson's, a forgotten Georgian, remains in my mind to this day: the evocation of the sea rolling on the shingle on the coast between Romney and Hythe:

> *The beach with all its organ stops*
> *Pealing again prolongs the roar*

Bartlett was a good watercolor painter. He dug out one of James Russell Lowell's poems, "The Vision of Sir Launfal," though why he chose that dim poem, I do not know, we went on to Tennyson, never learning by heart. Bartlett must have been formed in the late days of pre-Raphaelitism, for he introduced us to a form of writing then called half-print. He scrapped the school pens, made us use broad nibs and turn out stories, as near to the medieval script as possible. (This and German script, four years later, ruined my handwriting forever.) We had a magazine and newspaper.

Many of Bartlett's methods are now commonplace in English schools; in 1911 they were revolutionary. For myself, the sugar-bag blue cover of the *English Review* was decisive. One had thought literature was in books written by dead people who had been oppressively over-educated. Here was writing by people who were alive and probably writing at this moment. The author was not remote; he was almost with us. He lived as we did; he was often poor. And there was another aspect. In Ipswich I had been drawn to painting and now in poems and stories I saw pictures growing out of the print. Bartlett's picture of the *Hispaniola* lying beached in the Caribbean, on the clean swept sand, its poop, round house, mainsails, and foretops easily identified, had grown out of the flat printed words of *Treasure Island.* When we read *Kidnapped* he made us paint the Scottish moors. We laughed over *Tom Sawyer* and *Huckleberry Finn.* The art of writing became a manual craft as attractive—to a boy—as the making of elderberry pipes or carpentering. My imagination woke up. I now saw my grandfather's talk of Great Men in a new light. They were not a lot of dead Jehovahs far away; they were not even "Great"; they were men. I went up to a dirty secondhand book shop in Norwood, as often as I could cadge a penny off my mother, and out of the dusty boxes I bought paperbacks called *The Penny Poets.* One could have a complete edition of *Paradise Regained* (but not, for some reason, *Paradise Lost*), or Wordsworth's *Prelude,* the *Thanatopsis* (but what on earth was that?) of William Cullen Bryant, the poems of Cowper and Coleridge.

To encourage my mother to open her purse or to reward her with a present, I bought penny sheets of second-hand music for her. I was piqued by her laughter.

"This old stuff," she said, sitting down at the piano. "The Seventh Royal Fusiliers."

"The gallant Fusiliers, they march their way to glory," I sang out.

"You're flat," she said. "Where did you get it?"

I had found a collection of the worst patriotic songs of the Crimean War, full of soldierly pathos. The music sheets were very dirty and they smelled of hair oil, tea, and stale rooms.

That I understood very little of what I read did not really matter to me. (Washington Irving's *Life of Columbus* was as awful as the dictionary because of the long words.) I was caught by the passion for print as an alcoholic is caught by the bottle. There was a small case of books at home, usually kept in the backroom, which was called my father's study. Why he had to have a study we could not see. There was an armchair, a gate-legged table, a small rug, piles of business magazines usually left in their wrappers; the floor boards were still bare as indeed were our stairs; father had temporarily suppressed his weakness for buying on credit. I had not dared often to look much at his books. It is true I had read *Marriage on Two Hundred a Year*, because after all the quarrels in our house, marriage was a subject on which I had special knowledge. From the age of seven I often offered my parents bits of advice on how to live. I knew what the rent was and what housekeeping cost. I had also read *Paper Bag Cookery*—one of father's fads—because I wanted to try it. Now I saw *The Meditations of Marcus Aurelius* in leather: it defeated me. Wordsworth and Milton at least wrote in short lines with wide margins. I moved on to a book by Hall Caine called *The Bondman*. It appeared to be about a marriage and I noticed that the men and women talked in the dangerous adult language which I associated with *The Bad Girl of the Family*. *The Bondman* also suggested a doom—the sort of doom my mother sang about which was connected with Trinity Church and owing the rent.

Hall Caine was too thundery for me. I moved to Marie Corelli and there I found a book of newspaper articles called *Free Opinions*. The type was large. The words were easy, rather contemptibly so. I read and then stopped in anger. Marie Corelli had insulted me. She was against popular education, against schools, against Public Libraries, and said that common people like us made the books dirty because we never washed, and that we infected them with disease. I had never been inside a Public Library but I now decided to go to one. Mr. Bartlett had advised us to get notebooks to write down any thoughts we had about what we read. I got out mine and I wrote my first lines of English prose: hard thoughts about Marie Corelli.

This exhausted me and the rest of the notebook was slowly filled with copied extracts from my authors. I had a look at *In Tune with the Infinite.* I moved on to my father's single volume, India Paper edition, of Shakespeare's Complete Works and started at the beginning with the *Rape of Lucrece* and the sonnets and continued slowly through the plays during the coming year. For relief I took up Marie Corelli's *Master Christian* which I found more moving than Shakespeare and more intelligible than *Thanatopsis.*

On the lowest shelf of my father's bookcase were several new ornate and large volumes of a series called The International Library of Famous Literature. They were bound in red and had gold lettering. They had never been opened and we were forbidden to touch them. I think father must have had the job of selling the series, on commission, at one time. I started to look at them. There were photographs of busts of Sophocles and Shakespeare. There were photographs of Dickens, Thomas Hardy, of Sir James Barrie and Sir Edmund Gosse in deep, starched wing collars, of Kipling rooting like a dog at his desk and of G. K. Chesterton with his walking stick. There was Tolstoy behind his beard. The volumes contained long extracts from the works of these writers. I found at once a chapter from Hardy's *Under a Greenwood Tree;* and discovered a lasting taste for the wry and ironical. I moved on to Longinus's *Of the Sublime* and could not understand it. I was gripped by Tolstoy and a chapter from *Don Quixote.* In the next two or three years I read the whole of The International Library, on the quiet. These volumes converted me to prose. I had never really enjoyed poetry for it was concerned with inner experience and I was very much an extrovert and I fancy I have remained so; the moodiness and melancholy which fell on me in Dulwich and have been with me ever since, must have come from the disappointments of an active and romantic nature; the forms of Protestantism among which I was brought up taught one to think of life rigidly in terms of right and wrong and that is not likely to fertilize the sensibilities or the poetic imagination. The poet, above all, abandons the will; people like ourselves who were nearly all will burned up the inner life, had no sense of its daring serenity, and were either rapt by our active dramas or tormented by them; but in prose I found the common experience and the solid worlds where judgments were made and in which one could firmly tread.

An extract from *Oliver Twist* made me ask for a copy for Christmas. I put it in our one green armchair and knelt there reading it in a state of hot terror. It seized me because it was about London and the fears of the London streets. There were big boys at school who could grow up to be the Artful Dodger; many of us could have been Oliver; but the decisive thing must have been that Dickens had the excited mind, the terrors, the comic sense of a boy and one who can never have grown emotionally older than a boy is at the age of ten. One saw people going about the streets of London who could have been any of his characters; and right and wrong were meat to him. In all of Dickens, as I went on from book to book, I saw myself and my life in London. In Thackeray I found the gentler life of better-off people and the irony I now loved. To have been the young man in *The Virginians,* to have traveled as he did and to find oneself among affectionate, genial, and cultivated families who enjoyed their fortunes, instead of struggling for them, must be heaven. And I had seen enough in our family to be on the way to acquiring a taste for disillusion.

My mother's tales about her childhood made the world seem like a novel to me, and with her I looked back and rather feared or despised the present. The present was a chaos and a dissipation, and it was humiliating to see that the boys who lived for the minute and for the latest craze or adventure were the most intelligent and clear-headed. Their families were not claustrophobic, the sons were not prigs, as I was. There was a boy with a Japanese look to him—he had eyes like apple pips—who had introduced me to Wells's *Time Machine.* He went a step further and offered me his greatest treasures: dozens of tattered numbers of those famous stories of school life, *The Gem* and *The Magnet.* The crude illustrations, the dirty condition of the papers, indicated that they were pulp and sin. One page and I was entranced. I gobbled these stories as if I were eating pie or stuffing. To hell with poor self-pitying fellows like Oliver Twist; here were the cheerful rich. I craved for Greyfriars, that absurd Public School, as I craved for pudding. There the boys wore top hats and tail coats—Arthur Augustus D'Arcy, the toff, wore a monocle—they had feasts in their "studies"; they sent a pie containing a boot to the bounder of the Remove; they rioted; they never did a stroke of work. They "strolled" round "the Quad" and rich uncles tipped them a "fivah," which they spent on more food. Sometimes a shady foreign language master was seen to be in touch with a German spy. Very rarely did a girl appear in these tales.

The Japanese-looking boy was called Nott. He had a friend called Howard, the son of a compositor. *The Gem* and *The Magnet* united us. We called ourselves by Greyfriars names and jumped about shouting words like "Garoo." We punned on our names. When anything went wrong we said, in chorus:

"How-'ard! Is it Nott?"

—and doubled with laughter dozens of times a day as we "strolled" arm in arm on the way home from school.

I knew this reading was sin and I counteracted it by reading a short life of the poet Wordsworth. There was a rustic summer house at the end of our back garden. It had stained glass windows. Driving my brothers and sister out, I claimed it as my retreat and cell. When they kicked up too much noise I sat up on the thatched roof of the house from which, when life at Grasmere bored me, I had a good view of what other boys were doing in their gardens. I forgot about prose and said I was going to be a poet and "Dirty Poet" became the family name for me. Sedbergh is not far from the Lake Country: destiny pointed to my connection with Wordsworth. We had a common experience of Lakes and Fells. His lyrical poems seemed too simple and girlish to me: I saw myself writing a new *Prelude* or *Excursion*. Also the line "Getting and spending we lay waste our powers" struck home at our family, for my parents quarreled continually about money. I read that Wordsworth had been Poet Laureate: this was the ideal. To my usual nightly prayers that the house should not catch fire and that no burglar should break in, I added a line urging God to make me Poet Laureate "before I am twenty-one." This prayer lasted until I was sixteen.

One day Mr. Bartlett made this possibility seem nearer. He got us to put together a literary magazine. Nott and Howard efficiently produced a pair of thrillers, one set among the opium dens of Hong Kong. I got to work on a long poem. Finding—to my surprise—that Wordsworth was not a stirring model, I moved to Coleridge's *Cristabel*. My first line thrilled me. It ran: "Diana, goddess of the spectre moon." I turned in fifty or sixty lines of coagulated romantic imagery in this manner and waited for the startled applause, especially from Mr. Bartlett. There was silence. There was embarrassment. Nott and Howard were stunned by the poem. Ginger Reed, a little red-haired Cockney flea, skinny, ill, and lively, who skipped around cheeking me in the streets and clattering the hobnails of his brother's boots that were too heavy for his thin legs—Ginger Reed tore the poem to bits line by line: why call a "bird" Diana? Why "spectre"—was the "bird" dead? Metaphor and simile, I said. Stale, he said. I was very small, but he was smaller and people in Herne Hill might have been surprised to know that one urchin pestering another at a street corner were on the point of fighting about a poem, while a pale child with owlish glasses called Donald stood there as a kind of doleful referee. The thing to do was to wait for Bartlett, but he would not speak. At last I was driven to ask his opinion as he walked in the school yard.

"Too many long words," he said. And no more.

I was wretched. A gulf opened between myself and Coleridge.

To me, my Diana was a burst of genius. I have never had the sensation since.

I went home and sitting in our attic on a tin trunk, which I called my desk study, I finally gave up poetry for prose and started on my first novel. My father had sensibly given us the Children's Encyclopaedia and in that I had found some more Washington Irving, simplified and abridged from his book about the legends of the Alhambra. The thought of that ethereal Moorish girl rising from the fountain entranced me. Here was a subject: the story of that girl who rises and is caught in the wars of the Moors and the Spaniards. There was more than a boyish interest in war in this choice of subject. Nasty wars were boiling up in Edwardian Europe. We had had an illustrated history of the Boer War at home: and in the illustrated papers there had been dramatic pictures of contemporary wars in Greece and the Balkans, pictures of destroyed and muddy towns and fleeing people. The Balkan wars seeped into my novel. When I was short of invention—I could never make the Moorish girl do anything except wave her languorous arms—I put in a battle scene, usually a tragic defeat, ending with my stock device: a lament by the Moorish women looking on the battlefield for their dead. Laments had an intimate appeal; my mother lamented often in those days. Day after day I wrote, until my novel reached about 130 pages, and I showed some of it to my friends.

"How-'ard. Is it Nott?" they said, tactfully advising me to cut out the laments. I kept the MS. from Ginger Reed. He was spiteful in these months. He always came top in arithmetic and was leaving school to become a van boy: stunted, he was older than the rest of us, we discovered. He was over fourteen and he jeered bitterly at us. We were rich, he said. We had opportunities, he jeered, as he ate his bread and dripping (his breakfast), and danced about us in the schoolyard.

Then two bad things happened and their effect was to poison my life and was lasting. It took me many years to recover from them. Father discovered I was reading *The Gem* and *The Magnet*. To think that a son of a Managing Director of a Limited Company which had just paid off its debentures, a son who was always putting on the airs of a Professor, and always full of Mr. Bartlett This and Mr. Bartlett That: who had been brought up in the shadow of his grandfather's utterances about John Ruskin and possibly even deceived himself that he was John Ruskin, should bring such muck into the house.

We were sitting at tea. It was Sunday. The family looked at the criminal and not without pleasure. I had tried to force books on them. I had cornered them and made them listen to my poem and my novel. I had read *Thanatopsis* at them. I had made them play school, which they hated. I had hit out at the words Dirty Poet and had allowed no one near the tin trunk and, in fact, had put an onion in a jar of water on it, as a piece of Nature Study, to mark the intellectual claims of the spot. Naturally they couldn't help being a little pleased. My mother, always capricious, liable to treachery and perhaps glad not to be the center of a quarrel herself for once, betrayed me also.

"He reads them all day. Dozens of them. Dirty things."

"Where are they? Bring them down," said my father. I went upstairs and came back with about twenty or thirty grubby *Gems* and *Magnets.*

"Good godfathers," said my father, not touching the pile, for he hated dust and dirt. "I give you your Saturday penny and this is what you're doing with it. Wasting the money I earn. I suppose you think you're so superior because you have a father who has his own business and you spend right and left on muck like this."

"I borrowed them. A boy lent them to me."

"A man is known by the company he keeps," said my father. And getting up, his face greenish with disgust, he threw the lot in the fireplace and set fire to them.

"Walt, Walt, you'll have the soot down," screamed my mother. "You know we haven't had the sweep."

But father liked a blaze. What could I say to Howard and Nott?

"Why do you read that muck when you could be reading John Ruskin?"

"We haven't got any of Ruskin's books."

"He writes poetry. He wants to be a poet," said my brother Cyril.

"He's writing a book, all over the table instead of his homework," said my mother.

"No. Upstairs."

"Don't contradict your mother. What's this? So you are writing a book? I hope it will improve us. What is it? Where is it?"

"Upstairs," the traitors chimed. "Shall we go and get it?"

"No," I shouted.

"Go and get it."

"Oh, if he doesn't want us to see it . . ." my mother began.

"I suppose a boy would want his own father to see it," said my father. Anger put me on the point of tears. Very easily I cried when father reprimanded me.

I brought the manuscript and gave it to my father.

"The Alhambra—remember we used to go to the Alhambra, Beat?" he said.

"It's the Alhambra in Spain," I said scornfully.

"Oh, superior!" said my father. "Let's have a look at it."

And, to my misery, he began reading aloud. He had scarcely read ten lines before he came across the following line:

"She adjusted her robe with ostentatious care. She omited to wear a cloak."

"Ostentatious," exclaimed my father. "That's a big word—what does it mean?"

"I don't know," I sulked.

"You wrote a word and you don't know what it means?"

"It means sort of proud, showing off. ...." I could not go on. The tears broke out and I sobbed helplessly. I had got the word from Marie Corelli.

"Ostentatious," said my father. "I never heard of it. And what's this? 'Omited.' I thought they taught you to spell."

"Omitted," I sobbed.

"Don't bully the boy," said my mother. I tried to rescue myself in the Howard-Nott manner.

"O mite I have done better," I blubbered.

"O-mite, omit—it's a pun," I said and sent up a howl.

I took my novel back. I put it inside the tin trunk. Blackened by hatred, I did not touch it again. I hated my father. And one morning in the winter the hatred became intense or rather I decided I could never talk to him again about what went on in my mind.

It was an early morning of London fog. The room was dark and we had lit the gas. I was reading Shakespeare in bed. I had by now reached *Measure for Measure* when my father came in.

"Get out of bed you lazy hound," he said. "What are you reading?" He took the book and started reading himself and was perhaps startled by Claudio's proposal.

"Poetry," he said. Then very seriously and quietly said:

"Do you really want to be a poet?"

"Yes I do."

He went red with temper.

"If that's what you want," he shouted, "I have nothing more to say to you. I won't allow it. Get that idea out of your head at once."

Why my father raged against my literary tastes I never really knew. He had been very poor, of course, and really feared I would "starve in a garret." He wanted—in fancy only—to found a dynasty in business; and he heard no word of money in writing poetry. At this time he had many anxieties and the family, from my mother down, exasperated and tormented him. He was a perfectionist. He was also an egotist who had identified himself—as indeed I was doing—with an ideal state of things. And then there comes a time when a man of strong vitality finds it hard to bear the physical sight of his growing sons. He found it harder and harder; and he was to be even more severe with my brothers and my sister, especially the older of the three who adored him. We were at the beginning of a very long war; these were the first rumblings. One by one, we fell into secrecy. In self-preservation we told him lies.

He was behaving exactly to us as his own father had behaved to him; there was a strain of gritty, north country contempt and sarcasm in all of us.

Down at Rosendale Road we talked of football, "Jocks," and sex. "Jocks" were members of a small secret society who talked in a peculiar baby language they had invented or picked up from one of the Comics. I longed to be a Jock but was shut out. The anti-Bartlett campaign succeeded: the progressive movement was defeated and we were moved en bloc to a more conventional class, even more crowded. Mr. Williams, the geography master, taught the geography of India and told me I was Welsh: my name derived from Ap-Richard. I denied that I was Welsh. Boys who had lovingly called me Pritch, Prick, or even Shit, now called me Taffy and sang out Taffy was a Welshman, Taffy was a thief. There was an effusive Cockney music master, all roar and spit, who taught us to sing a song of Pope's. He sang out the words:

Where e'er you walk
Cool Giles shall fan the glide

in a fine voice. I at once took to reading Pope's *Essay on Man* during algebra.

The worst thing was that our new teacher was a woman. All the boys in the class hated her. Her figure was ridiculously beautiful, going in and out from bosom to waist and hips like a bottle; to walk behind her and see her lovely bottom sway made us giggle. One of the masters, a gingery hairy curly fellow like a barber was courting her. We esteemed that she was "hot" and that he "had it up" with her. I felt the desire to kick her. This woman had a high-class voice and finished herself for me by telling us that Bartlett was an out of date Impressionist in painting. I did a picture of Tower Bridge and she told me it was a mess. I told her I was not trying to put in every brick but that I was trying to get the "effect" of the bridge, not a copy. What, she asked, exactly did I mean by "effect"? "Well 'effect'" I said. "You have been badly taught," she said.

"Volume" and "shading" were what we had to aim for. Imagine: a whole hour drawing a pudding basin in pencil and then shading it. But Dexter, the draughtsman's son who sat next to me in this class, told me his father said she was right and that Bartlett was a slapdash old fool. A painting I had done of a Yorkshire moor in a storm was removed from the place of honor on the wall.

Holidays were getting near. The teacher said they were an opportunity to see unusual things. She would give a prize to the value of five shillings to the child who brought back a drawing of the most unusual thing he had seen. Five shillings! But how, since we never went away for holidays, would we see anything unusual? Five shillings—the books one could buy for that! I was nearly mad with determination to get it. I had a brilliant idea which I am afraid exposes the dirty cunning, the "deediness" as mother called it—and flightiness of my priggish character. I decided that museums were a store of unusual things. I dragged my brother and sister for a couple of miles across Dulwich Park because I had to look after the children—stopped them from playing on the way, with bribes of ginger beer, and got to Horniman's Museum. Oh sacred and blessed spot, oh temple of knowledge, oh secret Bore, I dragged the kids round the cases. Mr. Bartlett had been keen on stone arrowheads and flints, Uncle Arthur had gone in for fossils and quartz—I had bought a book on geology and had tried to memorize the name of rocks: the craze lasted a week or two—but what was unusual about them? And, in any case, how difficult for an "effect" artist like myself to draw things like these. I searched for something foreign, exotic, and simple. I found it. There was a collection of amulets from India. Quickly I drew the childishly simple shapes and noted the colors. I took the other children back home, got out my paints and did a full page of amulets, inventing some extra ones as I went along. Some I called Indian; at a venture, I lied and called some African. The whole swindle in yellows and purples looked pretty and salable.

My culture-snobbery and faking were successful. Most of the boys and girls in my class had forgotten to go in for the prize. Howard had spent his time selling newspapers; Nott had been to Somerset and had seen stalactites in caves but could not draw. Those self-indulgent rivals had been caught napping. They were not obsessional boys. I won the prize, the only one of my school life.

"And what would you like for your five shillings?" the teacher said.

"A book."

"That's good. Which book would you like? Henry? Conan Doyle?"

"No, Ruskin."

"What?" said the teacher. "He wrote a great many books." I did not know the titles of any of Ruskin's books.

"Any one. Some."

"You realize he was a social reformer and art critic?"

"On art," I said blindly, sucking up to her love of volume and shading.

The woman with the ludicrously beautiful figure, whom we mocked and whom I had wanted to kick, presented me a few weeks later with eight volumes of Ruskin—*Modern Painters, The Seven Lamps of Architecture, The Stones of Venice* and—most enlightening of all—an Index. I had blotted out the *Gem* and *Magnet* fiasco.

I went home and opened the first volume of *Modern Painters.* The title startled me. This surely could not have been the writer Grandfather admired. It contained nothing about social justice. I was faced by an utterly strange subject: art and the criticism of art. I had admired pictures for their silence and their peace, even their self-satisfaction as images. They were not—it now seemed—at peace at all. I struggled to understand the unusual words and nearly gave up; but I was kept going by Ruskin's bad temper, his rage against Claude and Poussin—whoever they might be—and his exaltation of Turner. He was in a passion. Until now I had never been inside Dulwich Gallery, but now I went. And there I stood in those empty polished rooms that sometimes smelled of the oil paint of a copyist who had left his picture on its easel, in Ruskin's world. Here were the Dutch, the Italians. Here was Rubens. Here was Mrs. Siddons as the Tragic Muse. I was happier than I had been in my life, but I was also oppressed. It was the old story, I was self-burdened. There was too much to know. I discovered that Ruskin was not so very many years older than I was when he wrote that book.

It took me a year to get through the first volume of *Modern Painters.* The second I skipped. The third bored me until I got to the chapter on the Pathetic Fallacy. This I read easily: in the conflict between painting and literature, literature always conquered. I was shocked to see Pope attacked. I was shamed to see that I was on the side of the Pathetic Fallacy. I had not realized that there was unrest in literature, too, and that one was allowed to attack "the great." Seeing that Homer was praised I bought Chapman's Homer from the second-hand box. How could Keats have been bowled over by it? Why no "wild surmise" for me? All the great poets have praised the *Iliad.* I was bored by it. Slowly Coleridge and Wordsworth drifted away into regions that were, evidently, unattainable.

There was presently talk at home of my sitting for a scholarship for a place at the Strand School, a State secondary school at Streatham. (Many a time I had walked over to Streatham Common in the belief that it was an approach to the Sussex Downs where Mr. Bartlett had found coltsfoot. There were only dandelions on Streatham Common.) Miss H.—as we called her—my father's partner, a woman, had been nagging my father about scholarships; and because of the Ruskin "prize" he was impressed and I was in a state of euphoric self-confidence.

Soon, father and I were on a bus going to Streatham. I was going to sit for the examination. I was impressed by being at a school where there was a dining hall and where boys could buy buns, chocolate, and drink cocoa in the break. They also wore long trousers. There was a touch of Greyfriars in this. I was sick with fright and had had diarrhea, of course, but I felt I could rely on my genius. But when I sat down to the examination papers I found that my genius was not being called upon. The effect of Mr. Bartlett's system was that I was totally unprepared and ignorant—even in English. I could answer scarcely any of the questions and I could hope only to get by in Scripture. There was a question about Noah and the Ark; something about the numbers of people aboard, size and location of the ark, the duration of the flood, and how many times the dove flew in and out and with what in its beak? I had inherited my father's dislike of a fact. I ignored the question and wrote at full speed a dramatic eyewitness account of the Flood, ending with that favorite device—a Lament. I made the drowning millions lament. A month later I heard the inevitable news: the genius, the inhabitant of a higher plane, had failed to win a scholarship.

I did not know how to bear the shame of this. It was made worse by hearing that I was older than all the other boys who were sitting. I could never sit again. I found it hard to face my brother. He who hated school, and except in carpentry always did badly—Cyril welcomed me to the brotherhood of failures.

Failure to win a scholarship was a blow to vanity and to hopes. For me it would be decisive. In those puzzled hours at the desk my future was settled. How often my grandfather and my father had urged me on with the joke, "Victor—always victorious." I wasn't and I began to be cowed by my morally pretentious Christian name and to hate it. I was never good at examinations and was never near the top of the class in spite of all my efforts. In English I was always near the bottom of the list. My memory was poor. Mr. Bartlett had scorned to teach English Grammar and I knew nothing of it until I learned French and German. I was bad at spelling and had—I have still—a bad handwriting. The most serious result of this failure was that it was now certain—although I did not realize this—that I would never go to the University. If I had passed I would have stayed at school until I was eighteen and would surely have got another scholarship to London University; probably I would have become a teacher or an academic. I had had a narrow escape. But I would have had friends whom I would have met again and again in life and, in university days, they would have helped as much as my tutors to put some order and direction to a drifting and chaotic mind.

CLAUDE BROWN

Claude Brown was born in Harlem in 1937. He became a member of the "Buccaneers," a Harlem gang, and spent two years at the Wiltwyck School for Boys. (James Agee, who is also represented in this anthology, wrote a superb screenplay for *The Quiet One,* about a boy very much like Claude Brown who had also been sent to Wiltwyck). Brown returned to Harlem and was soon in reform school. Somehow he survived his earlier experiences, graduated from Howard University in 1965, and published *Manchild in the Promised Land* in the same year. Of this book, from which the following selections are taken, *The New York Times* said, "This is a mature autobiography of the coming of age of one hidden human being, whose experience and generation are absolutely crucial to any future history of the American people."

Manchild in the Promised Land

"Run!"

Where?

Oh, hell! Let's get out of here!

"Turk! Turk! I'm shot!"

I could hear Turk's voice calling from a far distance, telling me not to go into the fish-and-chips joint. I heard, but I didn't understand. The only thing I knew was that I was going to die.

I ran. There was a bullet in me trying to take my life, all thirteen years of it.

I climbed up on the bar yelling, "Walsh, I'm shot. I'm shot." I could feel the blood running down my leg. Walsh, the fellow who operated the fish-and-chips joint, pushed me off the bar and onto the floor. I couldn't move now, but I was still completely conscious.

Walsh was saying, "Git outta here, kid. I ain't got no time to play."

A woman was screaming, mumbling something about the Lord, and saying, "Somebody done shot that poor child."

Mama ran in. She jumped up and down, screaming like a crazy woman. I began to think about dying. The worst part of dying was thinking about the things and the people that I'd never see again. As I lay there trying to imagine what being dead was like, the policeman who had been trying to control Mama gave up and bent over me. He asked who had shot me. Before I could answer, he was asking me if I could hear him. I told him that I didn't know who had shot me and would he please tell Mama to stop jumping up and down. Every time Mama came down on that shabby floor, the bullet lodged in my stomach felt like a hot poker.

Another policeman had come in and was struggling to keep the crowd outside. I could see Turk in the front of the crowd. Before the cops came, he asked me if I was going to tell them that he was with me. I never answered. I looked at him and wondered if he saw who shot me. Then his question began to ring in my head: "Sonny, you gonna tell 'em I was with you?" I was bleeding on a dirty floor in a fish-and-chips joint, and Turk was standing there in the doorway hoping that I would die before I could tell the cops that he was with me. Not once did Turk ask me how I felt.

Hell, yeah, I thought, I'm gonna tell 'em.

It seemed like hours had passed before the ambulance finally arrived. Mama wanted to go to the hospital with me, but the ambulance attendant said she was too excited. On the way to Harlem Hospital, the cop who was riding with us asked Dad what he had to say. His answer was typical: "I told him about hanging out with those bad-ass boys." The cop was a little surprised. This must be a rookie, I thought.

The next day, Mama was at my bedside telling me that she had prayed and the Lord had told her that I was going to live. Mama said that many of my friends wanted to donate some blood for me, but the hospital would not accept it from narcotics users.

This was one of the worst situations I had ever been in. There was a tube in my nose that went all the way to the pit of my stomach. I was being fed intravenously, and there was a drain in my side. Everybody came to visit me, mainly out of curiosity. The girls were all anxious to know where I had gotten shot. They had heard all kinds of tales about where the bullet struck. The bolder ones wouldn't even bother to ask: they just snatched the cover off me and looked for themselves. In a few days, the word got around that I was in one piece.

On my fourth day in the hospital, I was awakened by a male nurse at about 3 A.M. When he said hello in a very ladyish voice, I thought that he had come to the wrong bed by mistake. After identifying himself, he told me that he had helped Dr. Freeman save my life. The next thing he said, which I didn't understand, had something to do with the hours he had put in working that day. He went on mumbling something about how tired he was and ended up asking me to rub his back. I had already told him that I was grateful to him for helping the doctor save my life. While I rubbed his back above the beltline, he kept pushing my hand down and saying, "Lower, like you are really grateful to me." I told him that I was sleepy from the needle a nurse had given me. He asked me to pat his behind. After I had done this, he left.

The next day when the fellows came to visit me, I told them about my early-morning visitor. Dunny said he would like to meet him. Tito joked about being able to get a dose of clap in the hospital. The guy with the tired back never showed up again, so the fellows never got a chance to meet him. Some of them were disappointed.

After I had been in the hospital for about a week, I was visited by another character. I had noticed a woman visiting one of the patients on the far side of the ward. She was around fifty-five years old, short and fat, and she was wearing old-lady shoes. While I wondered who this woman was, she started across the room in my direction. After she had introduced herself, she told me that she was visiting her son. Her son had been stabbed in the chest with an ice pick by his wife. She said that his left lung had been punctured, but he was doing fine now, and that Jesus was so-o-o good.

Her name was Mrs. Ganey, and she lived on 145th Street. She said my getting shot when I did "was the work of the Lord." My gang had been stealing sheets and bedspreads off clotheslines for months before I had gotten shot. I asked this godly woman why she thought it was the work of the Lord or Jesus or whoever. She began in a sermonlike tone, saying, "Son, people was gitting tired-a y'all stealing all dey sheets and spreads." She said that on the night that I had gotten shot, she baited her clothesline with two brand-new bedspreads, turned out all the lights in the apartment, and sat at the kitchen window waiting for us to show.

She waited with a double-barreled shotgun.

The godly woman said that most of our victims thought that we were winos or dope fiends and that most of them had vowed to kill us. At the end of the sermon, the godly woman said, "Thank the Lord I didn't shoot nobody's child." When the godly woman had finally departed, I thought, Thank the Lord for taking her away from my bed.

Later on that night, I was feeling a lot of pain and couldn't get to sleep. A nurse who had heard me moaning and groaning came over and gave me a shot of morphine. Less than twenty minutes later, I was deep into a nightmare.

I was back in the fish-and-chips joint, lying on the floor dying. Only, now I was in more pain than before, and there were dozens of Mamas around me jumping up and screaming. I could feel myself dying in a rising pool of blood. The higher the blood rose the more I died.

I dreamt about the boy who Rock and big Stoop had thrown off that roof on 149th Street. None of us had stayed around to see him hit the ground, but I just knew that he died in a pool of blood too. I wished that he would stop screaming, and I wished that Mama would stop screaming. I wished they would let me die quietly.

As the screams began to die out—Mama's and the boy's—I began to think about the dilapidated old tenement building that I lived in, the one that still had the words "pussy" and "fuck you" on the walls where I had scribbled them years ago. The one where the super, Mr. Lawson, caught my little brother writing some more. Dad said he was going to kill Pimp for writing on that wall, and the way he was beating Pimp with that ironing cord, I thought he would. Mama was crying, I was crying, and Pimp had been crying for a long time. Mama said that he was too young to be beaten like that. She ran out of the house and came back with a cop, who stopped Dad from beating Pimp.

I told Pimp not to cry any more, just to wait until I got big: I was going to kill Dad, and he could help me if he wanted to.

This was the building where Mr. Lawson had killed a man for peeing in the hall. I remembered being afraid to go downstairs the morning after Mr. Lawson had busted that man's head open with a baseball bat. I could still see blood all over the hall. This was the building where somebody was always shooting out the windows in the hall. They were usually shooting at Johnny D., and they usually missed. This was the building that I loved more than anyplace else in the world. The thought that I would never see this building again scared the hell out of me.

I dreamt about waking up in the middle of the night seven years before and thinking that the Germans or the Japs had come and that the loud noises I heard were bombs falling. Running into Mama's room, I squeezed in between her and Dad at the front window. Thinking that we were watching an air raid, I asked Dad where the sirens were and why the street lights were on. He said, "This ain't no air raid—just a whole lotta niggers gone fool. And git the hell back in that bed!" I went back to bed, but I couldn't go to sleep. The loud screams in the street and the crashing sound of falling plate-glass windows kept me awake for hours. While I listened to the noise, I imagined bombs falling and people running through the streets screaming. I could see mothers running with babies in their arms, grown men running over women and children to save their own lives, and the Japs stabbing babies with bayonets, just like in the movies. I thought, Boy, I sure wish I was out there. I bet the Stinky brothers are out there. Danny and Butch are probably out there having all the fun in the world.

The next day, as I was running out of the house without underwear or socks on, I could hear Mama yelling, "Boy, come back here and put a hat or something on your head!" When I reached the stoop, I was knocked back into the hall by a big man carrying a ham under his coat. While I looked up at him, wondering what was going on, he reached down with one hand and snatched me up, still holding the ham under his coat with his other hand. He stood me up against a wall and ran into the hall with his ham. Before I had a chance to move, other men came running through the hall carrying cases of whiskey, sacks of flour, and cartons of cigarettes. Just as I unglued myself from the wall and started out the door for the second time, I was bowled over again. This time by a cop with a gun in his hand. He never stopped, but after he had gone a couple of yards into the hall, I heard him say, "Look out, kid." On the third try, I got out of the building. But I wasn't sure that this was my street. None of the stores had any windows left, and glass was everywhere. It seemed that all the cops in the world were on 145th Street and Eighth Avenue that day. The cops were telling everybody to move on, and everybody was talking about the riot. I went over to a cop and asked him what a riot was. He told me to go on home. The next cop I asked told me that a riot was what had happened the night before. Putting two and two together I decided that a riot was "a whole lotta niggers gone fool."

I went around the corner to Butch's house. After I convinced him that I was alone, he opened the door. He said that Kid and Danny were in the kitchen. I saw Kid sitting on the floor with his hand stuck way down in a gallon jar of pickled pigs' ears. Danny was cooking some bacon at the stove, and Butch was busy hiding stuff. It looked as though these guys had stolen a whole grocery store. While I joined the feast, they took turns telling me about the riot. Danny and Kid hadn't gone home the night before; they were out following the crowds and looting.

My only regret was that I had missed the excitement. I said, "Why don't we have another riot tonight? Then Butch and me can get in it."

Danny said that there were too many cops around to have a riot now. Butch said that they had eaten up all the bread and that he was going to steal some more. I asked if I could come along with him, and he said that I could if I promised to do nothing but watch. I promised, but we both knew that I was lying.

When we got to the street, Butch said he wanted to go across the street and look at the pawnshop. I tagged along. Like many of the stores where the rioters had been, the pawnshop had been set afire. The firemen had torn down a sidewall getting at the fire. So Butch and I just walked in where the wall used to be. Everything I picked up was broken or burned or both. My feet kept sinking into the wet furs that had been burned and drenched. The whole place smelled of smoke and was as dirty as a Harlem gutter on a rainy day. The cop out front yelled to us to get out of there. He only had to say it once.

After stopping by the seafood joint and stealing some shrimp and oysters, we went to what was left of Mr. Gordon's grocery store. Butch just walked in, picked up a loaf of bread, and walked out. He told me to come on, but I ignored him and went into the grocery store instead. I picked up two loaves of bread and walked out. When I got outside, a cop looked at me, and I ran into a building and through the backyard to Butch's house. Running through the backyard, I lost all the oysters that I had; when I reached Butch's house, I had only two loaves of bread and two shrimp in my pocket.

Danny, who was doing most of the cooking, went into the street to steal something to drink. Danny, Butch, and Kid were ten years old, four years older than I. Butch was busy making sandwiches on the floor, and Kid was trying to slice up a loaf of bologna. I had never eaten shrimp, but nobody seemed to care, because they refused to cook it for me. I told Butch that I was going to cook it myself. He said that there was no more lard in the house and that I would need some grease.

I looked around the house until I came up with some Vaseline hair pomade. I put the shrimp in the frying pan with the hair grease, waited until they had gotten black and were smoking, then took them out and made a sandwich. A few years later, I found out that shrimp were supposed to be shelled before cooking. I ate half of the sandwich and hated shrimp for years afterward.

The soft hand tapping on my face to wake me up was Jackie's. She and Della had been to a New Year's Eve party. Jackie wanted to come by the hospital and kiss me at midnight. This was the only time in my life that I ever admitted being glad to see Jackie. I asked them about the party, hoping that they would stay and talk to me for a while. I was afraid that if I went back to sleep, I would have another bad dream.

The next thing I knew, a nurse was waking me up for breakfast. I didn't recall saying good night to Jackie and Della, so I must have fallen asleep while they were talking to me. I thought about Sugar, how nice she was, and how she was a real friend. I knew she wanted to be my girl friend, and I liked her a lot. But what would everybody say if I had a buck-toothed girl friend. I remembered Knoxie asking me how I kissed her. That question led to the first fight I'd had with Knoxie in years. No, I couldn't let Sugar be my girl. It was hard enough having her as a friend.

The next day, I asked the nurse why she hadn't changed my bed linen, and she said because they were evicting me. I had been in the hospital for eleven days, but I wasn't ready to go home. I left the hospital on January 2 and went to a convalescent home in Valhalla, New York. After I had been there for three weeks, the activity director took me aside and told me that I was going to New York City to see a judge and that I might be coming back. The following morning, I left to see that judge, but I never got back to Valhalla.

I stood there before Judge Pankin looking solemn and lying like a professional. I thought that he looked too nice to be a judge. A half hour after I had walked into the courtroom, Judge Pankin was telling me that he was sending me to the New York State Training School for Boys. The judge said that he thought I was a chronic liar and that he hoped I would be a better boy when I came out. I asked him if he wanted me to thank him. Mama stopped crying just long enough to say, "Hush your mouth, boy."

Mama tried to change the judge's mind by telling him that I had already been to Wiltwyck School for Boys for two and a half years. And before that, I had been ordered out of the state for at least one year. She said that I had been away from my family too much; that was why I was always getting into trouble.

The judge told Mama that he knew what he was doing and that one day she would be grateful to him for doing it.

I had been sent away before, but this was the first time I was ever afraid to go. When Mama came up to the detention room in Children's Court, I tried to act as though I wasn't afraid. After I told her that Warwick and where I was going were one and the same, Mama began to cry, and so did I.

Most of the guys I knew had been to Warwick and were too old to go back. I knew that there were many guys up there I had mistreated. The Stinky brothers were up there. They thought that I was one of the guys who had pulled a train on their sister in the park the summer before. Bumpy from 144th Street was up there. I had shot him in the leg with a zip gun in a rumble only a few months earlier. There were many guys up there I used to bully on the streets and at Wiltwyck, guys I had sold tea leaves to as pot. There were rival gang members up there who just hated my name. All of these guys were waiting for me to show. The word was out that I couldn't fight any more—that I had slowed down since I was shot and that a good punch to the stomach would put my name in the undertaker's book.

When I got to the Youth House, I tried to find out who was up at Warwick that I might know. Nobody knew any of the names I asked about. I knew that if I went up to Warwick in my condition, I'd never live to get out. I had a reputation for being a rugged little guy. This meant that I would have at least a half-dozen fights in the first week of my stay up there.

It seemed the best thing for me to do was to cop out on the nut. For the next two nights, I woke up screaming and banging on the walls. On the third day, I was sent to Bellevue for observation. This meant that I wouldn't be going to Warwick for at least twenty-eight days.

While I was in Bellevue, the fellows would come down and pass notes to me through the doors. Tito and Turk said they would get bagged and sent to Warwick by the time I got there. They were both bagged a week later for smoking pot in front of the police station. They were both sent to Bellevue. Two weeks after they showed, I went home. The judge still wanted to send me to Warwick, but Warwick had a full house, so he sent me home for two weeks.

The day before I went back to court, I ran into Turk, who had just gotten out of Bellevue. Tito had been sent to Warwick, but Turk had gotten a walk because his sheet wasn't too bad. I told him I would probably be sent to Warwick the next day. Turk said he had run into Bucky in Bellevue. He told me that he and Tito had voted Bucky out of the clique. I told him that I wasn't going for it because Bucky was my man from short-pants days. Turk said he liked him too, but what else could he do after Bucky had let a white boy beat him in the nutbox? When I heard this, there was nothing I could do but agree with Turk. Bucky had to go. That kind of news spread fast, and who wanted to be in a clique with a stud who let a paddy boy beat him?

. . . .

The first thing I did when I got into the show that day was to yell out, "Forty thieves!" to see if any of my friends in the gang were there. That afternoon I got a loud "Yo!" from one of the front rows. It was Bucky. He hadn't been to school that day and had sneaked into the show about one o'clock. He had already seen the movie, but it was good, so he was seeing it over. "Goldie was in here a little while ago, but he hadn't been home for the past few nights, so he had to go and steal something to eat," he said. Bucky told me that he hadn't seen any of the other fellows all day. They must have been downtown stealing.

Bucky was about my age, had curly hair, was always dirty, like most of us, and had buck teeth. Of all the dirty kids on the block, Bucky was the dirtiest. He had just moved to our neighborhood around the first of the year.

Bucky had lots of sisters and brothers, and his mother was still having more sisters and brothers for him. He also had some sisters and brothers who, he said, lived with their aunts. These I had never seen. Bucky didn't have a father, and his mother was on relief. All the kids in Bucky's family knew when the relief check came. On that day, they would all follow Miss Jamie around until she cashed it. Then they would beg her to buy some food before she started drinking up the money. Every month when check day rolled around, Bucky and his brothers and sisters would always be arguing with their mother. Miss Jamie was forever telling them to wait someplace until she cashed the check, that she would come back and buy some food. But they all knew that if they ever let her out of their sight with that check, they wouldn't see her for days. When she did show up, she would tell them how she got robbed or how her pocket was picked or how she lost the money. So she would spend half of the day trying to duck the kids, and they would stick with her. If there was only one kid around, or even two, she could easily get away. She would usually go into a bar, where she knew the kids couldn't follow her, and she would leave the bar by another exit. When the kids got wise to this, one of them would start looking for the other exit as soon as she entered the bar. But even then, she could get away if there was only one at the exit she used. She would give him fifty cents as a bribe and jump into a cab.

Bucky was the only guy I knew who could stay out all night and not be missed. Sometimes he would go out and stay for days and still get home before his mother. Sometimes Bucky would go home and there would be nobody there. The lady next door always had the lowdown. The usual reason for the house being empty was that the welfare investigator had come by and had taken all the kids to the Children's Shelter. Whenever this happened while Bucky was away from home, he would go to the police station and tell them what had happened. After the policemen had gotten to know Bucky and were familiar with his home situation, he only had to walk in and they would send him to the Shelter without asking him anything. The Shelter was a second home to Bucky. He liked it more than his first home. At the Shelter, he always got three meals a day, and three meals beats none any way you look at it. Whenever I missed Bucky from around the block, I had a pretty good idea where he was, but he would always say that he was staying with his aunt in Brooklyn. That aunt was the great mystery in Bucky's life.

When Bucky moved into the neighborhood, I sort of adopted him. He had his first fight in the neighborhood with me, and since he was pretty good with his hands, we became friends after three fights. I used to take him home with me and feed him. After a while Bucky got to know what time we usually ate supper, and if he didn't see me on the street, he would come to my house looking for me. If I wasn't in, he would ask if he could come in and wait for me. He knew that somebody would offer him something to eat if he was there at suppertime. Dad started complaining about Bucky coming up to the house for supper every night. So Mama would tell Bucky to go downstairs and look for me if I wasn't there when he came by. When I brought him home with me, sometimes the family would slip into the kitchen one at a time to eat without his knowing it, or they would try to wait until he left. Bucky would never leave as long as he thought that we had not eaten supper. When Bucky was finally gone, Dad would start telling me how stupid I was and threatening to give my supper to Bucky the next time I brought him home with me. Dad said that Bucky had a roguish look about him and that he didn't trust him. Some of the fellows didn't like him either. They said he looked too pitiful.

That day after we saw the show, I went up to Bucky's house to show him a homemade that I had found a week before. I didn't have any bullets for it yet, but that wasn't important—I knew somebody I could steal them from. As I walked through the door—which was always open because the lock had been broken and Miss Jamie never bothered to have it fixed—I saw Bucky on the floor with his arm around his little sister's throat. He was choking her. Meanwhile, his big sister was bopping him on the head with a broom handle and they were all screaming. After I had watched the three-way fight for a minute or less, I started toward Dixie to grab the broom. Before I could get close enough to grab the broom handle, everything stopped. For a whole second, everything was real quiet. Dixie threw down the broom and started crying. Debbie was already crying, but I couldn't hear her because Bucky was still choking her. He let her go and started cursing. When Debbie got up, I saw what she and Dixie were crying over and what Bucky was cursing about. The three of them had been fighting over one egg, and the egg was broken in the scuffle.

Bucky had run out of the house cursing, and I was standing where he had left me. Dixie and Debbie were facing me on the other side of the room. They were staring at the broken egg on the floor, and their crying was getting louder all the time. I was staring at them and wondering why they were making so much fuss over one broken egg. They sure looked funny standing there with their mouths wide open and tears rolling down their dirty faces and into their mouths. I began to laugh and mimic them. Dixie threw the broom at me and missed. Knowing what they were going to do as soon as I left, I decided to get even with Dixie for throwing the broom at me. Before either of them realized what I was doing, I had stepped on the egg and was smearing it all over the floor. Debbie began to cry louder, and Dixie was all over me, scratching, biting, and hitting me with what seemed like ten hands. Without thinking, I started swinging. I didn't stop swinging until I heard Dixie crying again. She went over to what was left of that old ragged couch they had in the living room, threw herself down on it, and went on crying into the cushions. I went over and touched her on the shoulder and told her I was sorry. She only raised her head enough to scream as loud as she could and tell me to let her alone. I told her to wait there while I went to steal her some eggs. She yelled that she didn't want any eggs and that when her older brother got out of jail, she was going to get him to kick my ass.

Less than ten minutes after I had left Dixie crying on the couch, I walked in the house with a dozen eggs and a loaf of bread. Dixie was sitting up on the couch now. Her eyes were red, but she wasn't crying; her face still had tearstains on it, and her mouth was stuck out as if she were mad at somebody. Not saying anything. I walked over to her and offered her the eggs and the loaf of bread. I was standing in front of her holding out the eggs and bread. She just sat there staring at me as if she didn't believe it or as if she wondered how I had come by these things. Seeing that she needed a little encouragement, I pushed the eggs and bread against her chest saying, "Here, take it." She took them and started walking slowly toward the kitchen. It seemed as though she still didn't believe it was really happening, that if she should make a fast or sudden move, the eggs and bread would be gone. She carried the food to the kitchen like somebody carrying a large basin of water that was filled to the brim. When I heard Dixie moving about in the kitchen, I went in, feeling that everything was all right now and that she knew I hadn't played a joke on her.

Dixie was running some water into a small pot. She asked me if I wanted a boiled egg. I told her that I liked my eggs scrambled. She said the only grease in the house was some fish grease and if she scrambled the eggs in it, they would taste like fish. After she had put six eggs on the stove to boil, Dixie said she was sorry for scratching me and didn't mean what she had said about telling her brother to beat me up when he came home. I told her that I was sorry for laughing at her and that I hadn't meant to hit her so hard. I asked her if she wanted to make friends, and she said all right. We shook hands and started talking about the things we disliked in each other. She said I just thought I was too bad and was always messing with somebody. I told her that she was all right, but she should stop licking the snot off her lip when her nose was running. Also, I thought she looked crazy always pulling her bloomers up through her skirt.

While Dixie and I were testing out our new friendship, Debbie had come in and sat down. She just sat quietly and kept watching the pot. When Dixie got up and went over to the stove to turn the fire off beneath the pot, Debbie's eyes followed her. Dixie started cutting up eggs to make sandwiches, but I told her to just give me an egg and some salt. She made two sandwiches, one for herself and one for Debbie.

After the second round of eggs, Dixie sent Debbie downstairs to play. When Debbie had gone into the street, Dixie asked me if I wanted to play house, and I said okay. We got up from the milk crates that we had been sitting on in the kitchen. There were no chairs there. In fact, the only chair in the house was the one in the front room by the window. There had to be a chair in that spot. When Miss Jamie had money, she played numbers and waited all day long to hear what the first figure was. Mr. Bob, the number man, would come by and signal up to the window to let her know what each figure was as it came out.

When he gave the signal, Miss Jamie would either say something about the Lord and send one of the kids down for her money or say, "Oh-h-h, shit!" and send somebody down with some money to put on another figure . . . if she had any more money.

By the time Dixie and I reached the front room, we were old friends. She took off her bloomers without giving it a thought. She didn't want to lie down on the bed because it was wet from her little brothers sleeping there the night before. It didn't even bother her that her drawers were dirty and ragged. They looked as if she had been wearing them for months, but still she didn't ask me to turn around or close my eyes while she took them off. This meant we were real good friends now.

As I was leaving, I told Dixie that I would bring her something nice when I came back. She tried to get me to say what it was, and when she had failed at this, she said she didn't believe me anyway. But I knew she did and that she would be waiting for me to come back.

After she had finished telling me what a liar I was, I slapped her playfully and ran down the stairs. When I reached the street, I looked up and down the avenue for Bucky, but he wasn't around. So, I decided to wait in front of his house and let him find me.

Mr. Mitchell, the man who owned the fruit store next to Bucky's house, was afraid to go to the back of the store after seeing me sitting on the running board of a car in front of his store. Mr. Mitchell was a West Indian, and I didn't like him. I didn't like any West Indians. They couldn't talk, they were stingy, and most of them were as mean as could be. I like Butch, but I didn't believe that he was really a West Indian.

Mr. Mitchell was looking at me as if he thought I would jump up at any time and run away with his whole store. But I just sat there and looked right back at him. I thought about Mr. Mitchell and Mr. Lawson. Mr. Mitchell didn't seem to be a West Indian all the time, and he wasn't mean like Mr. Lawson. Mr. Lawson, who was the super of our house, was the meanest man on the Avenue. He was said to have killed half a dozen men. Dad had killed a man too, but that was for saying something nasty to Mama. I would have killed that bastard too. I think anybody would have killed him. Killing all those people wasn't what made Mr. Lawson mean. He was mean because he was a West Indian.

As I was sitting there on the running board of that car, I heard a voice that had always been pleasing to my ear as long as I could remember. It was little Pimp saying, "Sonny, Mama want you." Pimp was my favorite person in the whole family. Maybe that was because he was my only brother. Or maybe it was just because. Whenever I stayed away from home for days I missed him, and sometimes I would even go to the house of the lady who kept him, Margie, and Carole while Mama was working. I missed Margie and Carole too, but not as much as I missed Pimp. He was my brother, and that was different. I would always bring him something that I had stolen, like a cap gun or a water pistol. I was waiting for Pimp to grow up; then we could have a lot of fun together. Right now, all I could do was tell him about all the fun I was having outrunning the police, stealing everything I wanted, and sleeping in a different place every night. Man, I couldn't wait to teach him these things. That little nigger sure was lucky to have me for a brother. I threw my arm around Pimp and started choking him playfully as we started toward the house to see what Mama wanted me for.

When we got to the door, I stopped and told Pimp to be quiet. It was a habit of mine by now to listen at the door before going in. Whenever I heard a strange voice, I usually made a detour. But this day I was going in in spite of the strange voice. I knew it was safe even though it was strange, because it was a lady's voice. That meant that it couldn't be the cops or a truant officer, and I hadn't stolen anything from a lady that day, so it had to be just a visitor.

Mama was sitting in the living room on the studio cot drinking beer, and a light-skinned pretty lady was sitting in the big chair across from Mama, drinking beer too. I walked into the middle of the living room and stopped, staring at the lady who shouted out, "Is this Sonny Boy?"

When Mama answered, "Yeah, that's Sonny Boy," this woman just reached up and grabbed me with both hands, saying, "Boy, come here and kiss your aunt."

Before I could defend myself, she was smothering me to death between two gigantic breasts. I was let up for some air, but before I had taken two breaths, the lady was washing my face with sloppy kisses that stank from beer. I was getting mad and thinking that maybe I'd better tell her I didn't go for all that baby shit and that I didn't mean to have any more of it, aunt or no aunt. But when my long-lost aunt regained her senses and let me out of her bear hug, I wasn't mad any more. I had realized that this was just another one of those old crazy-acting, funny-dressing, no-talking people from down South. As I stood on the other side of the room looking at her, I was wondering if all the people down South were crazy like that. I knew one thing—I had never seen anybody from down there who looked or acted as if they had some sense. Damn, that was one place I never wanted to go to. It was probably eating corn bread and biscuits all the time that made those people act like that.

Mama started telling Aunt Bea how Pimp got his name, because Aunt Bea had said, "That sho don't sound like nothin' to be callin' no child." When Mama started getting labor pains while she was carrying Pimp, there was nobody around to get an ambulance but Minnie, the neighborhood prostitute. Minnie called an ambulance, but it was a long time coming, and Mama's pains were getting worse. Minnie got scared and ran out and got a cab and took Mama to the hospital.

All the way to the hospital, Minnie kept saying, "It better be a girl, 'cause I'm spending my last dollar on this cab, and I never gave a man no money in my life." Minnie was real proud to tell people that she had never had a pimp and would never give a nigger a dime. Well, when Mama came out of the operating room, Minnie was still out there with her fingers crossed and praying for it to be a girl. Minnie left the hospital cursing, but not before she had become a godmother and had named her godson Pimp. Mama told Minnie that she was sorry but that it must have been the Lord's will.

Minnie said, "That's all right, 'cause the cab fare was only seventy cents. And, anyway, he's such a cute little nigger, maybe he was born to be a pimp, and maybe it was in the cards for me to be the first one to spend some money on him." Minnie began teasing Mama about Pimp's complexion, saying, "Girl, you know you ain't got no business with no baby that light; it looks like it's a white baby. . . . I know one thing—that baby better start looking colored before your husband see him." Mama said all her children were born looking almost white. And that Carole was even lighter than that when she was born, but, that by the time she was five years old, she was the cutest little plump, dimple-cheeked black gal on Eighth Avenue. This was probably because my grandfather is more white than he is colored.

After Mama finished telling Aunt Bea how Pimp got his name, she started telling me and Pimp that Aunt Bea had a real nice farm down South. When she had told us all there was to tell about that real nice farm, Mama asked us if we wanted to go home with Aunt Bea when she left in a couple of weeks. Pimp said no because he knew that was what Mama wanted to hear. I said I wanted to go right away, because I had just heard about all those watermelon patches down South.

"In a couple of weeks, all you chillun goin' home with your Aunt Bea for the rest of the summer," Mama said.

I asked if I could have the beer bottle that was nearly empty. After I turned it up to my mouth and finished emptying it, I asked Pimp if he wanted to go to the show. We went into the kitchen to collect some more bottles to cash them in for show fare.

We could hear Mama and Aunt Bea talking in the living room. Mama was telling Aunt Bea how bad I was and that sometimes she thought I had the devil in me. Aunt Bea said that was probably true "'cause his granddaddy and his great-granddaddy on his daddy's side both had it." Next Aunt Bea was telling Mama how my great-grandfather, Perry Brown, had tied his wife to a tree and beat her with a branch until his arm got tired. Then she told Mama about what my grandfather, Mr. Son Brown, did to a jackleg preacher from Silver when he caught him stealing liquor from his still down in the Black Swamp. She said Grandpa circled around that old jackleg preacher and started shooting over his head with a shotgun and made the preacher run smack into a bear trap that he had set for whoever was stealing his liquor. After that the jackleg preacher only had one foot, and everybody said Mr. Son Brown shouldn't have done that to the preacher just for taking a little bit of whiskey.

I thought, Yeah, I guess there is a whole lotta devil in the Brown family and especially in Dad, 'cause he sure is mean.

Then I heard Aunt Bea ask Mama a familiar-sounding question: "Do you think somebody done work some roots on the po child?"

Mama said, "Lord, I sho hope nobody ain't work no roots on my child." Mama was quiet for a while, then she said, "They got some West Indian people around here who is evil enough to do anything to anybody, and they always 'fixing' somebody. I always tell that boy to stop playin' and fightin' with those West Indian chillun, but he just won't listen. Who knows? Maybe he done did sumpin to one-a those kids and they people found out about it and worked some roots on him. Anything might happen to that little nigger, 'cause he so damn bad. Lord, I ain't never seen a child in my life that bad. I know one thing—if I don't git that boy outta New York soon, my hair gonna be gray before I get thirty years old. Sumpin gotta be wrong with the boy, 'cause nobody in my family steal and lie the way he do, and none-a his daddy people ain't never been no rogues and liars like he is. I don't know who he coulda took all that roguishness at.

"Seem like nobody can't make him understand. I talk to him, I yell at him, I whip his ass, but it don't do no good. His daddy preach to him, he yell at him, he beat him so bad sometimes, I gotta run in the kitchen and git that big knife at him to stop him from killin' that boy. You think that might break him outta those devilish ways he got? Child, that scamp'll look Jesus dead in the eye when he standin' on a mountain of Bibles and swear to God in heaven he ain't gon do it no more. The next day, or even the next minute, that little lyin' Negro done gone and did it again—and got a mouthful-a lies when he git caught.

"And talk about sumpin mannish! I had to go to school with him one mornin' to see his teacher. I got the postcard on a Friday, and all that weekend I was askin' him what the teacher wanted to see me about, and all that weekend he was swearin' to some Gods and Jesuses I ain't never heard of before that he didn' know why in the world his teacher wanted to see me, unless somebody was tellin' lies on him again. And I told him, I said, 'Mind, now, my little slick nigger, you know I know you, and a lotta those lies people was tellin' on you was as true as what Christ told his disciples. Now, don't you let me go to that school and find out these lies they tellin' on you now got as much Gospel in 'em as those other lies had. 'Cause if I do, so help me, boy, I'm gonna take down your pants right there in that classroom and beat your ass until the Lord stop me.' He still kept sayin' he didn't do nothin' and had the nerve to poke out his lips and git mad at me for always blamin' him for sumpin he ain't did. You know that little scamp had me huggin' and kissin' him and apologizin' for what I said to him?

"So, Monday mornin' rolled around, and I went to school with him. I had to watch him close, had hold his hand from the minute he got up that mornin', 'cause I could tell by the look in his eye that if I took my eye offa him, that would be the last time I'd see him for the whole week. When I got to the school and talked to the teacher, I came to find out this Negro done took some little high-yaller girl in the closet one day when the teacher went outta the room. After he done gone and got mannish with this little yaller girl, he's gonna go and throw the little girl's drawers out the window. I almost killed that nigger in that classroom. As hard as people gotta work to get they kids clothes, he gon take somebody's drawers and throw 'em out the window. I bet you a fat man he never throwed nobody else clothes out no window. Ain't nothin' I kin do 'bout that high-yaller-woman weakness he got, 'cause he take that at his daddy. But I sho am glad they ain't got no little white girls in these schools in Harlem, 'cause my poor child woulda done been lynched, right up here in New York.

"They had him down there in one of those crazy wards in Bellevue Hospital, but they let him come home, so I guess it ain't nothin' wrong with his head. I think one-a dem doctors did think Sonny Boy was a little crazy though, 'cause he kept talkin' to me with all those big words, like he didn' want me to know what he was tellin' me. I don' know, maybe he didn' say Sonny Boy was crazy. It mighta been that he just don' know how to talk to regular people. You know, mosta those white doctors don' know how to talk to colored people anyway.

"Some of his teachers even said he was smart in doing his schoolwork and when he wasn't botherin' nobody. The trouble is that he's always botherin' somebody. He had one teacher, a little Jew-lady teacher, she was just as sweet as she could be. And she liked Sonny Boy and was always tryin' to be nice to him. She use to buy his lunch for him when he went lyin' to her about bein' hungry, after he done spend his lunch money on some ole foolishness. Well, one day she caught him lookin' up her dress, and she smacked him. Do you know that crazy boy hit her back? Yeah, I mean punch her dead in her face and made the poor lady cry. When I heard about it, I beat him for what seem like days, and I was scared to tell his daddy 'bout it, 'cause I know Cecil woulda killed him for doin' sumpin as crazy as that. And when I finished beating him, I told that nigger if I ever heard of him hitting or even talkin' back to that nice little Jew-lady again, I was gonna break his natural-born ass. Well, they throwed him outta that school right after that, so I guess he didn't git a chance to do that again.

"Yeah, sumpin is sho wrong with that boy, but I don' think he's crazy or nothin' like that, 'cause he got a whole lotta sense when it comes to gittin' in trouble. And when I stop to think about it, I don't believe nobody worked no roots on him, 'cause he got too much devil in him to be tricked by them root workers. But what coulda happen is that he went someplace and sassed some old person, and that old person put the bad mouth on him. Yeah, more'n likely that's what happened to him, 'cause he always sassing old people. I beat him and keep tellin' him not to talk back to people with gray hair, but that little devilish nigger got a head on him like rock. Lord, I don' know what to do with that boy. I just hope Pimp don't never git that bad."

When I got tired of hearing how bad I was and about the roots and the bad mouth, I took Pimp to the show. On the way to the show, Pimp asked me to tell him about roots. I didn't want to tell him that I didn't know, because he thought I knew everything, almost as much as God. So I started telling him things about roots and root workers based on the tales I had heard Mama tell about somebody working roots on somebody else "down home." I said, "Only people down South work roots, because you can't git roots around here." Pimp wanted to know what was wrong with the roots in the park. "Those ain't the right kinda roots," I said. "You have to git roots that grow down South. All kinda roots grow down there—money roots, love roots, good-luck roots, bad-luck roots, killin' roots, sick-makin' roots, and lotta other kinda roots."

"Sonny, do you know how to work roots?"

"Yeah, man, I can work some kinda roots, but some roots I'm not so sure about."

"Sonny, who teached you how to work roots?"

"Nobody. I just know 'cause I heard so much about it."

"Sonny, did you ever work any roots on anybody?"

"No, man, not yet."

"When you gonna work some on somebody?"

"When somebody who I can't beat make me real mad, that's when I'm gonna work some roots on somebody."

"You gonna work some roots on Daddy, Sonny?"

"No, man, he's too evil; you can't work roots on real evil people."

"Carole said God gon strike Daddy dead if he don't stop being so mean to us."

"Uh-uh, Pimp, I don't think God gon mess with Dad. 'Cause he woulda did it when Dad cut Miss Bertha husband throat that time or one-a those times when he beat me wit that ironing cord or that time when he cussed out the preacher. No, man, I don' think God gon mess wit Dad."

"Sonny, you think God is scared-a Daddy?"

"Man, I don' know. I know one thing—all the stuff he been doin' ain't nobody but the police been botherin' him."

"Maybe God gonna put the police on Daddy, huh, Sonny?"

"Yeah, man, maybe."

"Sonny, Margie said they got snakes down South and they bite people and the people die when the snakes bite 'em. Is that true, Sonny?"

"Yeah, it's true, but they don' bite everybody. They didn' bite Dad, and they didn' bite Mama, and I know a whole lotta people they didn' bite."

"Sonny, is the boogeyman down South too?"

"Man, how many times I done told you it ain't no boogeyman?"

"But Margie keep on sayin' it is."

"The next time she say it, punch huh in huh mout' real hard and she won't say it no more."

"Mama said the boogeyman comes around at night wit a big burlap sack and gits all bad kids and put in that burlap sack and nobody don't see 'em no more."

"Man, Mama's just try'n'-a scare you. You know it ain't no boogeyman, 'cause I told you so. You 'member all those times Mama and everybody use to say the boogeyman was gonna git me if I didn't stop bein' so bad? Well, I didn't git no gooder; I even got badder than I was then. Ain't no boogeyman got me yet. That's 'cause it ain't no boogeyman. Every place anybody even told me the boogeyman was, I went there and looked for him, but he ain't never been in none-a dem places. The next time somebody tell you the boogeyman is someplace, git you a big stick and go see him. If I'm around, come and get me and I'll show you it ain't no boogeyman."

"You ever been down South, Sonny?"

"Uh-uh not yet, but I know it ain't no boogeyman down there."

"They got crackers down there, ain't they, Sonny?"

"Yeah, Mama said they got crackers down South."

"Sonny, what is crackers? They ain't the kinda crackers you buy in the candy store, is they?"

"No, the crackers down South is white people, real mean white people."

"Is Mr. Goldman a cracker, Sonny?"

"No, he's a Jew."

"But he's white and look real mean."

"I know that, but some white people is crackers and some-a dem is Jews, and Mr. Goldman is a Jew. You see, Pimp, white people is all mean and stingy. If one-a dem is more stingy than he is mean, he's a Jew; and if he is more mean than he is stingy, then he's a cracker."

"But, Sonny, how kin you tell 'em?"

"That's easy. Just ask me. I'll tell you what they is."

"Sonny, I ain't goin' down South."

"Why ain'tcha?"

"'Cause they got snakes down dere, they got roots down dere, and they got crackers too. Uh-uh, I ain't goin' down dere. You goin', Sonny?"

"Yeah, I'm goin'."

"Why?"

"'Cause that judge said I better go."

Two weeks later, I was on my way down South for a summer vacation that lasted a year.

KATHERINE BUTLER HATHAWAY

Katherine Butler Hathaway was born in Baltimore in 1891. When she was five, she was stricken with a spinal disease and lay for ten years strapped almost constantly to a hard sloping bed with a halter around her neck to keep her head from sinking down on her chest. At fifteen, she was able at last to leave her bed. Still, she was misshapen, like the hunchbacked locksmith she had watched as a child, and after whom she named her autobiography, *The Little Locksmith*, from which the following selection comes. Although she never attained more stature than that of the normal ten-year-old, she married happily. She died Christmas Eve, 1942, shortly after completing *The Little Locksmith*.

The Disguise

When I was fifteen this horizontal life of night and day was ended. In that year I was pronounced cured; I was to get up at last and see things from a perpendicular and movable point of view, after watching them for so long from a horizontal and fixed one. Everything would look different, of course. Also, I knew that I myself would look different standing up from the way I had looked lying down. Why, at the great age of fifteen I didn't even know how tall I was! And I had begun to wonder secretly about my back. There was that unknown territory between my shoulders where the tuberculosis had lodged and burrowed for so long. How much it had disfigured me I didn't know. As I had grown older there had been a baffling silence in regard to that side of my illness, and I never dared to ask. Nobody guessed that I was secretly worrying about it, and I could not tell them. Nobody guessed, because, I suppose, I gave the impression of being such a happy, humorous child. But when I was alone in the room I sometimes slid my hand up under me to explore that fateful part. But my hand always got strangely panic-stricken and came hurrying back without making me any wiser than before. My hand seemed to be mortally afraid of that place, which remained therefore unknown, waiting for the day when I should get up and stand plainly revealed.

Although my mother had so often told me, when I was little, how lucky I was, as I grew older she never spoke of my being lucky. Instead, quite a different feeling seemed to come over her whenever she or anybody else spoke of my "trouble" as it was called. I must first explain that when I was young my mother seemed to me dull and uninteresting compared with my father. He and I were conscious of each other, almost as lovers are. Everything he said held my attention, and was interesting and essential to me. In comparison, my mother seemed to have to think and talk about a lot of unessential things, and her real self, for me, was swamped and obscured by them. I had a feeling that she didn't like unessential things, but that she didn't quite know how to manage them easily and get them out of the way. So she labored awkwardly, directing the house and servants, and she worried, and had to go to bed with sick headaches. Sometimes I felt very maternal toward her, she had such a hard time doing things that I thought looked quite easy. My own hands were so much more skillful than hers, for instance, that if she tried to make a paper doll for me she seemed to me like a clumsy younger child. She was not an artist, or a craftsman, like the rest of us, and so she thought we were much more wonderful than we were. I never saw her eyes really shine with happiness as much as they did when she was admiring us as artists, and treasuring all the things we made. Then she made herself, in comparison, seem humble and unimportant. In matters of our conduct as human beings she was relentless, and we feared her as we feared God. We learned very young to be good and to obey and to respect our father and mother. But when she was admiring us as artists she gave us a feeling of absolute freedom from authority. We were all for weighing and criticizing each other's works. We knew to a hair's breadth which was better than another, and why. But she liked everything we did, our good things and also the ones we would have torn up and thrown away. She gathered them all together and kept and treasured them, and her eyes shone over us with a pride and a tenderness that I shall never see again.

Because of this humble uncritical attitude of hers toward art, I didn't notice her very much, and when I did I often wished that she were more exciting and knew how to do things herself. But once in a great while, when somebody spoke of my illness or she mentioned it herself, she was all changed. I couldn't very well not notice her then. A terrific wave of pain sprang up in her blue eyes, and it was evident suddenly that the pain was always there, controlled, inside her, like something terribly alive, always ready to leap up and hurt her all over again. She never cried, but her self-control was worse than crying.

"I ought never to have *let* it happen! It was wicked! Wicked!" she would burst out. And then, immediately after, I witnessed the silent and to me awful struggle as for some reason she fought against the physical symptoms of her grief. Not a tear ever succeeded in getting past the barrier of her will, and not a sob. But during those few seconds when she could not trust herself to speak, and her gentian-blue eyes were fiercely widened to prevent the tears from coming into them as she stared away from me, out of the window, anywhere, away from me, and swallowed back that great lump of sadness and forced it away down into the secret part of her being, I was awe-struck and shaken, much more than I would have been to see her yield to tears. Her secretive Spartan way made crying seem like an enemy that one must never submit to. The awesome struggle that it cost her affected me almost as if I had been forced to watch her from a distance struggling all alone with a savage animal and managing by sheer force of her will and character to keep it at bay.

When she was like that I could not very well not notice her or think she was uninteresting. Then her aliveness frightened me. And I loved her more than I could possibly have told. I felt a furious will to cherish her and protect her and never to let her suffer, when I got old enough to influence or control her. Yet I could not show her what I felt. Besides being inarticulate myself, I knew that I had seen something in her that she thought I was too young to see or even to know about, and I knew I must pretend I hadn't seen it. It was not her concern for me that made me love her so much then. It was because I saw her in the grip of essential things, and she became alive and fiery and very brave. I felt humble before her, for myself and for all the rest of us toward whom she had made herself seem unclever and unimportant.

Although I felt an almost unbearable tenderness and love for her in those moments, I felt hatred and rebellion too. I hated and rejected the idea that there was anything tragic about my illness, or that she was to blame. I was angry because when she battled with those terrible surging tears I had to battle too. Watching her, I felt a violent emotion suddenly throbbing against my throat, surging and aching in my chest. For she seemed to waken something in me that was a disgusting traitor to my conscious self, a sorrow over my own plight that leaped up out of the depth of me, and answered her with a grieving that seemed to understand and match her own. I could love her piteous sorrow for me, but I loathed and despised it in myself. And I pushed it away from me with an almost masculine strength and confidence in my own soundness and well-being. This rebellion made me appear hard and cold toward her, just at the moment when I loved her most.

Yet I always longed to know intimately and adore and caress that real fiery self of hers. Why did she hide it from her children and almost from herself? It seemed as if she thought that if she ever once let her emotion escape from under her control its poignancy would be unbearable, and would destroy her and destroy us all. Whatever the reason, when these moments arrived they passed in fierce silence and aloofness. The hearts of the mother and the child ached in pity for each other, each separate, stoical, and alone.

So, lying still and watching her, I was tense and fighting for her, helping her with all my might not to be overcome by the enemy that was trying to make us both cry and break out into sobs. I knew that if anything could make her lose the battle it would be to have me be anything except the happy unconscious child she thought I was. And besides, except when she acted like this, I *was* happy. After all, what was there so sad about me and my illness? It was a mystery to me. I thought my mother's sadness must be just a phenomenon of mother love, which exaggerates everything.

When I got up at last, fifteen years old, and had learned to walk again, one day I took a hand glass and went to a long mirror to look at myself, and I went alone. I didn't want anyone, my mother least of all, to know how I felt when I saw myself for the first time. But there was no noise, no outcry; I didn't scream with rage when I saw myself. I just felt numb. That person in the mirror *couldn't* be me. I felt inside like a healthy, ordinary, lucky person—oh, not like the one in the mirror! Yet when I turned my face to the mirror there were my own eyes looking back, hot with shame. I had turned out after all, like the little locksmith—oh, not so bad, nearly—but enough like the little locksmith to be called by that same word.

What I felt that day did not fit in with the pleasant cheerful atmosphere of our family, any more than my horrors had fitted in. There was no place for it among us. It was something in another language. It was in the same language as my mother's suppressed panic-stricken grief, and I would have died rather than let that come to the surface of our cheerful life, for her to see and endure in me. And so from that first moment, when I did not cry or make any sound, it became impossible that I should speak of it to anyone, and the confusion and the panic of my discovery were locked inside me then and there, to be faced alone, for a very long time to come.

Here then was the beginning of my predicament. A hideous disguise had been cast over me, as if by a wicked stepmother. And I now had ahead of me, although I didn't know it, the long, blind, wistful struggle of the fairy tales. I had to wander stupidly and blindly, searching for I didn't know what, following fantastically wrong clues, until at last I might hit upon a magic that could set me free.

At the very beginning it was lucky for me that I found my brother Warren. Three things had ended suddenly all at the same time—my illness and my childhood and my father's life. When one thing ends another must begin. As I have already written, at the end of my illness there began my ignorant and lonely struggle to adapt myself to what I had seen in the mirror. At this same time my childhood ended and a thrilling ferment of new consciousness had begun to go on inside me which made me feel myself turning wonderfully into a haughty and grand young lady. Although my body was impeded in its growth and I was bewildered by its misfortune, my mind was not impeded. My mind grew independently of my body and independently of the shape of my body. It grew and behaved at first as if nothing were wrong with me anywhere. I was even more concerned at first with extricating myself from the disgrace of being considered a child than I was concerned with the fearful fact of my deformity. Now that I was up and walking around at last, like the rest of the world, I seemed to feel a fierce revenge against my bed and my invalid life, and especially against the bright little girl who had accepted it all so sweetly and submissively. I suddenly hated my adorable microscopic world, and all the little arts out of which with painstaking care I had constructed my joys. I hated the loving admiration of the grownups for me and everything I did. I felt fierce and rebellious and strong and mad toward them and myself. Something new had come into my mind, and it was like a labor agitator who furiously tries to destroy the docile contentment of workers who have so long adapted themselves to a narrow life that they do not even realize it is narrow. Out of loyalty to the new values that were dawning in me and making me, as I believed, into an entirely new person, I had to do cruel violence to the contented little girl. I had to emphasize my separateness from her in every possible way because the grownups persisted in clinging to her with an absurd devotion and insisting she was me. Whereas I knew with every part of myself that she was not me any more. I was through with her. I was through because a wonderful thing had happened to me. I had found suddenly that I was not frightened any more by the abstract ideas that had frightened the little girl so terribly in her bed. I had begun to fall at first gingerly and then boldly in love with the mystery of the Universe. Instead of wanting to curl my mind up and tuck it away in some cozy little place where it could never think those terrifying thoughts of death and birth and time, my mind suddenly wanted to reach out and embrace fearlessly those mysteries and become a conscious, proud part of them. It seemed to me that I had suddenly grown so tall that my head was among the stars. Relieved, by some miracle, of my cosmic fears, I felt an almost drunken sense of liberation, as if I had been released from a most abject slavery and admitted to the free and fearless aristocracy of the mind.

At this crucial time my father died, and on the day I lost him, after a long illness that had made him grow remote from me, I found my brother Warren. We sat side by side on the piazza of our house on the strange April morning when we became fatherless. We watched the undertakers coming up the steps into the house, and going busily back and forth between the house and their terrible high black carriage. I felt cruelly little sorrow, considering how very deeply my father had cherished and loved me, perhaps because his cultivating love had helped to create the little girl whom I was now intent on destroying. Instead, his death gave me an exultant happiness because it strengthened and intensified my new awareness and adoration of cosmic things. It made me feel mature and experienced and proud because I could see it in the radiance of the new daybreak that was in my mind. Death was another of the great and ordered mysteries of life, and, being so, it could never frighten me any more. In that revelation there was indescribable ecstasy and joy for the young mystic who was beginning to inhabit my mind and look out of my eyes.

Like every fifteen-year-old person, my mind was so new to thought, and I was consequently so naïve, that I examined everything that came before me with the feeling that it was an entirely new phenomenon and had never been examined by anybody before. And when I was struck that morning as we sat on the piazza by the thought that the noble mystery of death ought not to be intruded upon and degraded by these loathsome undertakers—officious, practical, busy little men like black ants running to and fro—I was thrilled and surprised by my own angry resentment. In my experience older people seemed to take everything for granted, and I found that I did not take the undertakers for granted; it also dawned on me that I must be a wild and revolutionary thinker. I thought I had hit upon a point of view that probably nobody else in the world had ever held before. It was a purifying, beautiful, joyous sensation of anger that I felt, and I knew for the first time that I could feel passionately about an idea. Something had blazed in me, and from the blaze I discovered a new element in myself, a combustible something that would always blaze again in defense of the mystery and sacredness in things, and against the queer, blind, blaspheming streak in human nature which instead of adoring, must vulgarize and exploit and insult life.

In my excitement I turned to my brother and burst out with some incoherent exclamation about how I hated the undertakers. To my astonishment he said that he knew how I felt, and that he hated them too. This was the first time that I had ever exchanged anything like an abstract idea with anyone, and I could feel my new self expand still more.

So my brother and I looked at each other that day with curiosity and surprise and each recognized in the other a new and unexpected friend. We had both deserted the two absorbed and happy children we had lately been, and in doing so we had lost each other. It was lucky for me that we met again at that moment, which, for me, would have been intolerably bewildering alone. We were just entering the period which is like a magic forest, into which nobody either older or younger than ourselves could possibly be admitted. We needed to escape from them, from all the others, because our turn had come. It was our precious turn to believe, deluded and untested as we were, that we and our generation were the elect—the only beings on earth whose vision of life was really pure and abstract, a mystic's vision. We had not yet allowed ourselves to be corrupted by any such despicable things as expediency or money. Our actions and plans were not yet crippled by any of the loathsome timidities and misrepresentations of common sense, or stifled altogether by the paralyzing fears by which children and old people are all degraded. From that time of awakening onward there was a wild enchantment crying and singing in my blood, the enchantment and excitement that come, by rights, with the flowering of the young human body and its short-lived perfection. My youthful singing blood did not seem to know the crazy fact that my body had stumbled against, and never could listen to it and learn it and take it in. My very joyous blood took it for granted that my body was unfolding simultaneously with my consciousness, and the song of my blood was so much a part of me that I forgot, over and over, and took it for granted too.

Over and over I forgot what I had seen in the mirror. It could not penetrate into the interior of my mind and become an integral part of me. I felt as if it had nothing to do with me; it was only a disguise. But it was not the kind of disguise which is put on voluntarily by the person who wears it, and which is intended to confuse other people as to one's identity. My disguise had been put on me without my consent or knowledge like the ones in fairy tales, and it was I myself who was confused by it, as to my own identity. I looked in the mirror, and was horror-struck because I did not recognize myself. In the place where I was standing, with that persistent romantic elation in me, as if I were a favored fortunate person to whom everything was possible, I saw a stranger, a little, pitiable, hideous figure, and a face that became, as I stared at it, painful and blushing with shame. It was only a disguise, but it was on me, for life. It was there, it was there, it was real. Every one of those encounters was like a blow on the head. They left me dazed and dumb and senseless every time, until slowly and stubbornly my robust persistent illusion of well-being and of personal beauty spread all through me again, and I forgot the irrelevant reality and was all unprepared and vulnerable again.

At this time of secret confusion it was lucky for me that I found my brother Warren. He acted as if he did not even see my disguise. He never mentioned it, he never explained how he felt. He merely treated me as if he saw in me the growing-up proud person that I felt myself to be.

SAMUEL L. CLEMENS

Samuel Langhorne Clemens was born in Florida, Missouri, in 1835. He took his famous pen name, Mark Twain, from the leadsman's call meaning "two fathoms"; it is perhaps the only name of a prominent American author, living or dead, which is a registered trademark. He became a riverboat pilot (which, as the following selection from *Life on the Mississippi* [1883] shows, is roughly equivalent to becoming the captain of a jetliner today). His greatest books, *The Adventures of Tom Sawyer* (1876) and *The Adventures of Huckleberry Finn* (1884), are often read and remembered as childhood adventures by child adventurers. These excerpts may encourage some readers to return to the tales of Tom and Huck to seek the dimension they may have missed the first time down the river. Mark Twain died in 1910.

A Cub Pilot

A Daring Deed

When I returned to the pilot-house St. Louis was gone, and I was lost. Here was a piece of river which was all down in my book, but I could make neither head nor tail of it: you understand, it was turned around. I had seen it when coming up-stream, but I had never faced about to see how it looked when it was behind me. My heart broke again, for it was plain that I had got to learn this troublesome river *both ways*.

The pilot-house was full of pilots, going down to "look at the river." What is called the "upper river" (the two hundred miles between St. Louis and Cairo, where the Ohio comes in) was low; and the Mississippi changes its channel so constantly that the pilots used to always find it necessary to run down to Cairo to take a fresh look, when their boats were to lie in port a week; that is, when the water was at a low stage. A deal of this "looking at the river" was done by poor fellows who seldom had a berth, and whose only hope of getting one lay in their being always freshly posted and therefore ready to drop into the shoes of some reputable pilot, for a single trip, on account of such pilot's sudden illness, or some other necessity. And a good many of them constantly ran up and down inspecting the river, not because they ever really hoped to get a berth, but because (they being guests of the boat) it was cheaper to "look at the river" than stay ashore and pay board. In time these fellows grew dainty in their tastes, and only infested boats that had an established reputation for setting good tables. All visiting pilots were useful, for they were always ready and willing, winter or summer, night or day, to go out in the yawl and help buoy the channel or assist the boat's pilots in any way they could. They were likewise welcomed because all pilots are tireless talkers, when gathered together, and as they talk only about the river they are always understood and are always interesting. Your true pilot cares nothing about anything on earth but the river, and his pride in his occupation surpasses the pride of kings.

We had a fine company of these river inspectors along this trip. There were eight or ten, and there was abundance of room for them in our great pilot-house. Two or three of them wore polished silk hats, elaborate shirt-fronts, diamond breastpins, kid gloves, and patent-leather boots. They were choice in their English, and bore themselves with a dignity proper to men of solid means and prodigious reputation as pilots. The others were more or less loosely clad, and wore upon their heads tall felt cones that were suggestive of the days of the Commonwealth.

I was a cipher in this august company, and felt subdued, not to say torpid. I was not even of sufficient consequence to assist at the wheel when it was necessary to put the tiller hard down in a hurry; the guest that stood nearest did that when occasion required—and this was pretty much all the time, because of the crookedness of the channel and the scant water. I stood in a corner; and the talk I listened to took the hope all out of me. One visitor said to another:

"Jim, how did you run Plum Point, coming up?"

"It was in the night, there, and I ran it the way one of the boys on the *Diana* told me; started out about fifty yards above the wood-pile on the false point, and held on the cabin under Plum Point till I raised the reef—quarter less twain—then straightened up for the middle bar till I got well abreast the old one-limbed cottonwood in the bend, then got my stern on the cottonwood, and head on the low place above the point, and came through a-booming—nine and a half."

"Pretty square crossing, an't it?"

"Yes, but the upper bar's working down fast."

Another pilot spoke up and said:

"I had better water than that, and ran it lower down; started out from the false point—mark twain—raised the second reef abreast the big snag in the bend, and had quarter less twain."

One of the gorgeous ones remarked:

"I don't want to find fault with your leadsmen, but that's a good deal of water for Plum Point, it seems to me."

There was an approving nod all around as this quiet snub dropped on the boaster and "settled" him. And so they went on talk-talk-talking. Meantime, the thing that was running in my mind was, "Now, if my ears hear aright, I have not only to get the names of all the towns and islands and bends, and so on, by heart, but I must even get up a warm personal acquaintanceship with every old snag and one-limbed cottonwood and obscure wood-pile that ornaments the banks of this river for twelve hundred miles; and more than that, I must actually know where these things are in the dark, unless these guests are gifted with eyes that can pierce through two miles of solid blackness. I wish the piloting business was in Jericho and I had never thought of it."

At dusk Mr. Bixby tapped the big bell three times (the signal to land), and the captain emerged from his drawing-room in the forward of the "texas," and looked up inquiringly. Mr. Bixby said:

"We will lay up here all night, captain."

"Very well, sir."

That was all. The boat came to shore and was tied up for the night. It seemed to me a fine thing that the pilot could do as he pleased, without asking so grand a captain's permission. I took my supper and went immediately to bed, discouraged by my day's observations and experiences. My late voyage's note-booking was but a confusion of meaningless names. It had tangled me all up in a knot every time I had looked at it in the daytime. I now hoped for respite in sleep; but no, it reveled all through my head till sunrise again, a frantic and tireless nightmare.

Next morning I felt pretty rusty and low-spirited. We went booming along, taking a good many chances, for we were anxious to "get out of the river" (as getting out to Cairo was called) before night should overtake us. But Mr. Bixby's partner, the other pilot, presently grounded the boat, and we lost so much time getting her off that it was plain the darkness would overtake us a good long way above the mouth. This was a great misfortune, especially to certain of our visiting pilots, whose boats would have to wait for their return, no matter how long that might be. It sobered the pilot-house talk a good deal. Coming up-stream, pilots did not mind low water or any kind of darkness; nothing stopped them but fog. But down-stream work was different; a boat was too nearly helpless, with a stiff current pushing behind her; so it was not customary to run down-stream at night in low water.

There seemed to be one small hope, however: if we could get through the intricate and dangerous Hat Island crossing before night, we could venture the rest, for we would have plainer sailing and better water. But it would be insanity to attempt Hat Island at night. So there was a deal of looking at watches all the rest of the day, and a constant ciphering upon the speed we were making; Hat Island was the eternal subject, sometimes hope was high and sometimes we were delayed in a bad crossing, and down it went again. For hours all hands lay under the burden of this suppressed excitement; it was even communicated to me, and I got to feeling so solicitous about Hat Island, and under such an awful pressure of responsibility, that I wished I might have five minutes on shore to draw a good, full, relieving breath, and start over again. We were standing no regular watches. Each of our pilots ran such portions of the river as he had run when coming up-stream, because of his greater familiarity with it; but both remained in the pilot-house constantly.

An hour before sunset Mr. Bixby took the wheel, and Mr. W. stepped aside. For the next thirty minutes every man held his watch in his hand and was restless, silent, and uneasy. At last somebody said, with a doomful sigh:

"Well, yonder's Hat Island—and we can't make it."

All the watches closed with a snap, everybody sighed and muttered something about its being "too bad, too bad—ah, if we could *only* have got here half an hour sooner!" and the place was thick with the atmosphere of disappointment. Some started to go out, but loitered, hearing no bell-tap to land. The sun dipped behind the horizon, the boat went on. Inquiring looks passed from one guest to another; and one who had his hand on the door-knob and had turned it, waited, then presently took away his hand and let the knob turn back again. We bore steadily down the bend. More looks were exchanged, and nods of surprised admiration—but no words. Insensibly the men drew together behind Mr. Bixby, as the sky darkened and one or two dim stars came out. The dead silence and sense of waiting became oppressive. Mr. Bixby pulled the cord, and two deep, mellow notes from the big bell floated off on the night. Then a pause, and one more note was struck. The watchman's voice followed, from the hurricane-deck:

"Labboard lead, there! Stabboard lead!"

The cries of the leadsmen began to rise out of the distance, and were gruffly repeated by the word-passers on the hurricane-deck.

"M-a-r-k three! M-a-r-k three! Quarter-less-three! Half twain! Quarter twain! M-a-r-k twain! Quarter-less—"

Mr. Bixby pulled two bell-ropes, and was answered by faint jinglings far below in the engine-room, and our speed slackened. The steam began to whistle through the gauge-cocks. The cries of the leadsmen went on—and it is a weird sound, always, in the night. Every pilot in the lot was watching now, with fixed eyes, and talking under his breath. Nobody was calm and easy but Mr. Bixby. He would put his wheel down and stand on a spoke, and as the steamer swung into her (to me) utterly invisible marks—for we seemed to be in the midst of a wide and gloomy sea—he would meet and fasten her there. Out of the murmur of half-audible talk, one caught a coherent sentence now and then—such as:

"There; she's over the first reef all right!"

After a pause, another subdued voice:

"Her stern's coming down just *exactly* right, by *George!*"

"Now she's in the marks; over she goes!"

Somebody else muttered:

"Oh, it was done beautiful—*beautiful!*"

Now the engines were stopped altogether, and we drifted with the current. Not that I could see the boat drift, for I could not, the stars being all gone by this time. This drifting was the dismalest work; it held one's heart still. Presently I discovered a blacker gloom than that which surrounded us. It was the head of the island. We were closing right down upon it. We entered its deeper shadow, and so imminent seemed the peril that I was likely to suffocate; and I had the strongest impulse to do something, anything, to save the vessel. But still Mr. Bixby stood by his wheel, silent, intent as a cat, and all the pilots stood shoulder to shoulder at his back.

"She'll not make it!" somebody whispered.

The water grew shoaler and shoaler, by the leadsman's cries, till it was down to:

"Eight-and-a-half! E-i-g-h-t feet! E-i-g-h-t feet! Seven-and—"

Mr. Bixby said warningly through his speaking-tube to the engineer:

"Stand by, now!"

"Ay, ay, sir!"

"Seven-and-a-half! Seven feet! *Six*-and—"

We touched bottom! Instantly Mr. Bixby set a lot of bells ringing, shouted through the tube, "*Now*, let her have it—every ounce you've got!" then to his partner, "Put her hard down! snatch her! snatch her!" The boat rapsed and ground her way through the sand, hung upon the apex of disaster a single tremendous instant, and then over she went! And such a shout as went up at Mr. Bixby's back never loosened the roof of a pilot-house before!

There was no more trouble after that. Mr. Bixby was a hero that night; and it was some little time, too, before his exploit ceased to be talked about by river-men.

Fully to realize the marvelous precision required in laying the great steamer in her marks in that murky waste of water, one should know that not only must she pick her intricate way through snags and blind reefs, and then shave the head of the island so closely as to brush the overhanging foilage with her stern, but at one place she must pass almost within arm's reach of a sunken and invisible wreck that would snatch the hull timbers from under her if she should strike it, and destroy a quarter of a million dollars' worth of steamboat and cargo in five minutes, and maybe a hundred and fifty human lives into the bargain.

The last remark I heard that night was a compliment to Mr. Bixby, uttered in soliloquy and with unction by one of our guests. He said:

"By the Shadow of Death, but he's a lightning pilot!"

Perplexing Lessons

At the end of what seemed a tedious while, I had managed to pack my head full of islands, towns, bars, "points," and bends; and a curiously inanimate mass of lumber it was, too. However, inasmuch as I could shut my eyes and reel off a good long string of these names without leaving out more than ten miles of river in every fifty, I began to feel that I could take a boat down to New Orleans if I could make her skip those little gaps. But of course my complacency could hardly get start enough to lift my nose a trifle into the air, before Mr. Bixby would think of something to fetch it down again. One day he turned on me suddenly with this settler:

"What is the shape of Walnut Bend?"

He might as well have asked me my grandmother's opinion of protoplasm. I reflected respectfully, and then said I didn't know it had any particular shape. My gun-powdery chief went off with a bang, of course, and then went on loading and firing until he was out of adjectives.

I had learned long ago that he only carried just so many rounds of ammunition, and was sure to subside into a very placable and even remorseful old smoothbore as soon as they were all gone. That word "old" is merely affectionate; he was not more than thirty-four. I waited. By and by he said:

"My boy, you've got to know the *shape* of the river perfectly. It is all there is left to steer by on a very dark night. Everything else is blotted out and gone. But mind you, it hasn't the same shape in the night that it has in the daytime."

"How on earth am I ever going to learn it, then?"

"How do you follow a hall at home in the dark? Because you know the shape of it. You can't see it."

"Do you mean to say that I've got to know all the million trifling variations of shape in the banks of this interminable river as well as I know the shape of the front hall at home?"

"On my honor, you've got to know them *better* than any man ever did know the shapes of the halls in his own house."

"I wish I was dead!"

"Now I don't want to discourage you, but—"

"Well, pile it on me; I might as well have it now as another time."

"You see, this has got to be learned; there isn't any getting around it. A clear starlight night throws such heavy shadows that, if you didn't know the shape of a shore perfectly, you would claw away from every bunch of timber, because you would take the black shadow of it for a solid cape; and you see you would be getting scared to death every fifteen minutes by the watch. You would be fifty yards from shore all the time when you ought to be within fifty feet of it. You can't see a snag in one of those shadows, but you know exactly where it is, and the shape of the river tells you when you are coming to it. Then there's your pitch-dark night; the river is a very different shape on a pitch-dark night from what it is on a star-light night. All shores seem to be straight lines, then, and mighty dim ones, too; and you'd *run* them for straight lines, only you know better. You boldly drive your boat right into what seems to be a solid, straight wall (you knowing very well that in reality there is a curve there), and that wall falls back and makes way for you. Then there's your gray mist. You take a night when there's one of these grisly, drizzly, gray mists, and then there isn't *any* particular shape to a shore. A gray mist would tangle the head of the oldest man that ever lived. Well, then, different kinds of *moonlight* change the shape of the river in different ways. You see—"

"Oh, don't say any more, please! Have I got to learn the shape of the river according to all these five hundred thousand different ways? If I tried to carry all that cargo in my head it would make me stoop-shouldered."

"*No!* you only learn *the* shape of the river; and you learn it with such absolute certainty that you can always steer by the shape that's *in your head,* and never mind the one that's before your eyes."

"Very well, I'll try it; but, after I have learned it, can I depend on it? Will it keep the same form and not go fooling around?"

Before Mr. Bixby could answer, Mr. W. came in to take the watch, and he said:

"Bixby, you'll have to look out for President's Island, and all that country clear away up above the Old Hen and Chickens. The banks are caving and the shape of the shores changing like everything. Why, you wouldn't know the point above 40. You can go up inside the old sycamore snag, now."[1]

So that question was answered. Here were leagues of shore changing shape. My spirits were down in the mud again. Two things seemed pretty apparent to me. One was, that in order to be a pilot a man had got to learn more than any one man ought to be allowed to know; and the other was, that he must learn it all over again in a different way every twenty-four hours.

That night we had the watch until twelve. Now it was an ancient river custom for the two pilots to chat a bit when the watch changed. While the relieving pilot put on his gloves and lit his cigar, his partner, the retiring pilot, would say something like this:

"I judge the upper bar is making down a little at Hale's Point; had quarter twain with the lower lead and mark twain[2] with the other."

"Yes, I thought it was making down a little, last trip. Meet any boats?"

"Met one abreast the head of 21, but she was away over hugging the bar, and I couldn't make her out entirely. I took her for the *Sunny South*—hadn't any skylights forward of the chimneys."

And so on. And as the relieving pilot took the wheel his partner[3] would mention that we were in such-and-such a bend, and say we were abreast of such-and-such a man's woodyard or plantation. This was courtesy; I supposed it was *necessity*. But Mr. W. came on watch full twelve minutes late on this particular night—a tremendous breach of etiquette; in fact, it is the unpardonable sin among pilots. So Mr. Bixby gave him no greeting whatever, but simply surrendered the wheel and marched out of the pilot-house without a word. I was appalled; it was a villainous night for blackness, we were in a particularly wide and blind part of the river, where there was no shape or substance to anything, and it seemed incredible that Mr. Bixby should have left that poor fellow to kill the boat, trying to find out where he was. But I resolved that I would stand by him anyway. He should find that he was not wholly friendless. So I stood around, and waited to be asked where we were. But Mr. W. plunged on serenely through the solid firmament of

---

[1] It may not be necessary, but still it can do no harm to explain that "inside" means between the snag and the shore.—M. T.

[2] Two fathoms. Quarter twain is $2\frac{1}{4}$ fathoms, $13\frac{1}{2}$ feet. Mark three is three fathoms.

[3] "Partner" is technical for "the other pilot."

black cats that stood for an atmosphere, and never opened his mouth.
"Here is a proud devil!" thought I; "here is a limb of Satan that would
rather send us all to destruction than put himself under obligations to
me, because I am not yet one of the salt of the earth and privileged to
snub captains and lord it over everything dead and alive in a steamboat." I presently climbed up on the bench; I did not think it was safe
to go to sleep while this lunatic was on watch.

However, I must have gone to sleep in the course of time, because
the next thing I was aware of was the fact that day was breaking, Mr.
W. gone, and Mr. Bixby at the wheel again. So it was four o'clock and
all well—but me; I felt like a skinful of dry bones, and all of them trying
to ache at once.

Mr. Bixby asked me what I had stayed up there for. I confessed
that it was to do Mr. W. a benevolence—tell him where he was. It took
five minutes for the entire preposterousness of the thing to filter into
Mr. Bixby's system, and then I judge it filled him nearly up to the chin;
because he paid me a compliment—and not much of a one either. He
said:

"Well, taking you by and large, you do seem to be more different
kinds of an ass than any creature I ever saw before. What did you
suppose he wanted to know for?"

I said I thought it might be a convenience to him.

"Convenience! D——nation! Didn't I tell you that a man's got to
know the river in the night the same as he'd know his own front hall?"

"Well, I can follow the front hall in the dark if I know it *is* the front
hall; but suppose you set me down in the middle of it in the dark and
not tell me which hall it is; how am *I* to know?"

"Well, you've *got* to, on the river!"

"All right. Then I'm glad I never said anything to Mr. W."

"I should say so! Why, he'd have slammed you through the
window and utterly ruined a hundred dollars' worth of window-sash
and stuff."

I was glad this damage had been saved, for it would have made me
unpopular with the owners. They always hated anybody who had the
name of being careless and injuring things.

I went to work now to learn the shape of the river; and of all the
eluding and ungraspable objects that ever I tried to get mind or hands
on, that was the chief. I would fasten my eyes upon a sharp, wooded
point that projected far into the river some miles ahead of me, and go
to laboriously photographing its shape upon my brain; and just as I was
beginning to succeed to my satisfaction, we would draw up toward it
and the exasperating thing would begin to melt away and fold back into
the bank! If there had been a conspicuous dead tree standing upon the
very point of the cape, I would find that tree inconspicuously merged

into the general forest, and occupying the middle of a straight shore, when I got abreast of it! No prominent hill would stick to its shape long enough for me to make up my mind what its form really was, but it was as dissolving and changeful as if it had been a mountain of butter in the hottest corner of the tropics. Nothing ever had the same shape when I was coming down-stream that it had borne when I went up. I mentioned these little difficulties to Mr. Bixby. He said:

"That's the very main virtue of the thing. If the shapes didn't change every three seconds they wouldn't be of any use. Take this place where we are now, for instance. As long as that hill over yonder is only one hill, I can boom right along the way I'm going; but the moment it splits at the top and forms a V, I know I've got to scratch to starboard in a hurry, or I'll bang this boat's brains out against a rock; and then the moment one of the prongs of the V swings behind the other, I've got to waltz to larboard again, or I'll have a misunderstanding with a snag that would snatch the keelson out of this steamboat as neatly as if it were a sliver in your hand. If that hill didn't change its shape on bad nights there would be an awful steamboat graveyard around here inside of a year."

It was plain that I had got to learn the shape of the river in all the different ways that could be thought of—upside down, wrong end first, inside out, fore-and-aft, and "thort-ships"—and then know what to do on gray nights when it hadn't any shape at all. So I set about it. In the course of time I began to get the best of this knotty lesson, and my self-complacency moved to the front once more. Mr. Bixby was all fixed, and ready to start it to the rear again. He opened on me after this fashion:

"How much water did we have in the middle crossing at Hole-in-the-Wall, trip before last?"

I considered this an outrage. I said:

"Every trip, down and up, the leadsmen are singing through that tangled place for three-quarters of an hour on a stretch. How do you reckon I can remember such a mess as that?"

"My boy, you've got to remember it. You've got to remember the exact spot and the exact marks the boat lay in when we had the shoalest water, in every one of the five hundred shoal places between St. Louis and New Orleans; and you mustn't get the shoal soundings and marks of one trip mixed up with the shoal soundings and marks of another, either, for they're not often twice alike. You must keep them separate."

When I came to myself again, I said:

"When I get so that I can do that, I'll be able to raise the dead, and then I won't have to pilot a steamboat to make a living. I want to retire from this business. I want a slush-bucket and a brush; I'm only fit for a roustabout. I haven't got brains enough to be a pilot; and if I had I wouldn't have strength enough to carry them around, unless I went on crutches."

"Now drop that! When I say I'll learn[4] a man the river, I mean it. And you can depend on it, I'll learn him or kill him."

A pilot must have a memory; but there are two higher qualities which he must also have. He must have good and quick judgment and decision, and a cool, calm courage that no peril can shake. Give a man the merest trifle of pluck to start with, and by the time he has become a pilot he cannot be unmanned by any danger a steamboat can get into; but one cannot quite say the same for judgment. Judgment is a matter of brains, and a man must *start* with a good stock of that article or he will never succeed as a pilot.

The growth of courage in the pilot-house is steady all the time, but it does not reach a high and satisfactory condition until some time after the young pilot has been "standing his own watch" alone and under the staggering weight of all the responsibilities connected with the position. When the apprentice has become pretty thoroughly acquainted with the river, he goes clattering along so fearlessly with his steamboat, night or day, that he presently begins to imagine that it is *his* courage that animates him; but the first time the pilot steps out and leaves him to his own devices he finds out it was the other man's. He discovers that the article has been left out of his own cargo altogether. The whole river is bristling with exigencies in a moment; he is not prepared for them; he does not know how to meet them; all his knowledge forsakes him; and within fifteen minutes he is as white as a sheet and scared almost to death. Therefore pilots wisely train these cubs by various strategic tricks to look danger in the face a little more calmly. A favorite way of theirs is to play a friendly swindle upon the candidate.

Mr. Bixby served me in this fashion once, and for years afterward I used to blush, even in my sleep, when I thought of it. I had become a good steersman; so good, indeed, that I had all the work to do on our watch, night and day. Mr. Bixby seldom made a suggestion to me; all he ever did was to take the wheel on particularly bad nights or in particularly bad crossings, land the boat when she needed to be landed, play gentleman of leisure nine-tenths of the watch, and collect the wages. The lower river was about bank-full, and if anybody had questioned my ability to run any crossing between Cairo and New Orleans without help or instruction, I should have felt irreparably hurt. The idea of being afraid of any crossing in the lot, in the *daytime,* was a

---

4"Teach" is not in the river vocabulary.

thing too preposterous for contemplation. Well, one matchless summer's day I was bowling down the bend above Island 66, brimful of self-conceit and carrying my nose as high as a giraffe's, when Mr. Bixby said:

"I am going below awhile. I suppose you know the next crossing?"

This was almost an affront. It was about the plainest and simplest crossing in the whole river. One couldn't come to any harm, whether he ran it right or not; and as for depth, there never had been any bottom there. I knew all this, perfectly well.

"Know how to *run* it? Why, I can run it with my eyes shut."

"How much water is there in it?"

"Well, that is an odd question. I couldn't get bottom there with a church steeple."

"You think so, do you?"

The very tone of the question shook my confidence. That was what Mr. Bixby was expecting. He left, without saying anything more. I began to imagine all sorts of things. Mr. Bixby, unknown to me, of course, sent somebody down to the forecastle with some mysterious instructions to the leadsmen, another messenger was sent to whisper among the officers, and then Mr. Bixby went into hiding behind a smoke-stack where he could observe results. Presently the captain stepped out on the hurricane-deck; next the chief mate appeared; then a clerk. Every moment or two a straggler was added to my audience; and before I got to the head of the island I had fifteen or twenty people assembled down there under my nose. I began to wonder what the trouble was. As I started across, the captain glanced aloft at me and said, with a sham uneasiness in his voice:

"Where is Mr. Bixby?"

"Gone below, sir."

But that did the business for me. My imagination began to construct dangers out of nothing, and they multiplied faster than I could keep the run of them. All at once I imagined I saw shoal water ahead! The wave of coward agony that surged through me then came near dislocating every joint in me. All my confidence in that crossing vanished. I seized the bell-rope; dropped it, ashamed; seized it again; dropped it once more; clutched it tremblingly once again, and pulled it so feebly that I could hardly hear the stroke myself. Captain and mate sang out instantly, and both together:

"Starboard lead there! and quick about it!"

This was another shock. I began to climb the wheel like a squirrel; but I would hardly get the boat started to port before I would see new dangers on that side, and away I would spin to the other; only to find perils accumulating to starboard, and be crazy to get to port again. Then came the leadsman's sepulchral cry:

"D-e-e-p four!"

Deep four in a bottomless crossing! The terror of it took my breath away.

"M-a-r-k three! M-a-r-k three! Quarter-less-three! Half twain!"

This was frightful! I seized the bell-ropes and stopped the engines.

"Quarter twain! Quarter twain! Mark twain!"

I was helpless. I did not know what in the world to do. I was quaking from head to foot, and I could have hung my hat on my eyes, they stuck out so far.

"Quarter-*less*-twain! Nine-and-a-*half*!"

We were *drawing* nine! My hands were in a nerveless flutter. I could not ring a bell intelligibly with them. I flew to the speaking-tube and shouted to the engineer:

"Oh, Ben, if you love me, *back* her! Quick, Ben! Oh, back the immortal *soul* out of her!"

I heard the door close gently. I looked around, and there stood Mr. Bixby, smiling a bland, sweet smile. Then the audience on the hurricane-deck sent up a thundergust of humiliating laughter. I saw it all, now, and I felt meaner than the meanest man in human history. I laid in the lead, set the boat in her marks, came ahead on the engines, and said:

"It was a fine trick to play on an orphan, *wasn't* it? I suppose I'll never hear the last of how I was ass enough to heave the lead at the head of 66."

"Well, no, you won't, maybe. In fact I hope you won't; for I want you to learn something by that experience. Didn't you *know* there was no bottom in that crossing?"

"Yes, sir, I did."

"Very well, then. You shouldn't have allowed me or anybody else to shake your confidence in that knowledge. Try to remember that. And another thing: when you get into a dangerous place, don't turn coward. That isn't going to help matters any."

It was a good enough lesson, but pretty hardly learned. Yet about the hardest part of it was that for months I so often had to hear a phrase which I had conceived a particular distaste for. It was, "Oh, Ben, if you love me, back her!"

LINCOLN STEFFENS

Lincoln Steffens, perhaps the most famous "muckraker" of the Progressive Era (from Teddy Roosevelt's presidency to the First World War), was born in San Francisco in 1866. He was expelled from military school for "drunkenness," but graduated from the University of California in 1889. He became the police reporter and later city editor of the *New York Evening Post*. With Upton Sinclair and other journalists, he aroused the conscience of a generation and encouraged basic reforms in American political and social life. The reforming instinct aroused by the muckrakers was smothered by World War I and later by the wet blanket of Republican "normalcy," but reemerged under Franklin Roosevelt in the 1930's. Steffens' most famous exposé is *The Shame of the Cities* (1904). He died in 1936. The following selection is from his *Autobiography,* published in 1931.

A Miserable, Merry Christmas

What interested me in our new neighborhood was not the school, nor the room I was to have in the house all to myself, but the stable which was built back of the house. My father let me direct the making of a stall, a little smaller than the other stalls, for my pony, and I prayed and hoped and my sister Lou believed that that meant that I would get the pony, perhaps for Christmas. I pointed out to her that there were three other stalls and no horses at all. This I said in order that she should answer it. She could not. My father, sounded, said that some day we might have horses and a cow; meanwhile a stable added to the value of a house. "Some day" is a pain to a boy who lives in and knows only "now." My good little sisters, to comfort me, remarked that Christmas was coming, but Christmas was always coming and grown-ups were always talking about it, asking you what you wanted and then giving you what they wanted you to have. Though everybody knew what I wanted, I told them all again. My mother knew that I told God, too, every night. I wanted a pony, and to make sure that they understood, I declared that I wanted nothing else.

"Nothing but a pony?" my father asked.

"Nothing," I said.

"Not even a pair of high boots?"

That was hard. I did want boots, but I stuck to the pony. "No, not even boots."

"Nor candy? There ought to be something to fill your stocking with, and Santa Claus can't put a pony into a stocking."

That was true, and he couldn't lead a pony down the chimney either. But no. "All I want is a pony," I said. "If I can't have a pony, give me nothing, nothing."

Now I had been looking myself for the pony I wanted, going to sales stables, inquiring of horsemen, and I had seen several that would do. My father let me "try" them. I tried so many ponies that I was learning fast to sit a horse. I chose several, but my father always found some fault with them. I was in despair. When Christmas was at hand I had given up all hope of a pony, and on Christmas Eve I hung up my stocking along with my sisters', of whom, by the way, I now had three. I haven't mentioned them or their coming because, you understand, they were girls, and girls, young girls, counted for nothing in my manly life. They did not mind me either; they were so happy that Christmas Eve that I caught some of their merriment. I speculated on what I'd get; I hung up the biggest stocking I had, and we all went reluctantly to bed to wait till morning. Not to sleep; not right away. We were told that we must not only sleep promptly, we must not wake up till seven-thirty the next morning—or if we did, we must not go the fireplace for our Christmas. Impossible.

We did sleep that night, but we woke up at six A.M. We lay in our beds and debated through the open doors whether to obey till, say, half-past six. Then we bolted. I don't know who started it, but there was a rush. We all disobeyed; we raced to disobey and get first to the fireplace in the front room downstairs. And there they were, the gifts, all sorts of wonderful things, mixed-up piles of presents; only, as I disentangled the mess, I saw that my stocking was empty; it hung limp; not a thing in it; and under and around it—nothing. My sisters had knelt down, each by her pile of gifts; they were squealing with delight, till they looked up and saw me standing there in my nightgown with nothing. They left their piles to come to me and look with me at my empty place. Nothing. They felt my stocking: nothing.

I don't remember whether I cried at that moment, but my sisters did. They ran with me back to my bed, and there we all cried till I became indignant. That helped some. I got up, dressed, and driving my sisters away, I went alone out into the yard, down to the stable, and there, all by myself, I wept. My mother came out to me by and by; she found me in my pony stall, sobbing on the floor, and she tried to comfort me. But I heard my father outside; he had come part way with her, and she was having some sort of angry quarrel with him. She tried to comfort me; besought me to come to breakfast. I could not; I wanted no comfort and no breakfast. She left me and went on into the house with sharp words for my father.

I don't know what kind of a breakfast the family had. My sisters said it was "awful." They were ashamed to enjoy their own toys. They came to me, and I was rude. I ran away from them. I went around to the front of the house, sat down on the steps, and, the crying over, I ached. I was wronged, I was hurt—I can feel now what I felt then, and I am sure that if one could see the wounds upon our hearts, there would be found still upon mine a scar from that terrible Christmas morning. And my father, the practical joker, he must have been hurt, too, a little. I saw him looking out of the window. He was watching me or something for an hour or two, drawing back the curtain never so little lest I catch him, but I saw his face, and I think I can see now the anxiety upon it, the worried impatience.

After—I don't know how long—surely an hour or two—I was brought to the climax of my agony by the sight of a man riding a pony down the street, a pony and a brand-new saddle; the most beautiful saddle I ever saw, and it was a boy's saddle; the man's feet were not in the stirrups; his legs were too long. The outfit was perfect; it was the realization of all my dreams, the answer to all my prayers. A fine new bridle, with a light curb bit. And the pony! As he drew near, I saw that the pony was really a small horse, what we called an Indian pony, a bay, with black mane and tail, and one white foot and a white star on his forehead. For such a horse as that I would have given, I could have forgiven, anything.

But the man, a disheveled fellow, with a blackened eye and a fresh-cut face, came along, reading the numbers on the houses, and, as my hopes—my impossible hopes—rose, he looked at our door and passed by, he and the pony, and the saddle and the bridle. Too much. I fell upon the steps, and having wept before, I broke now into such a flood of tears that I was a floating wreck when I heard a voice.

"Say, kid," it said, "do you know a boy named Lennie Steffens?"

I looked up. It was the man on the pony, back again, at our horse block.

"Yes," I spluttered through my tears. "That's me."

"Well," he said, "then this is your horse. I've been looking all over for you and your house. Why don't you put your number where it can be seen?"

"Get down," I said, running out to him.

He went on saying something about "ought to have got here at seven o'clock; told me to bring the nag here and tie him to your post and leave him for you. But, hell, I got into a drunk—and a fight—and a hospital, and—"

"Get down," I said.

He got down, and he boosted me up to the saddle. He offered to fit the stirrups to me, but I didn't want him to. I wanted to ride.

"What's the matter with you?" he said, angrily. "What you crying for? Don't you like the horse? He's a dandy, this horse. I know him of old. He's fine at cattle; he'll drive 'em alone."

I hardly heard, I could scarcely wait, but he persisted. He adjusted the stirrups, and then, finally, off I rode, slowly, at a walk, so happy, so thrilled, that I did not know what I was doing. I did not look back at the house or the man, I rode off up the street, taking note of everything—of the reins, of the pony's long mane, of the carved leather saddle. I had never seen anything so beautiful. And mine! I was going to ride up past Miss Kay's house. But I noticed on the horn of the saddle some stains like rain-drops, so I turned and trotted home, not to the house but to the stable. There was the family, father, mother, sisters, all working for me, all happy. They had been putting in place the tools of my new business: blankets, currycomb, brush, pitchfork—everything, and there was hay in the loft.

"What did you come back so soon for?" somebody asked. "Why didn't you go on riding?"

I pointed to the stains. "I wasn't going to get my new saddle rained on," I said. And my father laughed. "It isn't raining," he said. "Those are not rain-drops."

"They are tears," my mother gasped, and she gave my father a look which sent him off to the house. Worse still, my mother offered to wipe away the tears still running out of my eyes. I gave her such a look as she had given him, and she went off after my father, drying her own tears. My sisters remained and we all unsaddled the pony, put on his halter, led him to his stall, tied and fed him. It began really to rain; so all the rest of that memorable day we curried and combed that pony. The girls plaited his mane, forelock, and tail, while I pitchforked hay to him and curried and brushed, curried and brushed. For a change we brought him out to drink; we led him up and down, blanketed like a race-horse; we took turns at that. But the best, the most inexhaustible fun, was to clean him. When we went reluctantly to our midday Christmas dinner, we all smelt of horse, and my sisters had to wash their faces and hands. I was asked to, but I wouldn't, till my mother bade me look in the mirror. Then I washed up—quick. My face was caked with the muddy lines of tears that had coursed over my cheeks to my mouth. Having washed away that shame, I ate my dinner, and as I ate I grew hungrier and hungrier. It was my first meal that day, and as I filled up on the turkey and the stuffing, the cranberries and the pies, the fruit and the nuts—as I swelled, I could laugh. My mother said I still choked and sobbed now and then, but I laughed, too; I saw and enjoyed my sisters' presents till—I had to go out and attend to my pony, who was there, really and truly there, the promise, the beginning, of a happy double life. And—I went and looked to make sure—there was the saddle, too, and the bridle.

But that Christmas, which my father had planned so carefully, was it the best or the worst I ever knew? He often asked me that; I never could answer as a boy. I think now that it was both. It covered the whole distance from broken-hearted misery to bursting happiness—too fast. A grown-up could hardly have stood it.

SIX

KENNETH HINKLEY

Kenneth Hinkley was born in 1950 in Rumford, Maine. He is majoring in Agriculture and Life Sciences at the University of Maine in Orono. His essay first appeared in *Growing Up in Maine*, a collection of essays by Bowdoin College Upward Bound students published in 1968.

To Get Away

As I passed through that process of suddenly realizing that the world is real, although dark, gray, and blurry, called awakening, I heard below me in the kitchen-dining room the muffled clang-clanging of pans and dishes made daily by my father as he prepared his usual morning meal of fried eggs and toast chased down by a cup of hot coffee into which he put a heaping teaspoon of sugar.

I rolled over onto my back, tangling myself into the folds and wrinkles of the blanket and light quilt that served as bed-covers, to persuade myself that I was really awake and not still dreaming a gloomy dream where everything is colored in one shade of gray. I lay there staring at what I could see of the unfinished wooden ceiling above me and thought about the day to come and the things I had to do to make it complete. I thought with regret of the chores I had to do.

Since my mind could not focus itself on anything I enjoyed thinking about, except maybe the face of some girl I knew, I decided to rise and greet the day in my usual manner. I untangled myself from the jumble of quilt and blanket which seemed to be all edges and no corners. I found one and threw the covers off and swung my feet to the floor. There being an old carpet on the floor with about three inches of dust accumulated over a period of about six to eight months, I didn't mind standing on the floor, but the sub-zero weather chilled my bones through and through before I could even reach and get my cold-stiffened clothes on to hold in my body heat. It didn't usually take me more than a minute to get dressed in winter. I had a great urge to get near the stove.

At some point in this process, Dad finished his breakfast and put on his heavy outdoor wear and left for work in a neighboring town. He worked for a shoe company which makes high-heeled shoes for women. On some mornings the weather would be so cold the car wouldn't start and Dad would come back into the house cursing it and the weather.

"How many coals are there in that stove? That son-of-a-whore won't start."

He used the coals to put under the oil pan and warm the oil to make it flow more easily. But this didn't always work either and he would cuss and fume all the while he was trying to find out what the trouble was.

By the time I crossed the attic, descended the stairs, and crossed the cold linoleum of the floor of the room where we piled unused articles, I would be cold enough to make icicles if someone poured water over me.

Just before my father left (on mornings when there was no trouble), my mother would rise, throw on a housecoat, and busy herself with tidying up the kitchen—unless it was one of the many days that she didn't feel well. My mother has blood cancer, therefore she doesn't feel well a lot of the time. On such days, she would sit at the table and pour out her troubles upon me as I warmed myself beside the woodstove. I hardly ever listened, though, because I knew there wasn't anything I could do to help her.

The stove was an old cast-iron giant that seemed to spread itself into people's way when they tried to pass by. The oven door was left open when the oven wasn't in use and made a gaping red hole, like a giant yawning. One could see through the holes in the firebox wall into the fire. The heat it threw out, however, was hardly enough to heat the kitchen, to say nothing about the other four rooms downstairs or the attic. Once in a while we'd build a fire in the heater which squatted on the bricks of the false fireplace. The heat from this was a little more intense than that of the woodstove, but it didn't go any further. There were too many draft holes. Near any window or door one felt the wind driving through. Snow even blew onto the floor and, if it hadn't been swept up, would have set there for a week or more before it would melt.

We plugged the big draft holes with old rags or paper to keep the cold air out. Even though we did this, the heat from the stove or stoves could not warm the rooms. Many times we had to close the doors to the bedrooms on the ground floor to conserve heat for the kitchen and living room.

When I had thawed out by the woodstove, I would remove a bowl and a box of cereal from the cupboard and a spoon from the drawer and set them on the table at the spot nearest the stove. I would then fetch a pitcher of diluted canned milk from the cellarway (which was our only means of refrigeration, kept cool by the draft from the cellar below) and the sugar and sit down to eat.

I went through all this more by my sense of touch than sight, since the sun had not yet risen and the sky was only just beginning to lighten.

The house was illuminated by two or three kerosene-wick lamps which were placed in any place which seemed convenient. The glass chimney on top of a kerosene lamp is the most delicate part. It is easily broken in moving a lamp or, if one isn't careful in washing the chimney, a quick change of temperature will shatter it.

Sometimes I would sit in that thin light and read the cereal box, just to waste time so my breakfast would last longer. The longer I stayed near the woodstove the longer it would be before I went out into the cold. Some of the boxes would have information from different parts of the world on them, while others might have things which would only appeal to the mind of a youngster. There were at least two things which could be found on every box, the list of ingredients and the table of minimum daily requirements. I read them just to see if I could get my tongue around some of the big words they used. I never felt any more ready to face my chores after having all those important things my body needed to get through the day.

Pouring frozen and diluted canned milk on dry cereal is a mess. I would have to crack the ice with my spoon or, if it was too thick, I would set the pitcher on the back of the stove to soften the ice. Either way I would not wait for the ice to become completely dissolved and re-mixed with the milk, so I would have lumps of ice in my cereal where other people might have fruit. Finally, I would have to face my chores.

The chores were divided among the three of us boys who were old enough and strong enough to handle them. We had two other brothers, but one was excused for being too young and the other for being an almost complete cripple. The part of the chores that fell to me was one I disliked very much, no matter what it was. We usually rotated them among us, say, every week or so. On one week I would have to go out into the cold and pull logs or old timbers from a collapsed barn, throw them across a make-shift sawhorse or hard snowdrift (frozen solid by melting and refreezing) and cut them into sections about a foot long and carry them into the kitchen to fill the woodbox. I would always stop by the stove and warm myself between armloads.

Another week I would have to work inside the shed which we referred to as our "barn." We usually had one or two animals—a cow, or calf, a pony, or a couple of goats. I would have to clean the frozen manure from under the animal's feet, throw them some fresh hay, and give them some grain if there was any (which was very seldom). Our few chickens usually lived off our table scraps, which were very scanty. Many of the chickens did not live out the winter.

On the third week I would have to fill two ten-quart buckets with water from the well behind our house. This wasn't too bad a job except once in a while after you'd filled the evening's quota of water and settled as much as possible for the evening, someone would yell, "Waterboy! We need some water!"

Still, it was easy. You took two ten-quart buckets out into the back room where the well was, set them down, cranked down the bucket hanging in the well, let it fill, cranked it back up, poured the water into the pails, then carried them back into the kitchen. When the weather was very cold, however, the well froze over, and if it was too solid to be broken out with the bucket, I would grab the long stick, on the end of which was a once-sharp ice chipper, lower it into the well, and hang over the edge and chip out a hole in the ice large enough to lower the pail through and let it fill. Sometimes it would be frozen extremely solid, and chipping it would take a long time.

Usually about three trips would take care of the water needed for one day. Washing days were exceptions. On washing day it took about twelve to fifteen bucketsfull to suffice. Washing day occurred only once a week, unless my mother had nothing better to do and decided she wanted to do a washing. She would wait until we started filling the drinking pails and then say, "I think I'll do a washing today. So bring in the tub and fill it up." We would then bring in a large round tub and set it on the back of the kitchen stove and fill it up. After it was full, we poured more water into a smaller tub as rinse-water. How the last load of clothes came clean in this water after the other loads had all gone through it, I don't know. That water got dirty after the first load and more and more so after each additional load. Sometimes when I drained the washer there would be a pile of dirt—literal dirt—lying in the bottom.

No matter which of the three chores were assigned to me, I did it because I had to, not because I liked it at all. Any one of the three would require me to put on my shaggy jacket and cap which I wore to try to protect myself, although I always knew that they didn't do that much good. My mittens were either full of holes or extremely thin (or both) and kept no cold away from my fingers. Many a time I have removed my mittens after being out-of-doors and found my fingers numb with cold. The boots I wore were hand-me-downs which were absolutely no good when I got them. Most of the time I wore old rubber boots with no lining and about four or five holes in each one ranging from the size of a matchhead to an enormous tear.

After completing my chores, I would usually have about five or ten minutes before the school bus came. During that period, I would sit around the kitchen as light rose in the room and talk with my brothers and sisters about what had happened at school during the past few days. It was mostly just gossip, but then what do children in grade school talk about that isn't gossip?

On some mornings, if it wasn't too cold out or if the wind wasn't blowing to make the cold seem more intense, I would stand out by the road to await the arrival of the small two-toned green panelled pick-up used as a school bus. As I stood there, many thoughts raced through my mind. Many of these were just thoughts of temporary incidents, but there was one that kept re-occurring to me—I would be so glad to get away from this place. Sometimes I would stand there and look at the weather-beaten old run-down farmhouse which once had had a coat of white paint applied to it, but has not received one since we have lived there and wonder what I did to deserve to live in such a place as that. The shingles on the roof had all rotted and the snow and rain fell down through the house during a storm. There have been lots of mornings when I have awakened to find a small pile of snow either on the floor at the foot of my bed or on the bed itself.

Most of the windows were cracked or scratched and the frames were half-rotten. No one dared rap on one very hard for fear it would fall out. The sill under the front of the house was all rotted away and the floor had fallen away from the bottom of the door-joint. The floor of the porch had fallen down so that the pillars were no longer holding the roof and both of the two sets of steps leading onto it were either broken or loose.

My mother was always yelling, "Don't jump in the house or we'll end up down cellar!" Whenever anyone even so much as walked extra heavily, the floor would sag and rise under the strain and relaxation which are produced by walking.

I would keep telling myself that this is no place fit for anybody half-human to live in and that as soon as I was able to I would get out and go live where there were the comforts of electricity and automatic heat. I would go someplace where I could do what I wanted to do, rather than be stuck with barn chores every day and have almost no fun at all. I would get out of this rathole and go where there is something else.

But I would always come to and realize that the only way that I would ever get out without ruining my reputation by running away or by committing some serious crime would be just to go along with everything. So I did just that and I am now slowly breaking away from that unknown source that held me captive in this gloomy and depressing environment for so long. I am slowly becoming a free man to be able to choose what I want to, rather than have the environment force me to do things. It is now my choice whether I want to accomplish anything worthwhile or not. I now no longer have to shovel manure or carry water. I no longer have to wait for the school bus on cold winter mornings. I am now my own man.

DONNA VAN TASSELL

Donna Van Tassell was born in Milo, Maine, in 1950. She is majoring in English and Philosophy at the University of New Hampshire. Her essay appeared first in *Growing Up in Maine,* a collection of writings by Bowdoin College Upward Bound students published in 1968.

Home Thoughts

Half darkness gradually fading into dawn hung like fog in my room. If a pin dropped, I'd be its only witness. If a word was spoken, it was my own. The freshly starched white pillow on which I rested my head only accented my aloneness. I tossed and turned and retossed with self-pity.

Days came and left, leaving me silent. Each morning I awoke sure of my next movement. My mother would be rolled in her bed covers unaware that a new day had come and that the cat needed to be let in from out back where my step-father had chained him according to his custom shortly before work. I freed the cat and hurried to the greasiness of the kitchen to scramble eggs before it was too late and I'd go hungry again. No breakfasts had been allowed after seven-thirty ever since my mother's remarriage and I dared not alter her rule. Besides, the school bus was due at eight and unless I caught that I'd be trapped at home all day.

There was no mad rush to put on my coat, pick up my books, and bang out the door, as one normally expects. I was much too eager to leave not to be already on my mark and set to go.

A mile trip to school on rough and twisting road through the woods only takes a few minutes. Often I arrived in class with the words of my mother still ringing in my ears, "Aren't you ever going to get out of here?" or even more often, "Where's that damn bus?"

By the end of the first class I had usually lost myself and my problems in a book or a discussion and by the last class I secretly began dreading the three o'clock bell. I didn't need a clock to tell me what time it was, something inside of me fore-warned me.

Kitchen smells rarely greeted me as I idled through the front door but even less frequent was a word from anyone to assure me that human existence wasn't altogether foreign to that house, that surprisingly was by some few considered home. Perhaps the clatter of tin plates and plastic ones, the ring that glasses make, and the jingle jangle of silverware being sloshed in water was my welcome home each night.

Or perhaps the sound of one foot pressing upward always ahead of the other as I climbed the stairs leading to my bedroom was my only assurance that I was home.

Turning at a right angle from the stairs, walking mechanically to the big wooden dresser near my bed, flinging my books down in a nearby chair, and methodically changing my clothes were all ordinary movements on my part. Sometimes I found myself wondering what I would have done had someone rearranged those few pieces of furniture to which I turned every night.

Before supper I usually sprawled out on my cot with a book. And so I would read until either boredom or some particular words within my book made me drift off into some distant memory.

"My Lord, I think I saw him yesternight."

"Saw? Who?"

"My Lord, the King your father."

"Where was my father," I wondered. "Was he working or was he drunk somewhere." I looked down at my watch; it was five-thirty—five-thirty—Just four years ago I would have known where he was. He'd be home with mama and me up on the hill where we used to live. We'd all be sitting around the kitchen table eating and talking. It was always a good life back then before the divorce. I can't remember having any real problems then but now . . . now it was all changed. We never talked anymore; mama was always too busy or too tired. My step-father rarely spoke. It was almost like he was a complete stranger and the only thing I really knew about him was his face. Each night he came home from work, puttered with the familiar chores, sat down in his wooden rocking chair with his pipe tucked in his teeth and slept until supper. After supper he always returned to his chair or else mama and he went up the road to visit with his mother. Even there he slept. Rage and laughter looked bad on him. Whenever he put them on, I felt uncomfortable because they seemed unreal.

What would life have been like if I didn't know this man, my unwanted step-father? If only things hadn't changed and my real father was the man downstairs. But no, it was best not to think about it and so I forced myself to think of other things. I looked again at my book but my thoughts quickly returned to my family. I asked the question—"What would it be like?" Before the divorce there was carefreeness. I had a kitten for a pet and a back yard swing, and I'd chased June bugs, caught tadpoles, and hunted wild flowers. I went barefoot, picked berries, and rolled in clover that made my clothing sweet with scent. Even now I can close my eyes and picture life as it was. Now at twelve I wanted the things that twelve-year-olds are supposed to have. I wanted pretty dresses, not hand-me-downs; curls in my hair and jewelry just because everyone had them. I wanted to invite friends over to my house after school or go to theirs. Maybe even have a boyfriend.

A voice from my past urged me onward, to get up and conquer, to be that twelve-year-old of my dreams. I started up, pressed down the wrinkles from my clothing with my hands, started for the mirror to comb my hair, got there, and as the comb took its first sweep, the words of my mother came exploding in the air, "Get downstairs, supper's ready." I dropped the comb, walked to the door, turned back for just a moment, then went slowly down those stairs.

WILLIAM CARLOS WILLIAMS

William Carlos Williams, American poet, novelist, and physician, was born in Rutherford, New Jersey, in 1883. He practiced medicine in New Jersey all his life but also practiced writing during this time. In 1926 he was awarded the Dial prize for services to American Literature, and in 1946 he published the first four books of his major work, *Paterson.* The following selection comes from Williams' *Autobiography,* published in 1951. He died in 1963.

My Early Teens

One Fourth of July, when Uncle Carlos and my cousins Carlito and Raquel were here on a visit—I was nine or ten years old—we children were playing with a toy cannon, loading it with black powder, hammering a wad of damp paper down the muzzle, then putting the fuse from a firecracker into the touch hole to set it off. It made a very satisfactory *wham!* and we were delighted. We had done this several times but once the discharge didn't come off as planned. We had rammed the charge home with a hammer and a ten-penny nail as usual—in fact we had rammed it down extra hard for a good blast—the fuse was lit, but nothing happened. We waited a few moments to see that the fuse had burnt itself out, then I went forward to look. I leaned my face down to see why the fuse had expired. Instead of the charge exploding out of the muzzle of the cannon which, apparently, it couldn't do, we had packed it so hard, it flared up out of the touch hole right into my face and eyes!

I screamed that I was blind! My face was peppered with powder burns but, by the greatest of good luck, only the whites of my eyes were affected. No infection ensued. For weeks after I lay with bandages about my face while Raquel with a needle picked the powder grains from my cheeks, nose and forehead. For years there was one black spot on the sclera of my left eye between the iris and the inner canthus, but this too finally disappeared.

Kipp's woods, just over the back fence, was our wilderness. The fence itself was an object of delight to us with its wooden gate into the paths among the weeds. We seldom went through, however—but over it. You could sit on top with your feet on the upper rail and talk by the hour. I knew every tree in that wood, from the hickory where a squirrel had its hole to the last dogwood where in the fall the robins would gather for the red berries they are so fond of. We would hunt them with our BB rifles. They were not bad eating at that, though we were never good enough shots to get many.

But that wasn't what interested me most, nor was it the chestnuts we'd find about the big trees that were beginning to die of the blight. I saw Mr. Kipp and his colored man and dog take a wooden maul to the hickory of which I have spoken. They struck that tree with the maul until the squirrel appeared, then, at the right moment, hit the tree again so that the squirrel fell to the ground and the dog killed it. One day out behind the fence Charlie Newland had a little bitch on which someone else's dog was mounted and working. That wasn't it either.

What I learned was the way the moss climbed about a tree's roots, what growing dogwood and iron wood looked like; the way rotten leaves will mat down in a hole—and their smell when turned over—every patch among those trees had its character, moist or dry. I got to know the box turtle and the salamander and their spots and how the former hisses when annoyed.

It is a pleasure for me now to think of these things, but especially of the flowers I got to know in those precincts. It was a half-ashamed pleasure, I think. Jim Hyslop would be there to share those interests with me. The slender neck of the anemone particularly haunts me for some reason and the various sorts of violets—the tall blue ones, those with furry stems and the large, scarce, branching yellow ones, stars of Bethlehem, spring beauties, wild geranium, hepaticas with three-lobed leaves. My curiosity in these things was unbounded—secret, certainly. There is a long history in each of us that comes as not only a reawakening but a repossession when confronted by this world. To look up and see on a tree blooms, yellow and green, as large and heavy as the tulip, was something astonishing to me. The tassels of the chestnut—young and old trees, beggar's lice, spiders, shining insects—all these things were as much part of my expanding existence as breathing. I was comforted by them.

It was an unconscious triumph all day long to just be able to get out of doors and into my personal wild world. Jim, the "bugologist," was interested in insects and butterflies. I'd go with him on his forays. None of the others was interested. We never interfered with each other. I'd help him collect, but flowers and trees were my peculiar interest. To touch a tree, to climb it especially, but just to know the flowers was all I wanted.

Once I heard Mother calling me. I looked from the top branches of the beech tree at the back of our lot where I was rocking, swaying with a slow delightful motion back and forth. I couldn't imagine what was the matter with her.

"Willie, come down, come down," in a half-frightened voice. I climbed down thinking she wanted me to do some errand. No. It was just that I might fall.

Fall? Why Harry Howard used to go up into a cluster of oaks I knew, and still know, on Union Avenue, where his father had a carpenter shop, and from the top of one of them jump iike a squirrel into the branches of the tree adjacent and not fall. One day I jumped from the top of our outhouse, but when I landed my knees hit me on the chin with such force I was knocked sprawling.

Of course we were brats: lied, stole fruit and bits of lumber from new constructions, like any children. Always something new. Peter Kipp was our enemy and we his. One particularly pernicious thing we did was to run through his rye fields just when the grain was about to be harvested.

One day four or five of us were well into the field, the grain higher than our heads, when old man Kipp and his colored hand crept up on us. Jim, who wore glasses, had placed himself on the top rail of the nearby fence to keep watch for us, but he was too nearsighted to be of much help. I was farthest out into the field, with a building lath in my hands to push the grain down ahead of me. Jim yelled and fell off the fence backward before Kipp's brindled bull. We all made for the edge of the field nearest the woods. The others got away, but I ran right into Kipp's arms. He grabbed me by the throat, and, lifting me, half-threw, half-kicked me over the fence. I landed on my feet, lit out for cover and never looked back.

But we were not vicious. We didn't wish purposely to destroy, like those of a later generation, who finally drove the old man out of business by burning and uprooting his crops. For, as it was all part of the legend, we acknowledged our guilt but went back for more at the next opportunity.

One day we were playing ball on Elliot Place—at just about the spot where at midnight one day an owl struck me with a wing on the head as I was passing, the same place where at another time, I saw a small flock of cross-bills feeding (how old must I have been, between twelve and thirteen, I imagine, in the sixth grade?) when who should appear in the street but Lizzie Nevins and another girl in whom I was particularly, passionately interested. The other kids started to laugh and josh me, as Lizzie, grinning and loitering along the sidewalk, called to me to come over where they were standing. I was embarrassed, but finally went.

"Come on in the woods with us," she said, "I want to tell you something you want to know."

Well, in spite of my humiliation before the others and their disgust at my leaving the game, the three of us wandered off among the trees. Once there Lizzie said to me, "Wait here, a minute, her drawers are falling down."

So I waited while the two girls went behind a tree and refastened the garment. Then Lizzie began her game.

"Go ahead, you two. Go over there in the rye field if you want to and I'll watch. Go on. She wants you to. She told me she did. Go on!"

So we left her there, kids that we were, and groped our way out of sight into the green rye stalks, where we, who were under the same spell, sat down facing each other—too embarrassed even to open our mouths to ask a question.

WILLIAM TRACY

In 1946, when he was eleven, William Tracy went to live in Saudi Arabia, where his father worked for the Arabian American Oil Company. Mr. Tracy is now editor of the *Aramco World Magazine*, where the following essay first appeared.

A Boyhood in Ras Tanura

It always amused me to see people's reactions in the States when I told them where I lived. "Saudi Arabia?" they would say. "You mean in the desert?" And I would say, yes, in the desert, and they would say, "Well, gee, that must have been interesting!" Then they would hurry away to tell their friends about this oddball who grew up in an oil camp on the Arabian Gulf.

At the time I thought they really did consider it interesting. I didn't realize that to many people in the United States growing up anywhere but in America seemed more peculiar than interesting. "How," they sometimes asked, "can a boy grow up without, oh, football games on Saturday, snowstorms, ice skating, cutting the lawn in summer or burning leaves in the fall or going walking in the woods in the spring, or, well you know. . . ."

As it happened, I did not know, not really. I went to Saudi Arabia when I was only 11 years old. Oh, I do have vague memories of a few things in Illinois—frost on the windows, maybe, the smell of fresh cut grass, the Memorial Day parades, or the sight of tall trees against the sky. But for the vivid memories, the bright warm memories of boyhood, I have to go back to Saudi Arabia, to the night the plane from Cairo dropped out of the darkness onto the Dhahran airstrip, the night our new life in an old land began. . . .

It was 1946. The war was over—World War II, that is—and my mother, determined to join my father after a year's separation, had packed us off to New York and onto a freighter bound for Alexandria (it was called *The Black Warrior,* I remember). Then we took a train for Cairo and, after a week of false starts, a plane for Dhahran. When we landed we straggled across the airfield like a small untidy parade. My mother was first with my baby sister Sally cradled in one arm on a bulky WAC's purse. I was second, clutching her hand, and my brother Jimmy was last, trotting along at the end of a sort of leash with which, I felt, I had dragged him half way around the world.

It was terribly hot and very dark, I recall, and the loud speaker from the Dhahran Airfield was just broadcasting the beginning of "Inner Sanctum," one of my favorite programs at home. I remember the sound of the creaking door. And then I saw my father. He was standing on the apron waiting for us, a tall thin man, almost a stranger after our year's separation. He was dressed in white, I remember, and he had sunglasses strapped to his belt. We ran to meet him. . . .

Later, my father introduced us to the Snyders with whom we were to spend the night before going on to Ras Tanura, a new community where Aramco had built a refinery. One of the Snyders was a boy named Myles who was two years my senior and who, in the 15 minutes it took to drive to the Snyder house, became my closest friend.

"See those flames?" he asked in a low voice. I looked out through the darkness and saw the dancing lights of the gas flares from a gas-oil separator plant. "They're volcanoes," he said. "Live volcanoes, really!"

A few minutes later he pointed to the silhouette of twin minarets on a mosque near the road. "Cactus!" he hissed. "Saguaro cactus!"

And both times I believed him.

In the months to come, Myles was to teach me all sorts of new things: how to find green scorpions under driftwood on the beach, how to catch lizards behind the neck so that you weren't stuck with a writhing lizardless tail between your fingers. He was to introduce me to spiny-tailed "dabbs," meat-eating "warals" and suction-toed geckos; to desert hedgehogs and foxes, and even once—on a wilderness trip with a geologist—to a hunchbacked striped hyena. It would be Myles too who would, one year in Dhahran, lead me under the camp fence on daring hikes to distant flat-topped hills, and to the charred crater blasted by a misplaced Italian bomb. But that would come later. That first night he contented himself with making the new kid think that the flares were volcanoes. As I dozed off in the Snyders' living room, I heard his voice echoing in my head, "Live volcanoes, really!"

The next morning we headed for Ras Tanura in a four by four army surplus truck. We drove past Aramco's Dammam Seven, the company's first producing oil well, past pyramid-shaped Jabal Shamal on the left, and past the fishing villages of al-Khobar and Dammam. Later, we saw crystal white salt flats and scattered palm groves over which loomed towering dunes. As the truck drove along, occasionally shifting into four-wheel drive to push through patches of drifted sand, we saw flocks of long-haired black goats, clusters of low Bedouin tents, and the huge stiff-legged white donkeys of the Eastern Province, with spots of orange dye on their backs. We saw our first camel standing against the horizon and noted a sign by the road cautioning us that "camels have the right-of-way."

All this, which would become so familiar to us, was new that morning. Some of it, unstirred by centuries, had begun to disappear even then; all of it would change a little in the next few years. All except the searing heat and the scorching beige glare of the desert which reached halfway into the sky. Beside the road were the catalysts of the change; the high-tension power line, the flares of the gas-oil separator plants ("Live volcanoes," huh?) and the rows of pipelines with mounds of clay for the camel caravans to cross. Then the towers of the new refinery appeared beyond the long finger of Tarut Bay and we drove onto the narrow Ras Tanura headland to the house where we were to live.

We had one of the first group of 30 stucco family houses built in "American City," now Nejma. The houses, painted in brilliant colors as if to challenge the monotony of sand and sky, were arranged four deep along the shore. They had spacious yards of white beach sand, and patios of flat "faroush" stone taken from the bottom of the bay. From our dining room we could watch the changing moods and colors of the Gulf: misty silver and mirror-still at dawn, clear aquamarine and violet at mid-day, chalky green during a storm and washed lime-blue when the storm was over. It was unforgettably beautiful.

In Ras Tanura, in those days, most of the early facilities were located in temporary wooden barracks. There were a clinic, a laundry, a barbershop, a mail center, and a recreation hall in which were located a library, a snack bar, a billiard room and a bowling alley.

For the hard-hatted sheet metal construction workers, the recreation hall was the center of their off duty life. Here they balanced the day's sweat with a night of pre-prohibition beer drinking and high-stakes poker. Across the street was the Mess Hall which served all bachelors, including married men whose families had not yet arrived, and "bachelorettes," the first few nurses and secretaries who had been persuaded to come out to Saudi Arabia. Nearby were flood-lit tennis courts (used by us kids surreptitiously for roller skating). There was also an outdoor theater, with straw mat sides to keep out the strong north wind. We went to the movies winter and summer, although in winter it meant wrapping up in blankets. But often on mild nights in the spring and fall the sky and its stars offered a better show than the one on the screen.

The refinery, I remember, had just gone "on stream," as everyone soon learned to say, and little Ras Tanura began to celebrate its ever-increasing post-war production with splendid holidays on the beach every time we racked up a 100,000 or a 150,000-barrel day. These were most often Employe Association picnics with donkey races (the big white ones were safe bets), buried coin hunts for silver riyals and Indian rupees, and, on very special occasions such as the 4th of July, feasts of watermelon from al-Kharj, southeast of Riyadh.

Other big occasions in those days were the monthly (or sometimes semimonthly) arrivals of the refrigerator ships, for the ships brought fresh vegetables. I remember the sight of the women hurrying to the commissary carrying heavy canvas bags of clinking silver coins since paper money had not yet been introduced.

There was always construction underway and that meant lots of bricks and planks that enterprising boys could manage to "borrow" despite the efforts of the Safety Department to keep us at bay. Rightly or wrongly we considered Safety Department personnel and "Security" our mortal enemies. They discovered our board-covered tunnels beneath the sagebrush hillocks at the edge of town and bulldozed them under. They discouraged our long bicycle rides on the hard-packed beach at low tide by building a fence. They cut us off from the deserted coast where huge shells dried in the sun, where oar-tailed sea snakes warmed themselves on the sand and sand crabs tunneled below, leaving little castles by their front doors. We were never completely foiled, however, and swam outside the fence to walk as far as the magnificent sand dunes where we could somersault down to the bottom without harm, or play "king of the mountain."

Meanwhile, as we explored Ras Tanura and its environs, my mother was making a determined bid to tame the desert. In our first house the only garden we had was an accidental growth of tiny palm shoots that sprang up when dew dripped from the sloping roofs onto date pits left by construction workers who had made a habit of eating lunch in the shade of the house. But when we moved to a new house and when soil had been trucked in, Mother planted the beginnings of a garden and between the sandstorms which periodically swept across the beach wall, nursed it to life. First she planted a crop of alfalfa. Then she put in creepers of Bermuda grass which had to be poked into the earth one by one and painstakingly sprinkled with the hose each evening. Then she put on oleander bushes and tamarisk and acacia trees, buried dried seaweed and fish near the roots to fertilize them and, because of the wind and the shallow soil, tied them upright to sturdy poles. Some flowering plants could be obtained from the company's nursery: frangipani, climbing red, orange and purple bougainvillea, hardy periwinkle, dwarf poinsettia, but there were also four o'clocks grown from seeds sent out from my grandpa's farm in Ohio. I remember how strange Ras Tanura looked the first year green trees began to poke above the roofs all over town, throwing circles of shade onto the ground and softening the skyline.

Before then we had spent a year in Dhahran. It was the year my sister Sue was born. We lived in a house on a hill from which you could see the smoke from the flares on the island of Bahrain. On the other side of the house in Dhahran, I recall, lived a boy named Jim McCarthy who introduced me to an intriguing little book about the facts of life. Another neighbor, Louella Beckly, lent me scores of Carolyn Keene's Nancy Drew mystery stories. They were both "big kids" like Phil Braun, who could swim faster on his back than most of us could crawl. But big or little, there were plenty of them since the families in Saudi Arabia were young and large. There was always a new wing under construction at the school and new faces on the bus or at the mail center. Since someone was always leaving for long vacation or going "outside" to school, there were also familiar faces disappearing too. Myles Snyder, for one.

After the year in Dhahran we moved back to Ras Tanura and I made new friends. One was Joe Studholm and the other a boy named Jim Mandaville. Jim was a genius of many talents, we all knew, because he threw shoes at his brother Jack (who could pinch you with his toes when wrestling), identified desert plants and fragments of pottery, rode horses, and built radios and model airplanes. He was a "girl hater" at the time and a party hater. To his chagrin, his mother helped organize the Teen Club.

Since we lived on the shore, I guess it was inevitable that we would come to know the sea and its inhabitants. Some of us, at least, like D. T. Gray, my cousin, and Miles Jones, with whom I ranged up and down the coast in quest of all that it had to teach us.

Miles lived in a house in the Marine Terminal area on the tip of the Ras Tanura peninsula. Because the house was the oldest in town it was infested with earwigs and centipedes and for some reason that I can't remember we were convinced that there was a mongoose in the attic which had escaped from one of the tankers from India.

When D. T. and I spent the weekend with Miles we would hike across the narrow sand spit to the abandoned arrow-shaped palm frond fish traps there, and wade cautiously in the slimy sand, watching for sand dollars and sea urchins and feeling mud sharks and skates slither across our nervous toes. We caught baskets of fish for fertilizer and great blue crabs, and quantities of huge pink shrimp which we cleaned and ate doused in tomato catsup. We also decimated the population of a certain snail which had the bad luck of shutting itself in with a dime-sized trapdoor of some beauty which we called cat's-eye. We held our noses as we boiled kettles of them, pried their protective seal from the sticky body, dried them in the sun, and bathed them in glistening olive oil. We ran our fingers through piles of them like misers. They were too chalky to be valuable, of course, but to us they were priceless.

But great as it was, there was more to life than just leisure and mischief. There was also school. School then was held in a portable building on a steel frame that was hauled in on a truck and perched on four large concrete blocks. Sam Whipple was the principal but he was also our teacher, and our friend. He was short and balding and could run faster than any of the boys in junior high.

One day, when the seasonal wind had whipped around and under the school for several weeks, we felt a sudden window-rattling jolt and the building lurched. The sand had blown away from the base of one of the concrete supports. The Safety Department moved in at once and took precautions and put out bulletins, but we thought it had been great fun when all the volleyballs and baseball bats behind Mr. Whipple's desk began to roll lazily down to the far corner of the room.

In cool weather in our school we frequently went out on excursions, sometimes driving all day on sand tracks to the Hofuf oasis with its maze of caves and eroded sandstone pillars, its hot springs, donkey drawn wells, covered *suqs,* and old walls. We took the three step journey by dhow, rowboat, and donkey cart to Tarut Island where thousands of tiny turtles lived in the irrigation ditches beneath jungles of palms. We climbed like lizards over the crumbling Portuguese forts in Dammam and Qatif, and visited the last of the great winter encampments of the Bedouins.

Like all American boys, of course, we had a Boy Scout troop, but although we learned our first aid and Morse and semaphore in the prescribed fashion, our company trips were quite different. We always had an extra truck loaded with firewood and water. No amount of woodsman's lore would have provided either in that territory. In Tarut Bay we camped on uninhabited Za'al Island which was separated from the peninsula only by a broad mud flat and narrow reef channel, but gave us a splendid feeling of freedom and remoteness when the water rose and the tidal current was running. There we skinny-dipped and hunted tern's eggs, and at night herded schools of needlefish onto the beach by sweeping a powerful three-battery flashlight beam along the dark surface of the bay.

Ras Tanura was so small that having a party meant inviting every kid in camp. The girl hater clique was not big on "scissors," "walking the plank," "sardines," "inchy pinchy," or "country club." They once fled from a party with Nancy Bradfield's birthday cake in tow. But I think even the girl haters were secretly impressed by Mary Beth Harrity when she floated on her back in the Gulf. Of course she was a "big kid" and only came to Ras Tanura during vacations from the American Community School in Beirut, Lebanon. She brought back unbelievable stories about boarding school which we all believed and could hardly wait to experience for ourselves. In the meantime, enjoying our last year at home, we made dribble castles on the beach, threw sun-dried stinging jellyfish at each other, ran barefooted across melting asphalt roads, and chased locust swarms from the gardens, knocking them down with tennis rackets.

We thought ourselves to be a special breed of kids in those days. And maybe in some ways we were. We spoke Arabic, we had met the famous King Ibn Sa'ud. We knew real Bedouins and all of us had been around the world at least once. Our thick green passports were gay accumulations of visas and permits from as many nations as there were pages, and our arms and inoculation certificates were both full of shots. We had, furthermore, lived through the incomparable excitement of watching a town come to life in what, to us at least, was a new and exciting land.

But now, suddenly it was time to leave again—off to high school in Beirut. It wasn't really very far and we were coming back every holiday, but still, when the special red and silver Kenworth bus headed out to the airport that day, there was more than one red-eyed mother and silent father aboard.

We drove, I remember, past the same dunes, and the same palm groves, and even, I thought, the same herds of goats that I had seen that first day when we left the Snyders' house. My father had become noticeably quiet as we passed the halfway coast guard house and as Jabal Shamal appeared on the horizon, he began to fidget uneasily.

"Er, ah, Billy, . . ." We bounced past the gas flares ("Live volcanoes, really!"). "Well, Bill. . . ." We jolted past the main gate of Dhahran and down past the twin minarets ("saguaro cactus") towards the airfield. It was 1950. Had it only been four years? "Son," my father gulped and looked around and leaned towards my ear. A gargled whisper: "Is there, er, anything you'd like to know about, er . . . girls?"

Which is as good a place as any to end my memories, my bright warm memories of those, yes, innocent years growing up in Saudi Arabia.

JAMES BALDWIN

One of the most powerful writers of his generation, James Baldwin was born in New York City in 1924. Among his works are *Go Tell It on the Mountain* (1953), *Notes of a Native Son* (1955), from which the following selection is taken, *Giovanni's Room* (1956), *Nobody Knows My Name: More Notes of a Native Son* (1961), and, most recently, *Tell Me How Long the Train's Been Gone* (1968). His plays include *The Amen Corner* and *Blues for Mr. Charley.*

Notes of a Native Son

On the 29th of July, in 1943, my father died. On the same day, a few hours later, his last child was born. Over a month before this, while all our energies were concentrated in waiting for these events, there had been, in Detroit, one of the bloodiest race riots of the century. A few hours after my father's funeral, while he lay in state in the undertaker's chapel, a race riot broke out in Harlem. On the morning of the 3rd of August, we drove my father to the graveyard through a wilderness of smashed plate glass.

The day of my father's funeral had also been my nineteenth birthday. As we drove him to the graveyard, the spoils of injustice, anarchy, discontent, and hatred were all around us. It seemed to me that God himself had devised, to mark my father's end, the most sustained and brutally dissonant of codas. And it seemed to me, too, that the violence which rose all about us as my father left the world had been devised as a corrective for the pride of his eldest son. I had declined to believe in that apocalypse which had been central to my father's vision; very well, life seemed to be saying, here is something that will certainly pass for an apocalypse until the real thing comes along. I had inclined to be contemptuous of my father for the conditions of his life, for the conditions of our lives. When his life had ended I began to wonder about that life and also, in a new way, to be apprehensive about my own.

I had not known my father very well. We had got on badly, partly because we shared, in our different fashions, the vice of stubborn pride. When he was dead I realized that I had hardly ever spoken to him. When he had been dead a long time I began to wish I had. It seems to be typical of life in America, where opportunities, real and fancied, are thicker than anywhere else on the globe, that the second generation has no time to talk to the first. No one, including my father, seems to have known exactly how old he was, but his mother had been born during slavery. He was of the first generation of free men. He, along with thousands of other Negroes, came North after 1919 and I was part of that generation which had never seen the landscape of what Negroes sometimes call the Old Country.

He had been born in New Orleans and had been a quite young man there during the time that Louis Armstrong, a boy, was running errands for the dives and honky-tonks of what was always presented to me as one of the most wicked of cities—to this day, whenever I think of New Orleans, I also helplessly think of Sodom and Gomorrah. My father never mentioned Louis Armstrong, except to forbid us to play his records; but there was a picture of him on our wall for a long time. One of my father's strong-willed female relatives had placed it there and forbade my father to take it down. He never did, but he eventually maneuvered her out of the house and when, some years later, she was in trouble and near death, he refused to do anything to help her.

He was, I think, very handsome. I gather this from photographs and from my own memories of him, dressed in his Sunday best and on his way to preach a sermon somewhere, when I was little. Handsome, proud, and ingrown, "like a toe-nail," somebody said. But he looked to me, as I grew older, like pictures I had seen of African tribal chieftains: he really should have been naked, with war-paint on the barbaric mementos, standing among spears. He could be chilling in the pulpit and indescribably cruel in his personal life and he was certainly the most bitter man I have ever met; yet it must be said that there was something else in him, buried in him, which lent him his tremendous power and, even, a rather crushing charm. It had something to do with his blackness, I think—he was very black—with his blackness and his beauty, and with the fact that he knew that he was black but did not know that he was beautiful. He claimed to be proud of his blackness but it had also been the cause of much humiliation and it had fixed bleak boundaries to his life. He was not a young man when we were growing up and he had already suffered many kinds of ruin; in his outrageously demanding and protective way he loved his children, who were black like him and menaced, like him; and all these things sometimes showed in his face when he tried, never to my knowledge with any success, to establish contact with any of us. When he took one of his children on his knee to play, the child always became fretful and began to cry; when he tried to help one of us with our homework the absolutely unabating tension which emanated from him caused our minds and our tongues to become paralyzed, so that he, scarcely knowing why, flew into a rage and the child, not knowing why, was punished. If it ever entered his head to bring a surprise home for his children, it was, almost unfailingly, the wrong surprise and even the big watermelons he often brought home on his back in the summertime led to the most appalling scenes. I do not remember, in all those years, that one of his children was ever glad to see him come home. From what I was able to gather of his early life, it seemed that this inability to establish contact with other people had always marked him and had been one of the things which had driven him out of New Orleans. There was something in him, therefore, groping and tentative, which was never expressed and which was buried with him. One saw it most clearly when he was facing new people and hoping to impress them. But he never did, not for long. We went from church to smaller and more improbable church, he found himself in less and less demand as a minister, and by the time he died none of his friends had come to see him for a long time. He had lived and died in an intolerable bitterness of spirit and it frightened me, as we drove him to the graveyard through those unquiet, ruined streets, to see how powerful and overflowing this bitterness could be and to realize that this bitterness now was mine.

When he died I had been away from home for a little over a year. In that year I had had time to become aware of the meaning of all my father's bitter warnings, had discovered the secret of his proudly pursed lips and rigid carriage: I had discovered the weight of white people in the world. I saw that this had been for my ancestors and now would be for me an awful thing to live with and that the bitterness which had helped to kill my father could also kill me.

He had been ill a long time—in the mind, as we now realized, reliving instances of his fantastic intransigence in the new light of his affliction and endeavoring to feel a sorrow for him which never, quite, came true. We had not known that he was being eaten up by paranoia, and the discovery that his cruelty, to our bodies and our minds, had been one of the symptoms of his illness was not, then, enough to enable us to forgive him. The younger children felt, quite simply, relief that he would not be coming home any more. My mother's observation that it was he, after all, who had kept them alive all these years meant nothing because the problems of keeping children alive are not real for children. The older children felt, with my father gone, that they could invite their friends to the house without fear that their friends would be insulted or, as had sometimes happened with me, being told that their friends were in league with the devil and intended to rob our family of everything we owned. (I didn't fail to wonder, and it made me hate him, what on earth we owned that anybody else would want.)

His illness was beyond all hope of healing before anyone realized that he was ill. He had always been so strange and had lived, like a prophet, in such unimaginably close communion with the Lord that his long silences which were punctuated by moans and hallelujahs and snatches of old songs while he sat at the living-room window never seemed odd to us. It was not until he refused to eat because, he said, his family was trying to poison him that my mother was forced to accept as a fact what had, until then, been only an unwilling suspicion. When he was committed, it was discovered that he had tuberculosis and, as it turned out, the disease of his mind allowed the disease of his body to destroy him. For the doctors could not force him to eat, either, and, though he was fed intravenously, it was clear from the beginning that there was no hope for him.

In my mind's eye I could see him, sitting at the window, locked up in his terrors; hating and fearing every living soul including his children who had betrayed him, too, by reaching toward the world which had despised him. There were nine of us. I began to wonder what it could have felt like for such a man to have had nine children whom he could barely feed. He used to make little jokes about our poverty, which never, of course, seemed very funny to us; they could not have seemed very funny to him, either, or else our all too feeble response to them would never have caused such rages. He spent great energy and achieved, to our chagrin, no small amount of success in keeping us away from the people who surrounded us, people who had all-night rent parties to which we listened when we should have been sleeping, people who cursed and drank and flashed razor blades on Lenox Avenue. He could not understand why, if they had so much energy to spare, they could not use it to make their lives better. He treated almost everybody on our block with a most uncharitable asperity and neither they, nor, of course, their children were slow to reciprocate.

The only white people who came to our house were welfare workers and bill collectors. It was almost always my mother who dealt with them, for my father's temper, which was at the mercy of his pride, was never to be trusted. It was clear that he felt their very presence in his home to be a violation: this was conveyed by his carriage, almost ludicrously stiff, and by his voice, harsh and vindictively polite. When I was around nine or ten I wrote a play which was directed by a young, white schoolteacher, a woman, who then took an interest in me, and gave me books to read and, in order to corroborate my theatrical bent, decided to take me to see what she somewhat tactlessly referred to as "real" plays. Theatergoing was forbidden in our house, but, with the really cruel intuitiveness of a child, I suspected that the color of this woman's skin would carry the day for me. When, at school, she suggested taking me to the theater, I did not, as I might have done if she had been a Negro, find a way of discouraging her, but agreed that she should pick me up at my house one evening. I then, very cleverly, left all the rest to my mother, who suggested to my father, as I knew she would, that it would not be very nice to let such a kind woman make the trip for nothing. Also, since it was a schoolteacher, I imagine that my mother countered the idea of sin with the idea of "education," which word, even with my father, carried a kind of bitter weight.

Before the teacher came my father took me aside to ask *why* she was coming, what *interest* she could possibly have in our house, in a boy like me. I said I didn't know but I, too, suggested that it had something to do with education. And I understood that my father was waiting for me to say something—I didn't quite know what; perhaps that I wanted his protection against this teacher and her "education." I said none of these things and the teacher came and we went out. It was clear, during the brief interview in our living room, that my father was agreeing very much against his will and that he would have refused permission if he had dared. The fact that he did not dare caused me to despise him: I had no way of knowing that he was facing in that living room a wholly unprecedented and frightening situation.

Later, when my father had been laid off from his job, this woman became very important to us. She was really a very sweet and generous woman and went to a great deal of trouble to be of help to us, particularly during one awful winter. My mother called her by the highest name she knew: she said she was a "christian." My father could scarcely disagree but during the four or five years of our relatively close association he never trusted her and was always trying to surprise in her open, Midwestern face the genuine, cunningly hidden, and hideous motivation. In later years, particularly when it began to be clear that this "education" of mine was going to lead me to perdition, he became more explicit and warned me that my white friends in high school were not really my friends and that I would see, when I was older, how white people would do anything to keep a Negro down. Some of them could be nice, he admitted, but none of them were to be trusted and most of them were not even nice. The best thing was to have as little to do with them as possible. I did not feel this way and I was certain, in my innocence, that I never would.

But the year which preceded my father's death had made a great change in my life. I had been living in New Jersey, working in defense plants, working and living among southerners, white and black. I knew about the south, of course, and about how southerners treated Negroes and how they expected them to behave, but it had never entered my mind that anyone would look at me and expect *me* to behave that way. I learned in New Jersey that to be a Negro meant, precisely, that one was never looked at but was simply at the mercy of the reflexes the color of one's skin caused in other people. I acted in New Jersey as I had always acted, that is as though I thought a great deal of myself—I had to *act* that way—with results that were, simply, unbelievable. I had scarcely arrived before I had earned the enmity, which was extraordinarily ingenious, of all my superiors and nearly all my co-workers. In the beginning, to make matters worse, I simply did not know what was happening. I did not know what I had done, and I shortly began to wonder what *anyone* could possibly do, to bring about such unanimous, active, and unbearably vocal hostility. I knew about jim-crow but I had never experienced it. I went to the same self-service restaurant three times and stood with all the Princeton boys before the counter, waiting for a hamburger and coffee; it was always an extraordinarily long time before anything was set before me; but it was not until the fourth visit that I learned that, in fact, nothing had ever been set before me: I had simply picked something up. Negroes were not served there, I was told, and they had been waiting for me to realize that I was always the only Negro present. Once I was told this, I determined to go there all the time. But now they were ready for me and, though some dreadful scenes were subsequently enacted in that restaurant, I never ate there again.

It was the same story all over New Jersey, in bars, bowling alleys, diners, places to live. I was always being forced to leave, silently, or with mutual imprecations. I very shortly became notorious and children giggled behind me when I passed and their elders whispered or shouted—they really believed that I was mad. And it did begin to work on my mind, of course; I began to be afraid to go anywhere and to compensate for this I went places to which I really should not have gone and where, God knows, I had no desire to be. My reputation in town naturally enhanced my reputation at work and my working day became one long series of acrobatics designed to keep me out of trouble. I cannot say that these acrobatics succeeded. It began to seem that the machinery of the organization I worked for was turning over, day and night, with but one aim: to eject me. I was fired once, and contrived, with the aid of a friend from New York, to get back on the payroll; was fired again, and bounced back again. It took a while to fire me for the third time, but the third time took. There were no loopholes anywhere. There was not even any way of getting back inside the gates.

That year in New Jersey lives in my mind as though it were the year during which, having an unsuspected predilection for it, I first contracted some dread, chronic disease, the unfailing symptom of which is a kind of blind fever, a pounding in the skull and fire in the bowels. Once this disease is contracted, one can never be really carefree again, for the fever, without an instant's warning, can recur at any moment. It can wreck more important things than race relations. There is not a Negro alive who does not have this rage in his blood—one has the choice, merely, of living with it consciously or surrendering to it. As for me, this fever has recurred in me, and does, and will until the day I die.

My last night in New Jersey, a white friend from New York took me to the nearest big town, Trenton, to go to the movies and have a few drinks. As it turned out, he also saved me from, at the very least, a violent whipping. Almost every detail of that night stands out very clearly in my memory. I even remember the name of the movie we saw because its impressed me as being so patly ironical. It was a movie about the German occupation of France, starring Maureen O'Hara and Charles Laughton and called *This Land Is Mine*. I remember the name of the diner we walked into when the movie ended: it was the "American Diner." When we walked in the counterman asked what we wanted and I remember answering with the casual sharpness which had become my habit: "We want a hamburger and a cup of coffee, what do you think we want?" I do not know why, after a year of such rebuffs, I so completely failed to anticipate his answer, which was, of course, "We don't serve Negroes here." This reply failed to discompose me, at least for the moment. I made some sardonic comment about the name of the diner and we walked out into the streets.

This was the time of what was called the "brownout," when the lights in all American cities were very dim. When we re-entered the streets something happened to me which had the force of an optical illusion, or a nightmare. The streets were very crowded and I was facing north. People were moving in every direction but it seemed to me, in that instant, that all of the people I could see, and many more than that, were moving toward me, against me, and that everyone was white. I remember how their faces gleamed. And I felt, like a physical sensation, a *click* at the nape of my neck as though some interior string connecting my head to my body had been cut. I began to walk. I heard my friend call after me, but I ignored him. Heaven only knows what was going on in his mind, but he had the good sense not to touch me—I don't know what would have happened if he had—and to keep me in sight. I don't know what was going on in my mind, either; I certainly had no conscious plan. I wanted to do something to crush these white faces, which were crushing me. I walked for perhaps a block or two until I came to an enormous, glittering, and fashionable restaurant in which I knew not even the intercession of the Virgin would cause me to be served. I pushed through the doors and took the first vacant seat I saw, at a table for two, and waited.

I do not know how long I waited and I rather wonder, until today, what I could possibly have looked like. Whatever I looked like, I frightened the waitress who shortly appeared, and the moment she appeared all of my fury flowed toward her. I hated her for her white face, and for her great, astounded, frightened eyes. I felt that if she found a black man so frightening I would make her fright worth-while.

She did not ask me what I wanted, but repeated, as though she had learned it somewhere, "We don't serve Negroes here." She did not say it with the blunt derisive hostility to which I had grown so accustomed, but, rather, with a note of apology in her voice, and fear. This made me colder and more murderous than ever. I felt I had to do something with my hands. I wanted her to come close enough for me to get her neck between my hands.

So I pretended not to have understood her, hoping to draw her closer. And she did step a very short step closer, with her pencil poised incongruously over her pad, and repeated the formula: ". . . don't serve Negroes here."

Somehow, with the repetition of that phrase, which was already ringing in my head like a thousand bells of a nightmare, I realized that she would never come any closer and that I would have to strike from a distance. There was nothing on the table but an ordinary water-mug half full of water, and I picked this up and hurled it with all my strength at her. She ducked and it missed her and shattered against the mirror behind the bar. And, with that sound, my frozen blood abruptly thawed, I returned from wherever I had been, I *saw,* for the first time, the restaurant, the people with their mouths open, already, as it seemed to me, rising as one man, and I realized what I had done, and where I was, and I was frightened. I rose and began running for the door. A round, potbellied man grabbed me by the nape of the neck just as I reached the doors and began to beat me about the face. I kicked him and got loose and ran into the streets. My friend whispered, *"Run!"* and I ran.

My friend stayed outside the restaurant long enough to misdirect my pursuers and the police, who arrived, he told me, at once. I do not know what I said to him when he came to my room that night. I could not have said much. I felt, in the oddest, most awful way, that I had somehow betrayed him. I lived it over and over and over again, the way one relives an automobile accident after it has happened and one finds oneself alone and safe. I could not get over two facts, both equally difficult for the imagination to grasp, and one was that I could have been murdered. But the other was that I had been ready to commit murder. I saw nothing very clearly but I did see this: that my life, my *real* life, was in danger, and not from anything other people might do but from the hatred I carried in my own heart.

I had returned home around the second week in June—in great haste because it seemed that my father's death and my mother's confinement were both a matter of hours. In the case of my mother, it soon became clear that she had simply made a miscalculation. This had always been her tendency and I don't believe that a single one of us arrived in the world, or has since arrived anywhere else, on time. But none of us dawdled so intolerably about the business of being born as did my baby sister. We sometimes amused ourselves, during those endless, stifling weeks, by picturing the baby sitting within in the safe, warm dark, bitterly regretting the necessity of becoming a part of our chaos and stubbornly putting it off as long as possible. I understood her perfectly and congratulated her on showing such good sense so soon. Death, however, sat as purposefully at my father's bedside as life stirred within my mother's womb and it was harder to understand why he so lingered in that long shadow. It seemed that he had bent, and for a long time, too, all of his energies toward dying. Now death was ready for him but my father held back.

All of Harlem, indeed, seemed to be infected by waiting. I had never before known it to be so violently still. Racial tensions throughout this country were exacerbated during the early years of the war, partly because the labor market brought together hundreds of thousands of ill-prepared people and partly because Negro soldiers, regardless of where they were born, received their military training in the south. What happened in defense plants and army camps had repercussions, naturally, in every Negro ghetto. The situation in Harlem had grown bad enough for clergymen, policemen, educators, politicians, and social workers to assert in one breath that there was no "crime wave" and to offer, in the very next breath, suggestions as to how to combat it. These suggestions always seemed to involve playgrounds, despite the fact that racial skirmishes were occurring in the playgrounds, too. Playgrounds or not, crime wave or not, the Harlem police force had been augmented in March, and the unrest grew—perhaps, in fact, partly as a result of the ghetto's instinctive hatred of policemen. Perhaps the most revealing news item, out of the steady parade of reports of muggings, stabbings, shootings, assaults, gang wars, and accusations of police brutality, is the item concerning six Negro girls who set upon a white girl in the subway because, as they all too accurately put it, she was stepping on their toes. Indeed she was, all over the nation.

I had never before been so aware of policemen, on foot, on horseback, on corners, everywhere, always two by two. Nor had I ever been so aware of small knots of people. They were on stoops and on corners and in doorways, and what was striking about them, I think, was that they did not seem to be talking. Never, when I passed these groups, did the usual sound of a curse or a laugh ring out and neither did there seem to be any hum of gossip. There was certainly, on the other hand, occurring between them communication extraordinarily intense. Another thing that was striking was the unexpected diversity of the people who made up these groups. Usually, for example, one would see a group of sharpies standing on the street corner, jiving the passing chicks; or a group of older men, usually, for some reason, in the vicinity of a barber shop, discussing baseball scores, or the numbers, or making rather chilling observations about women they had known. Women, in a general way, tended to be seen less often together—unless they were church women, or very young girls, or prostitutes met together for an unprofessional instant. But that summer I saw the strangest combinations: large, respectable, churchly matrons standing on the stoops or the corners with their hair tied up, together with a girl in sleazy satin whose face bore the marks of gin and the razor, or heavy-set, abrupt, no-nonsense older men, in company with the most disreputable and fanatical "race" men, or these same "race" men with the sharpies, or these sharpies with the churchly women. Seventh Day Adventists and Methodists and Spiritualists seemed to be hobnobbing with Holyrollers and they were all, alike, entangled with the most flagrant disbelievers; something heavy in their stance seemed to indicate that they had all, incredibly, seen a common vision, and on each face there seemed to be the same strange, bitter shadow.

The churchly women and the matter-of-fact, no-nonsense men had children in the Army. The sleazy girls they talked to had lovers there, the sharpies and the "race" men had friends and brothers there. It would have demanded an unquestioning patriotism, happily as uncommon in this country as it is undesirable, for these people not to have been disturbed by the bitter letters they received, by the newspaper stories they read, not to have been enraged by the posters, then to be found all over New York, which described the Japanese as "yellow-bellied Japs." It was only the "race" men, to be sure, who spoke ceaselessly of being revenged—how this vengeance was to be exacted was not clear—for the indignities and dangers suffered by Negro boys in uniform; but everybody felt a directionless, hopeless bitterness, as well as that panic which can scarcely be suppressed when one knows that a human being one loves is beyond one's reach, and in danger. This helplessness and this gnawing uneasiness does something, at length, to even the toughest mind. Perhaps the best way to sum all this up is to say that the people I knew, felt, mainly, a peculiar kind of relief when they knew that their boys were being shipped out of the south, to do battle overseas. It was, perhaps, like feeling that the most dangerous part of a dangerous journey had been passed and that now, even if death should come, it would come with honor and without the complicity of their countrymen. Such a death would be, in short, a fact with which one could hope to live.

It was on the 28th of July, which I believe was a Wednesday, that I visited my father for the first time during his illness and for the last time in his life. The moment I saw him I knew why I had put off this visit so long. I had told my mother that I did not want to see him because I hated him. But this was not true. It was only that I *had* hated him and I wanted to hold on to this hatred. I did not want to look on him as a ruin: it was not a ruin I had hated. I imagine that one of the reasons people cling to their hates so stubbornly is because they sense, once hate is gone, that they will be forced to deal with pain.

We traveled out to him, his older sister and myself, to what seemed to be the very end of a very Long Island. It was hot and dusty and we wrangled, my aunt and I, all the way out, over the fact that I had recently begun to smoke and, as she said, to give myself airs. But I knew that she wrangled with me because she could not bear to face the fact of her brother's dying. Neither could I endure the reality of her despair, her unstated bafflement as to what had happened to her brother's life, and her own. So we wrangled and I smoked and from time to time she fell into a heavy reverie. Covertly, I watched her face, which was the face of an old woman; it had fallen in, the eyes were sunken and lightless; soon she would be dying, too.

In my childhood—it had not been so long ago—I had thought her beautiful. She had been quick-witted and quick-moving and very generous with all the children and each of her visits had been an event. At one time one of my brothers and myself had thought of running away to live with her. Now she could no longer produce out of her handbag some unexpected and yet familiar delight. She made me feel pity and revulsion and fear. It was awful to realize that she no longer caused me to feel affection. The closer we came to the hospital the more querulous she became and at the same time, naturally, grew more dependent on me. Between pity and guilt and fear I began to feel that there was another me trapped in my skull like a jack-in-the-box who might escape my control at any moment and fill the air with screaming.

She began to cry the moment we entered the room and she saw him lying there, all shriveled and still, like a little black monkey. The great, gleaming apparatus which fed him and would have compelled him to be still even if he had been able to move brought to mind, not beneficence, but torture; the tubes entering his arm made me think of pictures I had seen when a child, of Gulliver, tied down by the pygmies on that island. My aunt wept and wept, there was a whistling sound in my father's throat; nothing was said; he could not speak. I wanted to take his hand, to say something. But I do not know what I could have said, even if he could have heard me. He was not really in that room with us, he had at last really embarked on his journey; and though my aunt told me that he said he was going to meet Jesus, I did not hear anything except that whistling in his throat. The doctor came back and we left, into that unbearable train again, and home. In the morning came the telegram saying that he was dead. Then the house was suddenly full of relatives, friends, hysteria, and confusion and I quickly left my mother and the children to the care of those impressive women, who, in Negro communities at least, automatically appear at times of bereavement armed with lotions, proverbs, and patience, and an ability to cook. I went downtown. By the time I returned, later the same day, my mother had been carried to the hospital and the baby had been born.

For my father's funeral I had nothing black to wear and this posed a nagging problem all day long. It was one of those problems, simple, or impossible of solution, to which the mind insanely clings in order to avoid the mind's real trouble. I spent most of that day at the downtown apartment of a girl I knew, celebrating my birthday with whiskey and wondering what to wear that night. When planning a birthday celebration one naturally does not expect that it will be up against competition from a funeral and this girl had anticipated taking me out that night, for a big dinner and a night club afterwards. Sometime during the course of that long day we decided that we would go out anyway, when my father's funeral service was over. I imagine *I* decided it, since, as the funeral hour approached, it became clearer and clearer to me that I would not know what to do with myself when it was over. The girl, stifling her very lively concern as to the possible effects of the whiskey on one of my father's chief mourners, concentrated on being conciliatory and practically helpful. She found a black shirt for me somewhere and ironed it and, dressed in the darkest pants and jacket I owned, and slightly drunk, I made my way to my father's funeral.

The chapel was full, but not packed, and very quiet. There were, mainly, my father's relatives, and his children, and here and there I saw faces I had not seen since childhood, the faces of my father's one-time friends. They were very dark and solemn now, seeming somehow to suggest that they had known all along that something like this would happen. Chief among the mourners was my aunt, who had quarreled with my father all his life; by which I do not mean to suggest that her mourning was insincere or that she had not loved him. I suppose that she was one of the few people in the world who had, and their incessant quarreling proved precisely the strength of the tie that bound them. The only other person in the world, as far as I knew, whose relationship to my father rivaled my aunt's in depth was my mother, who was not there.

It seemed to me, of course, that it was a very long funeral. But it was, if anything, a rather shorter funeral than most, nor, since there were no overwhelming, uncontrollable expressions of grief, could it be called—if I dare to use the word—successful. The minister who preached my father's funeral sermon was one of the few my father had still been seeing as he neared his end. He presented to us in his sermon a man whom none of us had ever seen—a man thoughtful, patient, and forbearing, a Christian inspiration to all who knew him, and a model for his children. And no doubt the children, in their disturbed and guilty state, were almost ready to believe this; he had been remote enough to be anything and, anyway, the shock of the incontrovertible, that it was really our father lying up there in that casket, prepared the mind for anything. His sister moaned and this grief-stricken moaning was taken as corroboration. The other faces held a dark, non-committal thoughtfulness. This was not the man they had known, but they had scarcely expected to be confronted with *him;* this was, in a sense deeper than questions of fact, the man they had not known, and the man they had not known may have been the real one. The real man, whoever he had been, had suffered and now he was dead: this was all that was sure and all that mattered now. Every man in the chapel hoped that when his hour came he, too, would be eulogized, which is to say forgiven, and that all of his lapses, greeds, errors, and strayings from the truth would be invested with coherence and looked upon with charity. This was perhaps the last thing human beings could give each other and it was what they demanded, after all, of the Lord. Only the Lord saw the midnight tears, only He was present when one of His children, moaning and wringing hands, paced up and down the room. When one slapped one's child in anger the recoil in the heart reverberated through heaven and became part of the pain of the universe. And when the children were hungry and sullen and distrustful and one watched them, daily, growing wilder, and further away, and running headlong into danger, it was the Lord who knew what the charged heart endured as the strap was laid to the backside; the Lord alone who knew what one *would* have said if one had had, like the Lord, the gift of the living word. It was the Lord who knew of the impossibility every parent in that room faced: how to prepare the child for the day when the child would be despised and how to *create* in the child—by what means—a stronger antidote to this poison than one had found for oneself. The avenues, side streets, bars, billiard halls, hospitals, police stations, and even the playgrounds of Harlem—not to mention the houses of correction, the jails, and the morgue—testified to the potency of the poison while remaining silent as to the efficacy of whatever antidote, irresistibly raising the question of whether or not such an antidote existed; raising, which was worse, the question of whether or not an antidote was desirable; perhaps poison should be fought with poison. With these several schisms in the mind and with more terrors in the heart than could be named, it was better not to judge the man who had gone down under an impossible burden. It was better to remember: *Thou knowest this man's fall; but thou knowest not his wrassling.*

While the preacher talked and I watched the children—years of changing their diapers, scrubbing them, slapping them, taking them to school, and scolding them had had the perhaps inevitable result of making me love them, though I am not sure I knew this then—my mind was busily breaking out with a rash of disconnected impressions. Snatches of popular songs, indecent jokes, bits of books I have read, movie sequences, faces, voices, political issues—I thought I was going mad; all these impressions suspended, as it were, in the solution of the faint nausea produced in me by the heat and liquor. For a moment I had the impression that my alcoholic breath, inefficiently disguised with chewing gum, filled the entire chapel. Then someone began singing one of my father's favorite songs and, abruptly, I was with him, sitting on his knee, in the hot, enormous, crowded church which was the first church we attended. It was the Abyssinian Baptist Church on 138th Street. We had not gone there long. With this image, a host of others came. I had forgotten, in the rage of my growing up, how proud my father had been of me when I was little. Apparently, I had had a voice and my father had liked to show me off before the members of the church. I had forgotten what he had looked like when he was pleased but now I remembered that he had always been grinning with pleasure when my solos ended. I even remembered certain expressions on his face when he teased my mother—had he loved her? I would never know. And when had it all begun to change? For now it seemed that he had not always been cruel. I remembered being taken for a haircut and scraping my knee on the footrest of the barber's chair and I remembered my father's face as he soothed my crying and applied the stinging iodine. Then I remembered our fights, fights which had been of the worst possible kind because my technique had been silence.

I remembered the one time in all our life together when we had really spoken to each other.

It was on a Sunday and it must have been shortly before I left home. We were walking, just the two of us, in our usual silence, to or from church. I was in high school and had been doing a lot of writing and I was, at about this time, the editor of the high school magazine. But I had also been a Young Minister and had been preaching from the pulpit. Lately, I had been taking fewer engagements and preached as rarely as possible. It was said in the church, quite truthfully, that I was "cooling off."

My father asked me abruptly, "You'd rather write than preach, wouldn't you?"

I was astonished at his question—because it was a real question. I answered, "Yes."

That was all we said. It was awful to remember that that was all we had *ever* said.

The casket now was opened and the mourners were being led up the aisle to look for the last time on the deceased. The assumption was that the family was too overcome with grief to be allowed to make this journey alone and I watched while my aunt was led to the casket and, muffled in black, and shaking, led back to her seat. I disapproved of forcing the children to look on their dead father, considering that the shock of his death, or, more truthfully, the shock of death as a reality, was already a little more than a child could bear, but my judgment in this matter had been overruled and there they were, bewildered and frightened and very small, being led, one by one, to the casket. But there is also something very gallant about children at such moments. It has something to do with their silence and gravity and with the fact that one cannot help them. Their legs, somehow, seem *exposed*, so that it is at once incredible and terribly clear that their legs are all they have to hold them up.

I had not wanted to go to the casket myself and I certainly had not wished to be led there, but there was no way of avoiding either of these forms. One of the deacons led me up and I looked on my father's face. I cannot say that it looked like him at all. His blackness had been equivocated by powder and there was no suggestion in that casket of what his power had or could have been. He was simply an old man dead, and it was hard to believe that he had ever given anyone either joy or pain. Yet, his life filled that room. Further up the avenue his wife was holding his newborn child. Life and death so close together, and love and hatred, and right and wrong, said something to me which I did not want to hear concerning man, concerning the life of man.

After the funeral, while I was downtown desperately celebrating my birthday, a Negro soldier, in the lobby of the Hotel Braddock, got into a fight with a white policeman over a Negro girl. Negro girls, white policemen, in or out of uniform, and Negro males—in or out of uniform—were part of the furniture of the lobby of the Hotel Braddock and this was certainly not the first time such an incident had occurred. It was destined, however, to receive an unprecedented publicity, for the fight between the policeman and the soldier ended with the shooting of the soldier. Rumor, flowing immediately to the streets outside, stated that the soldier had been shot in the back, an instantaneous and revealing invention, and that the soldier had died protecting a Negro woman. The facts were somewhat different—for example, the soldier had not been shot in the back, and was not dead, and the girl seems to have been as dubious a symbol of womanhood as her white counterpart in Georgia usually is, but no one was interested in the facts. They preferred the invention because this invention expressed and corroborated their hates and fears so perfectly. It is just as well to remember that people are always doing this. Perhaps many of those legends, including Christianity, to which the world clings began their conquest of the world with just some such concerted surrender to distortion. The effect, in Harlem, of this particular legend was like the effect of a lit match in a tin of gasoline. The mob gathered before the doors of the Hotel Braddock simply began to swell and to spread in every direction, and Harlem exploded.

The mob did not cross the ghetto lines. It would have been easy, for example, to have gone over Morningside Park on the west side or to have crossed the Grand Central railroad tracks at 125th Street on the east side, to wreak havoc in white neighborhoods. The mob seems to have been mainly interested in something more potent and real than the white face, that is, in white power, and the principal damage done during the riot of the summer of 1943 was to white business establishments in Harlem. It might have been a far bloodier story, of course, if, at the hour the riot began, these establishments had still been open. From the Hotel Braddock the mob fanned out, east and west along 125th Street, and for the entire length of Lenox, Seventh and Eighth avenues. Along each of these avenues, and along each major side street—116th, 125th, 135th, and so on—bars, stores, pawnshops, restaurants, even little luncheonettes had been smashed open and entered and looted—looted, it might be added, with more haste than efficiency. The shelves really looked as though a bomb had struck them. Cans of beans and soup and dog food, along with toilet paper, corn flakes, sardines and milk tumbled every which way, and abandoned cash registers and cases of beer leaned crazily out of the splintered windows and were strewn along the avenues. Sheets, blankets, and clothing of every description formed a kind of path, as though people had dropped them while running. I truly had not realized that Harlem *had* so many stores until I saw them all smashed open; the first time the word *wealth* ever entered my mind in relation to Harlem was when I saw it scattered in the streets. But one's first, incongruous impression of plenty was countered immediately by an impression of waste. None of this was doing anybody any good. It would have been better to have left the plate glass as it had been and the goods lying in the stores.

It would have been better, but it would also have been intolerable, for Harlem had needed something to smash. To smash something is the ghetto's chronic need. Most of the time it is the members of the ghetto who smash each other, and themselves. But as long as the ghetto walls are standing there will always come a moment when these outlets do not work. That summer, for example, it was not enough to get into a fight on Lenox Avenue, or curse out one's cronies in the barber shops. If ever, indeed, the violence which fills Harlem's churches, pool halls, and bars erupts outward in a more direct fashion, Harlem and its citizens are likely to vanish in an apocalyptic flood. That this is not likely to happen is due to a great many reasons, most hidden and powerful among them the Negro's real relation to the white American. This relation prohibits, simply, anything as uncomplicated and satisfactory as pure hatred. In order really to hate white people, one has to blot so much out of the mind—and the heart—that this hatred itself becomes an exhausting and self-destructive pose. But this does not mean, on the other hand, that love comes easily: the white world is too powerful, too complacent, too ready with gratuitous humiliation, and, above all, too ignorant and too innocent for that. One is absolutely forced to make perpetual qualifications and one's own reactions are always cancelling each other out. It is this, really, which has driven so many people mad, both white and black. One is always in the position of having to decide between amputation and gangrene. Amputation is swift but time may prove that the amputation was not necessary—or one may delay the amputation too long. Gangrene is slow, but it is impossible to be sure that one is reading one's symptoms right. The idea of going through life as a cripple is more than one can bear, and equally unbearable is the risk of swelling up slowly, in agony, with poison. And the trouble, finally, is that the risks are real even if the choices do not exist.

"But as for me and my house," my father had said, "we will serve the Lord." I wondered, as we drove him to his resting place, what this line had meant to him. I had heard him preach it many times. I had preached it once myself, proudly giving it an interpretation different from my father's. Now the whole thing came back to me, as though my father and I were on our way to Sunday school and I were memorizing the golden text: *And if it seem evil unto you to serve the Lord, choose you this day whom you will serve; whether the gods which your fathers served that were on the other side of the flood, or the gods of the Amorites, in whose land ye dwell: but as for me and my house, we will serve the Lord.* I suspected in these familiar lines a meaning which had never been there for me before. All of my father's texts and songs, which I had decided were meaningless, were arranged before me at his death like empty bottles, waiting to hold the meaning which life would give them for me. This was his legacy: nothing is ever escaped. That bleakly memorable morning I hated the unbelievable streets and the Negroes and whites who had, equally, made them that way. But I knew that it was folly, as my father would have said, this bitterness was folly. It was necessary to hold on to the things that mattered. The dead man mattered, the new life mattered; blackness and whiteness did not matter; to believe that they did was to acquiesce in one's own destruction. Hatred, which could destroy so much, never failed to destroy the man who hated and this was an immutable law.

It began to seem that one would have to hold in the mind forever two ideas which seemed to be in opposition. The first idea was acceptance, the acceptance, totally without rancor, of life as it is, and men as they are: in the light of this idea, it goes without saying that injustice is a commonplace. But this did not mean that one could be complacent, for the second idea was of equal power: that one must never, in one's own life, accept these injustices as commonplace but must fight them with all one's strength. This fight begins, however, in the heart and it now had been laid to my charge to keep my own heart free of hatred and despair. This intimation made my heart heavy and, now that my father was irrecoverable, I wished that he had been beside me so that I could have searched his face for the answers which only the future would give me now.

MICHAEL LEONARD

Michael Leonard, a native of Boothbay Harbor, Maine, graduated from Bowdoin College in 1968. He is working on an advanced degree in Industrial Management at North Carolina State University. The following essay appeared first in *Quill: The Bowdoin College Literary Magazine* for Spring 1965.

Whale Hunt

It was the sound that brought me back to reality, a noise like hailstones or a hammer striking an iron roof. Then I knew that we were close to what we had been searching for the last few days. Being the lightest member of the crew, I had been given the mast watch. Now I began to search the horizon, my eyes making ever decreasing circles toward the boat.

The people who tell you whale hunting is gone forever and elaborate the dramatic side of the past should have been on the searing teak of the deck that day. The late part of Indian summer brought many things to the Maine coast. We had our harvest from the sea then in the form of lobsters and schools of fish that inhabited the peaceful inlets and quiet pine-encased coves. The fishermen set out seines to catch the vast schools of herring that leaped like silver flashes and swam like precision units in the shallows. The problem was that we were not the only ones after this catch. For weeks the men had been plagued by a whale which ripped through the cordage of their nets. The whale was only after food, and a captive meal kept him marauding our seines and destroying thousands of dollars worth of twine, and, in some cases, a man's chance to face the winter with something more than beans and salt fish.

My father had banded the fishermen together in one of our boats; it wasn't much to look at after ten months of work. The paint peeled off in yellow-white chunks, but only to show the heavy oak planks which are the symbol of Maine craftsmanship. Her insides weren't much better, permeated by the oppressive smell of rotten bait and decaying weed which none of us noticed but which made the tourists hold their breath and turn away with inflated cheeks and red faces. From the center of the cockpit rose the greasy Budda diesel. This was the fisherman's hope and security miles offshore, where an engine failure sometimes could mean a lonely death. We were in the second day of our search for the whale and, so far, no luck. However, the noise was as good as a sight, because we all knew it for a whale breathing. When whales blow after surfacing, it isn't the story book spout; it's a breath of vapor like a man's on a cold day and it has to rank among the world's worst smells: a cross between rotten eggs and old outhouses. As I searched the sparkling water, much clearer now that the summer boats were gone and the sand and weed had settled again, I knew I would never see the spout; it would be too small among the whitecaps, but turning to look at one of the many spruce-covered islands, I saw a glint like a mirror in the waves. There was no need to yell, even though I was about to burst from joy and excitement. Rather, I leaned over the mast hoops and pointed off to port. Suddenly the taciturn fishermen huddled around the engine were no more. My father sprang to the windward shrouds and up the mast. One man went forward, and two began to clear the harpoon line on the after deck. When my father was satisfied that the glint rolling along unaware was our target, he returned to the wheel and the pulsating chug of the diesel turned into a head-shattering roar as we came around and took up position behind the whale with the sun off our beam. The reflection was no longer blinding. We could all see the black head and dorsal fin rise rhythmically a few inches out of the water. We all also knew that there were probably thirty tons of living being under that spot. The whale dove just then, perhaps scared by the engine. My father gave up the wheel and went forward. In his right hand he held the ten foot pole with the sharp, malicious piece of metal at its tip. A few coils of line dangled from his left hand and ran along the deck like a sunburnt snake to the stern where the orange barrel with its staff and profusion of flags was set. We cruised for several minutes without seeing our quarry, then a shape like a giant black log rose from the depths ahead of us. We weren't in the 1950's any more; we were back more than half a century and there was a big man in sea boots and a navy wool jacket far from the bow on the thin wooden bridge of the tuna pulpit. He motioned slightly toward port; then toward himself. His commands, though silent, were obeyed as if a whip were over the men; they all knew that his word was law now. He slowly straightened up, his hands over his head clasping the shiny pole. He motioned again to the right, then his hands drove down in front and we heard the chunk of metal piercing unsuspecting blubber and bone. A thousand things exploded at once; my father yelled and the man at the wheel slammed the engine into full reverse. My father ducked behind the protective iron grating to avoid the loose harpoon pole which shot off to leeward like a javelin, and the man in the stern stepped back and punted the barrel into the foaming turbulence. We all rushed to the side as the bobbing orange blob started off toward Europe at a full eight knots. My father walked back to the cockpit, took over the wheel, and the men settled down, anticipating a long chase. After what seemed like hours the barrel stopped moving and bobbed peacefully in an ocean calmed by the approach of night. The men were tense again. Someone went forward to bring out the sheepskin case which held a .32 Winchester. This part was the most dangerous of the whole chase. The whale, although small, could still take the boat with him in his death flurry. His dark shape didn't seem as black or large as he slowly surfaced beside us. His tail flopped slightly, and the line which was wrapped around him disappeared in a circle of foamy red into his back. My father took the rifle and knelt over the gunwale. There was a crack; then the whale rolled fin up, dead. In the settling night the falling sun was reflected in his skin; we brought out ballast rocks and tied them to the line trailing from his body. The men looked at each other as he was cast adrift and disappeared in a swirling patch of milky red. They hated to kill anything unless it was a necessity, especially something so powerful and almost awesome.

The man with the rifle returned it carefully to its case, then took the wheel and said, "Michael, better turn on the running lights; we're going home."

RUBE MARQUARD

The great left-handed pitcher, Rube Marquard, played for John McGraw's New York Giants, who won three straight National League pennants (1911, 1912, 1913). During those three years, Marquard won seventy-three games and lost only twenty-eight, a better record than that of his great right-handed counterpart, Christy Mathewson (seventy-three wins, thirty-six losses). In 1912 he won nineteen straight games, still a major league record. But in 1914 he lost twelve consecutive games, an all-time New York Giant record! He won, however, over 200 games in the big leagues. The following story of how he made the majors was tape-recorded by Larry Ritter, who put together the wonderful baseball book, *The Glory of Their Times* (1966), which is not only a moving account of the early days of baseball as recalled by the men who played it, but an evocation of a raw, young, and optimistic America which will never be again.

I Become a Big Leaguer

> After twilight had gone, in the first darkness of the night, a freight train rumbled into the station. When the engine was switching cars on the sidetrack, he crept along the side of the train, pulled open the side door of an empty boxcar, and awkwardly and laboriously climbed in. He closed the door. The engine whistled. He was lying down, and in the darkness he smiled.
>
> —Jack London, *The Apostate*

My nickname being what it is, you probably automatically assume I must have been a country boy. That's what most people figure. But it's not so. Fact is, my father was the Chief Engineer of the city of Cleveland, and that's where I was born and reared.

Then how come I'm called "Rube"? Well, I'll get to that. But let me tell you about my father first. Like I say, he was the Chief Engineer of the city of Cleveland. As far as he was concerned, the only important thing was for me to get a good education. But as far back as I can remember all I could think of, morning, noon and night, was baseball.

"Now listen," Dad would say, "I want you to cut this out and pay attention to your studies. I want you to go to college when you're through high school, and I don't want any foolishness about it. Without an education you won't be able to get a good job, and then you'll *never* amount to anything."

"I already have a job," I'd say.

"You've got a job? What are you talking about?"

"I'm going to be a ballplayer."

"A ballplayer?" he'd say, and throw his hands up in the air. "What do you mean? How can you make a living being a ballplayer? I don't understand why a grown man would wear those funny-looking suits in the first place."

"Well," I'd answer, "you see policemen with uniforms on, and other people like that. They change after they're through working. It's the same way with ballplayers."

"Ha! Do ballplayers get paid?"

"Yes, they get paid."

"I don't believe it!"

And round and round we'd go. We'd have exactly the same argument at least once a week. Sometimes my grandfather—my father's father—would get involved in it. He liked baseball and he'd take my side.

"Listen," he'd say to my father, "when you were a youngster I wanted you to be something, too. I wanted you to be a stonecutter, same as I was when I came over from the old country. But no, you wouldn't listen. You wanted to be an engineer. So you became an engineer. Now Richard wants to be a baseball player. He's so determined that nothing is going to stop him. Let's give him a chance and see what he can do."

But Dad would never listen. "Ballplayers are no good," he'd say, "and they never will be any good."

And with that he'd slam the door and go outside and sit on the porch, and not talk to either my grandfather or me for the rest of the evening.

The thing is, I was always very tall for my age. I had three brothers and a sister, and my sister was the shortest of the five of us. She grew to be six feet two. So I was always hanging around the older kids and playing ball with them instead of with kids my own age. When I was about thirteen I used to carry bats for Napoleon Lajoie and Elmer Flick and Terry Turner and a lot of the other Cleveland Indians. They weren't called the Indians then. They were called the Cleveland Bronchos and then the Naps, after Napoleon Lajoie. After the regular season was over, a lot of them would barnstorm around the Cleveland area, and sometimes I'd be their bat boy.

Then later I even pitched a few games for Bill Bradley's Boo Gang. Bill Bradley was the Cleveland third baseman—one of the greatest who ever lived—and he also barnstormed with his Boo Gang after the season was over. So by the time I was only fifteen or sixteen I knew a lot of ballplayers, and I had my heart set on becoming a Big Leaguer myself.

One of my friends was a catcher named Howard Wakefield. He was about five years older than I was. In 1906 he was playing for the Waterloo club in the Iowa State League, and that summer—when I was only sixteen—I got a letter from him.

"We can use a good left-handed pitcher," the letter said, "and if you want to come to Waterloo I'll recommend you to the manager." I think Howard thought that I was at least eighteen or nineteen, because I was so big for my age.

I wrote Howard that my Dad didn't want me to play ball, so I didn't think he'd give me the money to go. If I asked him, he'd probably hit me over the head with something. Except for that, I was ready to go. Now if they could possibly arrange to send me some money for transportation. . . .

Well, pretty soon I got a telegram from the Waterloo manager. He said: "You've been recommended very highly by Howard Wakefield.

I'd like you to come out here and try out with us. If you make good, then we'll reimburse you for your transportation and give you a contract."

Of course, that wasn't much of an improvement over Howard's letter. So I went upstairs to my room and closed the door and wrote back a long letter to the manager, explaining that I didn't have any money for transportation. But if he sent me an advance right now for transportation, then I'd take the next train to Waterloo and he could take it off my salary later on, after I made good. I didn't have the slightest doubt that I would make good. And, of course, I didn't mention that I was only sixteen years old.

I mailed the letter to Iowa, and then I waited on pins and needles for an answer. Every day I had to be the first one to get at the mail, because if anyone else saw a letter to me from the Waterloo ball club that would have been enough to alert Dad to what was going on and I'd have been sunk. So every day I waited for the first sight of the mailman and tried to get to him before he reached the house.

As it turned out, I could have saved myself a lot of worrying. Because no letter ever came. Three weeks passed and still no answer. I couldn't understand what had gone wrong. Maybe it was against the rules to send transportation money to somebody not yet under contract? Maybe they didn't know how good I really was? Maybe this and maybe that.

Finally, I just couldn't stand it anymore. I gave some excuse to my folks about where I was going—like on an overnight camping trip with the Boy Scouts—and I took off for Waterloo, Iowa, on my own.

From Cleveland, Ohio, I bummed my way to Waterloo, Iowa. I was sixteen years old and I'd never been away from home before. It took me five days and five nights, riding freight trains, sleeping in open fields, hitching rides any way I could. My money ran out on the third day, and after that I ate when and how I could.

Finally, though, I arrived at my destination. It was early in the evening of the fifth day. The freight slowly drew into the Illinois Central station at Waterloo, Iowa, and just before it stopped I jumped off and went head over heels right in front of the passenger house. I hardly had time to pick myself up off the ground before the stationmaster grabbed me.

"What do you think you're doing?" he growled. "Come on, get out of here before I run you in."

"No," I said, "I'm reporting to the Waterloo ball club."

"You're what?" he says. "My God, did you ever wash your face?"

"Yes I did," I said, "but I've been traveling five days and five nights and I'm anxious to get to the ball park. Where do the ballplayers hang around?"

"At the Smoke Shop," he said, "down the street about half a mile.

If you walk down there probably whoever you're looking for will be there."

So I thanked him and told him I'd see that he got a free pass to the ball game as soon as I got settled, and started off for the Smoke Shop. It turned out that two brothers owned the Smoke Shop, and they also owned the ball club. One of them was behind the counter when I walked in. He took one look at me and let out a roar.

"What are you doing in here?" he yelled. "This is a respectable place. Get out of here."

"Wait a minute," I said. "I've got a telegram from the manager of the ball club to report here, and if I make good I'll get a contract."

"Are you kidding?" he said. "Who in the world ever recommended you?"

"Howard Wakefield did."

"Well," he said, "Wakefield is in back shooting billiards. We'll soon settle this!"

"I'd like to go back and see him," I said.

"Don't you go back there," he shouted. "You'll drive everybody out. Did you ever take a bath?"

"Of course I did," I said, "but I've bummed my way here and I haven't had a chance to clean up yet."

So he called to the back and in a minute out came Howard. "Holy Cripes!" he said. "What happened to you?"

I was explaining it to him when in came Mr. Frisbee, the manager, and I was introduced to him. "I received your telegram," I said. "I didn't have enough money to come first class or anything like that, but here I am."

"Keokuk is here tomorrow," he said, "and we'll pitch you."

"Tomorrow? You don't want me to pitch tomorrow, after what I've been through?"

"Tomorrow or never, young fellow!"

"All right," I said. "But could I have $5 in advance so I can get a clean shirt or something?"

"After the game tomorrow," he said, and walked away.

So Howard took me to his rooming house, and I cleaned up there and had something to eat, and they let me sleep on an extra cot they had.

The next day we went out to the ball park and I was introduced to the players and given a uniform that was too small for me. The Keokuk team was shagging balls while I warmed up, and they kept making comments about green rookies and bushers and how they'd knock me out of the box in the first inning. Oh, I felt terrible. I had an awful headache and I was exhausted. But I was determined to show them that I could make good, and I went out there and won that game, 6–1.

With that I felt sure I'd be offered a contract. So after the game I went to Mr. Frisbee and said, "Well, I showed you I could deliver the goods. Can we talk about a contract now?"

"Oh," he said, "Keokuk is in last place. Wait until Oskaloosa comes in this weekend. They're in second place. They're a tough team, and if you can beat them then we'll talk."

"Can't I get any money, any advance money, on my contract?" I asked him.

"You haven't got a contract," he said.

"All right," I said, and I didn't say another word.

That evening I didn't say anything to anybody. But when it got dark I went down to the railroad station, and the same stationmaster was there.

"Hey," he said, "you pitched a fine game today. I was there and you did a great job. What are you doing back here? Did you come to give me that free ticket you promised me?"

"No, I'm sorry," I said. "I'm going back home to Cleveland, and I want to know what time a freight comes by." And I explained to him everything that had happened.

He was very nice to me, and after we talked awhile he said, "Look, this train comes in at one o'clock in the morning and the engine unhooks and goes down to the water tower. When it does, you sneak into the baggage compartment, and meanwhile I'll talk to the baggage man before the engine gets hooked up again. Then when the train pulls out and is about five miles out of town he'll open the baggage door and let you out."

So that all happened, and when we were five miles out of town the door opened and the baggage man appeared. I talked with him all the way to Chicago, and as we got close to the yards he said to me, "OK, you better get ready to jump now. There are a lot of detectives around here and if you're not careful they'll grab you and throw you in jail. So once you get on he ground, don't hesitate. Beat it away from here as fast as you can."

The baggage man must have told the engineer about me, because we slowed down to a crawl just before we approached the Chicago yards, and off I jumped. I got out of there quick and took off down the street. I don't know what street it was, and I'm not sure where I was headed, but I do remember that I was awfully tired. It was the middle of the morning and I had hardly slept a wink the night before.

I'd walked about three or four blocks when I passed by a fire engine house. Evidently all the firemen were out at a fire, because the place was empty. I was tired, so I went in and sat down. Well, they had a big-bellied iron stove in there, and it was warm, and I guess I must have fallen asleep, because the next thing I knew a couple of firemen were shaking me and doing everything they could to wake me up. They called me a bum and a lot of other names, and told me to get out of there or they'd have me thrown in jail.

"I'm no bum," I said, "I'm a ballplayer."

"What, you a ballplayer! Where did you ever play?"

So I told them: Cleveland, around the sandlots, and in Waterloo, Iowa, too. And I told them all about it.

They still didn't really believe me. They asked me did I know Three-Fingered Brown, Tinker, Evers, Chance, and all those fellows.

"No," I said, "I don't know them. But some day I'll be playing with them, or against them, because I'm going to get in the Big Leagues."

"Where are you going now?" they asked me.

"Back home to Cleveland."

"Have you got any money?"

"No."

So they got up a little pool of about $5 and said, "Well, on your way. And use this to get something to eat."

I thanked them, and as I left I told them that some day I'd be back. "When I get to the Big Leagues," I said, "I'm coming out to visit you when we get to Chicago."

And home I went. I played around home all the rest of that summer, and then the next summer, 1907, I got a job with an ice-cream company in Cleveland. I made $25 a week: $15 for checking the cans on the truck that would take the ice cream away, and $10 a Sunday, when I pitched for the company team. It was a good team. We played the best semipro clubs in the Cleveland area, and I beat them all. I was only seventeen, but I hardly lost a game.

Then one day I got a postal card from the Cleveland ball club, asking me to come in and talk to them. Mr. Kilfoyl and Mr. Somers, the owners of the club, wanted to see me.

My Dad saw the card. "I see you still want to be a ballplayer," he said.

"Yes, I do. And I'm going to be a great one, too. You wait and see. Some day you're going to be proud of me."

"Yeah," he said, "proud of nothing."

But I went to the Cleveland club's office anyway, and Mr. Kilfoyl and Mr. Somers were both there.

"I received your card," I said. "You know, you got me in a little jam. My dad doesn't want me to be a ballplayer."

"Don't you worry," Mr. Kilfoyl said, "after you sign with us and get into the Big Leagues he'll think differently about it."

"Well," I said, "I'm not signing with you or anybody else until I hear what you're offering. I've been taken advantage of before, and it's not going to happen again. I know a lot of ballplayers and they always tell me not to sign with anybody unless I get a good salary. They all tell me you better get it when you're young, 'cause you sure won't get it when you're old."

"That's a lot of nonsense," Mr. Kilfoyl said. "Don't you worry. We'll treat you right. We'll give you $100 a month. That's a wonderful offer."

"I think he'll be overpaid," Mr. Somers says.

"I don't think that's so wonderful," I said. "And as for being overpaid, I get that much right now from the ice-cream company, and in addition I get to eat all the ice cream I want."

They wouldn't increase their price, and I wouldn't reduce mine, so I left and went home. On the way home, though, I stopped in this sporting-goods store at 724 Prospect Avenue. It was owned by Bill Bradley and Charlie Carr, and was a popular hangout for ballplayers. Bill Bradley, of course, played third base for Cleveland, and Charlie Carr managed and played first base for Indianapolis in the American Association.

When I walked in the door Bill Bradley said, "Hello, Big Leaguer, I understand the boss wants to sign you up."

"Not me," I said, "he wouldn't pay me as much as I already make with the ice-cream company."

"You know, I manage the Indianapolis club," Charlie Carr said.

"I know that."

"How would you like to sign with me?"

"You're in the minor leagues," I said. "If a major-league club won't pay me what I want, how could you do it?"

"How much do you want?"

I took a deep breath. "Two hundred a month."

"Wow! You want all the money, don't you!" he said.

"No, but you want a good pitcher, don't you?"

"Yes."

"Well," I said, "I'm one."

And darned if he didn't agree to it. So right then and there I signed my first professional contract, with Indianapolis of the American Association.

When I got home that night I had to tell my Dad about it, because I was to leave for Indianapolis the next day. Oh, that was a terrible night. Finally, Dad said, "Now listen, I've told you time and time again that I don't want you to be a professional ballplayer. But you've got your mind made up. Now I'm going to tell you something: when you cross that threshold, don't come back. I don't ever want to see you again."

"You don't mean that, Dad," I said.

"Yes I do."

"Well, I'm going," I said, "and some day you'll be proud of me."

"Proud!" he said. "You're breaking my heart, and I don't ever want to see you again."

"I won't break your heart," I said. "I'll add more years to your life. You wait and see."

So I went to Indianapolis. They optioned me out to Canton in the Central League for the rest of the 1907 season, and I won 23 games with them, which was one-third of all the games the Canton club won that year.

Next year—that would be 1908—I went to spring training with the Indianapolis club. We went to French Lick Springs, Indiana. After three weeks there we went back to Indianapolis and played a few exhibition games before the season opened. Well, believe it or not, the first club to come in for an exhibition game was the Cleveland team: Napoleon Lajoie, Terry Turner, Elmer Flick, George Stovall, and the whole bunch that I used to carry bats for. When they came on the field I was already warming up.

"Hey, what are you doing here?" a couple of them yelled at me. "Are you the bat boy here?"

"No," I said, "I'm a pitcher."

"You, a pitcher? Who do you think you're kidding?"

"Just ask Bill Bradley. He was there when I signed my first contract. You'll see, I'm going to pitch against you guys today, and I'm going to beat you, too."

"Beat us! Busher, you couldn't beat a drum!"

So then Bill Bradley came over and said hello. As he was leaving he said, "Richard, you're a nice boy, so I want to give you some advice before today's game. Be careful of the Frenchman." He meant Napoleon Lajoie. He said, "The Frenchman is very sharp and he's been hitting terrific line drives this past week. He's almost killed three of our own pitchers in practice, so there's no telling what he'll do in a real game, even if it is just an exhibition game."

I thanked him, of course, and went back to warming up. Well, I pitched the whole nine innings and beat them, 2–0. Lajoie got two hits off me, and I think George Stovall got a couple, but I shut them out—and I wasn't killed, either.

That night Charlie Carr called me over. "You know," he said, "a funny thing just happened. Mr. Somers, the owner of the Cleveland club, just came over to my hotel room and wanted to buy you. He offered me $3,500 for your contract with the understanding that you'd stay here all season, to get more experience, and then you would join the Cleveland club next year."

"Charlie," I said, "if you sell me to Somers I'm going right back to the ice-cream company. He had first chance to get me, and he wouldn't give me what I deserved. I won't play for Cleveland, no matter what."

"OK," he said, "don't worry. I won't sell you. Later on I'll be able to sell you for a lot more, anyway."

On opening day Kansas City was at Indianapolis, and I pitched the opening game. I won, 2–1, and that evening the story in the Indianapolis *Star* read like this: "The American Association season opened up today, and it was a beautiful game between two fine teams. Each had great pitching, with an eighteen-year-old right-hander pitching for Kansas City and an eighteen-year-old left-hander for the home team. The right-hander with Kansas City looks like he's going to develop into a great pitcher. They call him Smoky Joe Wood. But we have a left-hander with Indianapolis who is going places, too. He resembles one of the great left-handed pitchers of all time: Rube Waddell." And from that day on they nicknamed me "Rube."

I had a wonderful season that year with Indianapolis. I pitched 47 complete games, won 28 of them, led the league in most strikeouts, least hits, most innings pitched, and everything. Occasionally what I'd do would be reported in the Cleveland papers, and friends of mine would tell me that they'd pass by the house and see Dad sitting on the porch.

"Well, Fred," they'd say—that was my Dad's name, Fred—"did you see what your son Rube did yesterday?"

"Who are you talking about?" he'd say. "Rube who?"

"Your son, Richard."

"I told him baseball was no good," my Dad would reply. "Now they've even gone and changed his name!"

Anyway, I had a terrific year with Indianapolis, like I said. Late in the season we went into Columbus, Ohio, and Charlie Carr came up to me before the game.

"Rube," he said, "there are going to be an awful lot of celebrities here at the game today. The American and National Leagues both have an off-day, and they're all coming to see you pitch. If you pitch a good game I may be able to sell you before the night is out."

"For how much?" I asked.

"I don't know," he said, "but a lot. It depends on what kind of game you pitch."

"Will you cut me in?"

"No, I won't," he said. "You're getting a good salary and you know it."

"OK," I said, "I was only kidding anyway."

"I don't want you to get nervous today," he said.

"Nervous? Have I ever been nervous all season?"

"No," he said. "I've been in baseball a long time and I never saw anything like it. I never saw a kid like you, who can beat anybody and is so successful."

"Well," I said, "the reason I'm so successful is because I can beat anybody."

I went out there that day and I pitched one of those unusual games: no hits, no runs, no errors. Twenty-seven men faced me and not one of them got to first base. And that evening in Columbus they put me up for sale, with all the Big-League clubs bidding on me, like a horse being auctioned off. The Cleveland club went as high as $10,500 for my contract, but the Giants went to $11,000, and I was sold to them. At that time that was the highest price ever paid for a baseball player.

I reported to the New York Giants in September of 1908, as soon as the American Association season was over. I was eighteen years old and I was in the Big Leagues!

I came up too late in the season to make a trip to Chicago with the Giants that year, but the next season we made our first trip to Chicago the second week in June. And the first thing I did, as soon as I got there, was to make a beeline for that firehouse.

The only one there when I first got there was the lieutenant. I walked up to him and said, "Lieutenant, do you remember me?"

"Never saw you before in my life," he said.

"Well, remember about three years ago you caught me sleeping back of that stove there?"

"Oh, are you the kid from Cleveland that said he's a ballplayer?"

"Yes. Remember me? My name is Marquard, Richard Marquard."

"Of course. What are you doing here?"

"I'm in the Big Leagues," I said. "I told you when I got to the Big Leagues I was coming out to visit you."

"Well, I'll be darned," he said. "Who are you with?"

"Why, I'm with the New York Giants."

And boy, for years after that, whenever the Giants would come to Chicago I'd go out to that firehouse. I'd sit out front and talk for hours. The firemen would have all the kids in the neighborhood there . . . and all the families that lived around would stop by . . . and it was really wonderful. Everybody was so nice and friendly. Gee, I used to enjoy that. It was a great thrill for me.

Actually, every single day of all the years I spent in the Big Leagues was a thrill for me. It was like a dream come true. I was in the Big Leagues for eighteen years, you know, from 1908 through 1925. I was with the Giants until 1915, with the Dodgers for five years after that, with Cincinnati for one year, and then with the Boston Braves for four. And I loved every single minute of it.

The best years of all were those with the Giants. I don't mean because those were my best pitching years, although they were. In 1911 I won 24 games and lost only 7, and in 1912 I won 26. That's the year I won 19 straight—I didn't lose a single game in 1912 until July 8!

Actually, I won 20 straight, not 19, but because of the way they scored then I didn't get credit for one of them. I relieved Jeff Tesreau in the eighth inning of a game one day, with the Giants behind, 3–2. In the ninth inning Heinie Groh singled and Art Wilson homered, and we won, 4–3. But they gave Tesreau credit for the victory instead of me. Except for that it would have been 20 straight wins, not 19. Well, at any rate that record has stood up for a long time now. Over fifty years.

And, of course, I had other great years with the Giants, too. In 1914 I beat Babe Adams and the Pirates in a 21-inning game, 3–1. Both of us went the entire distance that day, all 21 innings. And in 1915 I pitched a no-hitter against Brooklyn and beat Nap Rucker, 2–0.

But that isn't why I remember my years with the Giants best. Maybe it's because that was my first club. I don't know. Whatever the reason, though, it was wonderful to be a Giant back then, from 1908 to 1915.

Take Mr. McGraw. What a great man he was! The finest and grandest man I ever met. He loved his players and his players loved him. Of course, he wouldn't stand for any nonsense. You had to live up to the rules and regulations of the New York Giants, and when he laid down the law you'd better abide by it.

I'll never forget one day we were playing Pittsburgh, and it was Red Murray's turn to bat, with the score tied in the ninth inning. There was a man on second with none out. Murray came over to McGraw—I was sitting next to McGraw on the bench—and he said, "What do you want me to do, Mac?"

"What do I want you to do?" McGraw said. "What are you doing in the National League? There's the winning run on second base and no one out. What would you do if you were the manager?"

"I'd sacrifice the man to third," Murray said.

"Well," McGraw said, "that's exactly what I want you to do."

So Murray went up to the plate to bunt. After he got to the batter's box, though, he backed out and looked over at McGraw again.

McGraw poked his elbow in my ribs. "Look at that so-and-so," he said. "He told me what he should do, and I told him what he should do, and now he's undecided. I bet he forgot from the bench to the plate."

Now, in those days—and I guess it's the same now—when a man was up there to bunt the pitcher would try to keep the ball high and tight. Well, it so happened that Red was a high-ball hitter. Howie Camnitz was pitching for Pittsburgh. He wound up and in came the ball, shoulder high. Murray took a terrific cut at it and the ball went over the left-field fence. It was a home run and the game was over.

Back in the clubhouse Murray was happy as a lark. He was first into the showers, and out boomed his wonderful Irish tenor, singing "My Wild Irish Rose." When he came out of the shower, still singing, McGraw walked over and tapped him on the shoulder. All of us were watching out of the corner of our eyes, because we knew The Little Round Man—that's what we used to call McGraw—wouldn't let this one go by without saying *something.*

"Murray, what did I tell you to do?" McGraw asked him.

"You told me to bunt," Murray said, not looking quite so happy anymore. "But you know what happened, Mac. Camnitz put one right in my gut, so I cow-tailed it."

"Where did you say he put it?"

"Right in my gut," Murray says again.

"Well," McGraw said, "I'm fining you $100, and you can try putting that right in your gut, too!" And off he went.

Oh, God, I never laughed so much in my life! Murray never did live that down. Years later something would happen and we'd yell to Murray, "Hey Red, is that right in your gut?"

There were a lot of grand guys on that club: Christy Mathewson and Chief Meyers, Larry Doyle and Fred Snodgrass, Al Bridwell and Bugs Raymond. Bugs Raymond! What a terrific spitball pitcher he was. Bugs drank a lot, you know, and sometimes it seemed like the more he drank the better he pitched. They used to say he didn't spit on the ball: he blew his breath on it, and the ball would come up drunk.

Actually, there was very little drinking in baseball in those days. Myself, I've never smoked or taken a drink in my life to this day. I always said you can't burn the candle at both ends. You want to be a ballplayer, be a ballplayer. If you want to go out and carouse and chase around, do that. But you can't do them both at once.

Of course, when we were on the road we had a nightly eleven o'clock bed check. At eleven o'clock we all had to be in our rooms and the trainer would come around and check us off. We'd usually have a whole floor in a hotel and we'd be two in a room. I always roomed with Matty all the while I was on the Giants. What a grand guy he was! The door would be wide open at eleven o'clock and the trainer would come by with a board with all the names on it. He'd poke his head in: Mathewson, Marquard, check. And lock the door. Next room, check, lock the door.

As far as I was concerned, I never drank a drop even when I was in show business. In 1912 I made a movie with Alice Joyce and Maurice Costello, and then I was in vaudeville for three years, Blossom Seeley and I. That's when she was my wife. It didn't work out, though. I asked her to quit the stage. I told her I could give her everything she wanted.

"No," she said, "show business is show business."

"Well," I said, "baseball is mine." So we separated.

How did I feel when I was traded from the Giants to the Dodgers? Well, not too bad. See, I traded myself. I didn't seem to be able to get going in 1915 after I pitched that no-hitter early in April, and late in the season McGraw started riding me. That was a very bad year for the Giants, you know. We were favored to win the pennant, and instead we wound up last. So McGraw wasn't very happy. After I'd taken about as much riding as I could stand, I asked him to trade me if he thought I was so bad.

"Who would take you?" he said.

"What do you mean?" I said. "I can still lick any club in the league." Heck, I wasn't twenty-six years old yet.

"Lick any club in the league?" McGraw said. "You couldn't lick a postage stamp."

"Give me a chance to trade myself, then," I said. "What would you sell me for?"

"$7,500," he answered.

"OK," I said, "can I use your phone?"

"Sure," he said. We were both pretty mad.

So I got hold of the operator and asked her to get me Wilbert Robinson, manager of the Brooklyn club. See, Robbie had been a coach with us for years before he became the Dodger manager in 1914. After a while she got Robbie on the phone.

"Hello," he says.

"How are you, Robbie?" I said.

"Fine," he said. "Who is this?"

"How would you like to have a good left-handed pitcher?"

"I'd love it," he said. "Who is this? Who's the man? Who are you going to recommend?"

"I'm going to recommend myself."

"Who are you?"

"Rube Marquard."

"Oh, what are you kidding around for, Rube?" he said. "I have to go out on the field and I don't have time to fool around."

"No, I'm serious," I said. "McGraw is right here and he says he'll sell me for $7,500. Do you want to talk to him?"

"Of course I do," Robbie said. And right then and there I was traded from the Giants to the Dodgers.

And, of course, we—the Dodgers, that is—won the pennant the next year, and I had one of the best years I ever had. I think I had an earned run average of about 1.50 in 1916. And then we won the pennant again in 1920. So everything worked out pretty well.

One day when I was pitching for Brooklyn I pitched the first game of a double-header against Boston and beat them, 1–0. I was in the clubhouse during the second game, taking off my uniform, when the clubhouse boy came in.

"Rube," he said, "there's an elderly gentleman outside who wants to see you. He says he's your father from Cleveland."

"He's not my father," I said. "My father wouldn't go across the street to see me. But you go out and get his autograph book and bring it in, and I'll autograph it for him."

But instead of bringing in the book, he brought in my Dad. And we were both delighted to see one another.

"Boy, you sure are a hardhead," he said to me. "You know I didn't mean what I said ten years ago."

"What about you, Dad?" I said. "You're as stubborn as I am. I thought you never wanted to see me again. I thought you meant it."

"Of course I didn't," he said.

After we talked a while, I said, "Did you see the game today?"

"Yes, I did," he said.

"Where were you sitting?" I asked him.

"Well, you know the man who wears that funny thing on his face?"

"You mean the mask? The catcher?"

"I guess so. Well, anyway, I was halfway between him and the number one—you know, where they run right after they hit the ball."

"You mean first base?"

"I don't know," he said. "I don't know what they call it. I was sitting in the middle there."

"How many ball games have you seen since I became a ballplayer, Dad?"

"This is the first one," he said.

Well, he stayed in New York with me for a few weeks, and we had a great time. Finally, he had to go back to Cleveland. After he'd left, the newspapers heard about my Dad and they wanted to know his address back home. So I gave it to them, and doggone if they didn't send reporters and photographers to Cleveland to interview him.

They took his picture and asked him a lot of questions. One of the things they asked him was whether he had ever played very much baseball himself.

"Oh, of course I did, when I was younger," he told them. "I used to love to play baseball. I used to be a pitcher, just like my son Richard—I mean like my son Rube."

"Are you proud of your son?" they asked him.

"I certainly am," Dad said. "Why shouldn't I be? He's a great baseball player, isn't he?"

E. B. WHITE

E. B. White was born in Mount Vernon, New York, in 1899. After service in the army in World War I, he graduated from Cornell in 1921. While at Cornell he took an English course from the illustrious William Strunk, Jr., and later helped reissue Strunk's "Little Book," *The Elements of Style*, a sane and concise guide to writing which is still used to effect in American classrooms. A frequent contributor to *The New Yorker*, E. B. White's writings include the wonderful children's story *Charlotte's Web* (1952) and *One Man's Meat* (1942), a collection of some of his finest essays, from which the following selection comes.

Once More to the Lake

One summer, along about 1904, my father rented a camp on a lake in Maine and took us all there for the month of August. We all got ringworm from some kittens and had to rub Pond's Extract on our arms and legs night and morning, and my father rolled over in a canoe with all his clothes on; but outside of that the vacation was a success and from then on none of us ever thought there was any place in the world like that lake in Maine. We returned summer after summer—always on August 1st for one month. I have since become a salt-water man, but sometimes in summer there are days when the restlessness of the tides and the fearful cold of the sea water and the incessant wind which blows across the afternoon and into the evening make me wish for the placidity of a lake in the woods. A few weeks ago this feeling got so strong I bought myself a couple of bass hooks and a spinner and returned to the lake where we used to go, for a week's fishing and to revisit old haunts.

I took along my son, who had never had any fresh water up his nose and who had seen lily pads only from train windows. On the journey over to the lake I began to wonder what it would be like. I wondered how time would have marred this unique, this holy spot—the coves and streams, the hills that the sun set behind, the camps and the paths behind the camps. I was sure that the tarred road would have found it out and I wondered in what other ways it would be desolated. It is strange how much you can remember about places like that once you allow your mind to return into the grooves which lead back. You remember one thing, and that suddenly reminds you of another thing. I guess I remembered clearest of all the early mornings, when the lake was cool and motionless, remembered how the bedroom smelled of the lumber it was made of and of the wet woods whose scent entered through the screen. The partitions in the camp were thin and did not extend clear to the top of the rooms, and as I was always the first up I would dress softly so as not to wake the others, and sneak out into the sweet outdoors and start out in the canoe, keeping close along the shore in the long shadows of the pines. I remembered being very careful never to rub my paddle against the gunwale for fear of disturbing the stillness of the cathedral.

The lake had never been what you would call a wild lake. There were cottages sprinkled around the shores, and it was in farming country although the shores of the lake were quite heavily wooded. Some of the cottages were owned by nearby farmers, and you would live at the shore and eat your meals at the farmhouse. That's what our family did. But although it wasn't wild, it was a fairly large and undisturbed lake and there were places in it which, to a child at least, seemed infinitely remote and primeval.

I was right about the tar: it led to within half a mile of the shore. But when I got back there, with my boy, and we settled into a camp near a farmhouse and into the kind of summertime I had known, I could tell that it was going to be pretty much the same as it had been before—I knew it, lying in bed the first morning, smelling the bedroom, and hearing the boy sneak quietly out and go off along the shore in a boat. I began to sustain the illusion that he was I, and therefore, by simple transposition, that I was my father. This sensation persisted, kept cropping up all the time we were there. It was not an entirely new feeling, but in this setting it grew much stronger. I seemed to be living a dual existence. I would be in the middle of some simple act, I would be picking up a bait box or laying down a table fork, or I would be saying something, and suddenly it would be not I but my father who was saying the words or making the gesture. It gave me a creepy sensation.

We went fishing the first morning. I felt the same damp moss covering the worms in the bait can, and saw the dragonfly alight on the tip of my rod as it hovered a few inches from the surface of the water. It was the arrival of this fly that convinced me beyond any doubt that everything was as it always had been, that the years were a mirage and there had been no years. The small waves were the same, chucking the rowboat under the chin as we fished at anchor, and the boat was the same boat, the same color green and the ribs broken in the same places, and under the floor-boards the same fresh-water leavings and dé-bris—the dead helgramite, the wisps of moss, the rusty discarded fishhook, the dried blood from yesterday's catch. We stared silently at the tips of our rods, at the dragonflies that came and went. I lowered the tip of mine into the water, tentatively, pensively dislodging the fly, which darted two feet away, poised, darted two feet back, and came to rest again a little farther up the rod. There had been no years between the ducking of this dragonfly and the other one—the one that was part of memory. I looked at the boy, who was silently watching his fly, and it was my hands that held his rod, my eyes watching. I felt dizzy and didn't know which rod I was at the end of.

We caught two bass, hauling them in briskly as though they were mackerel, pulling them over the side of the boat in a businesslike manner without any landing net, and stunning them with a blow on the back of the head. When we got back for a swim before lunch, the lake was exactly were we had left it, the same number of inches from the dock, and there was only the merest suggestion of a breeze. This seemed an utterly enchanted sea, this lake you could leave to its own devices for a few hours and come back to, and find that it had not stirred, this constant and trustworthy body of water. In the shallows, the dark, water-soaked sticks and twigs, smooth and old, were undulating in clusters on the bottom against the clean ribbed sand, and the track of the mussel was plain. A school of minnows swam by, each minnow with its small individual shadow, doubling the attendance, so clear and sharp in the sunlight. Some of the other campers were in swimming, along the shore, one of them with a cake of soap, and the water felt thin and clear and unsubstantial. Over the years there had been this person with the cake of soap, this cultist, and here he was. There had been no years.

Up to the farmhouse to dinner through the teeming, dusty field, the road under our sneakers was only a two-track road. The middle track was missing, the one with the marks of the hooves and the splotches of dried, flaky manure. There had always been three tracks to choose from in choosing which track to walk in; now the choice was narrowed down to two. For a moment I missed terribly the middle alternative. But the way led past the tennis court, and something about the way it lay there in the sun reassured me; the tape had loosened along the backline, the alleys were green with plantains and other weeds, and the net (installed in June and removed in September) sagged in the dry noon, and the whole place steamed with midday heat and hunger and emptiness. There was a choice of pie for dessert, and one was blueberry and one was apple, and the waitresses were the same country girls, there having been no passage of time, only the illusion of it as in a dropped curtain—the waitresses were still fifteen; their hair had been washed, that was the only difference—they had been to the movies and seen the pretty girls with the clean hair.

Summertime, oh summertime, pattern of life indelible, the fade-proof lake, the woods unshatterable, the pasture with the sweetfern and the juniper forever and ever, summer without end; this was the background, and the life along the shore was the design, the cottagers with their innocent and tranquil design, their tiny docks with the flagpole and the American flag floating against the white clouds in the blue sky, the little paths over the roots of the trees leading from camp to camp and the paths leading back to the outhouses and the can of lime for sprinkling, and at the souvenir counters at the store the miniature birch-bark canoes and the post cards that showed things looking a little better than they looked. This was the American family at play, escaping the city heat, wondering whether the newcomers in the camp at the head of the cove were "common" or "nice," wondering whether it was true that the people who drove up for Sunday dinner at the farmhouse were turned away because there wasn't enough chicken.

It seemed to me, as I kept remembering all this, that those times and those summers had been infinitely precious and worth saving. There had been jollity and peace and goodness. The arriving (at the beginning of August) had been so big a business in itself, at the railway station the farm wagon drawn up, the first smell of the pine-laden air, the first glimpse of the smiling farmer, and the great importance of the trunks and your father's enormous authority in such matters, and the feel of the wagon under you for the long ten-mile haul, and at the top of the last long hill catching the first view of the lake after eleven months of not seeing this cherished body of water. The shouts and cries of the other campers when they saw you, and the trunks to be unpacked, to give up their rich burden. (Arriving was less exciting nowadays, when you sneaked up in your car and parked it under a tree near the camp and took out the bags and in five minutes it was all over, no fuss, no loud wonderful fuss about trunks.)

Peace and goodness and jollity. The only thing that was wrong now, really, was the sound of the place, an unfamiliar nervous sound of the outboard motors. This was the note that jarred, the one thing that would sometimes break the illusion and set the years moving. In those other summertimes all motors were inboard; and when they were at a little distance, the noise they made was a sedative, an ingredient of summer sleep. They were one-cylinder and two-cylinder engines, and some were make-and-break and some were jump-spark, but they all made a sleepy sound across the lake. The one-lungers throbbed and fluttered, and the twin cylinder ones purred and purred, and that was a quiet sound too. But now the campers all had outboards. In the daytime, in the hot mornings, these motors made a petulant, irritable sound; at night, in the still evening when the afterglow lit the water, they whined about one's ears like mosquitoes. My boy loved our rented outboard, and his great desire was to achieve singlehanded mastery over it, and authority, and he soon learned the trick of choking it a little (but not too much), and the adjustment of the needle valve. Watching him I would remember the things you could do with the old one-cylinder engine with the heavy flywheel, how you could have it eating out of your hand if you got really close to it spiritually. Motor boats in those days didn't have clutches, and you would make a landing by shutting off the motor at the proper time and coasting in with a dead rudder. But there was a way of reversing them, if you learned the trick, by cutting the switch and putting it on again exactly on the final dying revolution of the flywheel, so that it would kick back against compression and begin reversing. Approaching a dock in a strong following breeze, it was difficult to slow up sufficiently by the ordinary coasting method, and if a boy felt he had complete mastery over his motor, he was tempted to keep it running beyond its time and then reverse it a few feet from the dock. It took a cool nerve, because if you threw the switch a twentieth of a second too soon you would catch the flywheel when it still had speed enough to go up past center, and the boat would leap ahead, charging bull-fashion at the dock.

We had a good week at the camp. The bass were biting well and the sun shone endlessly, day after day. We would be tired at night and lie down in the accumulated heat of the little bedrooms after the long hot day and the breeze would stir almost imperceptibly outside and the smell of the swamp drift in through the rusty screens. Sleep would come easily and in the morning the red squirrel would be on the roof, tapping out his gay routine. I kept remembering everything, lying in bed in the mornings—the small steamboat that had a long rounded stern like the lip of a Ubangi, and how quietly she ran on the moonlight sails, when the older boys played their mandolins and the girls sang and we ate doughnuts dipped in sugar, and how sweet the music was on the water in the shining night, and what it had felt like to think about girls then. After breakfast we would go up to the store and the things were in the same place—the minnows in a bottle, the plugs and spinners disarranged and pawed over by the youngsters from the boys' camp, the fig newtons and the Beeman's gum. Outside, the road was tarred and cars stood in front of the store. Inside, all was just as it had always been, except there was more Coca Cola and not so much Moxie and root beer and birch beer and sarsaparilla. We would walk out with a bottle of pop apiece and sometimes the pop would backfire up our noses and hurt. We explored the streams, quietly, where the turtles slid off the sunny logs and dug their way into the soft bottom; and we lay on the town wharf and fed worms to the tame bass. Everywhere we went I had trouble making out which was I, the one walking at my side, the one walking in my pants.

One afternoon while we were there at that lake a thunderstorm came up. It was like the revival of an old melodrama that I had seen long ago with childish awe. The second-act climax of the drama of the electrical disturbance over a lake in America had not changed in any important respect. This was the big scene, still the big scene. The whole thing was so familiar, the first feeling of oppression and a general air around camp of not wanting to go very far away. In midafternoon (it was all the same) a curious darkening of the sky, and a lull in everything that had made life tick; and then the way the boats suddenly swung the other way at their moorings with the coming of a breeze out of the new quarter, and the premonitory rumble. Then the kettle drum, then the snare, then the bass drum and cymbals, then crackling light against the dark, and the gods grinning and licking their chops in the hills. Afterward the calm, the rain steadily rustling in the calm lake, the return of light and hope and spirits, and the campers running out in joy and relief to go swimming in the rain, their bright cries perpetuating the deathless joke about how they were getting simply drenched, and the children screaming with delight at the new sensation of bathing in the rain, and the joke about getting drenched linking the generations in a strong indestructible chain. And the comedian who waded in carrying an umbrella.

When the others went swimming my son said he was going in too. He pulled his dripping trunks from the line where they had hung all through the shower, and wrung them out. Languidly, and with no thought of going in, I watched him, his hard little body, skinny and bare, saw him wince slightly as he pulled up around his vitals the small, soggy, icy garment. As he buckled the swollen belt suddenly my groin felt the chill of death.

WOODY GUTHRIE

Woody Guthrie, American composer and folk singer, was born in Okemah, Oklahoma, in 1912 and died in 1967. Like John Steinbeck in *The Grapes of Wrath*, Guthrie was a spokesman for the migrant workers of the depression years. He was a self-taught musician and never learned to read a note of music. He wrote, however, over a thousand songs, including "So Long, It's Been Good to Know You" and "This Land Is Your Land." The following selection is the first chapter of his autobiography, *Bound for Glory*. More of his writing is included in *Born to Win*.

Soldiers in the Dust

I could see men of all colors bouncing along in the boxcar. We stood up. We laid down. We piled around on each other. We used each other for pillows. I could smell the sour and bitter sweat soaking through my own khaki shirt and britches, and the work clothes, overhauls and saggy, dirty suits of the other guys. My mouth was full of some kind of gray mineral dust that was about an inch deep all over the floor. We looked like a gang of lost corpses heading back to the boneyard. Hot in the September heat, tired, mean and mad, cussing and sweating, raving and preaching. Part of us waved our hands in the cloud of dust and hollered out to the whole crowd. Others was too weak, too sick, too hungry or too drunk even to stand up. The train was a highball and had the right of way. Our car was a rough rider, called by hoboes a "flat wheeler." I was riding in the tail end where I got more dust, but less heat. The wheels were clipping it off at sixty miles an hour. About all I could hear above the raving and cussing and the roar of the car was the jingle and clink on the under side every time the wheels went over a rail joint.

I guess ten or fifteen of us guys was singing:

This train don't carry no gamblers,
Liars, thieves and big-shot ramblers;
This train is bound for glory,
This train!

"We would hafta git th' only goddam flat wheeler on th' whole dam train!" A heavy-set boy with a big-city accent was rocking along beside me and fishing through his overhauls for his tobacco sack.

"Beats walkin'!" I was setting down beside him. "Bother you fer my guitar handle ta stick up here in yer face?"

"Naw. Just long as yuh keep up th' music. Kinda songs ya sing? Juke-box stuff?"

"Much oblige, just smoked." I shook my head. "No. I'm 'fraid that there soap-box music ain't th' kind ta win a war on!"

"Little too sissy?" He licked up the side of his cigaret. "Wise-cracky, huh?"

"Hell yes." I pulled my guitar up on my lap and told him, "Gonna take somethin' more'n a dam bunch of silly wisecracks ta ever win this war! Gonna take work!"

"You don't look like you ever broke your neck at no work, bud!"
He snorted some fumes out of his nose and mashed the match down
into the dust with his foot. "What th' hell do you know 'bout work?"

"By God, mister, I work just as hard as you er th' next guy!" I held
the ends of my fingers up in his face. "An' I got th' blisters ta prove it!"

"How come you ain't drafted?"

"I never did get by those medical gents. Doctors and me don't see
eye to eye."

A blond-headed man about forty nudged me in the ribs with his
elbow on my left side and said, "You boys talkin' about a war. I got a
feelin' you're goin' to see a little spell of war right here in just a few
minutes."

"Makes ya think so?" I looked around all over the car.

"Boy!" He stretched out his feet to prop his self back up against
the wall and I noticed he was wearing an iron brace on his leg. "They
call me Cripple Whitey, th' Fight Spotter!"

"Fight spotter?"

"Yeah. I can spot a fist fight on the streets three blocks before I
come to it. I can spot a gang fight an hour before it breaks out. I tip off
the boys. Then they know how to lay their bets."

"Ya got a fight spotted now?"

"I smell a big one. One hell of a big one. Be some blood spilt. Be
about ten minutes yet."

"Hey! Heavy!" I elbowed the big boy on my right. "Whitey here
says he smells a big fight cookin'!"

"Awwww. Don't pay no 'tention to that crippled rat. He's just full
of paregoric. In Chicago we call 'im 'P. G. Whitey'! I don't know what
they call him here in Minnesota!"

"You're a goddam lyin' rat!" The cripple got up and swayed
around on the floor in front of us. "Get up! I'll cave your lousy dam
head in! I'll throw you out inta one of these lakes!"

"Easy, boy, easy." Heavy put the sole of his shoe in Whitey's
belly and held him back. "I don't wanta hit no cripple!"

"You guys watch out! Don't you stumble an' fall on my guitar!" I
eased over a little. "Yeah! You're some fight spotter! If you spot a fight
an' then it don't happen just when you said, why, you just pitch in and
start one yer self!"

"I'll crack that box over your dam curly head!" The cripple made a
step toward me, laughing and smearing cement dust down across his
face. Then he sneered and told me, "Goddam right! Hell yes! I'm a
bum! I gotta right ta be. Look at that gone leg. Withered away! You're
too dam low down an' sneakin' to make an honest livin' by hard work.
Sonofabitch. So you go into a saloon where th' workin' stiffs hang out,
an' you put down your kitty box an' play for your dam tips!"

I told him, "Go jump in one of these lakes!"

"I'm settin' right there!" He pointed at my guitar in my lap. "Right, by God, on top of you!"

I grabbed my guitar and rolled over three or four other fellows' feet and got out of Whitey's way just as he turned around and piled down backwards yelling and screaming at the top of his lungs. I stumbled through the car trying to keep my balance and hold onto my guitar. I fell up against an old man slumped with his face rubbing up against the wall. I heard him groan and say, "This is th' roughest bastardly boxcar that I ever swung into."

"Why doncha lay down?" I had to lean up against the wall to keep from falling. "How come ya standin' up this a way?"

"Rupture. It rides a little easier standin' up."

Five or six guys dressed like timberjacks brushed past us cussing and raving. "I can't stand this dust no longer!" "Out of our way, men!" "Let us by! We want to get to the other end of the car!"

"You birds won't be no better off in th' other end!" I hollered at them. The dust stung the roof of my mouth. "I tried it!"

A big husky gent with high boots and red wool socks rolled back on a pair of logger's britches stopped and looked me over and asked me, "Who in the hell are you? Don't you think I know how to ride a boxcar, sonny? I'm gettin' out of this wind!"

"Go ahead on, mister, but I'm tellin' ya, ya'll burn up back in that other end!" I turned again to the old man and asked him, "Anything I can do ta help ya?"

"Guess not, son." I could see by the look on his face that the rupture was tying him up in knots. "I was hopin' ta ride this freight on in home tonight. Chicago. Plumber there. But looks like I'll have ta get off at the next stop an' hit the highway."

"Purty bad. Well, it ain't a dam bit lonesome in here, is it?"

"I counted sixty-nine men in this car." He squinted his eyes and gritted his teeth and doubled over a little farther. "Might be, I counted wrong. Missed some of th' ones layin' down or counted some of them twice. Pretty close ta sixty-nine though."

"Jest like a car load of sheep headed fer th' packin' house." I let my knees bend in the joints a little bit to keep the car from shaking me to jelly.

A long tall Negro boy walked up and asked us, "You men know what's makin' our noses burn?" He was wearing a pair of work shoes that looked like they had seen Civil War service. "Eyes, too?"

"What?" I asked him.

"Cement dust. This heah cah wuz loaded down wid sack cement!"

"Shore 'nuff?"

"I bet I done sucked in three sacks of th' damn stuff!" He screwed his face up and mopped across his lips with his hands.

"I've breathed in more'n that! Hell, friend! You're talkin' to a livin', breathin' stretch of concrete highway!"

"Close as we is jammed an' packed in heah, we'z all gonna be stuck 'n' cemented together time we git outta dis hot box."

"Boys," the old man told both of us, "I hope we don't have no trouble while I'm in here. If somebody was ta fall on me or push me around, this rupture, I know, it would kill me."

"I'll he'p see to it dat nobody don't push nobody on toppa you, mistah."

"I'll break 'em of th' habit," I told both of them.

"What time of day is it? Must be fightin' time?" I looked around at the two.

"Mus' be 'roun' about two or three o'clock," the Negro boy told me, "jedgin' from that sun shinin' in th' door. Say! What's them two boys doin' yondah?" He craned his neck.

"Pourin' somethin' out of a bottle," I said, "right by that old colored man's feet. What is it?"

"Wettin' th' cement dust wid it. Strikin' a match now."

"Gasoline!"

"Ol' man's 'sleep. They's givin' 'im de hot foot!"

The flame rose up and burned in a little spot about the size of a silver dollar. In a few seconds the old man clawed at the strings of his bundle where he was resting his head. He kicked his feet in the dust and knocked little balls of fire onto two or three other men playing some poker along the back wall. They fought the fire off their clothes and laughed and bawled the kids and the old man both out.

"Hey! you old bastard! Quit bustin' up our card game!"

I saw one of the men draw back to hit the old man. Another player was grinning and laughing out to the whole crowd, "That wuz th' funniest dam sight I ever seen!"

The two boys, both dressed in overhalls, walked back through the crowd, one holding out the half-pint bottle. "Drinka likker, men? Who wantsa drinka good likker?" The boy with the bottle shoved it up under my nose saying, "Here, mister music man! Take a little snort! Then play somethin' good an' hot!"

"I been a needin' a little drink ta ease me on down ta Chicago." I wiped my hand across my face and smiled around at everybody. "I shore thank ya fer thinkin' 'bout me." I took the bottle and smelled of the gasoline. Then I sailed the bottle over a dozen men's heads and out of the door.

"Say, stud! Who daya t'ink youse are? Dat bottle was mine, see?" He was a boy about twenty-five, wearing a flop hat soaked through with some kind of dime-store hair oil. He braced his self on his feet in front of me and said again, "Dat bottle was mine!"

"Go git it." I looked him straight in the eye.

"Whattaya tryin' ta pull?"

"Well, since yer so interested, I'll jest tell ya. See, I might wanta lay down after while an' git a little sleep. I don't wanta wake up with my feet blistered. 'Cause then, dam yer hide, I'd hafta throw ya outta this door!"

"We was gonna use dat gas ta start a fire ta cook wid."

"Ya mean ta git us all in jail with."

"I said cook an' I mean cook!"

Then my colored friend looked the two boys over and said, "You boys, how long you been goin' roun' cookin' people's feet?"

"Keep outta dis! Stepinfetchit!"

"You cain't call me dat an' git by wid it, white boy!"

I put my shoulder against the colored boy and my hand against the white boy's arm, and told them, "Listen, guys! Goddamit! No matter who's mad at who, we jest cain't start a fight of no kind on this freight! These big Burlington dicks'll jail th' whole bunch of us!"

"Yaaa. Skeerd!"

"You're a dam liar! I ain't afraid of you ner twenty more like ya! But do you know what would of happened if these railroad bulls shook us down ta look at our draft cards, an' found you with that bottle of gasoline on ya? It'd be th' lockup fer you an' me an' all of th' rest of us!"

The old man with the rupture bit his lips and asked me, "Son, do you suppose you could get one of the men to move up out of the door and let me try to get a little breath of that fresh air? I feel like I've just got to get a little air."

The colored boy held the old man up while I walked over to the door and tapped a nice healthy-looking boy on the back. "Would you mind lettin' this old man ride in yer place there in th' door fer a little while? Sick. Rupture trouble."

"Not at all." The boy got up and set down back where the old man had been standing. He acted friendly and hollered at us, "I think it's about time we took turns ridin' in the doors. Let everybody have a whiff of that fresh air!"

Almost everybody in the car rolled over or stood up and yelled, "Hell yes!" "Turn about!" "I'm ready." "Too late, boys, I been dead an' buried in solid cement for two hours!" "Gimme air!" "Trot out yer frash airr!" Everybody mumbled and talked, and fifteen or twenty men pushed their way through the others to stand close to the doors, hoping to be first.

Heavy walked through a bunch of them saying, "Watch out. Men, let this Negro boy through with this old man. He's sick. He's needin' air. Back up a little. Make room."

"Who'n th' hell are you? Tubba lard! Dictater 'round here?" one boy popped off.

Heavy started for the man, but he slipped back in through the crowd. "All of you men get up! Let a new bunch get cooled off! Where's the old man that the boys put the hot foot on a few minutes ago? There you are! Hey! Come on! Grab yourself a hunk of this nice, fresh, cool climate! Set right there! Now, who's to be next?"

A red-eyed vino drunkard took a man by the feet and pulled him along the deck to the door. "My buddy. Ain't said a word since I loaded 'im in last night in Duluth. Bummed th' main stem fer two bits, then he scooped his flue."

A Mexican boy rubbed his head and got up from somewhere along the wall. He drank half of a quart vinegar jug of water and then sailed the bottle out the door. Then he set down and hung his feet out the door and rode along holding his head in his hands vomiting into the wind. In each door there was room for five men. The first ten being sick and weakly, we let them ride for about half an hour. Then they got up and ten more men took their seat for only fifteen minutes.

I was watching a bunch of men hold their fingers to their lips and shush each other to keep quiet. Every one of them haw-hawing and tittering under their breath and pointing to a kid asleep on the floor. He was about twenty. Little white cap from the ten-cent store, a pair of old blue washed-out pants, shirt to match, a set of dirty heels caked over with the dust of many railroads, and a run-over pair of low-cut shoes. He was hugging his bed roll and moving his lips against the wool blanket. I saw him dig his toes in the dust and kiss the bundle.

I walked over and put my foot in the middle of his back and said, "Wake up, stranger. Git ya some fresh air there in th' door!"

The men cackled and rolled in the dirt. They rared back and forth slapping their hands against their legs. "Ddrrreeeeeeeaaaammming of youuuu with your eyes so bluue!" One man was grinning like an ape and singing worse than that.

"What's th' boy dreamin' about so purty, music man?" another big guy asked me with his tongue in his cheek and eyes rolling.

"Leave th' boy alone," I told him back. "What th' hell do you dream about, freight trains?"

I set down with my back against the wall looking all through the troubled, tangled, messed-up men. Traveling the hard way. Dressed the hard way. Hitting the long old lonesome go.

Rougher than a cob. Wilder than a woodchuck. Hotter than a depot stove. Madder than nine hundred dollars. Arguing worse than a tree full of crows. Messed up. Mixed-up, screwed-up people. A crazy boxcar on a wild track. Headed sixty miles an hour in a big cloud of poison dust due straight to nowhere.

I saw ten men getting up out of the door and I took my guitar over and set down and stuck my feet out. The cold air felt good whipping up my pants leg. I pulled my shirt open to cool off across my waist and chest. My Negro friend took a seat by my side and told me, "I reckon we's 'bout due some frash air, looks like."

"Jest be careful ya don't use it all up," I kidded back at him.

I held my head in the wind and looked out along the lake shoreline with my ear cocked listening to the men in the car.

"You're a lyin' skunk!" one was saying. "I'm just as hard a worker as you are, any old day!"

"You're a big slobbery loafin' heel!"

"I'm th' best dadgum blacksmith in Logan County!"

"You mean you use ta was! You look like a lousy tramp ta me!"

"I c'n put out more manly labor in a minnit then you kin in a month!"

"Hay, there, you sot! Quit spittin' on my bed roll!"

"Yeah! Yeah! I know! I'm a woikin' stiff, too, see? But I ain't no good here! Yeah! I woiked thirteen years in th' same weave room! Breakout fixer on th' looms! Poil Harbor comes along. Big comp'ny gits alla de war orders. My place is a little place, so what happens? Just like dat! She closes down. An' I'm out on de freights. But I ain't nuttin' when I hit th' freights. Takes it all outta me. Nuttin'. But a lousy, dirty tramp!"

"If you're such a good weaver, mister, you can come back here and sew up my drawers! Ha! Ha! Ha!"

"Fancy pants! Whoooeee!"

"I plowed th' straightest row of corn in Missouri three years ago!"

"Yaaa! But, mister big shot, dey don't grow no corn in dese here boxcars, see! Yaaa! Dat's de last bitta woik yez ever done!"

"No Swede cut much timber as me, Big Swede! I cutta 'nuff of that white pine ta build up da whole town!"

"Quiet down! You dam bunch of liars, you! Blowin' off at yer head what all you can do! I hear this talk all up and down these railroads! You had a good job somewhere once or twice in your life, then you go around blabbin' off at your mouth for fifteen years! Tellin' people what all kinds of wonders you done! Look at you! Look at your clothes! All of the clothes in this car ain't worth three dollars! Look at your hands! Look at your faces! Drunk! Sick! Hungry! Dirty! Mean! Onery! I won't lie like you rats! An' I got on the best suit of clothes in this car! Work? Me work? Hell, no! I see somethin' I want, an' I just up an' take it!"

Looking back over my shoulder, I saw a little man, skinny, puny, shaking like he had a machine gun in his hands, raise up on his knees from the other end of the car and sail a brown quart bottle through the air. Glass shattered against the back of the well-dressed man's head. Red port wine rained all over me and my guitar and twenty other men that tried to duck. The man in the suit of clothes keeled over and hit the floor like a dead cow.

"I got my papers! I got my job already signed up!" The guy that slung the bottle was tromping through the car patting his chest and preaching. "I had a brother in Pearl Harbor! I'm on my way right this minute to Chicago to go to work rollin' steel to lick this Hitler bunch! I hope the gent with the nice suit on is restin' comfortable! But I ain't apologizing to none of you! I throwed that bottle! Want to make anythin' out of it?" He shook both fists and stood there looking at all of us.

I wiped my hands around over me where the wine was spilled. I saw everybody else was picking chips of glass out of their clothes and mumbling amongst themselves. "Crazy lunatic." "Hadn't ought ta done that." "Might of missed 'im, hit one of us."

The mumble got loud and broke into a crack like zigzag lightning. Little bunches of men circled around arguing. A few guys walked from bunch to bunch preaching over other fellows' shoulders. At the side of me a husky-looking man got up and said, "What all he says about Pearl Harbor and all is okay, men, but still he hadn't ought to have thrown that wine bottle. I'm going to walk back there and kick his rear good and proper just to teach him a lesson!"

Then from somewhere at my back a half-breed Indian boy dove out and tackled the husky man around the ankles and they tangled into a knot and rolled around over the floor, beating, scratching, and clawing. Their feet kicked other men in the face and other men kicked them back and jumped into the fight.

"You're not gonna hurt that little fella!"

"I'll kill you, Indian!"

"Hey! Watch who th' hell you're kickin'!"

Heavy split through the car knocking men out of his way hollering, "Hey! Cut it! Cut!"

"You fat pimp, keep outta dis!" A dirty-looking, dark-complected man was pulling a little oily cap down over his eyes and making for Heavy.

Heavy grabbed him by the throat and busted the back of his head up against the wall about a dozen times cussing, "I'll teach you that you cain't call no decent man a pimp! You snaky-looking hustler!"

All down the line it started and spread. "You said I wouldn't work fer my livin', huh? I'll bat your eyes out!"

"Who wuz it yez called da loafer?"

Shirts and pants ripped and it sounded like everybody was getting their duds tore off them.

"I didn't lak ya dam looks frum da very start!"

Five and then ten other couples dove in.

"Where's that low-life bastid that called me a bum?"

Men walked up and down the car pushing other men off of their feet, heaving others to one side, looking at the few that was still riding along on the floor.

"They're goin' an' blowin'!"

"There ye air, ye foul-mouth cur, you!"

I saw six or eight reaching down and grabbing others by their shirt collars, jerking them to the middle of the floor. Fists sailing in the air so fast I couldn't see which fist was whose.

"I knowed you was nuthin' but a lousy chiselin' snake when I first seen yuh climb on this train! Fight! Goddam yuh! Fight!"

Shoe soles cracked all around over the car and heads banged against the walls. Dust flew up in the air as if somebody was dumping it in with trucks.

"I'm a tramp, am I?"

Men's heads bobbed around in the dust like balloons floating on the ocean. Most everybody shut their eyes and gritted their teeth and swung wild haymakers up from the cement and men flattened out on the floor. Water bottles flew through the air and I could see a few flashes that I knew was pocketknife blades. Lots of the men jerked other men's coats up over their heads to where they couldn't see nor use their arms, and they fought the air like windmills, blind as bats. A hard fist knocked a fellow stumbling through the dust. He waved his hands trying to keep balanced, then fell, spilling all kinds of junk and trash out of his pockets over five or six other men trying to keep out of the fight. For every man who got knocked down, three more jumped up and roared through the mob taking sidelicks at any head that popped up.

"Boy!" My colored friend was shaking his head and looking worried. "You sho' as hell bettah not git yo' music box mixed up in dis!"

"I've got kicked in th' back about nine times. 'Nother good poke an' I'll sail plumb out this door inta one of them there lakes!" I was fighting to get myself braced again. "Here, let's me an' you hook our arms together so we can hold each other in th' dam car!" I clamped my hands together in front of me holding the guitar on my lap. "Be hell of a thing if a feller was ta git knocked outta this dern boxcar goin' this pace, wouldn't it? Roll a week. Hey! Look! Train's slowin' down."

"Believe she is at that." He squinted his eyes up and looked down the track. "She's slowin' down ta make a switch."

"I been lookin' fer you, mister music maker!" I heard somebody talking behind me. I felt a knee poking me in my back, each time hard enough to scoot me a little more out the door. "So ya thought I'd forgot about da bottla gas, huh? I t'ink I'll jist boot yez offa dis train!"

I tried to hold onto the colored boy's arm. "Watch out there, ya silly dam fool! What're ya tryin' ta do? Kick me out? I'll git up from here an' frail yore knob! Don't ya kick me again!"

He put his foot flat up against my shoulder blade and kicked me out the door. I swung onto the Negro's arms with both hands, and the leather strap of my guitar slipped out of my hold. I was holding both feet clear of the cinders down on the ground. When my guitar fell, I had to turn loose with one hand and grab it by the handle. The Negro had to hold onto the side of the door to hold his own self in the car. I seen him bend backwards as far as he could and lay down flat on the floor. This pulled me up within an inch or so of the edge of the door again, and I was about to get one arm inside. I knew he could pull me back in if I could make it that far. I looked down at the ground going past under me. The train was slowing down. The Negro and me made one more hard pull together to swing me back inside the door. "Hol' on! Boy!" he was grunting.

"No ya don't!' The young fellow bent down into a squatting position, heaving at the Negro's shoulders with both hands. "I'll jist kick da pair of yez out!"

The colored man yelled and screamed, "Hhhaaaayyy! Hhee-elllpp!"

"Goddam it, donnn't!" I was about to lose all of my strength in the left arm locked around the Negro's, which was the only thing between me and the six-by-three grave.

"Dis is where da both of yez hits de cinders! Good-bye! An' go ta hell!" He stuck his tongue out between his teeth and throwed every ounce of his weight against the colored man's shoulders.

Slowing down, the train jammed its air brakes and jarred every man in the boxcar off his feet. Men stumbled against each other, missed their licks, clawing and swinging their fists through the air. Two dozen hit the floor and knocked hide and hair and all off each other's heads. Blood flew and spattered everybody. Splinters dug into hands and faces of men tromped on the floor. Guys dove on their faces on top of strangers and grabbed handfuls of loose skin in their fingernails, and twisted until the blood caked into the dust. They rolled across the floor and busted their heads against the walls, knocked blind by the jar, with lungs and eyes and ears and teeth full of the cement. They stepped on the sick ones, ruptured the brave ones, walked on top of each other with loggers' and railroaders' spike shoes. I felt myself falling out of the Negro's hand hold.

Another tap on the brakes jerked a kink in the train and knocked the boy loose from his hold on the Negro's shoulders. The jar sent him jumping like a frog from where he was squatting, over me and the Negro both, and over the slope of the steep cinder grading, rolling, knocking and plowing cinders twenty feet to each side till like a wild, rolling truck tire he chugged into the water of the lake.

I pulled the Negro friend over the edge with me and both of us lit running with our feet on the cinders. I stumbled and took a little spill, but the colored boy run and managed to stay on his feet.

I made a run for the door of the same boxcar again, and put my hand down on an iron bolt and tried to run along with the train and swing myself up again. Men's hands reached out the door trying to grab me and help me in, but my guitar was going wild and I had to drop my hold on the bolt and trot off to the edge of the cinders. I was giving up all hopes of getting back in, when I looked behind me and saw my colored partner gripping onto the iron ladder on the end of the car. Holding the ladder with one hand, he was waving his other one in the air and yelling, "Pass me yo' guitah!"

As he went by me I got a running start on the cinders and held the guitar up to him. He caught it by the neck and clumb up onto the roof of the car. I swung the ladder and went over the top just at his heels.

"Hurry on up heah! You wanta see dat fella in th' lake?"

He pointed back down along the string of cars picking up speed again. "Off at d' side of dat little clump of trees there, there! Wadin' out yondah? See 'im? See! Boy, I bet you dat dip sobered 'im up!"

Both of us was standing side by side propping each other up. The roof of the car moved and bounced rougher than the floor inside.

The Negro friend grinned over at me with the sun in his eyes. He still hadn't lost his little greasy brown cap and was holding it down on his head while the wind made a few grabs at it. "Whoooee! Dat wuz a close one! Boy, you set fo' a good fas' ride on top? Sho' ain't no way gettin' back down inside dat cah when this roller gits ridin' ag'in!"

I squatted down cross-legged and took hold of the boards on the runwalk on top of the car. He laid down with his hands folded back of his head. We laughed at the way our faces looked with the cement all over them, and our eyes watering. The black coal dust from the locomotive made us look like white ghosts with black eyes. Lips chapped and cracked from the long ride in the hot sun and hard wind.

"Smell dat cool aih?"

"Smells clean. Don't it? Healthy!"

"Me 'n' you's sho' in fo' a soakin', ourselves!"

"Makes ya think?"

"I knows. Boy, up heah in dis lake country, it c'n cloud up an' rain in two seconds flush!"

"Ain't no rain cloud I can see!"

"Funny thing 'bout dese Minnesoty rain clouds. Evah cloud's a rain cloud!"

"Gonna go hard on my guitar." I played a few little notes without really noticing what I was doing. The air turned off cooler as we rolled along. A second later I looked up and saw two kids crawl from an open-top car just behind us: a tall skinny one about fifteen, and a little scrawny runt that couldn't be over ten or eleven. They had on Boy Scout looking clothes. The older one carried a pack on his back, and the little kid had a sweater with the sleeves tied together slung around his neck.

"Hiyez, men?" The tall one saluted and dumped his pack down a couple of feet from us.

The little feller hunched down and set picking his teeth with a rusty pocket knife, talking, "Been wid 'er long?"

I'd seen a thousand kids just like them. They seem to come from homes somewhere that they've run away from. They seem to come to take the place of the old stiffs that slip on a wet board, miss a ladder, fall out a door, or just dry up and shrivel away riding the mean freights; the old souls that groan somewhere in the darkest corner of a boxcar, moan about a twisted life half lived and nine tenths wasted, cry as their souls hit the highball for heaven, die and pass out of this world like the echo of a foggy whistle.

"Evenin', gentulmen, evenin'." The Negro boy raised up to a sitting position. "You gents is a little shade yo'ng t' be out siftin' th' cinders, ain't you?"

"C'n we help how old we are?" The biggest kid spit away into the wind without even looking where it would land.

"Me ole man's fault. Oughtta been bornt sooner," the little runt piped up.

The big one didn't change the expression on his face, because if he'd of looked any tougher, something would have busted. "Pipe down, squoit!" He turned toward us. "Yez hittin' fer de slaughter-house er Wall Street?"

"I don't git ya." I looked over at him.

"Chi? Er N'Yok?"

I tried to keep from busting out laughing in the kid's face. And I could see the colored boy turning his head the other way to hide a snicker. "Me," I answered the kid, "me, I'm headed fer Wall Street, I reckin." Then I thought for a minute and asked him, "'Bouts you boys goin'?"

"Chi."

"On da fly."

"Kin ya really beat it out on dat jitter box dere, mister?"

"I make a rattlin' noise."

"Sing on toppa dat?"

"No. Not on top of it. I stand up and hold it with this leather strap around my shoulder, or else I set down and play it in my lap like this, see?"

"Make anyt'ing wid it?"

"I've come purty close ta starvin' a couple of times, boys, but never faded plumb out of th' picture yet so far."

"Yeah?"

"Dat's bad."

I come down on some running notes and threw in a few sliding blues notes, and the kids stuck their ears almost down to the sound-hole, listening.

"Say ya hit da boog on dere, don'tcha?"

"Better boog all yez wants, sarg," the older kid said. "I dunno how dat box'll sound fulla wadder, but we gon'ta be swimmin' on toppa dis train here in about a minnit."

The Negro boy turned his head around toward the engine and whiffed of the damp air. "About one minnit's right!"

"Will it wreck dat music box?" The biggest kid stood up and threw his pack on his back. The coal dust had covered his face over in the days when this railroad was first laid, and a few drops of the spit and moisture from the lower streets of a lot of towns had been smeared like brushmarks in every direction around his mouth, nose and eyes. Water and sweat had run down his neck and dried there in long strings. He said it again: "Will de rain wreck dat rackit box?"

I stood up and looked ahead at the black smoke rolling out of the engine. The air was cool and heavy and held the big coil of smoke low to the ground along the side of the train. It boiled and turned, mixed in with the patches of heavy fog, and spun into all kinds of shapes. The picture in the weeds and bushes alongside the tracks was like ten thousand drunkards rolling in the weeds with the bellyache. When the first three or four splats of rain hit me in the face I said to the kids, "This water won't exactly do this guitar any good!"

"Take dis ole sweater," the smallest kid yelled at me. "'S all I got! Wrap it aroun' yer music! Help a little!" I blinked the water out of my eyes and waited a jiffy for him to pull the sweater from around his neck where he had tied the sleeves. His face looked like a quick little picture, blackish tobacco brown colors, that somebody was wiping from a window glass with a dirty rag.

"Yeah," I told him, "much oblige! Keep out a few drops, won't it?" I slipped the sweater over the guitar like a man putting clothes on a dummy in a window. Then I skint out of my new khaki shirt and put it on the guitar, and buttoned the buttons up, and tied the sleeves around the neck. Everybody laughed. Then we all squatted down in a little half circle with our backs to the rain and wind. "I don't give a dam how drippin' I git, boys, but I gotta keep my meal ticket dry!"

The wind struck against our boxcar and the rain beat itself to pieces and blew over our heads like a spray from a fire hose shooting sixty miles an hour. Every drop that blew against my skin stung and burned.

The colored rider was laughing and saying, "Man! Man! When th' good Lord was workin' makin' Minnesoty, He couldn' make up His mind whethah ta make anothah ocean or some mo' land, so He just got 'bout half done an' then He quit an' went home! Wowie!" He ducked his head and shook it and kept laughing, and at the same time, almost without me noticing what he was doing, he had slipped his blue work shirt off and jammed it over into my hands. "One mo' shirt might keep yo' meal ticket a little bettah!"

"Don't you need a shirt to keep dry?"

I don't know why I asked him that. I was already dressing the guitar up in the shirt. He squared his shoulders back into the wind and rubbed the palms of his hands across his chest and shoulders, still laughing and talking, "You think dat little ole two-bit shirt's gonna keep out this cloudbu'st?"

When I looked back around at my guitar on my lap, I seen one more little filthy shirt piled up on top of it. I don't know exactly how I felt when my hands come down and touched this shirt. I looked around at the little tough guys and saw them humped up with their naked backs splitting the wind and the rain glancing six feet in the air off their shoulders. I didn't say a word. The little kid pooched his lips out so the water would run down into his mouth like a trough, and every little bit he'd save up a mouthful and spit it out in a long thin spray between his teeth. When he saw that I was keeping my eyes nailed on him, he spit the last of his rainwater out and said, "I ain't t'oisty."

"I'll wrap this one around the handle an' the strings will keep dry that way. If they get wet, you know, they rust out." I wound the last shirt around and around the neck of the guitar handle. Then I pulled the guitar over to where I was laying down. I tied the leather strap around a plank in the boardwalk, ducked my head down behind the guitar and tapped the runty kid on the shoulder.

"Hey, squirt!"

"Whaddaya want?"

"Not much of a windbreak, but it at least knocks a little of th' blister out of that rain! Roll yer head over here an' keep it ducked down behind this music box!"

"Yeeehh." He flipped over like a little frog and smiled all over his face and said, "Music's good fer somethin', ain't it?"

Both of us stretched out full length. I was laying on my back looking straight up into the sky all gray and tormented and blowing with low clouds that whined when they got sucked under the wheels. The wind whistled funeral songs for the railroad riders. Lightning struck and crackled in the air and sparks of electricity done little dances for us on the iron beams and fixtures. The flash of the lightning knocked the clouds full of holes and the rain hit down on us harder than before. "On th' desert, I use this here guitar fer a sun shade! Now I'm usin' th' dam thing fer a umbreller!"

"T'ink I could eva' play one uv dem?" The little kid was shaking and trembling all over, and I could hear his lips and nose blow the rain away, and his teeth chatter like a jackhammer. He scooted his body closer to me, and I laid an arm down so he could rest his head. I asked him, "How's that fer a pillow?"

"Dat's betta." He trembled all over and moved a time or two. Then he got still and I didn't hear him say anything else. Both of us were soaked to the skin a hundred times. The wind and the rain was running a race to see which could whip us the hardest. I felt the roof of the car pounding me in the back of the head. I could stand a little of it, but not long at a time. The guitar hit against the raindrops and sounded like a nest of machine guns spitting out lead.

The force of the wind pushed the sound box against the tops of our heads, and the car jerked and buckled through the clouds like a coffin over a cliff.

I looked at the runt's head resting on my arm, and thought to myself, "Yeah, that's a little better."

My own head ached and pained inside. My brain felt like a crazy cloud of grasshoppers jumping over one another across a field. I held my neck stiff so my head was about two inches clear of the roof; but that didn't work. I got cold and cramped and a dozen kinks tied my whole body in a knot. The only way I could rest was to let my head and neck go limp; and when I did this, the jolt of the roof pounded the back of my head. The cloudbursts got madder and splashed through all of the lakes, laughing and singing, and then a wail in the wind would get a low start and cry in the timber like the cry for freedom of a conquered people.

Through the roof, down inside the car, I heard the voices of the sixty-six hoboes. There had been sixty-nine, the old man said, if he counted right. One threw his own self into the lake. He pushed two more out the door with him, but they lit easy and caught onto the ladder again. Then the two little windburnt, sunbaked brats had mounted the top of our car and were caught in the cloudburst like drowned rats. Men fighting against men. Color against color. Kin against kin. Race pushing against race. And all of us battling against the wind and the rain and that bright crackling lightning that booms and zooms, that bathes his eyes in the white sky, wrestles a river to a standstill, and spends the night drunk in a whorehouse.

What's that hitting me on the back of head? Just bumping my head against the roof of the car. Hey! Goddam you! Who th' hell do you think you're a hittin', mister? What are you, anyhow, a dam bully? You cain't push that woman around! What's all of these folks in jail for? Believing in people? Where'd all of us come from? What did we do wrong? You low-down cur, if you hit me again, I'll tear your head off!

My eyes closed tight, quivering till they exploded like the rain when the lightning dumped a truckload of thunder down along the train. I was whirling and floating and hugging the little runt around the belly, and my brain felt like a pot of hot lead bubbling over a flame. Who's all of these crazy men down there howling out at each other like hyenas? Are there men? Who am I? How come them here? How the hell come me here? What am I supposed to do here?

My ear flat against the tin roof soaked up some music and singing coming from down inside of the car:

This train don't carry no rustlers,
Whores, pimps, or side-street hustlers;
This train is bound for glory,
This train.

Can I remember? Remember back to where I was this morning? St. Paul. Yes. The morning before? Bismarck, North Dakota. And the morning before that? Miles City, Montana. Week ago, I was a piano player in Seattle.

Who's this kid? Where's he from, and where's he headed for? Will he be me when he grows up? Was I like him when I was just his size? Let me remember. Let me go back. Let me get up and walk back down the road I come. This old hard rambling and hard graveling. This old chuck-luck traveling. My head ain't working right.

Where was I?

Where in the hell was I?

Where was I when I was a kid? Just as far, far, far back, on back, as I can remember?

Strike, lightning, strike!

Strike, Goddam you, strike!

There's lots of folks that you cain't hurt!

Strike, lightning!

See if I care!

Roar and rumble, twist and turn, the sky ain't never as crazy as the world.

Bound for glory? This train? Ha!

I wonder just where in the hell we're bound.
Rain on, little rain, rain on!
Blow on, little wind, keep blowin'!
'Cause them guys is a singin' that this train is bound for glory, an'
I'm gonna hug her breast till I find out where she's bound.

6366   0